OXFORD IB DIPLOMA PROGRAM

SPORTS, EXERCISE AND HEALTH SCIENCE

COURSE COMPANION

John Sproule

OXFORD
UNIVERSITY PRESS

OXFORD
UNIVERSITY PRESS

Acknowledgments

The author and publisher would like to thank the following individuals and
organisations for granting permission to reproduce material:

Cover Photo: © Sebastian Kaulizki/Istock.com

Illustrations: Steve Evans and Q2A Media.

Photos: P30: Lisa S/Shutterstock; **P31:** Kyodo/Reuters, **P32:** FPG/Retrofile/
Getty Images; **P32:** Philippe Psaila/Science Photo Library; **P36:** Garo/Phanie/
Rex Features; **P37:** Ethan Daniels/Waterframe/Getty Images; **P40:** Picsfive/
Shutterstock; **P40:** Cheyennezj/Shutterstock; **P46:** Keystoneusa-ZUMA/Rex
Features; **P48:** Roberto Schmidt/Staff/AFP/Getty Images; **P53:** Monticello/
Shutterstock; **P53:** Goodmood Photo/Shutterstock; **P53:** Aleksandr Doodko/
Shutterstock; **P55:** Lou Linwei/Alamy/India Picture; **P57:** Voisin/Phanie/Rex
Features; **P57:** John Bryson/Photo Researchers/Getty Images; **P57:** Leungchopan/
Shutterstock; **P58:** Shutterstock; **P61:** National Health And Medical Research
Council; **P62:** www.oldwayspt.org; **P62:** www.oldwayspt.org/; **P62:** Bochkarev
Photography/Shutterstock; **P69:** Bsip, Laurent/B. Hop Ame/Science Photo
Library; **P69:** Dr P. Marazzi/Science Photo Library; **P70:** Saeed Khan/Staff/
AFP/Getty Images; **P72:** Hagen Hopkins/Stringer/Getty Images Sport/Getty
Images; **P72:** Photosport Int/Rex Features; **P72:** Sportgraphic/Shutterstock;
P77: Hamill And Knutzen (2009); **P77:** Hamill And Knutzen (2009); **P97:**
Sportgraphic/Shutterstock; **P108:** Goldenkb/Dreamstime; **P108:** Zadorozhnyi
Viktor/Shutterstock; **P109:** Dmitry Kalinovsky/Shutterstock; **P109:** Igor Sirbu/
Shutterstock; **P128:** Frank Waberführer/Fotolia; **P139:** Peter Weber/Shutterstock;
P158: Istvan Csak/Shutterstock; **P158:** Dmitry Berkut/Shutterstock; **P158:**
Adrian Dennis/Staff/AFP/Getty Images; **P158:** Philip Date/Shutterstock; **P158:**
Lehtikuva OY/Rex Features; **P175:** Volodymyr Goinyk/Shutterstock; **P175:**
Apdesign/Shutterstock; **P180:** Pierre Verdy/Staff/AFP/Getty Images; **P181:** John
Sproule; **P182:** Tim Wimborne/Reuters; **P182:** Tom Shaw/Staff/Getty Images
Sport/Getty Images; **P183:** Aleksey Ipatov; **P183:** Robert Harding Picture
Library Ltd/Alamy/India Picture; **P186:** John Green/BEI/Rex Features; **P187:** ©
Johan Copes Van Hasselt/Sygma/Corbis; **P187:** © SHOUT/Alamy; **P187:** Dudarev
Mikhail/Shutterstock; **P194:** EAPS Motorsport/Alamy; **P194:** Getty Images; **P195:**
Popperfoto/Getty Images; **P196:** Getty Images; **P216:** David Davies/PA Wire/
Press Association Images; **P222:** Matthew Lewis/Stringer/Getty Images Sport/
Getty Images; **P226:** David Rogers/Staff/Getty Images Sport/Getty Images; **P231:**
Supri Suharjoto/Shutterstock; **P231:** Rido/Shutterstock; **P238:** Simon Balson/
Alamy/India Picture; **P238:** Paparico/Dreamstime; **P273:** Hugh Routledge/Rex
Features; **P273:** Sipa Press/Rex Features; **P274:** Sipa Press/Rex Features; **P275:**
Flying Colours Ltd/Digital Vision/Getty Images; **P275:** Back Page Images/Rex
Features; **P271:** Jack Guez/Staff/AFP/Getty Images; **P280:** Redsnapper/Alamy/
India Picture; **P281:** Photoalto/Odilon Dimier/Photoalto Agency RF Collections/
Getty Images; **P281:** View China Photo/Rex Features; **P281:** Ian Waldie/Getty
Images Sport/Getty Images; **P281:** Mike Goldwater/Alamy/India Picture; **P281:**
Sonya Etchison/Shutterstock; **P281:** By Ian Miles-Flashpoint Pictures/Alamy/India
Picture; **P284:** Alan Edwards/Alamy/India Picture; **P299:** I S Farooqi, S O'Rahilly
(2005)/Nature Publishing Group; **P301:** Bliss, M. (2007)/Chicago Universirty
Press; **P303:** Nucleus Medical Art, Visuals Unlimited/Science Photo Library;
P321: Tek Image/Science Photo Library; **P321:** VAPRO®; **P321:** Andrew Lambert
Photography/Science Photo Library **P322:** Julian Finney/Getty Images Sport/Getty
Images; **P324:** St Bartholomew's Hospital/Science Photo Library; **P327:** Testing/
Shutterstock; **P327:** Nic Cleave Photography/Alamy/India Picture; **P327:** Julian
Finney/Getty Images Sport/Getty Images; **P327:** Erik Pendzich/Rex/Rex Features;
P327: Hindustan Times/Getty Images; **P327:** Alexander Ishchenko/Shutterstock;

P327: Antti Aimo-Koivisto/Rex Features; **P330:** Hannah Johnston/Getty Images
Sport/Getty Images; **P332:** © The Vegetarian Society; **P333:** Kraj41/Dreamstime;
P333: Giuliano Bevilacqua/Rex Features; **P356:** Siliconcoach Video Analysis
Software; **P357:** Cengage Learning Australia; **P357:** Philip Allen Updates.

Banner Images: Lightspring/Shutterstock; Bjorn Stefanson/Shutterstock;
Leungchopan/Shutterstock; Sportgraphic/Shutterstock; Olga Besnard/
Shutterstock; Istvan Csak/Shutterstock; Apdesign/Shutterstock; Fikmik/
Shutterstock; Andrey Yurlov/Shutterstock.Com; Rido/Shutterstock; Greg
Epperson/Shutterstock; Katatonia82/Shutterstock.Com; Jamie Roach/
Shutterstock.Com; Sebastian Kaulizki/Alamy; Testing/Shutterstock.

All other photography contributed by John Sproule and Edinburgh University.

The author and publisher are grateful to the following for permission to reprint
copyright material:

Annual Reviews, Inc (via CCC) for extract from A Bandura: 'Social Cognitive
Theory: An agentic perspective', 52 *Annual Review of Psychology* 1 (2001).

BMJ Publishing Group Ltd (via CCC) for figure from A M Edwards, C Wells
and R Butterly: 'Concurrent inspiratory muscle and cardiovascular training
differentially improves both perceptions of effort and 5000 m running
performance compared with cardiovascular training alone, 42 (10) *British Journal
of Sports Medicine* 823 (2008), copyright © 2008 BMJ Publishing Group Ltd and the
British Association of Sport and Exercise Medicine.

Elsevier (via CCC) for extract from Jonathan Wood: 'Record breaking or rule
breaking?', 11 (6) *Materials Today* (2008).

Independent News and Media for 'Too much choke ruins the Novotna engine'
by John Roberts, *The Independent*, 5.7.1993, copyright © The Independent 1993.

Reuters.com via PARS International for 'Penalty takers must ignore keeper,
study shows' by Kate Helland, Reuters.com, 7.7.2010, copyright © 2010 Thomson
Reuters. Thomson Reuters journalists are subject to an Editorial Handbook
which requires fair presentation and disclosure of relevant interests. All Rights
Reserved. Republication or redistribution is expressly prohibited without prior
written consent of Thomson Reuters.

Solo Syndication for 'Fatal dedication of man who ran himself to death' by Jaya
Narain, *Daily Mail*, 7.8.2002

World Health Organization (WHO) for summary of recommendations from
Global Recommendations on Physical Activity for Health (WHO, 2010) pp 20, 26, 31

Wolters Kluwer Health (via CCC) for figures from K Currell and A E
Jeukendrop: 'Superior Endurance Performance with Ingestion of Multiple
Transportable Carbohydrates', © 2001 by The American College of Sports
Medicine, 40 (2) *Medicine and Science in Sports & Exercise* 275 (2001); and from
K Spaccarotella and W Andzel: 'The Effects of Low Fat Chocolate Milk on
Postexercise Recovery in Collegiate Athletes', © 2011 by the National Strength
and Conditioning Association, 25 (12) *Journal of Strength and Conditioning Research*
3456 (2011).

Acknowledgement to the Biology department at UWCSEA (Dover), Singapore for
sharing their IA resources and providing support.

Although we have made every effort to trace and contact all copyright holders
before publication this has not been possible in all cases. If notified, the
publisher will rectify any errors or omissions at the earliest opportunity.

6.70

Course Companion definition

The IB Diploma Programme Course Companions are resource materials designed to support students throughout their two-year Diploma Programme course of study in a particular subject. They will help students gain an understanding of what is expected from the study of an IB Diploma Programme subject while presenting content in a way that illustrates the purpose and aims of the IB. They reflect the philosophy and approach of the IB and encourage a deep understanding of each subject by making connections to wider issues and providing opportunities for critical thinking.

The books mirror the IB philosophy of viewing the curriculum in terms of a whole-course approach; the use of a wide range of resources, international mindedness, the IB learner profile and the IB Diploma Programme core requirements, theory of knowledge, the extended essay, and creativity, action, service (CAS).

Each book can be used in conjunction with other materials and indeed, students of the IB are required and encouraged to draw conclusions from a variety of resources. Suggestions for additional and further reading are given in each book and suggestions for how to extend research are provided.

In addition, the Course Companions provide advice and guidance on the specific course assessment requirements and on academic honesty protocol. They are distinctive and authoritative without being prescriptive.

IB mission statement

The International Baccalaureate aims to develop inquiring, knowledgable and caring young people who help to create a better and more peaceful world through intercultural understanding and respect.

To this end the IB works with schools, governments and international organizations to develop challenging programmes of international education and rigorous assessment.

These programmes encourage students across the world to become active, compassionate, and lifelong learners who understand that other people, with their differences, can also be right.

The IB learner profile

The aim of all IB programmes is to develop internationally minded people who, recognizing their common humanity and shared guardianship of the planet, help to create a better and more peaceful world. IB learners strive to be:

Inquirers They develop their natural curiosity. They acquire the skills necessary to conduct inquiry and research and show independence in learning. They actively enjoy learning and this love of learning will be sustained throughout their lives.

Knowledgable They explore concepts, ideas, and issues that have local and global significance. In so doing, they acquire in-depth knowledge and develop understanding across a broad and balanced range of disciplines.

Thinkers They exercise initiative in applying thinking skills critically and creatively to recognize and approach complex problems, and make reasoned, ethical decisions.

Communicators They understand and express ideas and information confidently and creatively in more than one language and in a variety of modes of communication. They work effectively and willingly in collaboration with others.

Principled They act with integrity and honesty, with a strong sense of fairness, justice, and respect for the dignity of the individual, groups, and communities. They take responsibility for their own actions and the consequences that accompany them.

iii

Open-minded   They understand and appreciate their own cultures and personal histories, and are open to the perspectives, values, and traditions of other individuals and communities. They are accustomed to seeking and evaluating a range of points of view, and are willing to grow from the experience.

Caring   They show empathy, compassion, and respect towards the needs and feelings of others. They have a personal commitment to service, and act to make a positive difference to the lives of others and to the environment.

Risk-takers   They approach unfamiliar situations and uncertainty with courage and forethought, and have the independence of spirit to explore new roles, ideas, and strategies. They are brave and articulate in defending their beliefs.

Balanced   They understand the importance of intellectual, physical, and emotional balance to achieve personal well-being for themselves and others.

Reflective   They give thoughtful consideration to their own learning and experience. They are able to assess and understand their strengths and limitations in order to support their learning and personal development.

A note on academic honesty

It is of vital importance to acknowledge and appropriately credit the owners of information when that information is used in your work. After all, owners of ideas (intellectual property) have property rights. To have an authentic piece of work, it must be based on your individual and original ideas with the work of others fully acknowledged. Therefore, all assignments, written or oral, completed for assessment must use your own language and expression. Where sources are used or referred to, whether in the form of direct quotation or paraphrase, such sources must be appropriately acknowledged.

How do I acknowledge the work of others?
The way that you acknowledge that you have used the ideas of other people is through the use of footnotes and bibliographies.

Footnotes   (placed at the bottom of a page) or endnotes (placed at the end of a document) are to be provided when you quote or paraphrase from another document, or closely summarize the information provided in another document. You do not need to provide a footnote for information that is part of a 'body of knowledge'. That is, definitions do not need to be footnoted as they are part of the assumed knowledge.

Bibliographies   should include a formal list of the resources that you used in your work. 'Formal' means that you should use one of the several accepted forms of presentation. This usually involves separating the resources that you use into different categories (e.g. books, magazines, newspaper articles, Internet-based resources, CDs and works of art) and providing full information as to how a reader or viewer of your work can find the same information. A bibliography is compulsory in the extended essay.

What constitutes malpractice?
Malpractice is behaviour that results in, or may result in, you or any student gaining an unfair advantage in one or more assessment component. Malpractice includes plagiarism and collusion.

Plagiarism is defined as the representation of the ideas or work of another person as your own. The following are some of the ways to avoid plagiarism:

- Words and ideas of another person used to support one's arguments must be acknowledged.
- Passages that are quoted verbatim must be enclosed within quotation marks and acknowledged.
- CD-ROMs, email messages, web sites on the Internet, and any other electronic media must be treated in the same way as books and journals.
- The sources of all photographs, maps, illustrations, computer programs, data, graphs, audio-visual, and similar material must be acknowledged if they are not your own work.
- Works of art, whether music, film, dance, theatre arts, or visual arts, and where the creative use of a part of a work takes place, must be acknowledged.

Collusion is defined as supporting malpractice by another student. This includes:

- allowing your work to be copied or submitted for assessment by another student
- duplicating work for different assessment components and/or diploma requirements.

Other forms of malpractice include any action that gives you an unfair advantage or affects the results of another student. Examples include, taking unauthorized material into an examination room, misconduct during an examination, and falsifying a CAS record.

Contents

For answers to the exam questions in Chapter 18, please visit:

www.oxfordsecondary.co.uk/ibsport

Introduction

This book is the first Course Book available for the International Baccalureate Sport, Exercise and Health Science course. The subject is one of the most exciting ways to study and apply science, and this is reflected in the key aims of the course. For example, a knowledge and understanding of exercise science can play a prominent role in offering solutions to increasing levels of physical inactivity and globesity. This positions the study of Sport, Exercise and Health Science as a vital area of study in the 21st century for the inclusive and sustainable development of populations worldwide. Furthermore, major sporting events, such as the Olympics, the Asian games, the Pan American Games, the Paralympic games, the Rugby World Cup and the Soccer World Cup, highlight the importance of sports scientists in optimising mental and physical performance across time zones and in varied environmental conditions.

The curriculum model of the IB Sport, Exercise and Health Science course is divided into theory and practical work. Although not necessary, both the theoretical and practical components will be enhanced if considerable emphasis is placed on learning through the use of information and communication technology, such as dietary or motion analysis.

Section A: Core topics

The core syllabus covers anatomy, exercise physiology, energy systems, movement analysis, skill in sport, and measurement and evaluation of human performance. This exciting journey can be the gateway to a career in a host of sport, exercise and health-related professions.

Section B: Options

The four options available are:

(A) Optimising physiological performance
(B) Psychology of sport
(C) Physical activity and health
(D) Nutrition for sport, exercise and health

Section C: Practical experimental work and exam preparation

Chapter 17 will help to prepare you to put theory into practice - applied work in the laboratory and/or out in the field. One of the main aims of this section is to develop inquisitive, internationally-minded people with a natural curiosity. In preparation for examinations (Chapter 18), it is important that students clearly understand the difference between the command terms and objectives that form the individual assessment statements.

The worldwide growth of employment in sport, exercise and health-related jobs over the last four decades has been significant and exponential. Those students with aspirations for studying at college and university will find a wide range of undergraduate courses where a knowledge and understanding of this subject is relevant. A few examples include: Physical education, Coaching science, Physiotherapy, Public health and Applied sports science.

Writing this Course Book would not have been possible without a team approach. Thank you to my colleagues at the University of Edinburgh (Scotland), former colleagues at Loughborough University (England), UWIC (Wales) and Trinity University (Ireland), and the IB Diploma Programme teachers who have contributed in varying ways. In particular I would also like to thank John Bowers (England), Trevor Hayes (New Zealand), Donna Davies (Australia) Denise Stevenson (Singapore) and Maxine Small (Portugal) who have not only contributed but have done so with enormous goodwill, enthusiasm and interest - they continue to educate me towards global citizenship. Any errors and omissions are entirely mine and I welcome communication from you to point these out and to suggest improvements and updates for the next edition.

I would like to dedicate this book to those who have had the greatest impact on my life: in memory of my mother and father, Mary and Bob Sproule; to my wife Maggie who continues to do so much in return for so little; my two wonderful children Sean and Laura-Beth who mean everything to me; to my students who are a continual source of joy and inspiration, and Mr Kunalan - an inspirational Singaporean Physical Educator and Olympian. In my role as Head of Sport, Physical Education & Health Science at the University of Edinburgh it is a privilege to take forward the vision of Alec Peterson (born in Edinburgh) who was responsible for the birth of the IB educational system. In the words of the Greek goddess of victory, *JUST DO IT!*

John Sproule,
September 2012

CHAPTER 1

Musculoskeletal anatomy

OBJECTIVES

By the end of this chapter, students should be able to

→ describe the anatomy and function of the axial and appendicular skeleton

→ identify four types of bone

→ draw and identify the different parts of a long bone

→ outline the functions of cartilage, tendons and ligaments

→ define a joint and distinguish between different types of joint in relation to how much movement is possible

→ outline the features of a synovial joint

→ identify and describe the different types of synovial joint

→ distinguish between the different types of muscle

→ outline the general characteristics that are common to muscle tissue

→ describe the structure of skeletal muscle

→ define what the origin and insertion of a muscle is and identify these for a selection of muscles

→ use anatomical terminology to describe the location of bones and muscles.

Introduction

The musculoskeletal system is made up of the skeletal system which includes the bones and joints, and the muscular system which contains the muscles. When bones come together, they form joints. Muscles cross these joints and pull on the bones causing movement at the joints. Therefore, the musculoskeletal system plays a vital role in allowing you to do all the movements that are needed in daily life. To understand how bones and muscles are involved in sporting actions such as running, jumping up to spike a volleyball, kicking a football or throwing a javelin, it is important to know about the location and structure of specific muscles and bones, and to understand how they work together.

This chapter will introduce these topics and will provide a basis for future chapters that also refer to the musculoskeletal system.

Anatomical terminology

The body is made up of structures such as bones, muscles and organs, and is often divided into segments, for example the trunk, thigh and upper arm. The positions or locations of these structures are often described in relation to the positions of other body parts. In anatomy, there are a number of terms that

Inferior below or further away from the head

Superior above or nearer to the head

Proximal nearer to where a limb attaches to the body

Distal further away from where a limb attaches to the body

Posterior behind or nearer to the back

Anterior in front of or nearer to the front

Internal located inside or further away from the surface

External located on or near the surface

Lateral further away from the midline of the body

Medial closer to the midline of the body

TO DO

Use the terms in the glossary to describe the positions of different parts of the body. The body parts can be muscles, organs, limbs or any other structure you know the location of. For example, the lungs are internal to (inside) the ribcage.

TO DO

Stand in a relaxed position. Now stand in the anatomical body position. Can you think of any body parts that change location relative to each other when you stand in these two different positions?

are used for this purpose. Sometimes, these terms are included in the names of muscles or other structures in the body and this can give you a hint about their location. The terms that are commonly used appear in the glossary on the previous page.

The position of each of these structures can sometimes be affected by posture or how an individual stands. Reference positions allow you to clarify exactly what starting posture an individual is in. The anatomical body position is a commonly used reference position where the individual stands upright, facing straight ahead with the feet parallel and close together, and the palms facing forward (see Figure 1.1). The fundamental starting position is sometimes used - this is identical to the anatomical starting position except the arms are in a more relaxed position with the palms facing the body. These starting positions are also useful when describing and demonstrating joint movements (this will be covered in chapter 4).

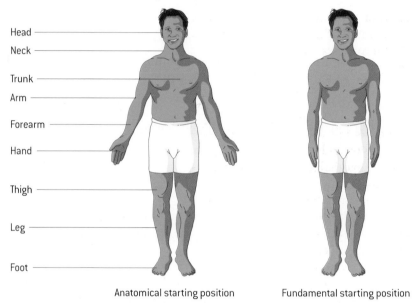

Head
Neck
Trunk
Arm
Forearm
Hand
Thigh
Leg
Foot

Anatomical starting position   Fundamental starting position

↑ Figure 1.1: Anatomical and fundamental body positions

Skeletal system

The skeletal system is made up of the bones, cartilage, ligaments and joints of the body, and accounts for approximately 20% of body weight. The skeleton roughly determines the shape and size of the body (although this is also affected by nutrition, physical activity and posture). There are 206 bones in the skeleton and it is divided into two parts: the axial skeleton and the appendicular skeleton (see Figure 1.2).

The axial skeleton contains 80 bones and includes the skull, ribs, sternum and vertebral column. The appendicular skeleton has 126 bones and includes the pectoral (shoulder) girdle, the pelvic (hip) girdle and the bones of the upper and lower extremities, i.e. the arms and legs. The pectoral and pelvic girdles attach the upper and lower extremities to the axial skeleton. The scapula and clavicle make up the pectoral girdle and the bones of the upper extremity include the humerus, ulna, radius, carpal bones, metacarpals and phalanges. The bones of the lower extremity include the femur, tibia, fibula, tarsal bones, metatarsals and phalanges.

The skeleton has several functions:

→ **Protection of the vital organs** The ribcage surrounds the heart and lungs, the skull encloses the brain, and the vertebrae surround the spinal cord.

- → **Support and maintenance of posture** The skeleton provides a framework for the body and each part bears the weight of all structures of the body above it. Note how the vertebral bones get bigger as you move down the body as they have to bear more weight. Also the bones of the lower extremities are larger than those in the upper extremities as humans walk on their feet rather than their hands.
- → **Providing attachment points for the muscles** Muscles run from one bone to another and they are connected to the bones via tendons. Bones are not completely smooth but have roughened areas or prominent landmarks where the tendons of muscles usually attach. When muscles and tendons contract, they pull on the bones causing movement at the joints.
- → **Storage and release of minerals such as calcium and phosphorus** These minerals are important for muscle contraction and nerve activity. They are released into the blood to maintain mineral homeostasis and so that they can be distributed to other parts of the body.
- → **Blood cell production or haemopoiesis** Red blood cells, white blood cells and platelets are produced in red bone marrow which is usually located in flat bones such as the ribs and sternum or in the ends of long bones such as the femur and humerus.
- → **Storage of energy** Lipids are stored in yellow bone marrow which is located inside long bones. These provide important chemical energy reserves.

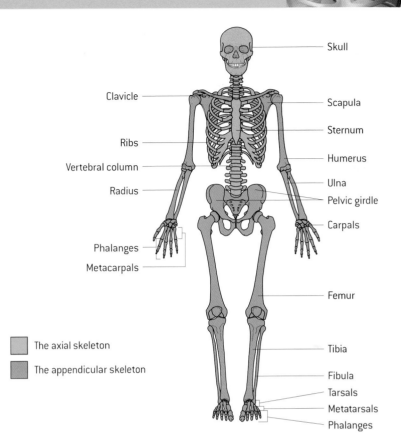

The axial skeleton

The appendicular skeleton

↑ Figure 1.2: Bones of the axial and appendicular skeleton

Axial skeleton

As already mentioned, the bones of the axial skeleton (skull, sternum, ribs and vertebral column) enclose important structures in the body and therefore their main function is to provide protection.

Skull

The skull sits on top of the vertebral column and is divided into the cranium and the face. As well as protecting the brain, the bones of the skull also protect the eyes and ears and contain the teeth.

Vertebral column

There are 33 vertebrae in the body, all stacked on top of each other to form the vertebral column. This column is very strong, but it is also very flexible as it bends anteriorly (forwards), posteriorly (backwards), laterally (to the side) and rotates. The vertebrae are divided into sections and together they make up about 40% of the total height of the body. In the neck region, there are seven cervical vertebrae. Underneath this, there are twelve thoracic, five lumbar, five sacral, and four coccygeal vertebrae. The sacral vertebrae are fused together to form one vertebra, as are the coccygeal vertebrae. This means that the cervical, thoracic and lumbar vertebrae can move relative to each other but the sacral and coccygeal vertebrae cannot.

To innervate to supply an organ or other body part with nerves

TO THINK ABOUT

Discs between the lumbar vertebrae are thicker than those between the cervical vertebrae. Why do you think this is?

TO THINK ABOUT

Slipped or herniated disc

Think of a jam donut. What happens when you squash it?

Now imagine the intervertebral disc as a jam donut where the annulus fibrosus is the doughy part and the nucleus pulposus is the jam. If there are cracks in the annulus fibrosus, the nucleus pulposus can squeeze through the gaps and, in some cases, may press on the spinal cord or the spinal nerves that are located near the disc. This can then cause pain in the areas of the body that are innervated by these nerves. This is often called a slipped disc even though the disc does not actually 'slip' but instead develops a crack or split. It can occur at any disc but occurs most commonly in the lower back.

The vertebrae in each section of the spine have a similar structure, but there are some specific differences in shape and function depending on where they are located.

→ Cervical vertebrae are the smallest and have more movement than the thoracic and lumbar vertebrae.
→ Thoracic vertebrae are less mobile because the ribs attach to the sides of each vertebra and therefore restrict movement.
→ Lumbar vertebrae are the biggest and strongest as they play a major role in weight-bearing and therefore absorb high compression loads.
→ Sacral vertebrae transmit weight from the body to the pelvis and the legs.

Figure 1.3 illustrates the features that are common to all vertebrae. The largest and flattest part of each vertebra is called the body. Towards the back of each vertebra there is a hole called the vertebral foramen. As the vertebrae are stacked on top of each other, these holes line up to form a canal along the length of the vertebral column; the spinal cord is located inside this canal. There is also a gap on either side of the vertebrae where the spinal nerves emerge from the spinal cord. Each spinal nerve innervates a different area of the body.

The bodies of the vertebrae do not actually touch each other as there is an intervertebral disc between each one. These discs have a tough outer ring of fibrocartilage called the annulus fibrosus, and a soft, gel-like, elastic structure in the middle called the nucleus pulposus. The discs make the vertebral column more flexible and they flatten and bulge out to the sides when they are compressed making them important shock absorbers.

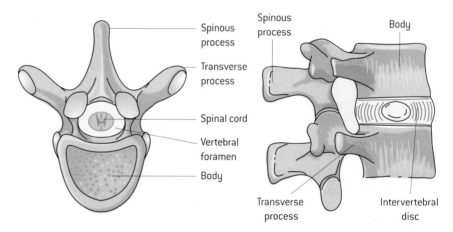

↑ Figure 1.3: Superior and lateral view of a typical vertebra

The vertebrae are arranged so that they provide the spine with four curves; these can be seen when looking at the vertebral column from the side (see Figure 1.4). The cervical and lumbar curves are anteriorly convex (curve outwards at the front) while the thoracic and sacral/coccygeal curves are anteriorly concave (curve inwards at the front). The thoracic and sacral curves are called primary curves as these are present in the curled up position of a foetus in the uterus. The cervical and lumbar curves are secondary curves as they develop later when a child can hold their head up (after three to four months) and stand upright (after twelve to fifteen months).

The curves increase the strength of the vertebral column, help maintain upright balance, and absorb shock during weight-bearing exercise. The other specific functions of the vertebral column are to support the head, enclose and protect the spinal cord, transmit weight from the body to the legs, and provide attachment points for the ribs and muscles of the back.

Anteriorly convex curves outwards at the front
Anteriorly concave curves inwards at the front

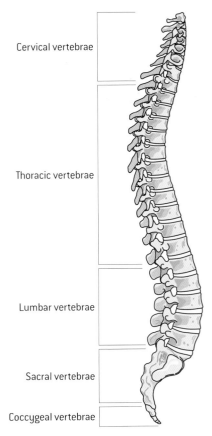

Cervical vertebrae

Thoracic vertebrae

Lumbar vertebrae

Sacral vertebrae

Coccygeal vertebrae

↑ Figure 1.4: Lateral view of the vertebral column

THEORY OF KNOWLEDGE

Correct posture is seen as a key element in maximising performance and the correct growth of humans. Investigate the use of yoga or pilates as a means for correct postural development.

TO THINK ABOUT

Problems with spinal curves
An exaggerated lumbar curve or large arch in the lower back is called lumbar lordosis. This is often associated with obesity, poor posture, tightness and/or weakness in the hip, back and abdominal muscles.

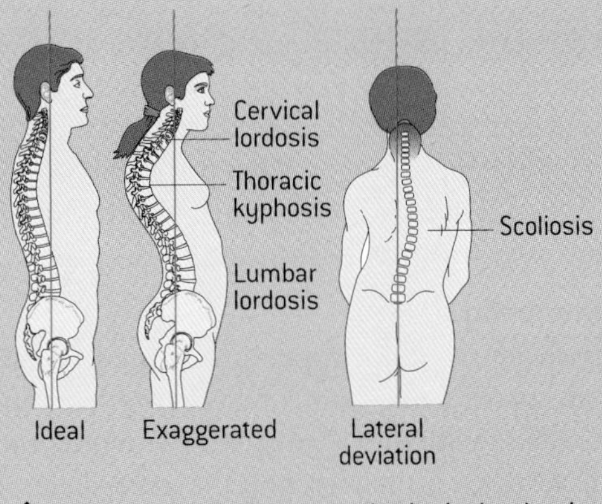

An exaggerated thoracic curve or excessively hunched shoulders is called kyphosis. This is associated with poor posture, tightness and/or weakness in the chest, neck and upper back muscles.

Cervical lordosis

Thoracic kyphosis

Lumbar lordosis

Scoliosis

Ideal   Exaggerated   Lateral deviation

↑ Figure 1.5: Ideal posture, lordosis, kyphosis and scoliosis

An excessive lateral curvature in the spine is called scoliosis. This may resemble an "S" or a "C" shape when looking at the spine from behind. If this is due to poor posture, muscle tightness and/or muscle weakness, it can be fixed. However, if it is congenital (present since birth) and due to a structural deformity such as a hemivertebra (half vertebra), surgery may be required.

Sternum and ribs

The sternum is a flat bone that starts at the bottom of the throat and runs about halfway down the chest in the center. The ribs are curved bones that articulate with the sternum at the front and the thoracic vertebrae at the back. There are 12 pairs of ribs in total. The first seven pairs are called true ribs as they attach directly to the sternum. Ribs 8 to 10 are called false ribs as they attach to rib 7 and therefore only attach indirectly to the sternum. Ribs 11 and 12 are floating ribs as they do not attach to the sternum—instead the tips can be felt at the lower part of the anterior ribcage. Together, the sternum, ribs and thoracic vertebrae form the thoracic cage. The intercostal muscles which are essential for breathing are located in-between the ribs, which is why any damage to the ribs also affects breathing.

Appendicular skeleton

While the main function of the axial skeleton is protection, the appendicular skeleton is mostly involved in movement.

Upper body

In the upper body, the pectoral (shoulder) girdles are formed by the clavicles and scapulae. The clavicles articulate with the sternum anteriorly and this is the only bony connection between the pectoral girdle and the axial skeleton. The scapulae are flat, triangular bones that are located posterior to the ribcage. The scapulae articulate with both the clavicle and the humerus.

The humerus is the bone in the upper arm and is a typical long bone, enlarged at the upper and lower ends. The upper end articulates with the lateral part of the scapula to form the shoulder joint, while the lower end articulates with the proximal ulna to form the elbow joint. The ulna is one of two long bones in the lower arm, the other being the radius. These bones lie parallel to each other with the ulna medial to the radius (in the anatomical body position). Between the bones, there is a layer of connective tissue called an interosseous membrane which keeps the bones together and helps to provide additional stability. Together these bones form the radioulnar joint where the bones rotate around each other.

At the wrist, the radius and ulna articulate with the carpal bones. These are short bones and are arranged closely together in two rows of four. The distal row articulates with the metacarpals of the hand, which in turn articulate with the proximal phalanges. Each finger has three phalanges while the thumb has only two. These bones form the individual joints within the fingers which allow very fine, specific movements.

Lower body

The structure of the upper and lower extremities is very similar. The pelvis is made up of three bones fused together—the ilium, ischium and pubis. It articulates with the sacrum and therefore provides the link between the lower extremities, i.e. the legs, and the axial skeleton.

There is one long bone in the upper leg called the femur which is enlarged at both the proximal and distal ends. The femur is the longest and heaviest bone in the body and it articulates with the pelvis in a hollow area called the acetabulum to form the hip joint. Distally, the enlarged femur articulates with the enlarged head of the tibia to form the knee joint. The tibia is the prominent bone found anteriorly in the lower leg—this is often called the shin bone. The fibula is another long bone which runs parallel and lateral to the tibia. Similarly to the upper limb, these bones are held together with an interosseous membrane.

The patella (or kneecap) is a small, triangular bone located at the front of the knee joint. The patella increases the leverage of the tendon of the quadriceps femoris muscle, maintains the position of the tendon when the knee is bent (flexed) and protects the knee joint.

At the ankle joint, the tibia and fibula articulate with the talus which is one of the tarsal bones. However, the most prominent tarsal bone is the calcaneus which forms the heel bone. The distal row of tarsals articulates with the metatarsals, which in turn articulate with the phalanges. Again, each toe has three phalanges except the big toe which has only two.

Bones

Figure 1.2 illustrates that the bones in the human body vary widely in size and shape. The main factor in determining the size and shape of bones is their location and function. The four main types of bones are long, short, flat and irregular.

→ **Long bones** usually have a long cylindrical shaft and are enlarged at both ends. They can be large or small but the length is always greater than the width. Long bones are the most important bones for movement. They include the femur, metatarsals and clavicle.
→ **Short bones** are small and cube-shaped and they usually articulate with more than one other bone. Short bones include the carpals of the hand and tarsals of the foot.
→ **Flat bones** usually have curved surfaces and vary from being quite thick to very thin. These bones provide protection and the broad surfaces also provide a large area for muscle attachment. Flat bones include the sternum, scapula, ribs and pelvis.
→ **Irregular bones** have specialized shapes and functions and include the vertebrae, sacrum and coccyx.

TO RESEARCH

Sesamoid bones
Another type of bone found in the body is the sesamoid bone. These are short bones embedded in tendons where large amounts of pressure develop.
→ Identify three areas of the body where sesamoid bones are found.
→ What is the largest sesamoid bone in the body?
→ It is embedded in the tendon of which muscle?
→ What is its main function?

TEST YOURSELF

Use a skeleton or a picture of a skeleton to help you with these tasks.
→ Identify the bones of the axial skeleton and the appendicular skeleton.
→ Indicate what type of bone each one is.
→ Most bones are not entirely smooth and have rough areas and prominent landmarks where muscles, tendons and ligaments often attach. See if you can feel the prominent bony landmarks on your arms, legs and trunk. Can you identify which bones these are?

Structure of bone

Bone contains a neatly arranged matrix of protein (collagen) fibers along with water and mineral salts. When the mineral salts accumulate in-between and around the collagen fibers, they crystallize and the tissue hardens. However, the collagen fibers also provide high tensile strength, in other words bone

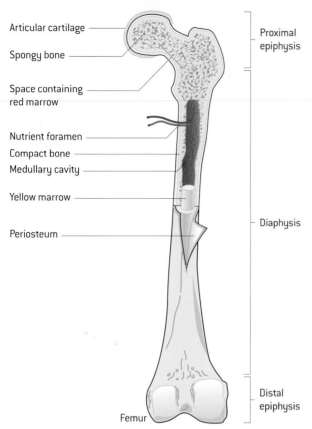

Articular cartilage

Spongy bone

Space containing
red marrow

Nutrient foramen

Compact bone

Medullary cavity

Yellow marrow

Periosteum

Proximal
epiphysis

Diaphysis

Distal
epiphysis

Femur

↑ Figure 1.6: Structure of a long bone

resists being stretched or torn apart. This structure has been likened to reinforced concrete where metal rods run through a block of concrete to reinforce it and give it strength.

The structure of bone can be described by examining a long bone (see Figure 1.6). The shaft or mid-section of a long bone is called the diaphysis and is made up of compact bone or hard bone. Compact bone is relatively solid and dense, it has few spaces and it is also found in the outer layer of most other types of bone. It is important for protection and support, and resists the stress of weight placed on long bones. The ends of the bone are called the proximal and distal epiphysis and these are made of cancellous or spongy bone. Cancellous bone has an irregular latticework structure (like honeycomb) where there are many spaces. Cancellous bone is also found in short, flat and irregular bones. As red bone marrow is stored in cancellous bone, blood cell production occurs here.

A thin layer of articular cartilage covers the ends of the bone where they articulate with other bones to form joints. The main functions of this cartilage are to reduce friction between the bones and absorb shock. The area of bone that is not covered by articular cartilage is covered instead by a thin, shiny white membrane called the periosteum. This forms the outer lining of bone and is important for bone growth, repair, nutrition and attachment of ligaments and tendons. The medullary (marrow) cavity is the space within the diaphysis where yellow bone marrow is stored. There is a small opening in the diaphysis called the nutrient foramen. Blood vessels pass through here, enter the medullary cavity and provide the bone marrow and compact bone with blood and nutrients.

THEORY OF KNOWLEDGE

Ballet dancers have on average a low bone mineral content (BMC), with elevated fracture risk, low body mass index (BMI) for age, and low energy intake. A 2011 study aimed at a better understanding of the interactions of these factors in young female ballet dancers (age 16 years; 60 Asians, 67 Caucasians), especially with regard to nutrition. They found that BMI for age was found to be normal in only 42.5% of the dancers, while 15.7% had a more or less severe degree of thinness. Food intake was below the recommendations for a normally active population in all food groups except animal proteins, where the intake was more than twice the recommended amount. In this population, with low BMI and intense exercise, BMC was low and associated with nutritional factors. They concluded that ballet schools should promote balanced diets and normal weight and should recognize and help dancers avoid eating disorders and delayed puberty caused by extensive dancing and inadequate nutrition. Eating disorders have been a contentious subject in the world of ballet for many years. In 2012 the artistic director of English National Ballet, Tamara Rojo, stated on the BBC news programme that dancers need to put on weight and that audiences want to see healthy looking women on stage.

(Burckhardt et al. 2011. "The effects of nutrition, puberty and dancing on bone density in adolescent ballet dancers". *Journal of Dance Medicine and Science*. Vol 15(2) (June), Pp. 51–60.)

Discuss how to change the mindset of some dancers to their nutritional needs for bone health.

Bone as a dynamic tissue

Bone is a dynamic tissue which means that it is constantly changing in response to activity levels or disuse. Bone cells are continually broken down and removed through a process called resorption and these cells are then replaced with new cells through bone deposition. If the amount of bone that is deposited equals the amount that is resorbed, then bone mass remains constant. An increase in bone mass results in increased strength while decreased bone mass is associated with decreases in strength.

Bone can alter its structure and properties if there is a change to the mechanical stress placed on it. The main types of mechanical stress are the skeletal muscles pulling on the bones and the effects of gravity. According to Wolff's law, bone in a healthy person or animal will adapt to the load it is placed under. This means that if a bone is exposed to a greater load, for example through training, there will be increased mineral salt deposits and greater production of collagen fibers to increase bone strength and the ability to resist this load. Athletes who repeatedly apply high stresses to the bones have noticeably higher bone mineral density and stronger bones compared to non-athletes.

In contrast, those who are sick and confined to bed, those who break a leg and are on crutches, or astronauts who are on space missions all experience restricted weight-bearing activity. This results in too much bone resorption and not enough bone deposition and can result in losses of up to 1% of bone mass per week as well as decreases in bone strength.

→ What are the bone cells that are involved in resorption and deposition called?
→ What precautions would an astronaut have to take immediately after returning to earth?
→ Identify a sport that would increase bone density in the lower limbs.
→ Identify a sport that would increase bone density in the upper limbs.
→ Can you think of any sports where bone mass or bone mineral density might be higher in one limb compared to the same limb on the opposite side of the body? Why would this happen?

Joints

A joint or articulation is where two or more bones come into contact or articulate with each other. The main function of joints is to increase mobility of the body and limbs. Think about how difficult it would be to play snooker, to do a free throw in basketball or to drink from a bottle if you had no elbow joint. The body contains several types of joints and these joints are classified according to a number of features. The most basic classification relies on the presence or absence of a joint cavity, in other words, if there is a gap between the articulating bones.

Joints are further classified depending on the shape of the articulating bones or the types of tissue that connect the bones together. The shape of the bones and subsequently the amount of movement allowed varies between joints, therefore the structure and function of joints are highly interrelated. Some joints allow little or no movement, others allow movement in one direction only, while others allow a wide range of movements in several directions.

Joint movement and stability

Joint movement is inextricably linked to joint stability. Generally, the more movement a joint has, the less stability it has and the greater the risk of injury. Several factors affect stability around the joints including:

→ the shape of the bones and whether they interlock with each other or not
→ the area over which the bones are in contact
→ the flexibility of the ligaments
→ the influence of other soft tissue structures (muscles, tendons, joint capsules etc.)

Depending on the joint, there can be numerous ligaments surrounding it. Ligaments are strong, flexible tissues that connect bone to bone. They can be in

TO RESEARCH

Range of motion varies between different joints and between individuals. Many factors can affect range of motion including the shape of bones and flexibility of the ligaments and muscles—these are the same factors that influence joint stability. Explain how other factors such as age, gender, muscle bulk, physical fitness, injury, work and exercise habits also affect range of motion.

TO THINK ABOUT

A dislocation is when the bones that form a joint come out of their normal alignment. It is often due to forceful movemnts or impact and results in damage to the joint capsule and surrounding muscles and ligaments. Identify a joint that is commonly dislocated.

the form of strap-like bands or round cords, and generally pass over joints. This allows them to provide stability and help maintain the normal bony arrangement. Ligaments restrain joint movements once they reach normal limits and resist movements that the joint was not designed for. For example, in the anatomical body position, there are ligaments located on the medial and lateral sides of the elbow joint. Their function is to resist sideways movements of the elbow.

While ligaments are generally very strong, they can be torn if they are suddenly and violently stretched. Also, they are not very elastic and they take a long time to return to their original length after they have been stretched. If they are stretched abnormally for prolonged periods, they may be permanently damaged and may never return to their original length. This means that they can no longer provide stability for joints and there is an increased risk of joint injury.

Types of joints

There are three main types of joints: fibrous, cartilaginous and synovial. Fibrous and cartilaginous joints have no joint cavity whereas synovial joints do.

Fibrous joints have a thin layer of fibrous tissue connecting the edges of the two bones. This is continuous with the periosteum and no movement is allowed at these joints. An example would be between the sutures in the skull.

In cartilaginous joints, the bones can be separated by a fibrocartilage disc (e.g. the intervertebral disc located between adjacent vertebrae), or by a thick layer of hyaline cartilage (e.g. connecting the ribs to the sternum). There is limited movement allowed at these joints.

Synovial joints are the most commonly occurring joints in the body and are the most important joints for mobility. They have several distinctive features as you can see from Figure 1.7.

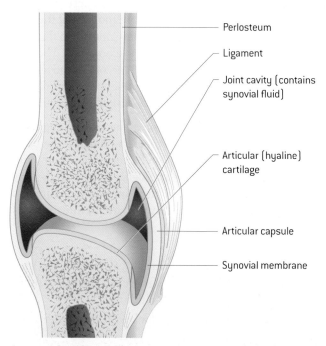

Perlosteum

Ligament

Joint cavity (contains synovial fluid)

Articular (hyaline) cartilage

Articular capsule

Synovial membrane

↑ Figure 1.7: Structure of a synovial joint

→ The space between the bones is called the joint (articular) cavity.
→ A smooth, white layer of articular cartilage covers the articulating surfaces of the bones. This is usually hyaline cartilage but can occasionally be

TO RESEARCH

In which joint do you think articular cartilage would be thickest? Why?

fibrocartilage. The main functions of cartilage are to reduce friction, absorb shock and protect the bones. It varies in thickness depending on the amount of stress that it is exposed to. Cartilage can wear away from normal wear and tear or overuse (osteoarthritis) and, when it does, the bones grate on each other causing friction and pain during movement.

→ A sleeve-like structure called an articular capsule surrounds the joint. This capsule is flexible enough to allow joint movements to take place while the tensile strength protects the joint from dislocation. In some joints, the fibers of these capsules are arranged in parallel bundles to form ligaments which provide additional support.

→ The inside of the capsule is lined by a synovial membrane that secretes synovial fluid. This fluid has the consistency and appearance of uncooked egg whites which makes it quite viscous, however it does become more fluid with movement. It lubricates the joint cavity, reduces friction and provides nutrients to the cartilage.

→ Menisci are semi-lunar discs of fibrocartilage that are found between some articulating bones, for example between the femur and tibia in the knee joint. The shapes of these bones are not very well matched, but these menisci allow the bones to fit together more tightly. This provides greater cushioning and stability to the joint.

→ Bursae are small fluid-filled sacs found where two structures rub against each other, for example between ligament and bone, between tendon and bone, or between skin and bone. As bursae are lined by a synovial membrane, they provide lubrication to the structures and therefore reduce friction. Bursae are found in areas of high stress all over the body.

Types of synovial joint

Most joints in the body are synovial joints and they can be classified further depending on how much movement is allowed. The main types of synovial joints are gliding, hinge, pivot, condyloid, saddle, and ball and socket joints.

→ Of all the synovial joints, gliding joints have the least amount of movement. The surfaces of the bones are flat or slightly curved and they glide back and forth and from side to side across each other. Gliding joints are found between the tarsal bones and between the carpal bones.

→ Hinge joints bend (flex) or straighten (extend) in one direction only, for example the elbow joint. Similar movements take place at the knees and in the small joints between the phalanges of the fingers and toes. Usually the surface of one bone is convex and it fits into a reciprocally shaped concave surface.

→ In a pivot joint, one bone forms a ring in which the other bone rolls or pivots allowing rotation of the joint, for example the radius rotates around the ulna at the radioulnar joint.

→ Condyloid joints are formed where an oval or egg-shaped convex surface fits into a reciprocally shaped concave surface. For example, they are found between the radius and carpal bones of the wrist and allow movement in two directions (you can move your wrist both up-and-down and from side-to-side).

→ In a saddle joint, the bones are shaped like a saddle and a rider sitting in the saddle. An example of a saddle joint is found between the metacarpal of the thumb and the carpal bone next to it. These joints can move in two directions (side-to-side and up-and-down).

→ Ball and socket joints can move in all directions and therefore have the greatest amount of movement. They are formed when the sphere shaped head of one bone fits into a rounded cavity on the other bone, for example the shoulder and hip joints.

TO DO

For each of the major joints in the body, identify the type of joint it is and in which directions you can move it.

JOINT	DESCRIPTION	DIAGRAM
Gliding joint e.g. between the tarsal bones and between the carpal bones	Usually flat or slightly curved bones	
Hinge joint e.g. elbow joint	A convex surface fits into a concave surface	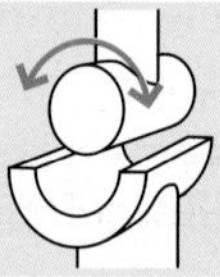
Pivot joint e.g. radioulnar joint	Rounded surface of one bone rolls around in a ring formed by bone and ligament	
Condyloid joint e.g. between the radius and carpal bones	Oval or egg shaped convex surface fits into a reciprocally shaped concave surface	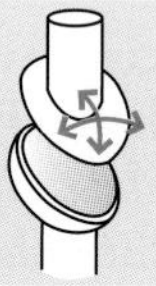
Saddle joint e.g. between the carpal bone and metacarpal of the thumb	A saddle shaped bone fits against another bone shaped like the legs of a rider sitting in the saddle	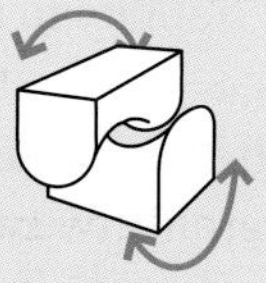
Ball and socket joint e.g. shoulder joint	Sphere shaped head of one bone fits into a rounded cavity on the other bone	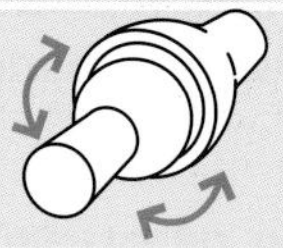

↑ Figure 1.8: Types of synovial joint

TO RESEARCH

Mobility and stability of the shoulder and hip joints
Both the hip and shoulder are ball and socket joints; however their structures are very different which affects movement and therefore stability. Look at the diagrams of the shoulder and hip joints and think back to the factors that affect joint stability.

→ Based on bony structure, which joint do you think is most mobile? Which is most stable? Explain your answers.
→ What other factors do you think might influence this?
→ How do mobility and stability influence function of the shoulder and hip joints?
→ What effect do these have on injury risk?

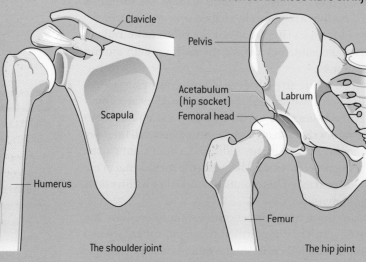

↑ Figure 1.9: Shoulder and hip joints

Muscular system

There are over 600 muscles in the human body and these vary in size, shape and structure. Together they make up about 40-50% of the weight of the body.

Types of muscle

There are three types of muscle: skeletal, cardiac and smooth. These have different functions and are located in different parts of the body.

Skeletal muscle is under voluntary control and has a striated appearance, which means that it has alternating dark and light bands that are visible if you examine it under a microscope. Skeletal muscle has tendons that attach mostly to bone and therefore the main function of this type of muscle is to move the skeleton.

Cardiac or heart muscle is also striated but it is under involuntary control therefore it contracts without you having to consciously think about it.

Smooth muscle lines the walls of blood vessels and hollow organs such as the stomach and intestines. It is also involuntary but it does not have a striated appearance like skeletal and cardiac muscle.

Muscle has four main functions:

→ Movement occurs through the interaction of bones, skeletal muscles and joints. When skeletal muscles contract, they exert forces on tendons which then pull on the bones causing joint movement.

→ Muscles also move substances within the body. For example, smooth muscles help move food through the gastrointestinal tract, cardiac muscle pumps blood to all the tissues in the body and skeletal muscle helps return venous blood to the heart.

→ When postural muscles contract they help to stabilize and maintain body positions. For example, the posterior neck muscles contract to keep the head in an upright position otherwise it would fall forwards. Therefore muscles can be active even if there seems to be no movement at the joint.

→ When muscles contract either voluntarily or involuntarily (as with shivering) they can generate up to 85% of body heat.

Striated appearance of light and dark stripes

TEST YOURSELF

As mentioned earlier, different body parts are often named according to their location. Muscle names often give an indication of their shape, size, structure, appearance or action. Recognizing and understanding the meaning of these terms can make it easier to remember muscle names and to understand more about their structure and function.

Below are examples of some muscles that will be covered in the next section. What information do the names give you about the size, location and structure of these muscles?

→ gluteus maximus
→ pectoralis major
→ trapezius
→ vastus lateralis
→ rectus abdominus
→ tibialis anterior
→ triceps brachii

13

In this chapter, the main focus is on the larger skeletal muscles that are important for movement of the joints.

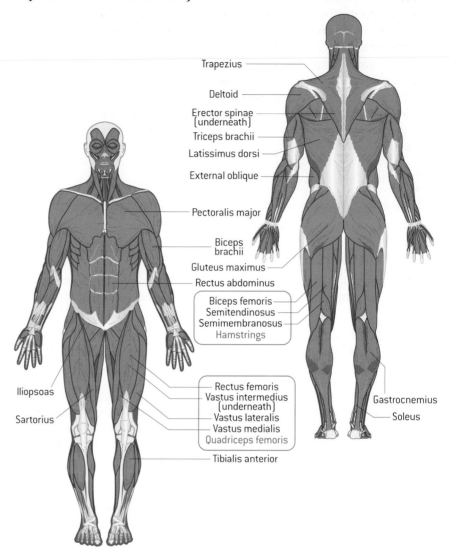

Trapezius
Deltoid
Erector spinae (underneath)
Triceps brachii
Latissimus dorsi
External oblique
Pectoralis major
Biceps brachii
Gluteus maximus
Rectus abdominus
Biceps femoris
Semitendinosus
Semimembranosus
Hamstrings
Iliopsoas
Rectus femoris
Vastus intermedius (underneath)
Vastus lateralis
Vastus medialis
Quadriceps femoris
Sartorius
Gastrocnemius
Soleus
Tibialis anterior

↑ Figure 1.10: Superficial and deep muscles of the body

Properties of muscle tissue

The properties of muscle include contractility, extensibility and elasticity.

→ Contractility is the ability of muscle to contract and generate force when it is stimulated by a nerve. Muscle tissue is the only tissue in the body that has this property. Muscles are usually arranged in pairs so that when one muscle is contracted or shortened, the opposing muscle is stretched.

→ The ability of muscle to be stretched beyond its normal resting length is called extensibility.

→ Elasticity is the muscle's ability to return to its original resting length after the stretch is removed.

To illustrate this, think about what happens when you lift a glass to drink some water. First, a nerve sends a signal to the muscle on the front of the arm (biceps brachii) telling it to contract. The muscle shortens using the property of contractility. As the elbow bends, the muscle on the back of the arm (triceps brachii) is stretched and lengthens thus demonstrating the property of extensibility. When the arm is lowered again, the triceps goes back to its original length because of elasticity.

TO THINK ABOUT

An average muscle fiber can shorten to about 50% of its original resting length and stretch to about 150% of the original resting length.

Structure of skeletal muscle

Fascia is a type of connective tissue that is located in-between and surrounding other tissues of the body such as muscles and bones. Fascia is made up of fibrous tissue, adipose (fatty) tissue and fluid. It can be superficial, for example just under the skin, or deep, for example when it surrounds the muscles and attaches to bones. In general, skeletal muscles work together in groups to carry out specific actions rather than working independently. They are divided into compartments that contain groups of muscles which have the same function. Each compartment is surrounded by fascia and the same nerve innervates all of the muscles in the compartment.

There are three layers of fascia in each individual skeletal muscle. These are called the epimysium, perimysium and endomysium (see Figure 1.11).

→ The epimysium is the outer layer which covers the entire muscle.

→ The perimysium surrounds bundles of muscle fibers or fascicles. These fascicles are long, cylindrical and vary in length and width depending on the muscle.

→ The endomysium is the layer of fascia that surrounds the individual muscle fibres.

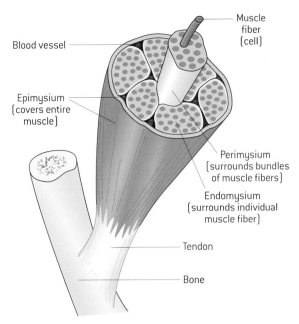

↑ Figure 1.11: Structure of muscle

When a muscle is viewed under a microscope, thousands of long, cylindrical muscle fibers can be seen lying parallel to one another. Looking at these more closely reveals smaller structures called myofibrils which have light and dark bands and give the muscle the striated appearance that was mentioned earlier. These are arranged into a series of functional units called sarcomeres. Sarcomeres contain bands of contractile proteins called actin and myosin and are very important for muscle contraction. The structure and function of these sarcomeres will be covered in more detail in chapter 4.

When a muscle is trained through exercise or increased activity, the muscle will get bigger or experience hypertrophy due to an increase in the number of myofibrils. When a muscle is not used, the number of myofibrils will decrease and it will waste away or atrophy. Atrophy commonly occurs in people who are confined to bed because of illness or who cannot use a limb because it is in a cast.

When these layers of fascia continue on beyond the muscle fibers, they form tendons which are tough, flexible bands of fibrous connective tissue connecting muscle to bone. Tendons can be in various forms such as a rounded cord or a broad, flat sheet called an aponeurosis. Groups of tendons can also be enclosed in tubes of fibrous connective tissue called tendon sheaths such as those found in the wrist. These sheaths contain synovial fluid, which helps to reduce friction as the tendons move back and forth across each other. Tendons are very strong and transmit the forces generated by muscles to bone, therefore they play an important role in muscle contraction and joint movement. The fleshy middle section of the muscle is called the muscle belly and this becomes prominent when the muscle contracts.

Unlike ligaments and tendons, muscles have a good nerve and blood supply. The nerves that bring the impulses from the central nervous system to the muscle are called motor neurons. These neurons release neurotransmitters into the blood which stimulate the muscle to contract and produce force. There is also a rich network of capillaries which provide the muscle with oxygen, nutrients and calcium and remove waste products. This means that muscles are good at repairing damage, for example if a muscle is pulled or strained.

Actin and myosin contractile proteins responsible for movement

TO THINK ABOUT

Some researchers use bed-rest to simulate the effects of physical inactivity. A study by Belavy et al. (2009) examined the rate of atrophy in the individual leg muscles during eight-week-long bed-rest. Magnetic resonance scanning was used to measure leg muscle volume on the first day of bed-rest and then at two-week intervals. They found that the leg muscles *reduced* in volume. For example, the soleus muscle reduced in volume by 6% after two weeks, by 9% after four weeks, by 12% after six weeks, and by 16% after eight weeks. Why might this have implications for prolonged spaceflight?

Origin and insertion of muscles

As already mentioned, muscles generally have a tendon on each end and these attach to roughened areas or prominent landmarks on the bone. Most muscles cross over one joint and are involved in movement at that joint, however some muscles cross two joints and can therefore influence movement at both joints.

The two ends of the muscle, or the attachment points, are called the origin and the insertion. Generally, one attachment stays fixed while the other moves. The origin is usually the more proximal attachment, i.e. the end that is closest to the center of the body, and this is usually the bone that stays fixed. The insertion is usually the more distal attachment, i.e. the end furthest away from the center of the body, and this is usually the movable bone. The major muscles of the trunk, upper extremities and lower extremities will be covered in this chapter. The muscle actions will be identified briefly in this section and then described in more detail in chapter 4.

Muscles of the trunk

The trunk muscles are quite large and powerful and they play an important role in stability. Anterior muscles include the rectus abdominus and external obliques, while the main posterior muscle is the erector spinae.

The rectus abdominus is the most superficial muscle in the anterior trunk (see Figure 1.12). Superficial means that it is located on or near the surface of the body. There are two of these muscles running upwards from the pubis to the ribs and sternum on either side of the midline of the trunk. These muscles have several tendinous lines going across them which give the characteristic "six-pack" appearance. When these muscles contract, they pull the trunk forwards, for example when doing abdominal crunches.

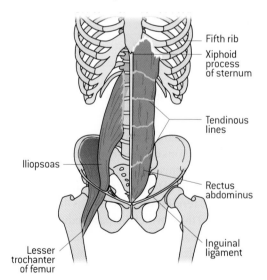

Fifth rib

Xiphoid process of sternum

Tendinous lines

Iliopsoas

Rectus abdominus

Lesser trochanter of femur

Inguinal ligament

↑ Figure 1.12: Rectus abdominus. Notice the tendons that are located running across the rectus abdominus that form the "six-pack".

The external obliques are located on the side and front of the trunk, just under the rectus abdominus (see Figure 1.13). They originate on the lower eight ribs and run down to insert onto the ilium. These muscles are involved in sideways bending movements and rotation and, therefore, they are trained when doing oblique abdominal exercises.

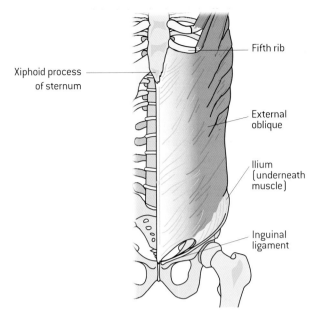

Xiphoid process of sternum

Fifth rib

External oblique

Ilium (underneath muscle)

Inguinal ligament

↑ Figure 1.13: External obliques

The erector spinae muscles are a series of overlapping muscles that run alongside most of the spine (see Figure 1.14). Some of the muscles originate on the ilium and lumbar vertebrae, some originate on the thoracic vertebrae and ribs, while others start on the cervical vertebrae. As they insert at different points along the vertebrae they have an overlapping structure. When these muscles contract, they pull the trunk into extension so that the person is leaning backwards.

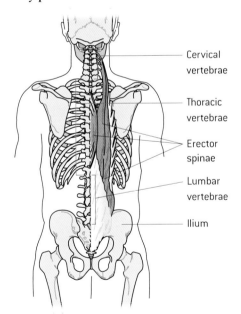

Cervical vertebrae

Thoracic vertebrae

Erector spinae

Lumbar vertebrae

Ilium

↑ Figure 1.14: Erector spinae

MUSCLE	ORIGIN	INSERTION
Rectus abdominus	Pubis	5th to 7th ribs and sternum
External obliques	Lower eight ribs	Ilium
Erector spinae	Ribs, cervical, thoracic and lumbar vertebrae, ilium	Ribs, cervical, thoracic and lumbar vertebrae

↑ Table 1.1: Origin and insertion of selected muscles of the trunk

Muscles of the upper extremity

The upper extremity muscles are vital in many sports such as tennis, baseball, cricket and javelin. Some muscles stabilize the pectoral girdle which is important as it allows the other muscles around the shoulder to generate higher levels of force. Muscles of the anterior upper extremity include deltoid, pectoralis major and biceps brachii, while the trapezius, latissimus dorsi and triceps brachii are located posteriorly.

The deltoid muscle is one of the most prominent and useful shoulder muscles. It originates on the scapula posteriorly and clavicle anteriorly, and inserts onto the lateral humerus (see Figure 1.15). Therefore, it covers the anterior, superior and posterior parts of the shoulder giving it a rounded appearance. As the fibers run across the joint in several directions, it is involved in most shoulder movements.

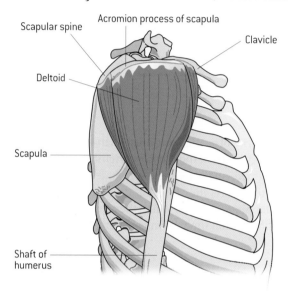

↑ Figure 1.15: Deltoid

The pectoralis major originates on the clavicle, sternum and anterior ribs and covers the entire anterior chest region (see Figure 1.16). The tendon of this muscle forms the front of the armpit and it inserts to the inside of the humerus. This muscle is involved in all shoulder movements where the arm is brought forwards or upwards.

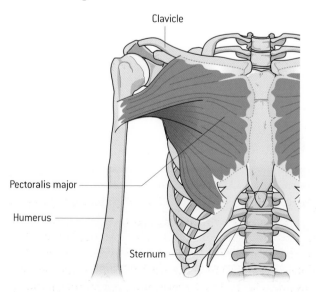

↑ Figure 1.16: Pectoralis major

The biceps brachii muscle has two heads (hence *bi*-ceps) which originate on the scapula (see Figure 1.17). The muscle runs down the anterior aspect of the upper arm and inserts onto the radius and ulna just below the elbow joint. The biceps crosses the shoulder joint and the elbow joint which means it is involved in both shoulder and elbow movement; specifically it flexes or brings the arm upwards at the shoulder and bends (flexes) the elbow.

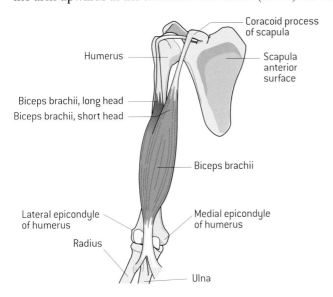

↑ Figure 1.17: Biceps brachii

The trapezius muscle is a triangular-shaped muscle located on the posterior neck and upper back (see Figure 1.18). The origin is at the base of the skull and along the cervical and thoracic vertebrae, and it inserts onto the clavicle and scapula. Its main action is to raise the shoulders, however it also controls the movements of the scapula which is important to allow powerful shoulder joint movements to take place.

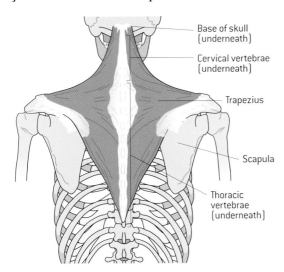

↑ Figure 1.18: Trapezius

The latissimus dorsi muscle is a large muscle located on the back. Its origin runs from the sacrum and ilium up along the lumbar and thoracic vertebrae (see Figure 1.19). The tendon of this muscle forms the posterior border of the armpit and inserts onto the inside of the humerus close to the insertion of the pectoralis major. The latissimus dorsi brings the arm backwards (into extension) and rotates the arm inwards. This makes it a very important muscle in rowing, swimming and boxing and is highly developed in athletes from these sports.

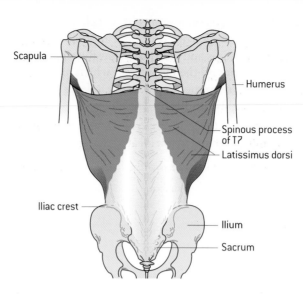

↑ Figure 1.19: Latissimus dorsi

The triceps brachii muscle is located on the posterior upper arm and the origin has three heads (hence *tri*-ceps) on the scapula and humerus (see Figure 1.20). The insertion point is on the bony prominence on the proximal and posterior ulna (often referred to as the tip of the elbow). Like the biceps muscle, the triceps is involved in both shoulder and elbow movement where it extends or moves the arm backwards at the shoulder and straightens the elbow.

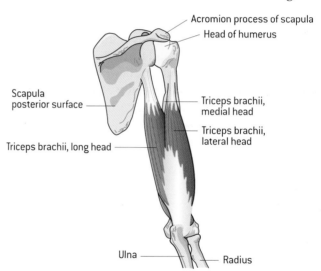

↑ Figure 1.20: Triceps brachii

MUSCLE	ORIGIN	INSERTION
Deltoid	Scapula, clavicle	Lateral humerus
Pectoralis major	Sternum, clavicle, anterior ribs	Humerus
Biceps brachii	Scapula	Radius, ulna
Trapezius	Cervical and thoracic vertebrae, base of skull	Clavicle, scapula
Latissimus dorsi	Sacrum, ilium, thoracic and lumbar vertebrae	Humerus
Triceps brachii	Scapula, humerus	Ulna

↑ Table 1.2: Origin and insertion of selected muscles of the upper extremity

Muscles of the lower extremity

The lower extremity muscles are generally bigger than the upper extremity muscles. This is because they have to bear the weight of the entire body and forcefully push off the ground to move the body forwards and upwards when walking. The iliopsoas, sartorius, quadriceps (rectus femoris, vastus intermedius, vastus medialis, vastus lateralis) and tibialis anterior are located anteriorly. The gluteus maximus, hamstrings (biceps femoris, semitendinosus, semimembranosus), gastrocnemius and soleus are located posteriorly.

Iliopsoas is a deep muscle which originates on the lumbar vertebrae and ilium and attaches to the inner femur (see Figure 1.21).

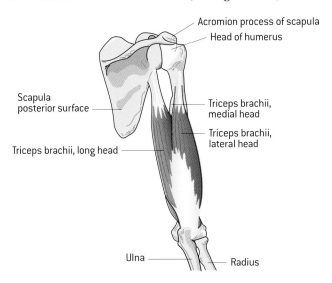

↑ Figure 1.21: Iliopsoas

Sartorius runs from the ilium to the medial tibia and is the longest muscle in the body, crossing both the hip and knee joints (see Figure 1.22). Both the iliopsoas and the sartorius bring the thigh upwards at the hip while the sartorius also bends the knee.

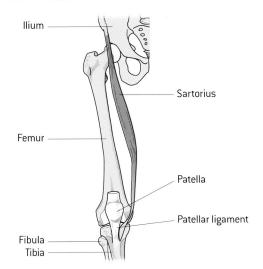

↑ Figure 1.22: Sartorius

There are four muscles in the quadriceps muscle group (rectus femoris, vastus medialis, vastus lateralis, vastus intermedius) which cover the front and sides of the thighs (see Figure 1.23). Rectus femoris originates on the ilium while the three vasti muscles originate on the femur. As the names suggest, vastus lateralis is located on the lateral thigh, vastus medialis is located on the medial thigh, and vastus intermedius is located between these and underneath the rectus femoris. The tendons of these four muscles join together to form a common tendon known as the quadriceps tendon which inserts into the patella. The quadriceps tendon continues below the patella as the patellar ligament and inserts onto the anterior and upper tibia. The quadriceps muscles straighten the knee joint and therefore are very important in sports which involve jumping or kicking.

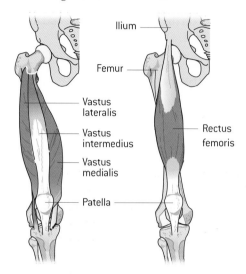

↑ Figure 1.23: Quadriceps

Tibialis anterior is located on the front of the lower leg. It runs between the tibia and fibula down the leg where it inserts onto the first metatarsal and tarsal bones of the foot (see Figure 1.24). When this muscle contracts, it pulls the toes towards the shins and is therefore used in walking and running.

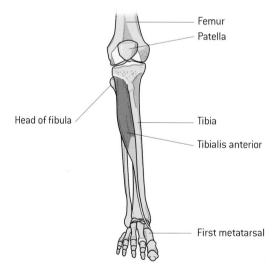

↑ Figure 1.24: Tibialis anterior

Gluteus maximus is a large muscle which covers the posterior hip and buttocks (see Figure 1.25). It originates on the sacrum, ilium and coccyx and inserts on to the upper part of the lateral femur. When this muscle contracts, it moves the thigh backwards at the hip into extension.

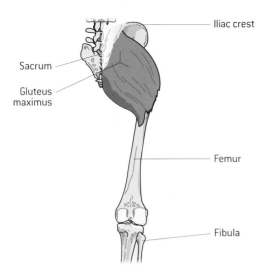

Sacrum

Gluteus
maximus

Iliac crest

Femur

Fibula

↑ Figure 1.25: Gluteus maximus

There are three muscles in the hamstring group (biceps femoris, semitendinosus, semimembranosus) and they are all located on the posterior thigh (see Figure 1.26). They all originate on the ischium, however they attach on different sides of the knee—the biceps femoris inserts on the head of fibula and lateral tibia, while the semitendinosus and semimembranosus insert on the medial tibia. As they cross both the hip and knee joints, they extend the hip and flex the knee. These muscles are powerfully used when running and kicking; as a result hamstring strains are common in sprinters and footballers.

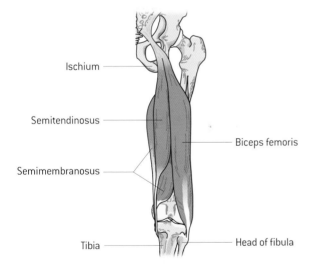

Ischium

Semitendinosus

Semimembranosus

Tibia

Biceps femoris

Head of fibula

↑ Figure 1.26: Hamstrings

The two main muscles in the calf are the gastrocnemius and the soleus (see Figures 1.27 & 1.28). The gastrocnemius is the most superficial of the two muscles and is the most prominent particularly when standing or walking on tiptoe. It has two heads which originate on the posterior femur and the muscle crosses both the knee joint and the ankle joint making it a two-joint muscle. The soleus originates on the posterior tibia and fibula and is located underneath the gastrocnemius. The tendons of both muscles join together to form the Achilles tendon, which attaches to the calcaneus (heel bone).

Chapter 1   MUSCULOSKELETAL ANATOMY

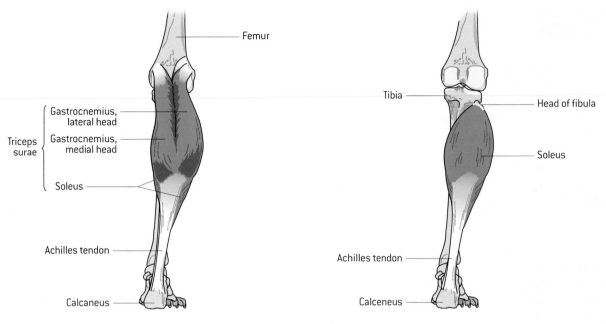

↑ Figure 1.27: Gastrocnemius   ↑ Figure 1.28: Soleus

THEORY OF KNOWLEDGE

A 2012 cross-sectional survey of girls from Pune (India) has shown that individuals from lower socio-economic groups tend to have low bone mineral density as compared to those from higher socio-economic groups.

(Khadilkar et al. 2012. "Poor bone health in underprivileged Indian girls: an effect of low bone mass accrual during puberty." *Bone*. Vol 50. Pp 1048–1053)

Explain why socio-economic factors may have a negative effect on the bone status of adolescents in developing countries.

MUSCLE	ORIGIN	INSERTION
Iliopsoas	Lumbar vertebrae, ilium	Inner femur
Sartorius	Ilium	Medial tibia
Quadriceps → Rectus femoris → Vastus lateralis → Vastus medialis → Vastus intermedius	 Ilium Femur Femur Femur	Patella and upper tibia (for all four)
Tibialis anterior	Lateral tibia	First metatarsal and first cuneiform (one of the tarsal bones)
Gluteus maximus	Posterior ilium, sacrum and coccyx	Lateral femur
Hamstrings → Biceps femoris → Semitendinosus → Semimembranosus	 Ischium, femur Ischium Ischium	 Fibula, lateral tibia Medial tibia Medial tibia
Gastrocnemius	Posterior femur	Calcaneus (one of the tarsal bones) via Achilles tendon
Soleus	Posterior tibia and fibula	Calcaneus via Achilles tendon

↑ Table 1.3: Origin and insertion of selected muscles of the lower extremity

24

→ The axial skeleton includes the skull, sternum, ribs and vertebrae. Its main function is protection.

→ The appendicular skeleton includes the pelvic and pectoral girdles and all the bones of the upper and lower extremities. The main function is movement.

→ The four main types of bone are long, short, flat and irregular.

→ Long bones have a diaphysis, epiphysis, articular cartilage, periosteum, medullary cavity, and nutrient foramen. Different parts of a long bone contain compact and cancellous bone.

→ Joints can be classified as fibrous, cartilaginous and synovial depending on if there is a joint cavity and how much movement is allowed. Synovial joints can be further subclassified depending on the shape of the bones and type of movement allowed.

→ The features of a synovial joint include the joint cavity, joint capsule, synovial membrane, articular cartilage, bursae and menisci.

→ There are three types of muscle—skeletal, cardiac and smooth.

→ The main properties of muscle are contractility, extensibility and elasticity.

→ Skeletal muscle is made up of sarcomeres which fit together in series to form myofibrils. They contain actin and myosin which give muscle its characteristic striated appearance. Individual muscle fibers are grouped together to form fascicles, which in turn are grouped together to form muscles. Groups of muscles with similar functions are grouped together in compartments.

→ The different levels of muscle are surrounded by layers of fascia called endomysium, perimysium and epimysium.

→ The origin and insertion of muscles refer to where they attach to bones.

Self-study questions

1   Assume the anatomical starting position. Identify the bone that is:
   → proximal to the phalanges
   → anterior to the distal end of the femur
   → posterior to the clavicle
   → distal to the femur
   → inferior to the third rib
   → lateral to the tibia
   → medial to the radius
   → superior to the first thoracic vertebrae.

2   Name the bones that make up the:
   → axial skeleton
   → appendicular skeleton.

3   What bones form the pelvic girdle?

4   What is the longest bone in the body?

5   What are the functions of the skeletal system?

6   What are the functions of the vertebral column?

7   Name the types of bone. Which type is most important for movement?

8   Identify the type of bone that each of the following bones would be–patella, metacarpals, cervical vertebrae, sternum, radius, sacrum, tarsals.

9   How do the axial and appendicular skeletons differ in terms of their main function?

10 In which bones is compact bone usually found?

11 In which bones is cancellous bone usually found?

12 What are the ends and the shaft of a long bone called?

13 What would you find in the medullary cavity of a long bone?

14 What factors affect the stability of a joint?

15 Name and briefly describe the types of synovial joint that are found in the body. Which type of joint has most movement?

16 How do fibrous, cartilaginous and synovial joints differ?

17 What type of joint is the elbow joint?

18 Where is articular cartilage found and what is its function?

19 Where is synovial fluid found and what is its function?

20 Where are bursae commonly found? Describe them and their function.

21 A tendon connects _____ to _____.

22 A ligament connects _____ to _____.

23 Name the important shoulder joint muscles.

24 Name the important hip joint muscles.

25 What is the longest muscle in the body?

26 What muscle is well developed in rowers?

27 Identify the muscle that goes:

→   from the ilium, lumbar, sacral and thoracic vertebrae across the lower and middle back to the humerus

→   from the ischium and femur to the lateral tibia

→   from the lumbar, thoracic and cervical vertebrae and ribs up along the length of the spine

→   from the anterior sternum and clavicle to the humerus

→   from the anterior tibia and fibula to the tarsals

→   from the scapula down along the anterior humerus to the radius and ulna.

28 Name and briefly explain the properties of muscle.

29 Name the layers of fascia found in muscle and identify where they are found.

30 What gives muscle its characteristic striated appearance?

31 Which muscles make up the calf? Which is the most superficial?

32 How many muscles are in the quadriceps muscle group? Name them.

33 How many muscles are in the hamstrings muscle group? Name them.

34 Label the bones on the following diagram.

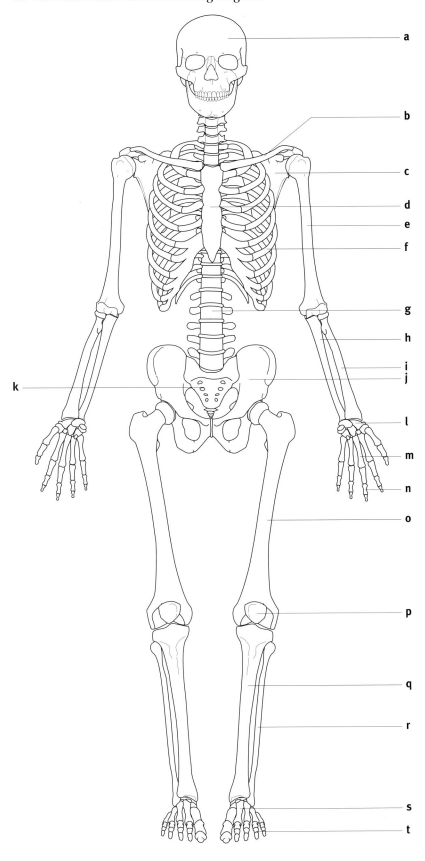

a

b

c

d

e

f

g

h

i

j

k

l

m

n

o

p

q

r

s

t

35 Label the features of this long bone.

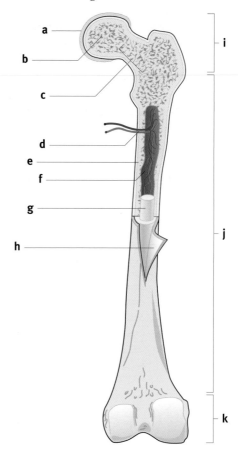

36 Label the features of this synovial joint.

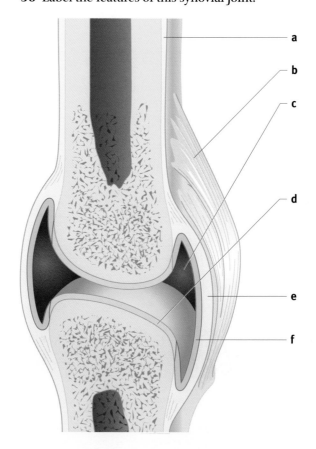

DATA BASED QUESTION

Bone mineral density (BMD) gives an estimate of bone mass. Several longitudinal studies in the US measured fracture risk, BMD and annual change in BMD at the neck of the femur. This paper presents results from these studies and examines if there were any racial differences in these measures.

	Black females	White females	Black males	White males
Mean BMD (g.cm^{-2})	0.75	0.65	0.86	0.75
Annual change in BMD (%)	−0.19	−0.51	−1.1	−2.1
Fracture risk (per 1,000)	4.1	10.1	3.1	4.3

Source: Hochberg, M.C. 2007. "Racial Differences in Bone Strength." *Transactions of the American Clinical and Climatological Association*. Vol 118. Pp 305–15.

1 Is the risk of fracture higher in blacks or whites?

2 Identify what factors may contribute to this increased risk.

3 Suggest ways in which the level of BMD can be increased?

CHAPTER 2

Cardio-respiratory exercise physiology

OBJECTIVES

By the end of this chapter students should be able to:

→ introduce the concept of homeostasis

→ describe the structure and function of the ventilatory system

→ consider the relative importance of static and dynamic lung volumes

→ explain the processes of gas exchange and transport

→ state the structure and function of blood cells

→ describe the structures and functions of the cardiovascular system

→ detail the main responses of the ventilatory and cardiovascular systems during exercise, including how training affects these responses

→ discuss the importance of blood pressure and redistribution of blood flow

→ introduce the functional importance of maximal oxygen uptake ($\dot{V}O_2$max)

→ identify some of the factors that contribute to differences in $\dot{V}O_2$max.

Introduction

> 66 Even when all is known, the care of a man is not yet complete, because eating alone will not keep a man well; he must also take exercise. For food and exercise, while possessing opposite qualities, yet work together to produce health. 99
>
> Hippocrates

Physiology is the study of how the human body functions and has intrigued mankind for centuries. Advances in technology have allowed us to explore in ever greater detail, progressing our knowledge and understanding to reinforce quite how remarkable the human body is. Exercise presents an excellent model to demonstrate just how effectively the systems within the body are regulated and interact with each other. Importantly, the same processes apply to everyone across a very wide spectrum, from elderly people trying to complete activities of daily living, to a highly trained athlete competing at the very top levels of sport.

THEORY OF KNOWLEDGE

Haile Gebrselassie is a long-distance runner who was born in 1973 in Asella, Arsi Province, Ethiopia. He was one of 10 children. During his childhood, Gebrselassie grew up on a farm and had to run 10 kilometers daily to go to school (carrying his books) which laid the foundation for his running career. In 1995, he ran 5000 meters in 12:44.39 and broke the world record (12:55.30). This world record at the Weltklasse meet in Zürich was voted 'Performance of the Year' by Track and Field News magazine. At the 1996 Atlanta Olympics, Gebrselassie won his first Olympic gold in the 10 000 meter race. A couple of years later, in Hengelo, Netherlands, he set a 10 000 meter world record of 26:22.75. He entered the 2000 Sydney Olympics and became the third man in history to successfully defend an Olympic 10 000 meter title. In 2005, Gebrselassie went undefeated in all of his road races, which included a British All-Comers record in the 10 000 meters at Manchester, a win in the Amsterdam Marathon by setting the record for the fastest marathon time in the world for 2006 (2:06:20), and a new world best for 10 miles in Tilburg, Netherlands (44:24). Gebrselassie decided not to take part in the 2008 Beijing Olympics due to high air pollution levels in the city.

A central theory of human physiology is homeostasis, defined as maintenance of a constant internal environment. The underpinning theory in its current format was detailed in Walter Cannon's seminal book *The Wisdom of the Body* (1932). It is based on the stability of several key variables, achieved by changes in a number of physiological systems. It has since become apparent that many systems within the body are continuously working in a highly coordinated manner to keep a large number of variables at, or as close as possible to, resting levels. Exercise presents a number of challenges to the homeostasis of the body and successful completion of exercise requires the systems within the body to function together, tightly regulating the conditions of the internal tissues.

The cardiovascular and ventilatory systems are examples of such systems that work together to regulate variables such as the oxygen content of arterial blood, acid-base status and core body temperature, to name a few. The transport of oxygen is an excellent illustration of the body's systems in action during exercise and this will present a common theme while studying the cardiovascular and ventilatory responses to exercise in this chapter. Indeed, the rate at which oxygen is taken into the body and used (known as oxygen uptake, $\dot{V}O_2$) is an excellent indicator of how well these systems are working together.

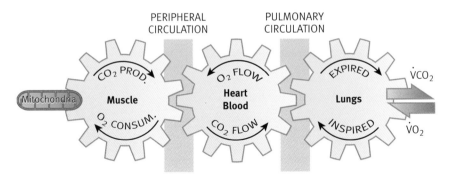

↑ Figure 2.1: A version of Wasserman's three cogs, illustrating the stages in the process from oxygen being taken in and used (oxygen uptake $-\dot{V}O_2$) with the carbon dioxide then being produced and removed (carbon dioxide output $-\dot{V}CO_2$)

Figure 2.1 shows how oxygen is transported from the atmosphere to exercising muscles for use in the aerobic energy systems. Note the representation of the systems as cogs that are required to fit together and work dependent on one

Homeostasis maintenance of a constant internal environment

Gas exchange the transfer of oxygen and carbon dioxide between the systems

another. Note also the importance of oxygen and carbon dioxide transfer between the systems, known as gas exchange (taking place in the shaded areas where the cogs meet).

In healthy humans these cogs work well at rest, irrespective of age. During exercise, when more oxygen is required by the active muscles, we can establish how well the systems are integrating by directly analysing the breathing responses and air content to calculate $\dot{V}O_2$. This makes $\dot{V}O_2$ a valuable marker of physiological function and an exercise physiologist will measure this during exercise to evaluate health and fitness. The relevance applies to a patient with some form of respiratory or cardiovascular disease where exercise capacity is seriously compromised, as well as to the highly trained endurance athlete where adaptations to training have greatly increased exercise capacity.

KEY POINT

The ventilatory and cardiovascular systems work together in a highly coordinated manner to increase oxygen delivery during exercise. This is part of the body continuously trying to maintain a constant internal environment (homeostasis).

TO THINK ABOUT
The exercise test

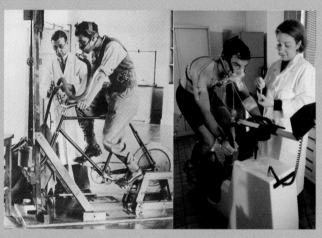

Tests of physiological responses to exercise have changed considerably. Early experiments were interested in learning what happens to try and further understand the interaction of systems. Most testing was confined to research projects in specialist labs, using early forms of heart monitoring and gas exchange equipment on people who performed controlled exercise attached to considerable amounts of equipment.

Nowadays, exercise tests are routinely conducted in a very wide range of settings: physical screening of employees to confirm fitness to do a job (e.g. emergency services or military); health testing in hospitals to determine causes or impact of illness, as well as responses to treatment; monitoring of athletes to evaluate levels of fitness and responses to training.

Advances in technology mean that physiological responses to exercise can now be measured using a variety of online systems that are often portable and wireless. This removes many of the constraints on what can easily be achieved, further enabling the study of exercise physiology in action. The demands of many forms of exercise have now been well characterized, such that sport and exercise scientists can develop various methods of optimizing performance through interventions such as training, nutrition and cooling.

Ventilatory system

The first stage in the oxygen transport system is the breathing in of oxygen-rich air through the mouth or nose and into the lungs. The action of breathing is mostly an involuntary process, although we can control it by choice to an extent, e.g. holding your breath when under water or trying to blow up a balloon.

The basis of air movement by breathing during rest and exercise is a principle of physics. A substance, air in this case, will flow from an area of higher pressure to an area of lower pressure. Therefore, for inhalation (breathing in) to occur the air pressure in the lungs needs to be lower than in the atmosphere. At rest this is almost entirely caused by contraction of the muscular diaphragm (Figure 2.2) at the base of the chest cavity (thorax). The diaphragm pulls downwards and, because of a vacuum between the lungs, chest walls and diaphragm, this increases the volume of the lungs. This increase in lung volume reduces the pressure in the lungs causing air to flow from the atmosphere into the lungs to balance the pressure gradient.

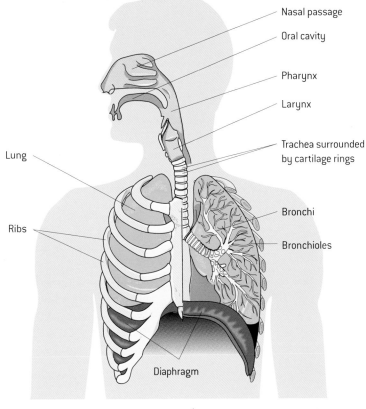

↑ Figure 2.2: Anatomy of the ventilatory system

At rest, the exhalation (breathing out) process is passive (no energy required) as the diaphragm relaxes and therefore recoils back to its original position without any conscious muscular work. This recoil naturally reduces the volume of the lungs, increasing the pressure to greater than that of the atmosphere, causing air to flow back out again. The cycle then repeats and during exercise the principle remains the same.

However, during exercise when more oxygen is needed by the active muscles and more carbon dioxide is being produced by the muscles, more air needs to be inhaled and exhaled at a faster rate. To achieve this, some additional muscles in the chest wall (external intercostal muscles), abdomen, and even the shoulders, can assist with increasing the lung volume during inhalation. Furthermore, contraction of these muscles during exhalation will also compress the lungs faster and more forcefully than the natural recoil. This is therefore an active process, requiring energy to fuel the muscles of the chest and abdomen.

The inhaled air initially passes through the conducting airways (the nasal and oral passageways, and the larger airways such as the trachea and bronchi) and although no gas exchange takes place here, the air is warmed, moistened and filtered by the lining of the airways.

The airways continuously branch into smaller bronchioles and eventually end in small air sacs, each one known as an alveolus. This is where gas exchange takes place, with oxygen and carbon dioxide moving across the very thin barrier that separates the alveoli from the passing blood for further transport.

The lungs are ideally designed for gas exchange as they cover a very large surface area (millions of alveoli make a total of approximately 50-100 m², equivalent to around half a tennis court), have a good blood supply, and have a very thin total distance between the alveoli and blood (0.4 µm).

KEY POINT

The movement of air in and out of the lungs is achieved by repeated contraction and relaxation of muscles in the base of the chest cavity (diaphragm) and chest wall to alternately increase and decrease the volume of, and therefore pressure in, the lungs.

What do lung volumes tell us about fitness?

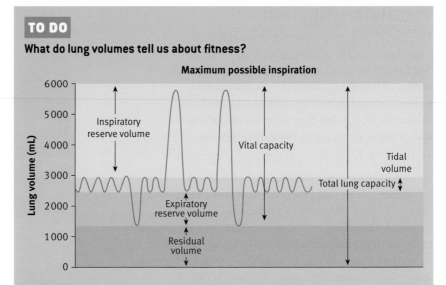

The above trace shows the change in volume during some resting breaths and some forced breaths (where the person breathes in and out as much as possible). From the above trace, define the following terms:

→ vital capacity
→ residual volume
→ tidal volume
→ total lung capacity
→ inspiratory and expiratory reserve volumes.

Interestingly, when we compare trained and untrained people of similar size, it becomes clear that these lung volumes are not something that can be trained and are not related to aerobic fitness. They are mostly determined by natural body size and age/health status.

In contrast, the rate at which the air can be exhaled is a very sensitive marker of lung function. For example, the maximum volume that can be breathed out in one second (Forced Expiratory Volume in one second, FEV_1) is often used as a test of dynamic lung volume.

An interesting area for research at present is whether training the respiratory muscles can assist performance. In contrast to original ideas in this field, there is some suggestion that training these muscles with special resisted breathing devices can improve long duration endurance performance by making breathing easier without any changes in lung volume.

Gas exchange

Gas exchange in the lungs, as well as in other body tissues, takes place according to another passive process known as diffusion. This is another basic principle of physics. Gas will move along a gradient from an area of higher partial pressure to lower partial pressure. Partial pressure is similar to concentration, but represents the pressure exerted by a single gas (e.g. oxygen) within a mixture (e.g. air, blood or tissue fluid).

In the lungs, the air breathed in is high in oxygen and low in carbon dioxide. The blood being pumped to the lungs from the active tissues via the heart is lower in oxygen and higher in carbon dioxide. Therefore, oxygen will diffuse from the alveolus into the blood, and carbon dioxide will diffuse from the blood into the alveolus (Figure 2.3). The blood leaving the lungs, now high in oxygen and low in carbon dioxide, will be pumped to the tissues via the heart. At the tissues where oxygen is being used up and carbon dioxide produced, the pressure gradients will drive oxygen from blood into tissues and carbon dioxide from tissues into blood.

During exercise, the pressure gradient at the tissues and lungs becomes greater as more oxygen is being used up and more carbon dioxide is being produced (Figure 2.3). The challenge for the lungs is to maintain resting partial pressures in the alveoli. This is achieved by breathing out the air with less oxygen and more carbon dioxide and then breathing in fresh air to maintain the pressure gradients for diffusion to occur. Otherwise the exercise could not be sustained for long.

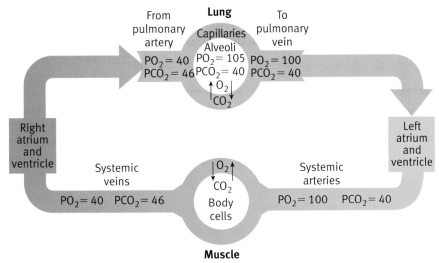

↑ Figure 2.3: Simplified version of partial pressure differences between lungs, blood and tissues (all partial pressures are in the units of mmHg)

Ventilation during exercise

The minute ventilation ($\dot{V}_E$) describes the volume of air being exhaled per minute (and inhaled as we don't store air).

$\dot{V}_E$ is determined as the product of the size of each breath (V_T = tidal volume) multiplied by the number of breaths per minute (B_f = breathing frequency).

$$\dot{V}_E \text{ (L.min}^{-1}) = V_T \text{ (L.breath}^{-1}) \times B_f \text{ (breaths.min}^{-1})$$

TO DO

Complete the table below that presents some data collected during an exercise test.

		EXERCISE INTENSITY DURING RUNNING AT PROGRESSIVELY FASTER SPEEDS						
	Rest	8 km.h^{-1}	10 km.h^{-1}	12 km.h^{-1}	14 km.h^{-1}	16 km.h^{-1}	18 km.h^{-1}
V_T (L.br^{-1})	0.67	2		3.3	3.6		4
B_f (br.min^{-1})	12		22.3	24.2		30	38
$\dot{V}_E$ (L.min^{-1})	8	40	58		98	115	

↑ Table 2.1: Comparison of $\dot{V}_E$, V_T and B_f values at rest and during incremental exercise

As exercise intensity increases, how is the increased ventilation achieved?

During exercise $\dot{V}_E$ typically increases by increasing both V_T and B_f (Table 2.1) to maintain resting gas partial pressures in the lungs and arterial blood supply to the active tissues. As the exercise becomes harder the ventilation increases further, such that in healthy individuals the homeostasis of arterial partial pressure of oxygen is preserved, even at maximal exercise intensities (with the exception of some highly trained athletes). This very tight regulation raises the question of how the ventilation response to exercise is controlled.

Despite a very large amount of research conducted on this topic, there is no single factor in the body that regulates ventilation alone. Instead, researchers have identified a number of factors that can stimulate or inhibit ventilation according to the conditions, e.g. gas partial pressures, acidity, temperature, hormones. The relative contribution of these factors during exercise depends on the characteristics of the exercise, such as intensity, duration and environmental conditions. For example, we know that when exercising at altitude, where the atmospheric partial pressure of oxygen is reduced, receptors that are sensitive to the oxygen content of the blood stimulate increased ventilation. However, at sea level, in the majority of individuals, arterial oxygen content is kept constant. So, although oxygen can be a contributing factor, it would appear that during exercise the ventilation response is actually more sensitive to carbon dioxide increases, particularly during high intensity exercise.

KEY POINT

Ventilation increases in response to the increasing intensity of exercise to maintain resting oxygen and carbon dioxide levels in the arterial blood supplying exercising muscles. This is achieved by increasing breathing depth and rate. The control of ventilation is very complex and no single factor is responsible, although carbon dioxide plays an important role.

TO THINK ABOUT

Examples of the importance of CO_2

The term hyperventilation refers to an increase in ventilation above what is actually required to meet the oxygen demand of the exercise. Such a response means that we exhale more carbon dioxide than necessary and arterial blood levels of carbon dioxide fall. Such a drop in carbon dioxide will reduce our drive to breathe and there are two very different ways in which we can demonstrate this.

Rebreathing

In the past, some people recommended breathing into a paper bag when someone has had a 'panic attack'. The theory behind this advice was that when a person suffers from an acute period of heightened anxiety he or she will hyperventilate. This causes a drop in arterial carbon dioxide which reduces the stimulus to breathe, which in turn can cause the sensation of further panic as the person becomes confused and further hyperventilates making the situation worse.

This is not caused by an excess of oxygen being detected by the brain. By breathing in and out of a paper bag the person breathes some of the carbon dioxide back in and this builds up over a few breathing cycles to restore arterial carbon dioxide levels. Provided the person is able to reduce their state of anxiety their breathing should return to normal.

NOTE: This explanation and practice only applies when there is no further pathological cause for the hyperventilation, otherwise rebreathing could actually cause further problems and place the person at increased risk. This is why current first aid guidance advises against using such rebreathing techniques.

Cardiovascular system

Blood

During exercise the primary function of blood is transport to and from various tissues, whether it be transport of gases, nutrients, waste products, hormones or even heat. The total volume of blood in the body is around 5 litres for a 70 kilogram male. Approximately 55% of this blood is fluid known as plasma which contains some dissolved substances, and the remainder is blood cells and platelets.

The primary role of platelets (< 1% of blood volume) is to assist in the process of repair following injury, but the blood cells have a variety of roles. White blood cells (< 1% of blood volume), known as leucocytes, are primarily involved in immune function, protecting the body from infection. Trillions of red blood cells, known as erythrocytes, make up around 40-45% of the blood volume which is known as the hematocrit, although the exact value is dependent on factors such as how well trained an individual is and gender.

The increased volume of carbon dioxide produced during exercise is transported from the muscles to the lungs for exhalation, partly dissolved in blood but mostly in the temporary form of bicarbonate. Oxygen is less soluble in the plasma; only a few per cent of the total oxygen delivered to the active muscles is transported this way. Instead, oxygen temporarily attaches to an iron-rich pigment in the blood called hemoglobin. In the lungs where there is high partial pressure, oxygen easily binds to the hemoglobin. In the active muscle where partial pressure is lower, oxygen detaches and diffuses from the blood into the active tissues. The deoxygenated red blood cells then return to the lungs (via the heart) where more oxygen can bind.

If hemoglobin concentration can be increased by manipulating the hormone erythropoietin (EPO) responsible for stimulating red blood cell production, then more oxygen can be transported and aerobic exercise performance will improve. This is the reason behind many endurance athletes often living and/ or training at altitude, where less oxygen availability naturally stimulates more hemoglobin production so that when athletes return to sea level they can perform better.

Unfortunately, there are also illegal methods that are abused in sport to achieve the same goal. For example, blood doping involves removing some blood from an athlete weeks before a competition and storing it while the athlete's hemoglobin is restored naturally by EPO stimulation. Then just before the competition the stored blood is reintroduced so that hemoglobin concentration is higher than normal, more oxygen can be transported and exercise performance is better. Or athletes can be injected with synthetic EPO to achieve the same goal without even removing blood. The detection of synthetic EPO or blood doping abuse remains a very significant challenge for the World Anti-Doping Agency (WADA), as significant immediate benefits can be achieved for athletes (see chapter 9).

Circulation

Blood is transported around the body through an extensive network of blood vessels. These include the following:

→ **Arteries** These are vessels which are relatively large in diameter. They have thick muscular walls as there is considerable pressure exerted from the oxygen-rich blood in these vessels. They are responsible for transport away from the heart to tissues. (Tip: remember that *a*rteries take blood *a*way from the heart.) Arteries then branch into narrower arterioles.

→ **Capillaries** Supplied by the arterioles, these are very narrow vessels with very thin walls. They form an extensive branching network through tissues and are the sites of exchange between blood and tissues.

→ **Veins** The capillaries link to larger vessels called venules and then larger veins which are the vessels that deliver mostly deoxygenated blood back towards the heart. They are less muscular and fibrous than arteries as pressure is lower, so they are flexible and contain valves to prevent back-flow.

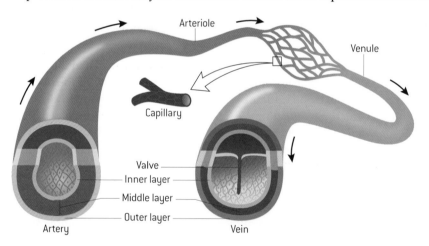

↑ Figure 2.4

The pump at the center of the cardiovascular system is the heart, which is a sequence of chambers enclosed by walls of specialist muscle fibers called cardiac muscle fibers. The heart is the link between two distinct loops of circulation (look at the central cog in Figure 2.1).

→ The pulmonary circulation delivers deoxygenated blood from the right side of the heart to the lungs for oxygenation and then back to the left side of the heart.

→ The systemic circulation delivers this oxygenated blood from the left side of the heart to the other tissues of the body where oxygen is used up, and then delivers deoxygenated blood back to the right side of the heart for the cycle to continue. This includes the heart itself which consists of specialized muscle tissue and therefore needs to be supplied with essential blood through the coronary arteries. Any disruption to the coronary arteries will result in a heart attack as the cardiac muscle is starved of oxygen and therefore cannot function correctly.

The cardiac cycle

The heart can be considered a four-chamber double-pump system. The left and right sides of the heart work in parallel simultaneously. Each has an atrium that first receives blood from a vein and then pushes it into a larger and thicker-walled ventricle. The ventricle then pushes blood out of the heart into an artery for transport away from the heart.

There are a series of valves between chambers that close and open by force in response to a highly coordinated sequence of muscle contractions. The valves ensure that the system operates in one direction and enable heart muscle contractions to increase pressure in the chambers for ejection of blood (either from an atrium into a ventricle, or from a ventricle into an artery and away from the heart).

Unlike other muscular contractions in the body, the cardiac cycle does not require a nerve stimulation to make the heart muscle contract. This means that the heart makes itself contract and this is called a myogenic contraction. The sequential contractions of the chambers are initiated from a specialist group of cells called the pacemaker (or sinoatrial node, SAN), found in the wall of the right atrium. However, before detailing the stages of the cardiac cycle it is important to point out that the pacemaker firing rate is heavily influenced by many factors.

As well as direct hormonal stimulation (e.g. adrenaline) or manipulation by drugs, the autonomic nervous system (involuntary) can speed up or slow down the pacemaker firing rate by adjusting the relative contributions from the sympathetic and parasympathetic branches respectively. This involuntary control is an example of systems responding to a range of stimuli to try and maintain homeostasis, by increasing or decreasing the release of specific chemicals called neurotransmitters. For example, when exercise begins the parasympathetic stimulation is reduced (this normally keeps the heart rate low) and the sympathetic stimulation is increased, resulting in increased heart rate.

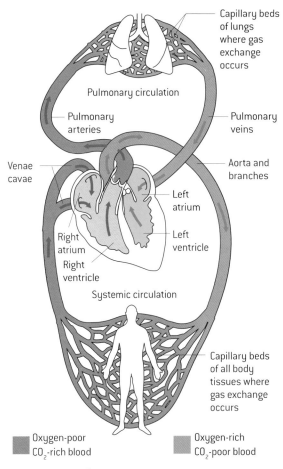

↑ Figure 2.5

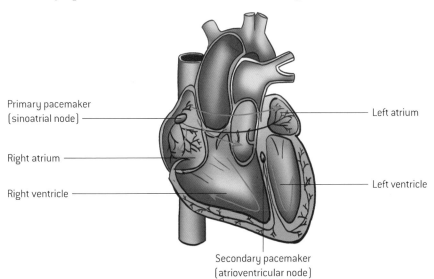

↑ Figure 2.6

The pacemaker sends an impulse through the walls of the atria (left and right sides) to a second group of specialist cells called the atrioventricular (AV) node (Figure 2.6). This rapid conduction of the impulse causes the muscles in the walls of the atria to contract simultaneously, increasing the pressure in the atria and forcing blood from the atria, through the AV valves, into the ventricles. The AV valves then close.

Following a very brief delay, the impulse is then conducted rapidly via a bundle of specialist cells called the Bundle of His. These cells rapidly conduct the impulse along the very fast conducting Purkinje fibers that spread the impulse along the ventricle walls. This impulse now causes the fibers in the ventricle walls to contract simultaneously, increasing the pressure in the ventricles and forcing blood up and out through the main arteries leaving the heart.

The semi-lunar valves at the openings into the main arteries now close, and while the ventricles relax the cycle has already started again with the atria filling with blood returning to the heart ahead of the pacemaker firing.

Blood pressure

In order for blood to flow around the body we have so far recognized the importance of the heart pumping the blood. We have mentioned the contraction and relaxation of the chamber walls to cause changes in the pressure exerted on the blood to drive it through and out of the heart and around the body. Accordingly, if we directly measure the pressure in the blood vessels leaving the heart (arteries), it fluctuates according to the different phases of the cardiac cycle, between very high peaks as the ventricle contracts and forces blood out, to troughs were the ventricle is relaxing and no blood is being pumped out (semi-lunar valves are closed). These represent what are known as the systolic (contracting) and diastolic (relaxing) pressures respectively.

In a resting, healthy adult the typical values would be in the range of 120 mmHg (systolic) to 80 mmHg (diastolic), described as "120 over 80 mmHg". This is the ideal balance to permit efficient emptying and filling of the heart, but with enough pressure in the system to maintain blood flow to the tissues of the body. The pressure (and extent of the fluctuations) lessens as the blood goes from the arteries to arterioles and then capillaries. The pressure in the venules and veins is comparatively low and consistent, but it is the arterial pressure that is most important and this is what is routinely measured by physicians.

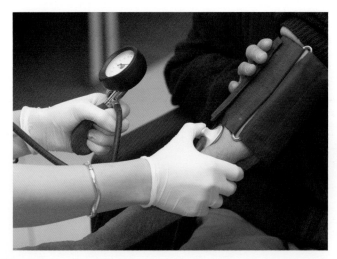

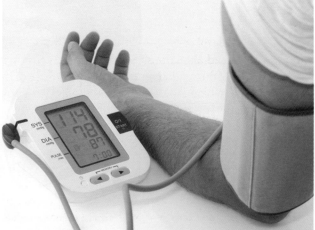

TO DO

Interpret blood pressure readings

Blood pressure can be measured manually using an adjustable pressure cuff (that can be inflated or deflated gradually to restrict blood flow) attached to a pressure measuring device (a sphygmomanometer) and a stethoscope (to listen to an artery for what are known as the Korotkoff sounds). Alternatively, there are many commercially available automatic blood pressure measuring devices, but the principle is exactly the same.

The cuff is inflated to a pressure higher than systolic pressure (around 150–180 mmHg in a healthy young person) to stop blood flow through the artery as it is compressed (there will be no sound in the artery below the cuff). The cuff is then very slowly allowed to deflate. As the systolic pressure is reached a tapping sound can be heard as blood is intermittently able to get through the blocked artery immediately after each heart contraction only—the systolic pressure is noted at this point. With further deflation the sounds will disappear as full blood flow is restored—at this point the diastolic pressure is noted.

	ACTIVITY	DIASTOLIC PRESSURE (mmHg)	SYSTOLIC PRESSURE (mmHg)
80 kg healthy male	*Rest*	75	116
	Running	80	180
	Lifting	150	240
100 kg unhealthy male	*Rest*	95	150

The table above presents data for a healthy trained 80 kg male at rest and performing two different actions (running fast, a dynamic activity; trying to lift a very heavy object, static but very high forces), as well as resting data for another untrained and unhealthy individual. Answer the following questions.

1   What effect does dynamic exercise have on blood pressure?
2   What effect does static exercise have on blood pressure?
3   Why is one higher than the other?
4   What difference is there between the two participants at rest?
5   Elevated blood pressure is known as hypertension. Why would a higher blood pressure present a challenge that may result in health complications?

Blood flow distribution

During exercise, and even at rest, the diameter of the arteries, arterioles and opening/closing of capillaries needs to be carefully regulated to keep blood pressure at a sufficient level to ensure cardiovascular function. This is achieved by involuntary control of the smooth muscle which lines the walls of the arteries and arterioles, and also around tiny sphincters throughout the network of capillaries. If all of this smooth muscle relaxed then there would not be sufficient pressure to return blood to the heart and the cardiac cycle could not function. Therefore, the nervous system and cardiovascular system interact carefully so that there is sufficient relaxation of some vessel walls and contraction of others to ensure that enough blood is passing through all organs requiring exchange, yet blood pressure is maintained.

During exercise the muscles that are being used become the main demand on blood flow, as more oxygen and nutrients are required and more waste products and heat need to be removed. Therefore, in addition to the increases in cardiac output (below), more blood is directed towards the active muscles by dilating the arterioles supplying the muscles and opening more of the capillary network within the muscles. However, to prevent a resulting catastrophic drop in blood pressure throughout the whole system, the vessels supplying other organs in the body constrict and many of the capillaries are closed so that blood flow is reduced to these organs.

As shown in Figure 2.7, some essential organs such as the brain and heart are protected so that they still have sufficient supply (life could be compromised if either had insufficient blood flow), but active muscles can demand as high as 90 per cent of the total blood flow during exercise compared to only 20% at rest.

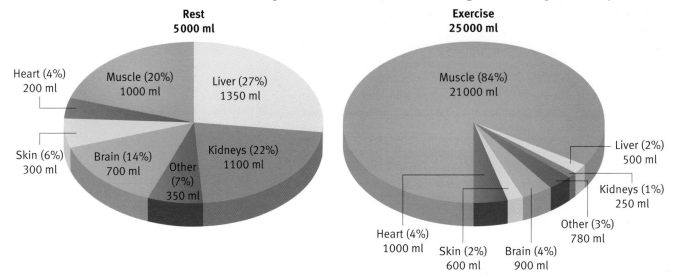

↑ Figure 2.7

Acute cardiovascular responses to exercise

With ventilatory responses deemed to be sufficient to maintain efficient gas exchange in healthy individuals, even during maximal exercise, the cardiovascular system is crucial to maintain function and attempt to maintain homeostasis in the face of the exercise challenge. Previous sections have highlighted various ways in which this is achieved to an extent, but it is the responses of the heart to dynamic exercise that can truly be considered "central". Accordingly, the responses of the heart are very accurately regulated according to the demands of the exercise.

This is nicely illustrated by exploring the increase of blood flow out of the heart during exercise and how this is achieved. Cardiac output is defined as the amount of blood ejected from the left side of the heart (and therefore supplying the whole body except the lungs) in litres per minute. Cardiac output is determined by how quickly the heart is beating (heart rate in beats per minute) and the amount of blood being ejected with each contraction (stroke volume in millilitres per beat), according to the following equation:

$$\text{Cardiac output} = (\text{Heart rate} \times \text{Stroke volume}) \div 1000$$

In order to achieve the increases in cardiac output required during exercise the heart beats faster (increased heart rate) and the heart fills and empties more during each contraction (increased stroke volume). As exercise becomes progressively harder, the heart rate and stroke volume both increase until their respective maximum rate and volume are achieved. As maximum cardiac output is reached so too is exhaustion and exercise cannot continue at this intensity (see section below).

In contrast, during prolonged sub-maximal exercise at a fixed intensity (endurance activities), the cardiac output is maintained at the same level throughout as the demand stays constant with stroke volume and heart rate at values higher than rest. Interestingly, however, while cardiac output stays constant eventually the heart rate starts to increase slightly and progressively. This is known as cardiovascular drift and reflects a decline in stroke volume, primarily due to changes in thermoregulation.

TO DO

The table below shows the cardiovascular responses during dynamic whole-body exercise for 2 adult males of similar age (20 years old) and size (1.8 m, 70 kg), but one is sedentary and the other is a well-trained endurance athlete. Data reflect 3 levels of exercise intensity: rest; sub-maximal exercise (Sub-max.) walking at the same speed; and maximal exercise (Max.) at the point of exhaustion.

	INTENSITY	UNTRAINED ADULT MALE	TRAINED ADULT MALE
Heart rate (beats.min^{-1})	Rest	75	50
	Sub-max.	110	80
	Max.	197	195
Stroke volume (ml.beat^{-1})	Rest	60	90
	Sub-max.	85	112
	Max.	120	190
Cardiac output (L.min^{-1})	Rest	4.6	4.5
	Sub-max.	9.4	9.0
	Max.	19.7	32.2

1 Evaluate the effect of training on the cardiovascular responses to sub-maximal and maximal dynamic exercise.
2 Aside from any differences in training status, predict any differences that you would expect if the data in the above table were compared to an adult female.

TO THINK ABOUT

Sub-maximal cardiovascular responses are different in children and adults. Both boys and girls have a lower cardiac output than adults at a given absolute sub-maximal rate of work. This lower cardiac output is attributable to a lower stroke volume, which is partially compensated for by a higher heart rate. The table below shows the data from a study comparing cardiovascular responses to cycling and treadmill running in 7–9 year old children versus 18–26 year old adults.

	CARDIAC OUTPUT L.min^{-1}		STROKE VOLUME ml		HEART RATE beats.min^{-1}	
	CHILD	ADULT	CHILD	ADULT	CHILD	ADULT
Cycle 60 W	9.4	12.4	61.9	126.8	153.1	97.8
Run 3 mph	6.7	12.3	57.3	135.7	116.0	92.0

Differences in sub-maximal cardiovascular responses between children and adults are related to the smaller hearts and a smaller amount of muscle doing a given rate of work in the children.

Functional capacity of the cardiorespiratory systems

It is clear that the response of the human body to exercise requires the successful integration and regulation of a number of systems in the body. There are limits to how hard theses systems can be pushed and this is reflected in the varied durations and intensities of exercise that people can tolerate. The most commonly used marker of an individual's aerobic fitness brings us back to the importance of $\dot{V}O_2$ discussed at the start of this chapter.

Maximal oxygen uptake ($\dot{V}O_2$max) quantifies the maximum rate that an individual can take in and use oxygen. The $\dot{V}O_2$ is directly assessed by measuring the gas concentration and volume of air being breathed out at progressively increasing intensities of exercise. As the oxygen demand increases so too does the $\dot{V}O_2$, until the person approaches their limit, that is their $\dot{V}O_2$max. At this time, even if intensity (and therefore oxygen demand) is further increased, the $\dot{V}O_2$ cannot increase any further and the person will stop exercising as they can no longer continue.

For this reason, the $\dot{V}O_2$max is sometimes known as aerobic capacity and this is why it is a parameter of interest for physiologists working with both severely limited patients and elite endurance athletes. The patients will have a very low $\dot{V}O_2$max and therefore cannot cope with what may seem relatively easy exercise to us. Whereas the elite endurance athletes will have very high $\dot{V}O_2$max values and are therefore capable of the impressive endurance performances that we see in high performance sport.

Fick equation

In maximum exercise the Fick equation summarises the important relationship between maximum cardiac output, maximum arterio-venous oxygen difference, and $\dot{V}O_2$ max:

$\dot{V}O_2$max = Maximum cardiac output $\times$ Maximum aterio-venous oxygen difference

As well as a larger cardiac output, other positive endurance training adaptations include both a more effective blood "shunting" (redistribution) and increases in skeletal muscle microcirculation (ratio of capillaries to muscle fiber). This helps to increase tissue oxygen extraction during intense exercise for both children and adults. Higher heart rates in children compared to adults during sub-maximal exercise do not fully compensate for the smaller stroke volume of the children. Children have a smaller cardiac output relative to adults at a given sub-maximal exercise oxygen consumption. As a result, the arterio-venous oxygen difference increases to meet the oxygen requirements of the children.

During sub-maximal exercise a higher arterial-mixed venous O_2 difference [$(a\text{-}v)O_2$] in children also helps compensate for their lower cardiac output compared to adults to achieve a similar $\dot{V}O_2$. The table below shows the data from a study comparing responses to cycling and treadmill running in 7–9 year old children versus 18–26 year old adults.

TO DO

From the data provided in the table, use the Fick equation to calculate the $\dot{V}O_2$max of children and adults when cycling at 60 W.

	CARDIAC OUTPUT $L.min^{-1}$		$(A\text{-}V)O_2$ ml per 100 ml	
	CHILD	ADULT	CHILD	ADULT
Cycle 60 W	9.4	12.4	11.1	8.9
Run 3 mph	6.7	12.3	8.7	8.4

When comparing $\dot{V}O_2$max values between different populations it is crucial to recognise that the values can be expressed in two formats:

→ **absolute** $\dot{V}O_2$max is reported in $L.min^{-1}$
→ **relative** $\dot{V}O_2$max is the same value but normalised according to body mass in $ml.kg^{-1}.min^{-1}$.

For activities that are considered weight-bearing it is more appropriate to use the relative $\dot{V}O_2$max values as this makes an attempt to account for individual differences in size and mass. This is important as differences in size and mass explain the majority of the variability in absolute $\dot{V}O_2$max values between individuals, due to factors such as active muscle mass, heart size, blood volume etc.

For example, an untrained healthy adult with a body mass of 70 kg may have an absolute $\dot{V}O_2$max of 3.0 $L.min^{-1}$, which means a relative $\dot{V}O_2$max of 42.9 $ml.kg^{-1}.min^{-1}$ (3.0 × 1000 to convert L to ml, then divide by 70kg). In contrast a 58 kg female hockey player may also have an absolute $\dot{V}O_2$max of 3.0 $L.min^{-1}$, yet her relative $\dot{V}O_2$max of 51.7 $ml.kg^{-1}.min^{-1}$ reflects her training adaptations that mean she will be able to run at faster speeds and for longer than the untrained male. Highest values of $\dot{V}O_2$max have been recorded in cross-country skiers (over 90 $ml.kg^{-1}.min^{-1}$ in males and over 75 $ml.kg^{-1}.min^{-1}$ in females), however in those who are seriously ill the values can be considerably lower than even 20 $ml.kg^{-1}.min^{-1}$. The general pattern is therefore for relative $\dot{V}O_2$max to reflect cardio-respiratory fitness, although it must be recognised that there is still a lot of individual variation and these are population averages. For 20-year old males, an untrained healthy relative $\dot{V}O_2$max may be 40-45 $ml.kg^{-1}.min^{-1}$, with moderately trained in the range 45-55 $ml.kg^{-1}.min^{-1}$, professional team sport athletes 50-60 $ml.kg^{-1}.min^{-1}$ and top endurance athletes higher than 65 $ml.kg^{-1}.min^{-1}$. Changes in size between these groups mean that the training effects on absolute $\dot{V}O_2$max will be less obvious.

Gender

Regardless of training status gender also has an effect. Absolute $\dot{V}O_2$max values are considerably lower in age-matched females, primarily due to the size differences. However, even when expressed in relative terms active, healthy adult females typically have lower $\dot{V}O_2$max values than males. For 20-year old females an untrained healthy range may be 35-40 $ml.kg^{-1}.min^{-1}$, moderately trained 40-50 $ml.kg^{-1}.min^{-1}$, professional team sport athletes 45-55 $ml.kg^{-1}.min^{-1}$ and endurance athletes higher than 55-60 $ml.kg^{-1}.min^{-1}$. The primary factors that contribute to these gender differences are related to body composition (dividing by body mass does not account for the naturally higher percentage of non-oxygen-using body fat in females) and hemoglobin concentration to a lesser extent (males have slightly more hemoglobin than females).

Age

A further important factor that influences $\dot{V}O_2$max is age. During childhood and adolescence absolute $\dot{V}O_2$max increases according to patterns of growth and maturation, peaking in the early 20s for males and mid-teens for females. So children typically have much lower absolute $\dot{V}O_2$max values than adults due to their size. However, when the values are normalized to body mass male children and adolescents have very similar values to healthy adults, i.e. relative $\dot{V}O_2$max is very similar in male adults and children. Does this mean that a trained boy should be able to run a marathon in the same time as trained man? Children of course could not achieve such fast times and this nicely illustrates that normalising $\dot{V}O_2$max to body mass cannot fully explain differences in actual endurance performance, for a variety of reasons. In females the patterns of growth and maturation are clearly different (typically peaking earlier by a few years and with more accumulation of body fat and less muscle mass during puberty) and the effects on $\dot{V}O_2$max reflect this. In girls absolute $\dot{V}O_2$max increases with growth, peaking in the mid-teens. However, relative $\dot{V}O_2$max actually tends to decrease from early-teens in girls, partly due to the changes in body composition, potentially in addition to changes in physical activity patterns.

From adulthood, in males and females, the relative $\dot{V}O_2$max typically declines by approximately 1% each year on average. This reflects a gradual decline in the maximum heart rate that can be achieved, although again changes in physical activity patterns may contribute. So, for a healthy untrained 20-year-old with a $\dot{V}O_2$max of 45 ml.kg^{-1}.min^{-1} natural ageing would mean that at 45 and 70 years old the $\dot{V}O_2$max would be expected to have declined to 35.0 and 27.2 ml.kg^{-1}.min^{-1} respectively. This implies a steady decline in endurance capacity as we get older and any illness or injury will speed-up this decline. However, very importantly this does not mean that all elderly people have very low $\dot{V}O_2$max values and limited endurance capacity. Although the size of training response gets lower as we get older, physical exercise can still induce significant improvements in $\dot{V}O_2$max in the elderly such that a trained 65-year-old may well have a higher $\dot{V}O_2$max than an untrained and over-weight 30-year-old. Indeed Masters athletes compete all over the world until the end of their lives. A remarkable example is that of Fauja Singh, a 100-year-old Briton who completed the Toronto Waterfront marathon in 2011.

Type of exercise

A final factor that can further influence recorded values for $\dot{V}O_2$max is the type of exercise that is being performed. Within the same individual the highest rate of oxygen uptake that is recorded will be different dependent on whether the person is running or cycling for example. As more muscle mass is being used during running (compared to cycling the upper body and postural muscles are being used more as this is a weight-bearing activity) it would be expected that a higher $\dot{V}O_2$max would be recorded compared to cycling. This is the main reason underpinning why the highest observed values are in cross-country skiers compared to runners - as cross-country skiing places more oxygen demand on the upper-body, in addition to the lower-body and postural muscles that are working hard in both types of exercise.

What limits $\dot{V}O_2$max?

Although we can see from Figure 2.1 that a limitation could occur anywhere in the oxygen transport system when $\dot{V}O_2$max is reached, it is widely believed that in the majority of healthy individuals the primary limitation is the capacity of the cardiovascular system to deliver oxygen. There are exceptions to this rule, including illness and extremely high aerobic fitness levels, but in most cases it is believed that the ventilation system and oxygen use at the muscle do not cause someone to reach $\dot{V}O_2$max.

How does training increase $\dot{V}O_2$max?

The training responses that can be seen following a period of aerobic training support the idea that training can increase $\dot{V}O_2$max. The increases in $\dot{V}O_2$max that are observed are underpinned, at least in part, by training-induced changes in the heart and cardiovascular system (central adaptations), as well as being helped by some changes within the muscle (peripheral adaptations). Centrally, the main training response is an increase in stroke volume at sub-maximal and maximal values. In contrast, the heart rate response becomes lower at sub-maximal intensities and the maximum heart rate is actually unchanged with training, it just isn't reached until the person is working harder than before training (their capacity has improved).

The mechanism responsible for the increased stroke volume is mainly an increase in the volume of the left ventricle, meaning that more blood can fill the ventricle ahead of each contraction. As well as some changes in the blood, the muscles also develop more capillaries so that more blood can supply oxygen to the exercising muscles. In terms of oxygen use, there are also some adaptations that occur within the muscle itself to increase the amount of oxygen being extracted from the blood as it passes. Collectively, these central and peripheral adaptations permit an individual to exercise harder as their $\dot{V}O_2$max has increased.

KEY POINT

$\dot{V}O_2$max is the maximal rate of oxygen uptake and represents someone's maximal aerobic capacity. It is affected by factors such as training status, age and gender.

KEY POINT

Aerobic training can increase $\dot{V}O_2$max. The main mechanism is an increased stroke volume, although other adaptations in the cardiovascular and muscular systems also contribute.

TO DO

'To become an Olympic champion you must choose the right parents!'
Said by a very famous Swedish exercise physiologist Per-Olof Astrand.

Evidence from training studies suggests that at least some of the variation in $\dot{V}O_2$max between individuals can be explained by genetic variation. However, there is little doubt that training can have a positive impact on $\dot{V}O_2$max. This raises a classic question of fitness—is it due to nature (genetics) or nurture (training)?

Some very insightful research has compared the training adaptations of identical twins with non-identical twins. Interestingly, both improved but the responses were more similar in the identical than non-identical twins, despite identical training programmes and similar initial fitness levels.

→ Why does such research imply that genetics must at least play some part?
→ Why did using twins in both groups help to answer the nature versus nurture question?

A good way to think of this is that each person may have a 'ceiling' $\dot{V}O_2$max that is determined by their genes, but this will only become limiting once that person has trained and increased their $\dot{V}O_2$max as much as possible. Therefore, people with a low untrained $\dot{V}O_2$max cannot blame their genes as they have not reached their genetic ceiling.

THEORY OF KNOWLEDGE

Since the 1960s, East African athletes have clearly dominated endurance events, holding all of the male world records over distances from 3000m to marathons and many of the female world records over this range as well. Genetics has recently been explored in an attempt to explain why athletes with origins from a few tribes in Kenya and Ethiopia have been so successful. Interestingly, it appears that genetics may play a role, but does not adequately explain the pattern. Explore what other geographical, physiological, training, psychosocial, economic and cultural factors could also contribute to their success.

SUMMARY

→ Homeostasis is the maintenance of a constant internal environment.
→ The ventilatory and cardiovascular systems function together to maintain homeostasis during exercise.
→ Ventilation functions to ensure that blood leaving the lungs is oxygenated and low in carbon dioxide. Breathing occurs by repeated contraction and relaxation of muscles around the chest cavity.
→ No single factor controls the ventilation response, although carbon dioxide plays an important role.
→ Static lung volumes are more related to size than health or fitness, although dynamic volumes are more functional and sensitive to illness.
→ Gas exchange in the lungs and tissues occurs by diffusion from higher partial pressure to lower partial pressure, through thin capillary, alveoli and cell walls.
→ During exercise ventilation is increased by increasing the depth and frequency of breathing.
→ Blood consists of fluid (plasma) and cells with various functions including transport. Oxygen attaches to hemoglobin in red blood cells for transport.
→ The circulation system is made up of a pump (the heart) and a series of blood vessels, whose diameter and opening can be controlled by smooth muscle in the walls and sphincters.
→ The heart contains four chambers (two atria and two ventricles), with the left side supplying blood to the systemic circulation and the right side supplying the pulmonary circulation.
→ A heartbeat consists of a series of carefully coordinated contractions of the heart muscle tissue to eject blood from chamber to chamber and out of the heart. The initial impulse is generated within the heart itself, but the rate of firing can be controlled by other factors.
→ Blood pressure must be maintained to ensure blood flow is high enough. This is achieved through constriction and relaxation of vessel walls and sphincters. During exercise this ensures that more blood is diverted away from other organs towards the muscle.
→ Total blood flow (cardiac output) increases in proportion to the intensity of exercise up to a maximum value. This is achieved by increasing heart rate and stroke volume.
→ $\dot{V}O_2$max is the maximal rate of oxygen uptake achieved during maximal aerobic exercise.
→ Training, age and gender all affect someone's $\dot{V}O_2$max. Training increases $\dot{V}O_2$max primarily through increases in maximal stroke volume, although other peripheral adaptations can also contribute.

Self-study questions

1   Why might a doctor be interested in assessing $\dot{V}O_2$ in an exercise test?

2   Describe the process of breathing and comment on how exercise affects this process.

3   Insert **higher** or **lower** and **from** or **to** into the correct places in the following statements.

> → The partial pressure of oxygen is .... in arterial blood supplying exercising muscles than in the muscle tissue. Therefore, oxygen will diffuse .... the blood .... the muscle.

> → The partial pressure of carbon dioxide is .... in the lungs (alveoli) than in the blood returning from exercising muscles. Therefore, carbon dioxide will diffuse .... the lungs .... the blood.

4   What is the name of the pigment that binds oxygen for transport in the blood? Which type of blood cell is it found in?

5   Draw and label the four chambers of the heart, including the valves.

6   List the names of the specialist cells found in the heart that generate and then relay the electrical signal that causes the heart to contract.

7   Explain what will happen to the smooth muscles in the arterioles and capillaries within active muscle, compared to within the kidney during exercise.

8   Describe the responses of heart rate, stroke volume and hence cardiac output during exercise.

9   Define $\dot{V}O_2$max and discuss why it is considered to be of functional importance from a health and sports perspective.

10 How does aerobic training increase $\dot{V}O_2$max?

DATA BASED QUESTION

Thirteen children (9–10 years old) completed two tests to determine their $\dot{V}O_2$ peak (litre/min). The "ramp" test involved cycling for 3 min at 10 W and then increasing the workload by 10 W per min. The "supra-maximal" test commenced with 2 min cycling at 10 W, and then involved cycling at 105% of the peak power achieved during the "ramp" test. Both tests stopped when the children had a drop in cadence below 60 rpm for five consecutive seconds, despite encouragement to maintain the required workload. Their physiological responses are shown in the table below.

Peak physiological responses during the ramp and supra-maximal tests

Variable	Ramp test	Supra-maximal test
$\dot{V}O_2$ peak (L.min^{-1})	1.690 (0.284)	1.615 (0.307)
Heart rate peak (beats.min^{-1})	202 (7)	196 (8)
RER peak	1.11 (0.06)	1.07 (0.13)
Cardiac output peak (L.min^{-1})	15.10 (4.82)	14.64 (4.51)
Oxygen extraction peak (ml. min^{-1} per 100 ml)	12.61 (2.57)	12.28 (2.50)

Data are reported as mean (SD).

(Source: adapted from Barker et al. 2011. "Establishing maximal oxygen uptake in young people during a ramp cycle test to exhaustion." *British Journal of Sports Medicine*. Vol 45. Pp 498–503.)

1   State which test resulted in:

    i)   the highest $\dot{V}O_2$ peak   (1 mark)

    ii) the highest heart rate   (1 mark)

    iii) the lowest cardiac output.   (1 mark)

2   Distinguish between the standard deviations for:

    i)   RER peak   (2 marks)

    ii) oxygen extraction peak.   (2 marks)

3   Suggest reasons for the different physiological responses to the two tests.   (4 marks)

CHAPTER 3

Nutrition and energy systems

By the end of this chapter students should be able to:

→ list the macronutrients and micronutrients

→ outline the roles of macronutrients and micronutrients

→ describe the chemical composition and basic structure of a glucose molecule, triacylglycerol molecule and protein molecule

→ distinguish between saturated and unsaturated fatty acids and between essential and non-essential amino acids

→ understand the concept of a healthy balanced diet

→ describe current recommendations for a healthy balanced diet

→ state the energy content of 100 grams of carbohydrate, fat, and protein

→ discuss how the recommended energy distribution of macronutrients differ between endurance athletes and non-athletes

→ outline the terms metabolism, anabolism, and catabolism

→ understand the metabolism of carbohydrate and fat

→ outline the metabolic pathways of carbohydrate and fat metabolism

→ explain the role of insulin, glucagon and adrenaline in the carbohydrate and fat metabolism

→ explain the role of insulin and muscle contraction on glucose uptake during exercise

→ reproduce the ultrastructure of a mitochondrion

→ define the term cell respiration

→ describe metabolic pathways that supply energy

→ explain the role of ATP in muscle contraction

→ explain the phenomena of oxygen deficit and excess post-exercise oxygen consumption (EPOC)

→ discuss the characteristics of the energy systems and their contribution during exercise

→ evaluate the contributions of the energy systems during different types of exercise.

Introduction

The knowledge of the importance of food for growth and health is as old as human history. The choice of what to eat and drink is not only influenced by biological needs but also by the environment as it determines quality, quantity and balance of food supply.

Figure 3.1 shows the relationship between the human body (internal environment), external environment (for example, culture and economics), nutritional requirements and health. Although health is also influenced by other factors than nutrition, for example, lifestyle, nutrition is a powerful and modifiable factor for health promotion.

An optimal nutritional status results in normal development, good health and a high quality of life. Undernutrition (hunger), malnutrition (for example, vitamin deficiency) and overnutrition (obesity) can cause impaired growth and/or development, and diseases.

> **"Our food should be our medicine and our medicine should be our food."**
> Hippocrates, 400BC

> **"These small things—nutrition, place, climate, recreation—are inconceivably more important than everything one has taken to be important so far."**
> Friedrich Nietzsche

> **"I saw few die of hunger; of eating, a hundred thousand."**
> Benjamin Franklin, 18th century

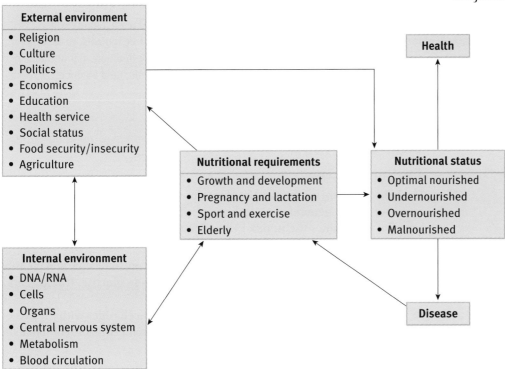

↑ Figure 3.1: The relationship between nutrition, environment and health

Food consists of a combination of several nutrients that influence the function of the human body. The combination and amount of nutrients a person takes in determine health and well-being. We eat food which is then digested and its nutrients absorbed in the gut system. Nutrients are transported via the blood stream and metabolized in the cells of different organs. Naturally nutrients do not function in isolation. They interact with each other in food, in the digestive system, in the blood and in the final site of function, the cell.

Nutrients are classified into macronutrients and micronutrients. Macronutrients are nutrients that our body needs in larger amounts to maintain health. These include carbohydrate, fat, protein and water. Micronutrients, vitamins and minerals are required in smaller amounts. The function and main food sources of macro- and micronutrients are summarized in Table 3.1.

TYPE OF NUTRIENT	FOOD SOURCES	FUNCTIONS
Macronutrients		
Carbohydrate	Cereals, sweeteners, root crops, pulses, vegetables, fruit, dairy products	Fuel, energy storage, cell membrane, DNA, RNA
Fat	Meat, milk, dairy products, eggs, fish oil, vegetable seeds, nuts, vegetable oil	Fuel, energy storage, cell membrane, hormones, precursor of bile acid
Protein	Meat, fish, milk, dairy products, eggs, pulses, cereals	Structure, transport, communication, enzymes, protection, fuel
Water	Beverages, fruits, vegetables	Medium for biochemical reactions, transport, thermoregulation, excretion, lubrication
Micronutrients		
Vitamins	Fruits, vegetables, fatty fish (e.g. salmon, mackerel), fish oil, liver, meat	Energy release from macronutrients, metabolism, bone health, blood health, immune function, eyesight
Minerals and trace elements	Meat, fish, milk, dairy products, salt, cereals, fruits, vegetables, water	Mineralization of bones and teeth, blood oxygen transport, defence against free radicals, co-factors for energy metabolism, muscle function, maintenance of acid-base balance and cellular fluid balance

↑ Table 3.1: Nutrients, food sources and functions

Macronutrients

Carbohydrates

Carbohydrates are synthesized by plants from water and carbon dioxide using sun energy. The general chemical composition of carbohydrates is $(CH_2O)_n$ where n determines the number of molecules that influence body function and impact on health.

→ **Monosaccharides** The simplest form is made of one molecule and is easily absorbed by the human body. Examples include glucose, fructose and galactose.

→ **Disaccharides** Two monosaccharides form disaccharides with the loss of one molecule of water. For example, sucrose is a glucose-fructose combination (Figure 3.2).

→ **Oligosaccharides** These are carbohydrates with three to nine molecules, for example, maltodextrin.

→ **Polysaccharides** These are molecule chains longer than 10 molecules, for example starch and glycogen.

Di-, oligo- and polysaccharides need to be broken down to monosaccharides in the gut before they can be absorbed and transported to the organs. Some oligo- and polysaccharides are indigestible or poorly digestible and are called dietary fibre. Mostly found in the cellular walls of plants such as cellulose, these carbohydrates play an important role in the prevention of diseases.

The main function of carbohydrates is to act as metabolic fuels and energy stores. In the cells,

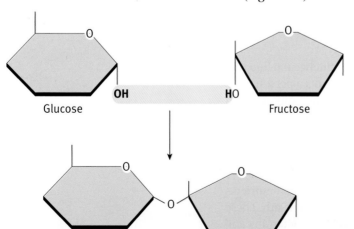

↑ Figure 3.2: Formation of sucrose from glucose and fructose by removal of water (condensation reaction)

carbohydrate (glucose) is oxidized back into water and carbon dioxide. This reaction produces energy that is used for further metabolic processes requiring yet more energy. All living cells contain carbohydrates and, on a worldwide basis, carbohydrates represent the most widespread source of food energy. In plants carbohydrate is stored as starch and in animals in the form of glycogen. One hundred grams of carbohydrate yield 1,760kJ (kilo joule). Later in this chapter you will find out that carbohydrates are an important source of energy for intense and prolonged periods of exercise.

The major food sources vary in different areas of the world. The variability depends on availability and cultural preference. A list of the major carbohydrate sources in different countries is shown in Table 3.2. Carbohydrates are also used to build structures such as cell membranes in the body and to synthesize DNA and RNA.

Joule a unit of energy. In nutrition, joule (J) is the energy obtained from food that is available through cell respiration

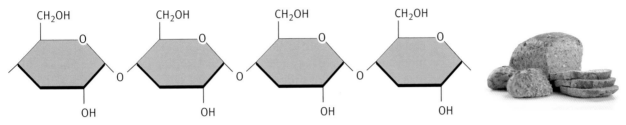

a Structure of amylose, a form of starch—a sugar storage compound in plants. Oxygen bridges link the glucose subunits.

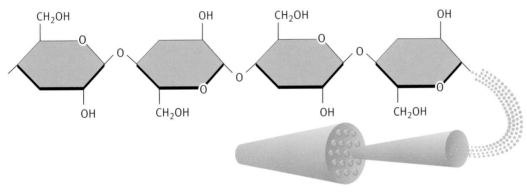

b Structure of cellulose, in cellulose fibers, chains of glucose monomers stretch side by side and hydrogen-bond at—OH groups. Together the bonds stabilize the chains in bundles that are organized in fibers. Like many other organisms, humans lack the enzymes required to digest cellulose, which is a component of plant-derived products such as cotton thread used in clothing.

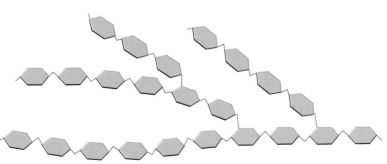

c Glycogen, the form in which excess glucose is stored in the human body (and other animals). It is especially abundant in the muscles and liver.

↑ Figure 3.3: Comparison of the polysaccharides a) starch, b) cellulose and c) glycogen

COUNTRY	MAJOR CARBOHYDRATE SOURCE
China	Rice
Ireland	Potato
Mexico	Maize
Nigeria	Cassava
Italy	Wheat
Oceania	Sweet potato

↑ Table 3.2: Major carbohydrate sources in different countries

Fat

Dietary fat is found in a variety of animal and plant sources (Table 3.1). The major dietary fats are triglycerides, phospholipids and sterols. Triglycerides make up to 95 per cent of dietary fat and one molecule consists of one glycerol molecule and three fatty acids (Figure 3.4). These fatty acids can be identical or a combination of different fatty acids. The structure of the fatty acids determines the characteristic and biological function of triglycerides.

Some fatty acids are classified as essential because our body is lacking in the enzymes necessary to synthesize them and therefore depends on their supply through food. Essential fatty acids are found in plant oil such as from sesame seeds, corn, linseeds and walnuts.

Fatty acids are a chain of carbon atoms with hydrogen attached, and a methyl group (CH_3) and a carboxyl group (COOH) on each end (Figure 3.4). There are different kinds with different structures.

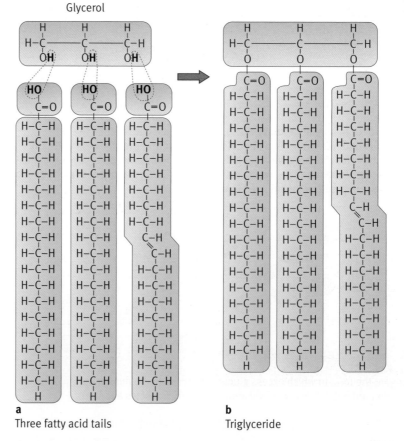

a
Three fatty acid tails

b
Triglyceride

↑ Figure 3.4: Formation of triglycerides from glycerol and three fatty acids with removal of water

- → **Saturated fatty acids (SFA)** with the maximal number of hydrogen atoms (four) on each carbon atom.
- → **Unsaturated fatty acids** where two hydrogen atoms are missing form double bonds between two carbon atoms and become unsaturated.
- → **Monounsaturated fatty acids (MUFA)** with a single double bond in the chain.
- → **Polyunsaturated fatty acids (PUFA)** shaped by multiple double bonds.
- → **Omega-3 fatty acids** PUFAs that have the first double bond located between the third and fourth carbon atom from the methyl end.
- → **Omega-6 fatty acids** PUFAs that have their first double bond located between the sixth and seventh carbon atom from the methyl end.

Research has shown that an optimal balance of omega-3 and omega-6 fatty acids in the diet is important to maintain adequate inflammatory and immunological responses.

Fat is an important source of food energy. The intake of 100 grams of fat provides 4000kJ; about three times more than carbohydrates. Triglycerides can be stored in adipose tissue which builds up an energy store over a prolonged period of time. Later in this chapter you will find out that although fat cannot be used during high intensity exercise, it is an important source of energy in the recovery period between high intensity exercise, as well as during prolonged exercise.

Moreover, fat in adipose tissue provides physical protection of vital organs and helps to control body temperature (thermal insulation). Dietary fat also plays a major role in the synthesis of hormones, vitamin D (sterols) and cell membranes (sterols, phospholipids). Fats are important for the transport of fat-soluble vitamins.

KEY POINT

Essential fatty acids are called "essential" because our bodies can't synthesize or create them so we have to get them from the food we eat.

TO THINK ABOUT

Food manufacturing alters dietary fat

Biscuits, chocolate, cakes and margarines are produced with fat that has been altered by the food manufacturers to make it solid at room temperature. Mono- and polyunsaturated fats, mainly plant oils, are converted into saturated fat by adding hydrogen atoms to the double bonds. This process is called hydrogenation. Hydrogenation also changes the position of hydrogen atoms on the remaining

↑ Cakes and biscuits contain harmful fatty acids

double bonds. In the naturally occurring *cis* form, the two hydrogen atoms are attached on the same side of the double bond. This form is changed into a *trans* form where the hydrogen atoms are placed on opposite sites of the double bond. *Trans* fatty acids are known to harm the body in the same way as an excess of saturated fatty acids in the diet.

Proteins

Proteins are the second most abundant compounds in the body (water is the most abundant). Proteins are formed by amino acids, compounds made of carbon atoms, nitrogen atoms, oxygen atoms and hydrogen atoms. Most amino acids are characterized by the same central structure (Figure 3.5) and a side chain that distinguishes the physical and chemical properties. Amino acids are linked in chains through peptide bonds. Each protein has a characteristic amino acid composition. Twenty amino acids have been identified as being required for the synthesis of proteins. Of the twenty, eight are essential and need to be provided in the diet. Table 3.3 lists the essential amino acids.

ESSENTIAL AMINO ACIDS
Isoleucine
Leucine
Lysine
Methionine
Phenylalanine
Threonine
Tryptophan
Valine

↑ Table 3.3 Essential amino acids

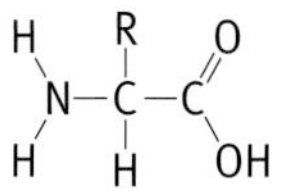

↑ Figure 3.5: Basic structure of amino acids (R indicates another atom or molecular structure attached to the carbon atom)

Foods rich in proteins are meat, fish, milk, dairy products, eggs, pulses and cereals. The quality of proteins in the diet depends on whether all essential amino acids are included. In pulses and grains we find proteins that are lacking in essential amino acids. Pulses are short in isoleucine and lysine. Grains lack methionine and tryptophan. The quality of these proteins is low. In order to avoid diseases, pulses and grains should be combined as part of the diet.

Proteins are also a source of energy; the metabolism of 100 grams of protein yields 1720kJ. The functional activity of proteins is determined by their structure, size and shape. Proteins have a wide range of functions in the body. They can be summarized in four functional groups:

→ **Structural** muscles, bones, skin, cells
→ **Transport/communication** plasma proteins, hormones, receptors, neurotransmitters
→ **Protective** antibodies, mucus, anti-inflammatory proteins
→ **Enzymatic** digestion, metabolic pathways, O_2 and CO_2 transport

Dietary protein deficiency is common in developing countries and a cause of undernutrition. A lack of protein in the diet is associated with impairment in growth and development, life-threatening diseases and death. In the western world usually overconsumption of protein occurs because the main protein source is meat. The digestibility of animal protein is higher than the digestibility of plant proteins.

Protein-energy malnutrition in children

Children are in the process of growing and developing. For example, in the first year of life a child triples its body weight and increases its height by 50 per cent. Growth and development require energy and proteins which must be provided by food. A child needs much more energy in relation to body weight than an adult. When children do not get enough macronutrients they will suffer from protein-energy malnutrition. This form of malnutrition can cause extreme wasting where children appear like 'skin and bone' (syndrome called marasmus), where children have abnormal amounts of water under the skin and in the body (syndrome called kwashiorkor) or both (syndrome called marasmic kwashiorkor). Children who suffer from malnutrition are more likely to have impaired growth, suffer from infection, disabilities and die at a young age. Malnutrition is not only caused by inadequate diet but also by environmental factors, infectious diseases, and poverty.

Questions:

1   What are the factors that influence adequate nutrition?
2   What are the consequences of a lack of carbohydrate, fat and protein in the diet?
3   Why are children at greatest risk of suffering from undernutrition/malnutrition?

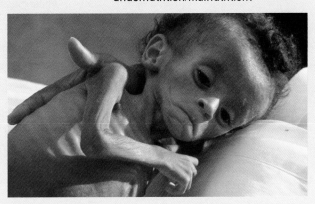

↑ Young children, one nourished to the optimal level and the other malnourished

Water

Water is essential to all forms of life. The functions of water in humans are varied.

In the cells, water acts as a medium for vital biochemical reactions. Outside cells it plays a role in the following:

→   transport of nutrients, metabolites, waste products, hormones, and respiratory gases
→   thermoregulation (sweat) and excretion (urine, faeces)
→   cell–cell and cell–environment communication
→   lubrication of joints and sliding surfaces.

An adult body contains about 35–45 liters of water. Water balance is strongly regulated in the body. A high water intake balances out water losses through increased production of urine and sweat. However, both an excess and a deficiency of water can harm the body and threaten life.

Micronutrients

Vitamins

Vitamins are organic compounds that are vital for health and well-being and are found in fruits, vegetables and some meat. They are regulators in processes of energy release from food and important co-factors in various chemical reactions. Vitamins are grouped into water-soluble and fat-soluble vitamins. As the name indicates water-soluble vitamins are soluble in water and therefore an overdose is not toxic in healthy individuals for most vitamins. They are simply excreted with the urine.

❝ **The dose makes the poison.** ❞
Paracelsus, 15th century

In contrast, excessive intake of fat-soluble vitamins can result in poisoning because they can be stored in adipose tissue and the liver. An overdose of those vitamins, however, is rare and only needs to be considered under particular conditions (for example, during pregnancy). Table 3.4 lists the water- and fat-soluble vitamins and their food sources. All vitamins are classified as essential and need therefore to be supplied in food.

There are two compounds that are considered to be vitamins but they can be synthesized by the body. Vitamin D is produced through precursors in the skin in combination with sunlight and the B vitamin niacin is synthesized from the amino acid tryptophan.

VITAMINS	FOOD SOURCES
Vitamin C	Citrus fruits, green vegetables
B vitamins (e.g. B$_{12}$, folic acid)	Whole grains, pulses, seeds, vegetables, meat, fish, milk, eggs
Vitamin E	Whole grains, seeds, nuts, fatty meat, plant oils, green leafy vegetables
Vitamin D	Fatty fish, fish oil, liver, beef, egg yolk
Vitamin A	Yellow, orange and red fruits and vegetables, green vegetables
Vitamin K	Green leafy vegetables, milk, liver

↑ Table 3.4: Water-soluble (blue) and fat-soluble (orange) vitamins and their food sources

Major minerals and trace elements

Minerals and trace elements are inorganic compounds that must be supplied through food and fluids. The main sources are meat, fish, milk, dairy products, cereals and green leafy vegetables. Minerals are distinguished from trace elements by the occurrence in the body with approximately 4 per cent of body mass consisting of minerals while trace elements make up approximately 0.001% of body mass.

They also differ in the amount that is required in the diet for the maintenance of health. Optimal mineral intake varies between grams and milligrams per day and those for trace elements between milligrams and micrograms per day. Minerals and trace elements are involved in processes that range from maintaining bone and blood health to the release of energy, muscle function and maintenance of cellular fluid balance.

The minerals that the body needs are:

→ calcium (Ca)
→ chloride (Cl)
→ magnesium (Mg)
→ sodium (Na)
→ potassium (K)
→ phosphorus (P)

The trace elements that the body needs are:

→ iron (Fe)
→ iodine (I)
→ fluoride (F)
→ zinc (Zn)
→ selenium (Se)
→ copper (Cu)
→ chromium (Cr)
→ manganese (Mn)
→ molybdenum (Mb)

↑ Daily consumption of colourful fruits and vegetables provides essential vitamins important for health and well-being

TO RESEARCH

Choose five of the minerals or trace elements listed opposite and find out what the daily recommended intake of each is.

KEY POINT

Food consists of different nutrients that play different roles in contributing to our health and well-being. We need to eat a range of foods to get all the nutrients we need.

Dietary advice for a healthy balanced diet

Dietary advice can range from the anecdotal saying "an apple a day keeps the doctor away" to scientifically derived amounts of nutrient intake. Once the essential nutrients were understood and established, quantitative advice for individual macro- and micronutrients were developed. These types of dietary advice are dietary recommendations for a population's daily intake of nutrients.

Broader dietary advice for the individual's general nutritional well-being is given by dietary guidelines. For example, in the UK the "Five a day" campaign is an example of a dietary guideline to promote the consumption of five portions of fruit and vegetable per day. The five-a-day campaign also exists in the USA, New Zealand, Germany, and as an equivalent in Australia. In France, five portions of fruit and vegetables are also recommended but not promoted in the form of a five-a-day campaign. The current fruit and vegetable recommendations are based on the WHO guidelines on fruit and vegetable intake of 400 g per day: http://www.who.int/dietphysicalactivity/fruit/en/index2.html

Dietary recommendations

Dietary recommendations set standards for what constitutes an adequate intake of essentials nutrients to promote health. They are developed by governments and health authorities based on scientific evidence to assess whether the diet of a population or a population subgroup meets the nutritional needs. The amount of nutrients varies based on age, gender, activity level and change during pregnancy and lactation.

The adequate nutrient intake is chosen so that the needs of 97.5 per cent of the population are met. In the case of the total energy intake, however, a value adequate for 50 per cent of the population is considered. This is because over time even a small imbalance of energy intake over energy expenditure would lead to individuals becoming overweight or even obese and would cause severe health problems.

The methods used to determine nutritional requirements are:

→ observation of nutrient intake in a healthy population
→ observation of nutrient intake in a diseased population
→ studies on the maintenance of the balance of nutrients in the body
→ studies that involve removing or adding a nutrient from the diet
→ measurement of nutrient levels in biological tissues or fluids
→ measurement of nutrient-specific biological markers
→ animal experiments.

Internationally, there is no agreement about dietary recommendations. Different countries prefer their country-specific recommendations. The methods used to identify the level of an adequate intake of nutrients vary between countries. The availability of new research data in one country and not in another also contributes to different dietary recommendations. For example, the intake of carbohydrate as percentage of total daily energy intake for an adult is set in North America at 45-65 per cent, in Japan at 50-70 per cent, and in the UK at 50 per cent. In 2003, the World Health Organization and the Food and Agriculture Organization of the United Nations developed dietary goals for both developed and developing countries for the prevention of long-term chronic diseases (Table 3.5).

Balanced diet a diet that provides all nutrients in the right amount in order to maintain health and prevent nutrient excess or deficiency diseases

Dietary recommendations recommended amounts of essential nutrients in the diet

Dietary guidelines recommended amounts of foods, food groups or meals

THEORY OF KNOWLEDGE

A balanced diet which provides all nutrients in sufficient amounts is important for human development and health. In some countries and cultures people do not consume meat (vegetarian diet) or base their diet on plant derived foods only (vegan diet).

1 Discuss the concept of a balanced diet in the context of different religions and cultures.
2 Evaluate how people who follow a vegetarian or vegan diet ensure a balanced diet.

Dietary recommendation

In Table 3.5 you see the global dietary recommendations for fat, carbohydrate, protein, and salt. The recommendation for carbohydrate intake, for example, is higher than that from a single developed country (e.g. USA, see text above) because of the high risk of under- and malnutrition in developing countries.

1 What could be the rationale for countries to use their own dietary recommendation rather than the international one?
2 What is the advantage of an international dietary recommendation over a national recommendation?

DIETARY FACTOR	DIETARY RECOMMENDATION (% OF TOTAL ENERGY OR g/day)
Total fat	15–30%
Saturated fatty acids (SFA)	<10%
Polyunsaturated fatty acids (PUFA)	6–10%
Omega-6 polyunsaturated fatty acids	5–8%
Omega-3 polyunsaturated fatty acids	1–2%
Trans fatty acids	<1%
Monounsaturated fatty acids (MUFA)	Difference of total fat minus (SFA + PUFA + trans fatty acids)
Total carbohydrate	55–75%
Sugars	<10%
Dietary fibre	>25g
Protein	10–15%
Sodium Chloride (salt)	<5g

↑ Table 3.5: International dietary recommendation for fat, carbohydrate, protein, and salt

Dietary guidelines

Dietary guidelines can differ between countries. However, all have the primary aim of promoting the health of the population. In a food pyramid food groups that should be eaten the most are placed on the bottom and those that should be eaten the least on the top. Recommendations for water and other beverages are illustrated outside the food pyramid.

1 Describe the differences between the dietary guidelines of the two regions shown in Figure 3.7.
2 Why do the food guides differ between countries?
3 Based on the food pyramids, what are the principles of a healthy balanced diet?

Dietary guidelines

Dietary guidelines target foods, food groups or meals and are set by a country to guide its people towards a healthy balanced diet. The development of dietary guidelines can be based on dietary recommendations—it can be a practical interpretation of nutrient intake recommendations. Figure 3.6 shows how the scientific knowledge of a healthy diet is converted into a practical guideline. Dietary guidelines are influenced by sociocultural factors of the country including:

→ religious beliefs
→ social norms
→ preparation preferences
→ food consumption patterns
→ food availability
→ food security
→ income
→ food prices.

The visual presentation used to illustrate dietary guidelines differs between countries as well as the advice given on the food groups that should be eaten most or least. Most graphical images illustrate the proportion of fluids, fruits, vegetables, cereals, milk, dairy products, eggs, meat, fish, oil and sweets in the diet. Visual presentations used range from a food pyramid (e.g. Australia), a food tower (Korea) and a food circle (Finland) to a spinning top (Japan), a rainbow (Canada) and a food plate (UK).

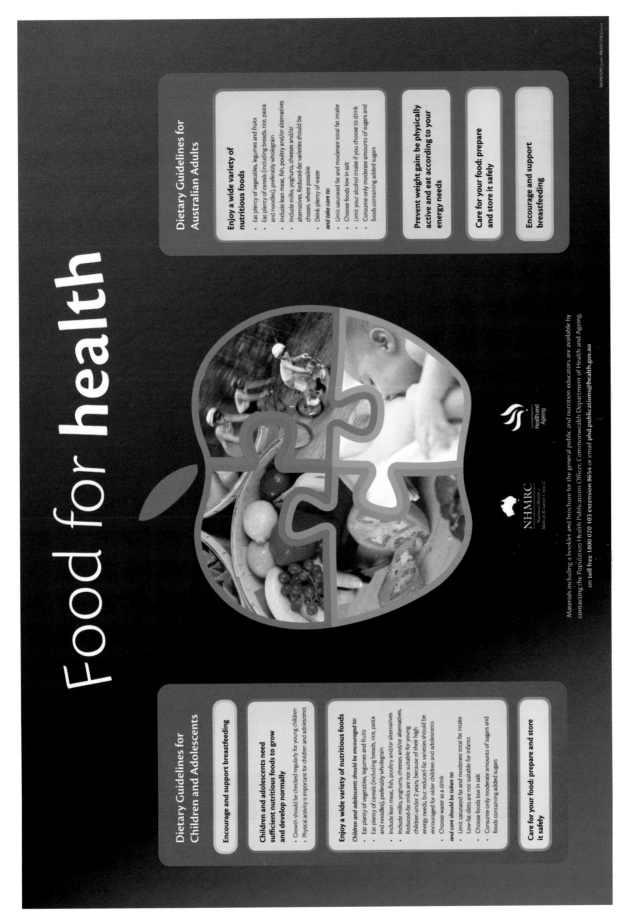

↑ Figure 3.6: Dietary guidelines for Australians (http://www.nhmrc.gov.au/guidelines/publications/n29-n30-n31-n32-n33-34)

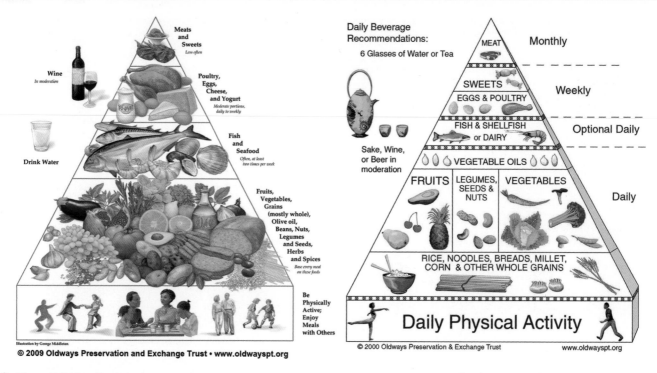

↑ Figure 3.7: Visualization of region-specific dietary guidelines in the form of a Mediterranean (left) and Asian (right) food pyramid

TO THINK ABOUT

Population-specific recommendations—Endurance athletes versus non-athletes

> ❝The more glycogen, the further and faster the player ran.❞
>
> Kirkendall, 1993

An optimal level of nutrition is essential for the health and performance of an athlete. The diet of an athlete needs to meet the increased physiological requirements. The most important differences between a non-athletic population and athletes are the increased energy and fluid requirements of athletes. The nutritional needs vary between the type of sport and the periods of training, competition and recovery.

An endurance athlete (e.g. marathon runner) needs far more carbohydrates in the diet than a non-athlete in order to meet the energy requirements for high intensity events and to delay the onset of fatigue. Most of the total daily

energy intake is provided by carbohydrates which lead to proportional lower energy intake from proteins and fat (Table 3.6). Nevertheless, the protein intake should be slightly increased in endurance athletes compared to non-athletes in order to maintain, build and repair muscle mass and connective tissue. Slightly more protein is also required to synthesize certain hormones and enzymes. Dietary fat recommendations for endurance athletes are also slightly higher than for non-athletes. This is because dietary fat is a source of energy, fat-soluble vitamins and essential fatty acids which are crucial for athletic performance. The recommendation for water intake in endurance athletes is that they should drink to replace the fluid lost through sweat. As endurance athletes sweat more than non-athletes the water intake is higher in athletes.

NUTRIENTS	NON-ATHLETE FROM NORTH AMERICA		ENDURANCE ATHLETE	
	(% OF TOTAL ENERGY)	G/KG BODY WEIGHT	(% OF TOTAL ENERGY)	G/KG BODY WEIGHT
Carbohydrate	45–65%	3–6 g/kg	55–75%	6–10 g/kg
Protein	10–15%	0.8–1 g/kg	10–35%	1.2–1.4 g/kg
Fat	15–30%	–	20–35%	–

↑ Table 3.6: Comparison of the recommended daily dietary energy distribution from carbohydrate, protein and fat for non-athletes and endurance athletes

Metabolism of macronutrients

Energy metabolism

Not all energy that is stored in food is available for metabolism in humans. Some components such as fibre cannot be digested and absorbed. This energy is lost in faeces. Even if nutrients are digestible there are metabolic pathways whose end products still contain energy. One example is the production of urea and ammonia in the metabolism of protein. These compounds still contain energy which is lost in the urine. Only the metabolizable energy of food is relevant for the energy metabolism of the human body.

The amount and composition of carbohydrates, fat and proteins in the diet determine the availability of energy. Macronutrients that can be stored easily in the body such as fat in adipose tissue are metabolized more slowly than proteins for which the body lacks any storage capacity. Therefore after eating a meal containing all macronutrients, the body will metabolize proteins first, then carbohydrates followed by fat.

Metabolism can be defined as all chemical processes in living organisms required for the maintenance of life. Metabolism consists of two phases: anabolism and catabolism. They are defined as follows.

→ **Anabolism** The constructive phase of metabolism where smaller molecules are converted to larger molecules. For example, glucose molecules convert to glycogen.
→ **Catabolism** The destructive phase of metabolism where larger molecules are converted to smaller molecules. For example, triglycerides convert to glycerol and fatty acids. Aerobic catabolism refers to processes which require oxygen. Anaerobic catabolism is independent of the presence of oxygen.

Carbohydrate metabolism

Carbohydrates are digested to the monosaccharides glucose, fructose and galactose. These are absorbed into the blood stream and transported to the liver. In the liver fructose and galactose are converted to glucose. From there glucose is transported to the other organs.

In the cytosol of all cells the breakdown of glucose takes place. The process is called glycolysis and involves many reactions. The reactions are regulated by the enzymes hexokinase, phosphofructokinase and pyruvate kinase.

Glycolysis leads to the metabolism of glucose to pyruvate and the production of energy in the form of adenosine triphosphate (ATP). When oxygen is available pyruvate enters mitochondria where it is oxidized to carbon dioxide and water. Under anaerobic conditions (for example, in brief, high intensity exercise) pyruvate is converted to lactate. Lactate is either transported back to the liver where glucose is reformed or oxidized to pyruvate in the muscles.

In liver and muscle cells glucose is converted to glycogen when the diet provides more glucose than the tissue requires. Glycogen is the storage form of glucose. In a process called glycogenesis many glucose molecules are linked together to form glycogen.

When the body needs more glucose than is ingested glycogen is broken down and glucose (liver) and glucose-6-phosphate (muscle) can serve as metabolic fuel. This process is called glycogenolysis. The muscle glycogen is only used to deliver an immediate energy source for the muscle, while the liver glycogen provides glucose for all the other organs.

KEY POINT

Glucose is broken down to provide energy. This process is known as glycolysis (the breakdown of glucose to pyruvate). Glucose that is not used immediately is stored as glycogen. This conversion of glucose to glycogen is called glycogenesis. When the energy stored in the glycogen is needed it is turned back into glucose. This process is known as glycogenolysis (the conversion of glycogen to glucose).

Draw your own diagram to show the relationship between the following:

→ Liver
→ Muscle
→ Blood stream
→ Food
→ Glucose
→ Glycogen
→ Lactate
→ CO_2
→ Water
→ Glycolysis (aerobic, anaerobic)
→ Glycogenolysis
→ Glycogenesis

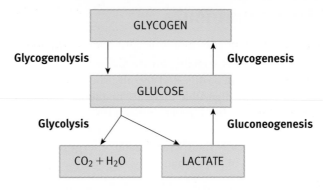

↑ Figure 3.8: Pathways in carbohydrate metabolism

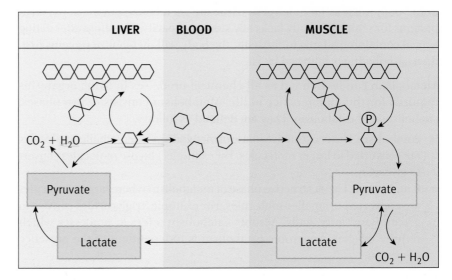

↑ Figure 3.9: Liver and muscle play an important role in carbohydrate metabolism

Fat metabolism

The energy-yielding process in the fat metabolism is the β-oxidation of fatty acids. β-oxidation occurs in the mitochondria to which fatty acids are transported with the support of the shuttle enzyme carnitine. Fatty acids are gradually broken down to acetyl CoA molecules by shortening the fatty acid chain. This β-oxidation of fatty acids involves a repeat cycle of four reactions, reducing the fatty acid chain by two carbons on each cycle. This already generates energy but more energy is released when acetyl CoA is further metabolized to citrate in the Krebs cycle.

The Krebs cycle is a series of chemical reactions that occurs in the mitochondria which involves the oxidation of acetyl CoA to produce a large quantity of ATP. During this process carbon dioxide is formed.

The oxidation differs slightly depending on the chain length of fatty acids, whether they have double bonds and how many of them. Research in both animals and humans has shown that the body prefers to metabolize mono- and polyunsaturated fatty acids over the metabolism of saturated fatty acids. This is important for the choice of type of fat in the diet which can prevent chronic diseases such as those affecting the arteries of the heart. The reason is that the slower the oxidation of fatty acids, the longer they remain in the blood stream. Fatty acids contribute to reactions that form cholesterol which subsequently can be placed in the vessel wall.

Eating more fat than the body requires leads to excess fat being stored as triglycerides in adipose tissue and skeletal muscles. The adipose tissue can be found under the skin and between organs. Stored fat provides energy when energy supply is not immediately available from the diet or glycogen pools. Lipolysis is the process of releasing triglycerides from the body's stores. Triglycerides supported by enzymes are converted into glycerol and fatty acids. Fatty acids are then available for the energy-generating β-oxidation.

Hormonal regulation of energy metabolism

Energy metabolism is controlled by many hormones. These hormones include insulin, glucagon, adrenalin, cortisol and growth hormones.

After you have eaten a meal the glucose concentration in the blood rises. This is a signal for the pancreas to secrete insulin from its β-cells. Insulin increases the transport of glucose into the cell, especially into skeletal muscle cells and liver cells by the translocation of glucose transporters from intracellular (i.e. from within the cell) to the surface (Figure 3.10).

The fast uptake of glucose in the blood inhibits the release of glucose from the liver and muscle stores and promotes the synthesis of glycogen in the liver and muscle. Insulin stimulates glycolysis to lower blood glucose levels after a meal to signal energy availability to all organs. It inhibits gluconeogenesis (the conversion of protein or fat into glucose) and promotes glycogenesis (the conversion of glucose to glycogen). Insulin also inhibits lipolysis in fat stores and the breakdown of proteins (it also promotes the synthesis of proteins).

During a prolonged period with no food intake (fasting) or exercise the blood glucose concentration decreases which causes the secretion of the hormone glucagon. Glucagon is secreted by the α-cells of the pancreas and acts in the opposite way to insulin. It stimulates the glycogenolysis and synthesis of glucose which increases the glucose level in the blood—a sign that glucose is transported to the organs for the utilization of energy. Glucagon also activates the lipolysis of triglycerides in fat stores which subsequently contributes to the energy supply. A low blood glucose concentration also stimulates adrenalin which acts as glucagon in the processes of glycogen breakdown and lipolysis.

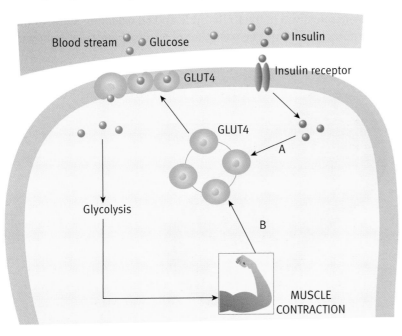

← Figure 3.10: Mechanisms of glucose uptake into skeletal muscle. (A) insulin-stimulated glucose uptake, (B) muscle contraction-stimulated glucose uptake. GLUT 4: glucose transporter 4

TO THINK ABOUT

Blood sugar testing using a blood glucose monitor provides an easy, accurate and self-administered method to assess the concentration of glucose in the blood. This is important for people with diabetes where the blood glucose regulation by insulin is impaired. Both a high and a low blood sugar concentration can be harmful.

Muscle glucose uptake during exercise

In the very first moment of muscle contractions creatine phosphate stores will be used to provide energy. During exercise of light to moderate intensity, energy is derived from glucose, initially from anaerobic glycolysis until the aerobic system can convert stored glucose into energy. In order to maintain the energy supply by glucose the muscle increases the uptake of glucose from the blood. Muscle contraction stimulates the translocation of glucose transporters from the inner cell storage pool to the cell membrane but in a different way to insulin (Figure 3.10). The insulin-induced transporter translocation takes place during phases of no exercise (i.e. rest). Exercise lowers the concentration of insulin in the blood and therefore reduces its function in glucose transport.

THEORY OF KNOWLEDGE

Research on the role of carbohydrates for exercise and particularly endurance performance became the foundation for the dietary practice for many athletes. A high carbohydrate diet improves endurance performance and carbohydrate intake during exercise delays fatigue.

1   Investigate the use of sport drinks and energy bars as means for carbohydrate intake during endurance performance.
2   Discuss the development of a multimillion dollar industry of sports nutrition products which evolved from the knowledge of the effect of carbohydrate on performance, and how this industry can influence future research.

Energy systems

All cells in the human body require a source of energy to perform biological work. This includes all the processes involved in growth and maintenance of function. Muscle cells also require a source of energy to produce force during muscle contraction.

Mitochondria are cell components that have an important role in energy provision for cells and they are the only site in which oxygen is used. With the exception of red blood cells, mitochondria are present in all human cells. The proteins of the electron transport chain are located in the inner membrane and the enzymes involved in the Krebs cycle and fat oxidation are within the matrix of a mitochondrion. The structure of a mitochondrion is shown in Figure 3.11.

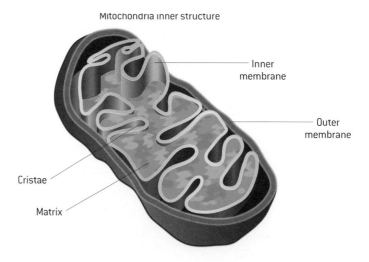

Mitochondria inner structure

Inner membrane

Outer membrane

Cristae

Matrix

↑ Figure 3.11: Ultrastructure of a mitochondrion

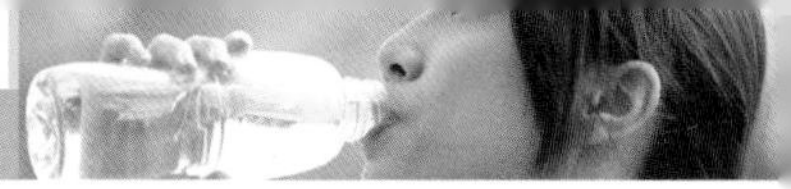

The energy currency of the cells—ATP

In cells, catabolic reactions take place that convert biochemical energy from organic molecules into a molecule called adenosine triphosphate (ATP). The controlled release of energy in the form of ATP is called cell respiration.

Figure 3.12 shows the structure of an ATP molecule. The bonds between the three inorganic phosphate groups are very energy-rich. This energy is released when an ATP molecule is combined with water.

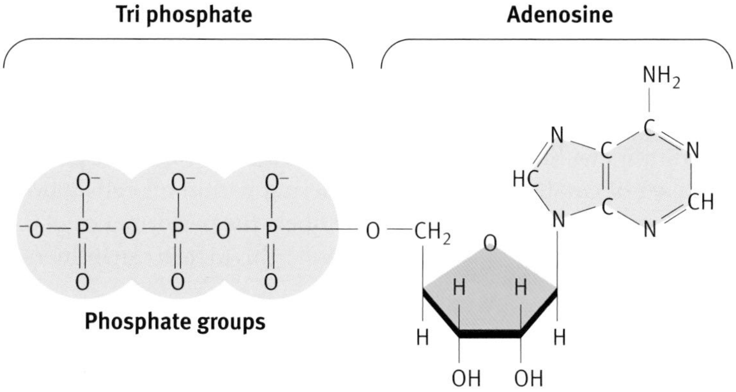

↑ Figure 3.12: Chemical structure of adenosine triphosphate (ATP)

As a result ATP loses the last phosphate group from the chain. This separation releases large amounts of energy (Figure 3.13). In the reverse process called phosphorylation, ATP can be synthesized by adding a phosphate group to the compound adenosine diphosphate (ADP).

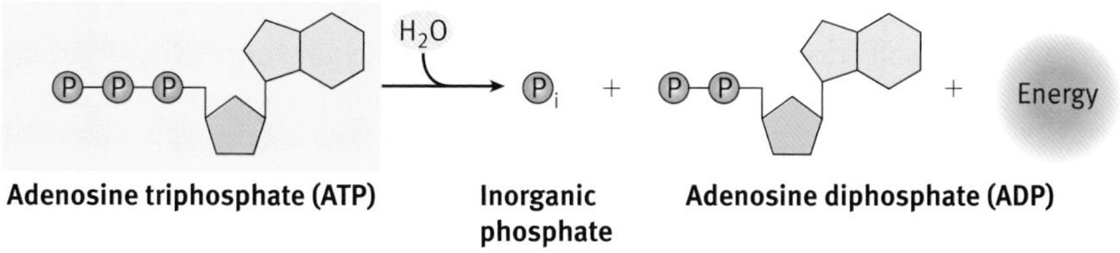

↑ Figure 3.13: Energy is released from ATP when a phosphate group splits away

The ATP molecule is at the center of energy metabolism as it connects anabolic and catabolic reactions. For example, chemical energy ingested as food can be stored in the body as glycogen or fat. However, making use of this available energy means that the chemical energy must be transferred to ATP first. Chemical energy in this form can now be used to drive reactions and processes in the body which require energy (Figure 3.14). This universal process has meant that ATP is often referred to as the energy currency of the cell.

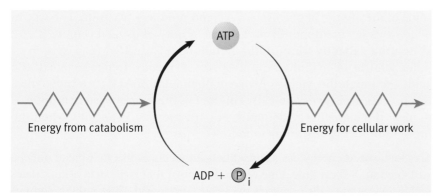

↑ Figure 3.14: Involvement of ATP in energy provision for cells

Adenosine triphosphate (ATP) a molecule created from biochemical energy in organic molecules by catabolic reactions

Cell respiration the controlled release of energy in the form of ATP

THEORY OF KNOWLEDGE

The knowledge on energy metabolism and energy systems and how nutrition influences sport performance was primarily investigated in small animals, mainly mice, rats and hamsters.

1 Discuss ethical concerns related to research in animals.
2 Justify the relevance of knowledge obtained from experiments with rodents to the human metabolism.

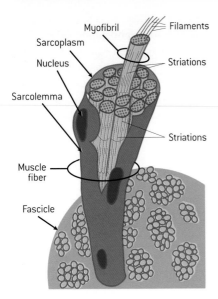

↑ Figure 3.15: A muscle fiber

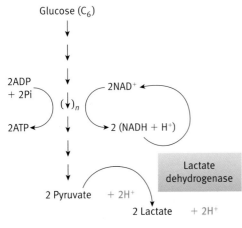

↑ Figure 3.16: Anaerobic use of glucose

Energy for muscle contraction

One important process in the body that requires lots of energy is muscle contraction. Each muscle fiber making up a muscle is in itself a single elongated cell. All muscle fibers have the biochemical capacity to produce ATP using energy sources such as carbohydrates and fats. When a muscle fiber is stimulated to contract by the nervous system the contractile protein molecules within it (e.g. actin and myosin) use ATP to provide the chemical energy to drive the contraction process. Since muscle-driven movement is central to sport and exercise, it is ATP within muscle fibers that provide all energy to make this possible.

In muscle there is sufficient ATP present to allow just two seconds of muscular activity. This means any exercise lasting longer than about two seconds must be using ATP from another source. This source of ATP comes from a range of biochemical pathways within the muscle cell itself called the energy systems. This refers to a set of catabolic reactions occurring within all cells whose principal function is generating ATP. In muscle fibers the performance of the energy systems influences the contraction of muscle; this in turn can influence our ability to perform different types of exercise.

Anaerobic energy systems
Creatine phosphate system

Creatine phosphate, like ATP, is another high energy chemical compound. Although it is present within muscle it cannot be used directly to drive muscle contraction. However, the chemical energy liberated by the following reaction (the creatine kinase reaction) is sufficient to synthesize ATP.

$$\text{Creatine phosphate} + \text{ADP} + \text{H}^+ \leftrightarrow \text{Creatine} + \text{ATP}$$

Creatine phosphate (PCr), in combination with the two seconds' worth of ATP already in muscle, dominates the provision of energy for muscle contraction when we first begin to exercise. This chemical reaction can occur very quickly and so it is also important during hard exercise. For hard exercise ATP is needed at a fast rate, for example, when we perform a sprint. Note that the reaction can go in both directions; this means at rest when we recover from exercise ATP can be used to refill our store of PCr in muscle.

Although fast, the capacity of the creatine phosphate system is short-lived. Your PCr stores (along with existing ATP) only make meaningful contribution to your muscles' energy needs for up to the first 20 seconds of all-out exercise. However, the weakening of PCr does not mean we have to stop—it means other ways of providing ATP must become available.

Lactic acid system

Glycolysis is a metabolic pathway present in the cytoplasm of all cells. This means all cells have the ability to use carbohydrate. Glycolysis releases some of the energy in glucose as ATP and produces pyruvate. The way in which this occurs depends on the availability of oxygen (Figure 3.16). When the capacity for aerobic metabolism is limited (e.g. oxygen or mitochondria are in limited supply) pyruvate is converted to lactate (lactic acid). Although this yields only a small amount of ATP (two molecules) this process occurs very quickly. This means this energy system is optimal to meet the high energy demands of hard exercise, especially when the input from PCr is beginning to fade.

This high speed energy has a consequence though, as like PCr it can only be sustained for a short time. One reason for this is that lactic acid accumulates within muscle and reduces muscle pH as it is a strong acid. This causes discomfort but also reduces the ability of muscle to contract and we begin to slow down.

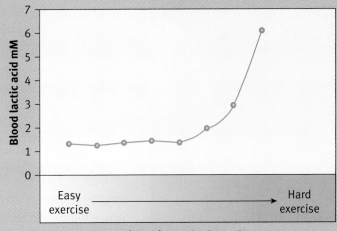

TO THINK ABOUT

The lactate molecules produced in muscle during exercise are transported out of muscle in the blood circulation. Increased concentrations of lactic acid in either muscle or blood are an indicator that anaerobic glycolysis has been used as a key energy system. One very simple way of observing this involves taking tiny blood samples drawn from the fingertip or earlobe and analysing the blood using an automatic, portable lactate analyser to measure the concentration. The graph below shows concentration of lactate in the blood of our cyclist after performing eight progressively faster periods of cycling.

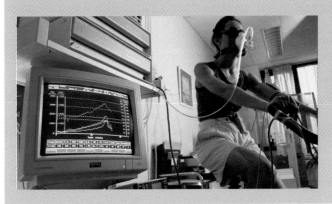
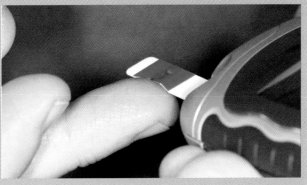

The data in the panel above suggests that during more moderate levels of exercise our cyclist is not relying heavily on anaerobic glycolysis. Therefore other energy systems must be supplying sufficient ATP to keep the pedals turning at the more gentle levels of exercise.

Aerobic systems

The mitochondria of cells accommodate the biochemical processes of aerobic metabolism including the Krebs cycle and the electron transport chain. This aerobic energy system can produce ATP from all the main food groups of our diet. Although carbohydrates and fats are the principal energy substrates, proteins are also used and contribute around 15 per cent of resting energy metabolism.

Glucose oxidation

The final product of glycolysis, pyruvate, has a different fate depending upon metabolic conditions in cells (Figure 3.17). During less demanding metabolic conditions pyruvate is converted to acetyl CoA. This compound enters the Krebs cycle in the mitochondria where chemical reactions that involve oxygen convert it to water and carbon dioxide. During glycolysis and the Krebs cycle hydrogen ions are released. Specific coenzymes bind the hydrogen ions and carry them to the electron transport chain where energy

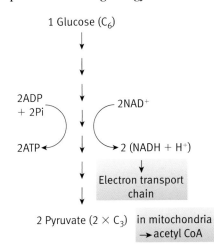

↑ Figure 3.17 Aerobic glucose oxidation

KEY POINT

When we begin exercise it is the anaerobic systems that dominate energy provision. The pre-existing ATP within the muscle provides energy during the first 2 seconds, creatine phosphate's contribution fades after the first 20 seconds after which increasing activation of the lactic acid system dominates energy provision. This too is short lived and as exercise continues an increasing activation of the aerobic energy system means that it quickly dominates energy provision.

KEY POINT

Fats can only be used during aerobic activities, not high intensity, anaerobic activities.

69

↑ Exhausted runners

is produced. This energy is needed to form ATP as described in the section The energy currency of the cell – ATP.

Fat oxidation

Free fatty acid molecules enter the mitochondria and a process called β-oxidation sequentially removes two-carbon units from the fatty acid chains. The enzymes of the β-oxidation are in the matrix of the mitochondria and this process produces acetyl CoA which shares the same fate in oxidative metabolism as that produced from glucose. Unlike carbohydrate, fat cannot in any way be used anaerobically.

Oxygen deficit and excess post-exercise oxygen consumption (EPOC)

Struggling to complete hard exercise leaves us feeling fatigued afterwards. Even at rest we continue to breathe hard for some time. When exercise begins abruptly the demand for ATP is immediate, being met initially with ATP stores, quickly followed by PCr and anaerobic glycolysis, the lactic acid system. These energy systems are activated more quickly than the aerobic energy system which takes longer to react.

The body needs oxygen from the moment we begin to exercise. The body gets into an oxygen deficit because oxygen need and oxygen supply do not match in the first moment of exercise. During recovery from exercise oxygen utilization continues at a rate greater than that needed at rest. This is referred to as excess post-exercise oxygen consumption (EPOC). Part of this is to offset the consequences of anaerobic metabolism during the early phase of exercise. However, additional oxygen demands persist during recovery, needed for processes such as the restoration of tissue and myoglobin oxygenation, the cost of respiration that remains elevated, and a whole range of other physiological factors that keep metabolism elevated even when exercise has ceased. Post-exercise tissue repair which is one of the foundations of the training response has an energy cost too. Figure 3.18 shows how ATP cost and oxygen use result in an oxygen deficit at the beginning of exercise and EPOC at recovery after exercise.

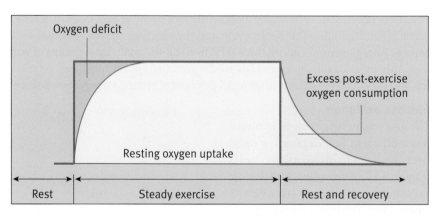

--- ATP cost

--- Oxygen use

↑ Figure 3.18: Oxygen deficit and excess post-exercise oxygen consumption

Characteristics of the energy systems and their contributions during exercise

During exercise all fuel sources and the energy systems which use them come into play to meet the demand for ATP. The rate at which the energy systems can synthesize ATP varies with fat oxidation being the slowest, and creatine phosphate being the fastest. Therefore it makes sense that the faster energy systems dominate when ATP is required at high rates such as those needed to support high intensity exercise (Figure 3.19).

Glucose (anaerobic and/or aerobic) is important across the full range of exercise intensities. However, fatty acids are only used during lower intensity exercise. Above about 90 per cent of maximal exercise no free fatty acids are used at all. Conversely creatine phosphate only contributes during brief, high intensity exercise; it no longer contributes after 20 seconds of all-out exercise.

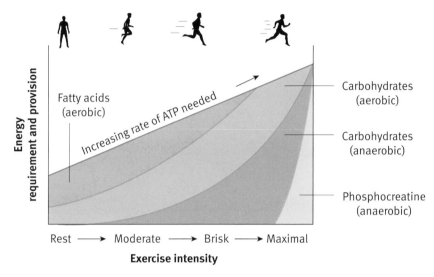

↑ Figure 3.19: The relationship between exercise intensity and rate of energy (ATP) demand. Both the overall rate of ATP production and the mechanism of its synthesis change with intensity.

Of course exercise is never that simple, we rarely maintain a constant pace or rate of work. There may be repeated bursts of high intensity activity, for example, during team games in which anaerobic metabolism (lactic system and creatine phosphate system) are used, broken up by periods of lower effort in which recovery can occur. Similarly during longer, seemingly constant pace running speed may change, with bursts of faster running at the start and a sprint for the finish line.

In summary, the contraction of muscle during exercise of any type and level of intensity requires ATP. The high rate of mechanical work required during intense exercise requires a high rate of ATP provision. This can only be achieved by the fast metabolic processes of the lactic acid system and PCr. The slower processes associated with aerobic metabolism are active during longer, slower exercise efforts. Figure 3.20 illustrates the relative contribution of the energy systems during different types of exercise.

KEY POINT

Because oxygen needs and oxygen supply differ during the transition from rest to exercise, your body experiences oxygen deficit.

During the initial minutes of recovery at the end of exercise, oxygen consumption remains elevated temporarily. There are several reasons for this including:

→ oxygen is required to rebuild the ATP and PCr stores
→ during the initial phase of exercise some oxygen is borrowed from hemoglobin and myoglobin, and that oxygen must be replenished
→ respiration remains elevated to help "clear out" any excess CO_2 that has accumulated in the tissues during exercise
→ participation in exercise elevates body temperature and there is an oxygen cost to help cool the body (through increased breathing rate, for example).

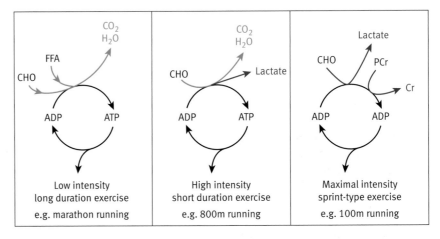

↑ Figure 3.20: Relative contributions to ATP synthesis during three different types of exercise effort. The red content represents aerobic metabolism and the blue anaerobic metabolism. CHO: carbohydrates (glucose); FFA: free fatty acids; PCr: creatine phosphate; Cr: creatine.

TEST YOURSELF

Contribution of the different energy systems during different types of sport

1 Evaluate the dominating energy systems during
   a rugby
   b Tour de France cycling
   c high jump.

2 Label the diagram according to the type of sport on the x-axis and energy systems (different colour boxes). Choose between the systems ATP/PCr, lactate or glucose + fat.

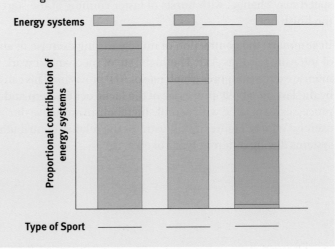

THEORY OF KNOWLEDGE

In aesthetic, weight-dependent and endurance sport, some athletes are engaged in disordered eating behaviour to improve their appearance and performance. Christy Henrich (USA) was a world class artistic gymnast who died in 1994 at the age of 22 years from multiple organ failure caused by 7 years suffering from an eating disorder (anorexia nervosa). It is said that she was told by a national judge to lose weight in order to increase her chances to win the upcoming Olympic Games. Her death raised awareness of unhealthy eating practice in gymnastics and its consequences on health.

1 Investigate whether knowledge of harmful dieting has changed the eating practice of athletes in aesthetic sport today.
2 Discuss, from an ethical standpoint, the role of national and international sport committees in promoting a low body weight in certain sports.

SUMMARY

→ An optimal nutritional status is important for development, growth, performance, and health.
→ A balanced diet is essential to ensure an optimal nutritional status and is defined as a diet that provides the right amount of each of the nutrients carbohydrate, fat, proteins and water (macronutrients) as well as vitamins, minerals and trace elements (micronutrients).
→ Governments and international organizations provide dietary recommendations for an adequate intake for all nutrients that are essential for the promotion of health. Dietary guidelines help the population to put dietary recommendations and the concept of a "balanced diet" into practice.
→ Nutritional requirements vary between population subgroups. For example, an athlete needs more fluids and energy from macronutrients than a non-athlete.
→ Carbohydrates and fat are the dominant energy sources in food.
→ Our body depends on the supply of energy from food which is converted into adenosine triphosphate (ATP) in biochemical pathways.
→ The metabolism either breaks large molecules down (catabolism) to release energy or synthesizes larger molecules from smaller ones (anabolism) to store energy.
→ Energy from carbohydrates can be stored in the form of glycogen in the liver and skeletal muscles. Energy from fat can be stored in form of triglycerides in adipose tissue and skeletal muscle.
→ Muscle contraction is an important energy-requiring process. Different energy systems are accessed to provide energy in the form of ATP.
→ The anaerobic energy systems are the ATP/creatine phosphate system and the lactate system. These provide energy quickly for a short time. The aerobic systems are glucose and fat oxidation which make energy available for a long period after a delayed onset.
→ In muscle fibers the performance of the energy systems influences the contraction of muscle; this in turn can influence our ability to perform different types of exercise.

Self-study questions

1 Identify $C_6H_{12}O_6$.
2 State the smallest chemical unit of proteins and what it is made of.
3 Distinguish between an essential and a non-essential amino acid.

4   Outline what is meant by the term *glycogenolysis*.

5   State the two main sites for glycogen storage in the human body.

6   Distinguish between saturated and unsaturated fatty acids.

7   State the functions of fat stored in adipose tissue.

8   Evaluate the amount of energy stored in dietary carbohydrate, protein and fat.

9   Distinguish between dietary recommendations and dietary guidelines.

10 List the food groups most dietary guidelines refer to.

11 List six forms of energy.

12 Outline the terms *metabolism*, *anabolism* and *catabolism*.

13 Discuss the role of insulin during exercise.

14 Discuss the role of muscle contraction and insulin in blood glucose uptake.

15 Explain the role of adrenaline in metabolism.

16 Define the term *cell respiration*.

17 Evaluate the relative contributions of the pathways for ATP production:

  a   in short-duration, intense exercise (e.g. lifting a heavy weight)

  b   during a 20 minute steady-state, low-intensity jog.

DATA BASED QUESTION

In a study by Currell and Jeukendrup eight trained cyclists consumed either water (placebo – P), a glucose drink (G) or a glucose-fructose drink (GF) before and during 120 min of sub-maximal cycling (55% of peak power), followed by a time trial in which subjects had to complete a set amount of work as quickly as possible. Researchers tested the effect of the beverages on power output as measure of performance during the time trial.

Source: Currell, AK., Jeukendrup, A.E. 2008. "Superior endurance performance with ingestion of multiple transportable carbohydrates." *Medicine & Science in Sports & Exercise*. Vol 40, number 2. Pp 275–81.

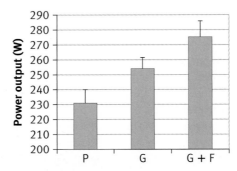

1   Compare the effect of glucose versus water ingestion on the power output during the cycling time trial.   (3 marks)

2   Discuss the benefits of sufficient carbohydrate consumption before, during and after endurance performance in relation to muscle glycogen stores.   (6 marks)

CHAPTER 4

Movement analysis

By the end of this chapter students should be able to:

→ identify the components of a motoneuron

→ explain how muscle fibers and motoneurons combine to form motor units

→ describe how motor units are innervated to create muscle forces

→ explain the sliding filament theory of muscular contraction

→ define the planes of movement and axes of rotation of the human body

→ explain concentric, eccentric and isometric muscle contraction

→ analyse the roles of muscles during joint actions

→ understand the principles of leverage and mechanical advantage

→ distinguish between first, second and third class levers

→ define kinetics and kinematics

→ state Newton's three laws of motion

→ apply Newton's laws of motion to sport and exercise

→ understand the impulse–momentum relationship and its application to sport and exercise

→ define center of mass and center of gravity

→ appreciate the important factors in projectile motion

→ understand drag and lift forces in the flight of objects in sport

→ explain the role of angular momentum in rotation of the human body in sport.

Introduction

The human body is made up of bones, joints and muscles which allow it to perform a wide range of movements. Understanding how muscles contract and how they move the bones around the joints is critical to understanding sport and exercise. Furthermore, the movements of the body (and of sporting implements) are underpinned by Newton's laws of motion which relate forces to motion. It is not possible to analyse sporting techniques or physical activity without a sound appreciation of these laws of motion, whether your aim is to improve performance, reduce the risk of injury or create new techniques.

Terms such as force, power, velocity, torque and energy all have specific meanings and a correct understanding of these and other mechanical quantities will allow accurate and informative analyses of human movement.

> **"Mechanical science is the noblest and above all other, the most useful, seeing that by means of it, all animated bodies which have movement perform all their actions."**
> Leonardo da Vinci (1452-1519)

Neuromuscular function

The nervous system is made up of millions of nerve fibers, all carrying minute electrical signals. The central nervous system (CNS) consists of the brain and spinal cord and is where most sensing and control takes place. The peripheral nervous system is the arrangement of nerves extending from the spinal column to the limbs and other parts of the body.

Sensory neurons carry signals to the central nervous system from receptors that sense various factors such as body temperature, blood pressure, blood oxygen and carbon dioxide levels as well as many other variables. These neurons are sometimes called afferent neurons.

Motoneurons are those nerves which carry information from the central nervous system to the muscles and which signal muscles to contract or relax. There are about 200 000 motoneurons in the human body and they are often called the efferent system.

Interneurons link the afferent neurons to the motoneurons, and have either an excitatory or inhibitory effect on the neural signals.

Afferent neurons neurons that carry sensory information

Efferent system the motoneurons that carry information to the muscles

Structure of neurons

The neuron consists of various components which have different functions in the transmission of nerve signals. The structure of a motoneuron is shown in Figure 4.1.

The soma, or cell body, is contained within the spinal cord or in clusters just outside it called ganglia. Dendrites link the neuron to other neurons and allow information to flow between different nerves. The axon is the main component of nerve signal transmission. It is similar to an electrical wire and has a cover made of myelin, a protein that makes sure the electrical signal is insulated from surrounding tissues. The myelin covering has gaps in it called nodes of Ranvier and these aid transmission of the information.

At the end of the neuron where it meets the muscle cell the axon is unmyelinated. The neuron joins the muscle fiber at the neuromuscular junction or motor end plate and there is actually a gap between neuron and muscle fiber called the synapse, across which transmission of the electrical nerve signal stimulates the muscle.

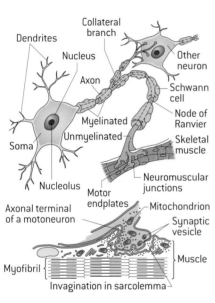

↑ Figure 4.1: Structure of a motoneuron

The motor unit

A motor unit is a single motoneuron and the muscle fibers which it innervates. The number of muscle fibers per motoneuron may be as high as 2,000 (for example, in the gluteus maximus on the back of the hip) or a small as 10 (for example, in the eye). A large number of muscle fibers per motoneuron allows a single motoneuron to cause the muscle to generate large forces; a small number of muscle fibers per motoneuron gives small forces but great precision. The number of muscle fibers stimulated by one motoneuron is called the innervation ratio.

When the motor unit is innervated by the motoneuron all of its muscle fibers contract at once. This is called the all-or-nothing response—all of the muscle fibers attached to one motoneuron are either relaxed or contracted.

Motor unit a single motoneuron and the muscle fibers which it innervates

Types of motor unit

Although all human muscles contain the three types of muscle fibers described in Chapter 1, there are three types of motor unit.

→ **Type I** slow twitch motor units consist of mainly type I (slow twitch) muscle fibers and have fairly slow nerve transmission speeds and small muscle forces. However, they can maintain contractions for a long time, as they are fatigue resistant.

→ **Type IIa** fast twitch oxidative motor units consist mainly of type IIa muscle fibers and have fast neural transmission times and stronger contraction forces and are also resistant to fatigue.

→ **Type IIb** motor units generate the fastest contraction times and largest forces, but these fatigue at a high rate and so cannot maintain contractions for a long period of time.

Type I motor units would therefore be useful for events requiring small forces over a long time period such as walking or jogging. Type IIa motor units would be more appropriate for activities which require larger forces but still occur over a long time, such as swimming and cycling. Type IIb motor units produce very large forces very quickly so would be critical in sprinting, jumping, throwing and weightlifting.

Mechanics of muscle contraction

As mentioned in chapter 1, when seen under a microscope, muscle fiber sarcomeres appear striped or *striated*. These cross-striations are due to the overlap of actin and myosin proteins in the muscle fiber. The detail of the muscle fibers and sarcomeres is shown in Figure 4.2.

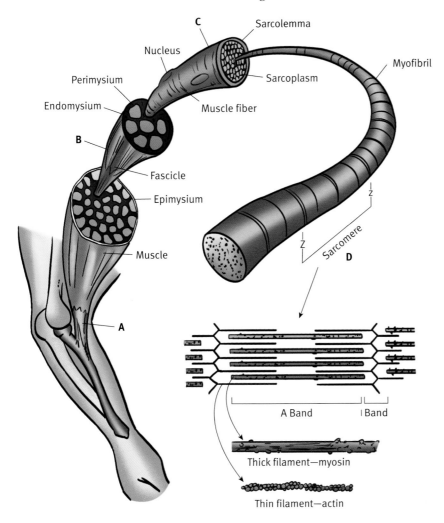

↑ Figure 4.2

Muscular contraction starts with an electrical impulse, generated either voluntarily from the brain or by reflex, which travels along a motoneuron to

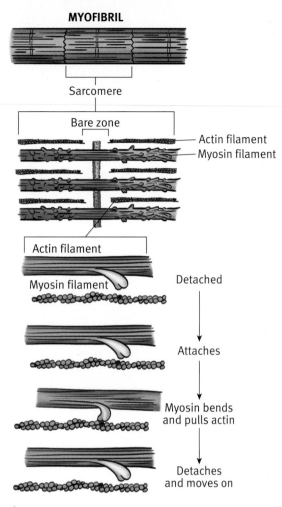

MYOFIBRIL

Sarcomere

Bare zone

Actin filament
Myosin filament

Actin filament

Myosin filament

Detached

Attaches

Myosin bends
and pulls actin

Detaches
and moves on

↑ Figure 4.3

the neuromuscular junction of the motor unit. At the neuromuscular junction or motor end plate, there is a space between the end of the neuron and the muscle fibers. This is called a synapse. When the signal reaches this synapse, a chemical called acetylcholine is released. This changes the electrical state of the muscle and causes a signal called the action potential to travel along the muscle fibers.

The action potential travels through the muscle fibers down the T-tubules, and stimulates the sarcoplasmic reticulum to release calcium ions (Ca^{2+}). This opens the binding sites on the actin molecules and the heads of the myosin molecules move out towards these sites. The heads of the myosin molecules are shaped a little like golf clubs and it is the ends of the heads that attach to the actin. Attached to the myosin head is a chemical called adenosine triphosphate (ATP) and this is split chemically into adenosine diphosphate (ADP) and phosphate. At the same time, the head of the myosin "bends" thus sliding the actin along a little relative to the myosin.

The myosin is then released from the actin and fresh ATP can join the myosin head. If the electrical signal is still present, fresh calcium will also be available, and the myosin heads can bind to the next sites on the actin. Thus the actin has been pulled along parallel to the myosin. This happens repeatedly while the neural signal is active, thus the muscle contracts by the sliding of the actin relative to the myosin. This is known as the sliding filament theory and was first proposed by Huxley in 1957. Muscle fibers are made up of many thousands of actin and myosin molecules, and the sliding of all of these makes the muscle contract.

When the nerve is no longer stimulated, acetylcholine is removed by acetylcholine esterase, calcium goes back into the sarcoplasmic reticulum and the myosin heads move back to their resting positions away from the actin.

Control of muscle force

When a muscle is signalled to contract, the central nervous system will usually control the force of contraction so that the body segment will move appropriately. This might require a very large force (such as in the quadriceps muscles during kicking) or a small force (such as when writing). The control of the muscle force can be carried out by recruiting the motor units in two ways.

The size principle is when smaller motor units are recruited first and only when larger forces are required are large motor units stimulated. However, in activities that require very large forces, this principle may not be effective. Therefore, the frequency of motor unit innervation can also be varied, with a higher rate of activation causing a higher force in the muscle. This is called frequency or rate coding of motor unit recruitment.

Measuring muscle activation

It is useful to be able to monitor the electrical activation of motor units, so that factors such as timing of contraction, force of contraction and fatigue can be assessed. This is carried out with electromyography (EMG). Electrodes are either inserted into the muscle (rare when looking at sport and exercise due to the invasive nature of the insertion) or are placed on the surface of the skin above the muscles of interest.

The electrodes are then connected to an amplifier and the action potential which innervates the muscle can be recorded, usually by computer. The "raw" EMG signal shows a signal above and below the resting baseline, indicating the depolarization and repolarization of the motor units. When the muscle contracts, the amplitude (size) of the signal increases; as the motor units are recruited and when it relaxes the signal returns to base level.

Further calculations may be applied to the raw EMG signal to help understanding of the muscle contractions.

→ Firstly, the raw EMG may be rectified—this makes all the negative signals positive, and this makes calculation of the mean average much easier. The mean average can be used to give the overall strength of a contraction.

→ Secondly, a linear envelope (or low pass filter) can be applied to the raw EMG—this shows an outline of each muscle contraction and makes it clearer to see when each "burst" starts and ends.

→ Thirdly, the total signal can be added up for each muscle contraction, and this is called integrated EMG. This gives a total amount of muscle activity for all of the muscle contractions of interest.

→ Finally, the raw EMG can be transformed into frequency information. This shows the rate of firing of the muscle, and can be used to examine fatigue.

a

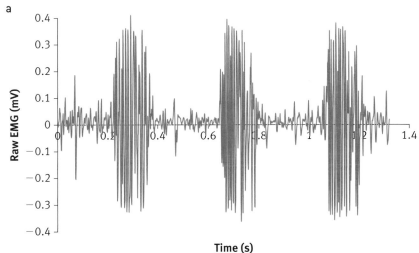

b

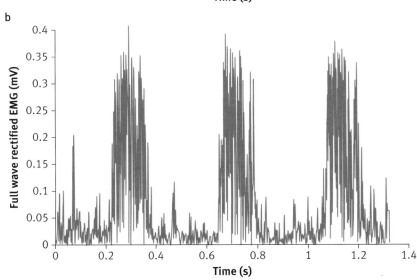

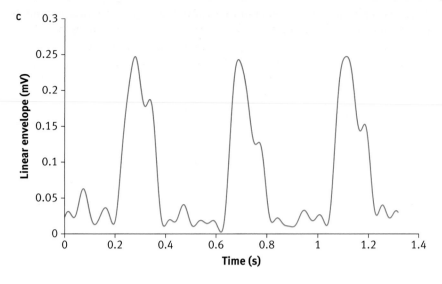

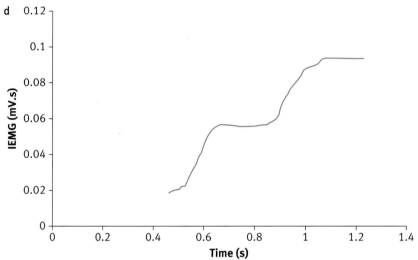

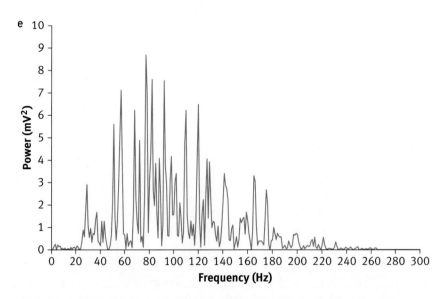

↑ Figure 4.4: Electromyogram from biceps brachii muscles performing three contractions showing: **a** raw EMG, **b** full-wave rectified EMG, **c** linear envelope, **d** integrated EMG and **e** frequency spectrum.

Although EMG seems an attractive method of measuring muscle activity, it is not straightforward. Fat, fluid and skin have a filtering effect on the signal as it travels between the muscle being studied and the surface electrodes. This reduces the size of the signal and also spreads it out, making it difficult to identify what is happening at the motor units. Also, the movement of the muscles under the skin in dynamic contractions means that the EMG may be recording electrical activity from different parts of the muscle, or even from different muscles, as the body segments move. There are also electrical signals from other devices (such as fluorescent lights) and from motion of the cables used to transmit the EMG signal that can interfere with the recordings, and make it difficult to distinguish the required information from the electrical "noise".

Therefore, there is not a direct linear relationship between muscle force and the recorded EMG, except occasionally in simple static (isometric) contractions where the body segment does not move although the muscle is contracting (such as holding a weight). The above factors also affect the EMG signal when examining changes in the frequency spectrum to determine the effects of muscle fatigue. Hence EMG is a useful research tool, but the signals should be analysed bearing in mind the complications noted above.

Joint and movement type

The musculoskeletal system is the arrangement of bones, joints and muscles that permits movement of the human body in sports and exercise. The body segments are articulated by the synovial joints at which two or more bones meet. Usually, movement consists of rotation of one segment relative to another at the joint. This rotation is caused by forces originating from the muscles, other parts of the body, or external actors (such as gravity, sporting implements or other people). Understanding the movements possible at the joints and how the muscles control these movements is crucial for us to be able to analyse human activity in sport and exercise.

Movements of synovial joints

Synovial joints can be classified depending on how many axes of rotation the bones have. The structure of synovial joints was discussed in chapter 1, and this chapter will explain how this structure permits movements around particular axes.

→ **Non-axial** In gliding joints (e.g. between the carpal bones in the palm of the hand) the bones simply slide in relation to each other. Therefore, there are no axes of rotation in this type of joint.

→ **Uniaxial** In hinge joints (e.g. the elbow) and pivot joints (e.g. the radioulnar joint) there is only one axis of rotation. This means that the structure of the bones at the joint restricts rotation to movement around one axis only.

→ **Biaxial** At condylar joints (e.g. the knee) and saddle joints (e.g. the base of the thumb) there are two axes of rotation and therefore the bones can move in two different ways.

→ **Traxial** Ball and socket joints such as the shoulder and hip allow rotation around three axes. Therefore, these bones permit the greatest movement, as they allow the limbs attached at them to move through a large volume of space.

When segments of the human body move, it is very useful to be able to describe the movements precisely and concisely. Therefore, there is a system of naming the movements of the body's segments that it is used in sport, exercise and medicine. Knowledge of these terms will greatly assist description and analysis of motion, as well as promote greater understanding between sports scientists, physical educators, coaches and sports medicine practitioners.

Axes of rotation and planes of movement of the human body

There are several planes and axes which provide a reference for describing the motion at the joints as well as movement of the whole body. These axes and planes use the anatomical terminology introduced in chapter 1.

There are three fundamental axes of rotation:

→ the anteroposterior axis (going from front to back)
→ the transverse axis (going from left to right)
→ the vertical axis (going from top to bottom).

For the whole body, these axes pass through the center of gravity as shown in Figure 4.5.

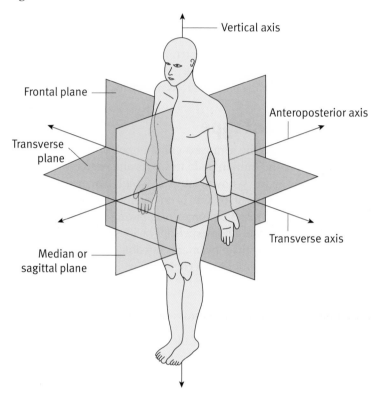

↑ Figure 4.5: Axes of rotation and planes of movement of the human body

For individual joints these axes pass through the joint center. Of course, at some joints (particularly triaxial joints) the axis of rotation may be at some oblique angle and not about one of the reference axes, depending on the position of the static bone and the motion of the moving bone at the joint. Also, at individual joints, practitioners may refer to the "longitudinal axis" meaning the axis from the proximal to the distal ends of the moving bone at the joint.

Movement of the body's segments at the joints can be considered to be in three planes. Of course, it is possible to move in a combination of two or more of these planes. When applied to the whole body, these planes go through the center of gravity (see Figure 4.5) and are:

→ the frontal plane (cuts the body front from back)
→ the sagittal or median plane (cuts the body left from right)
→ the transverse plane (cuts the body top from bottom).

These planes can also refer to movements at individual joints.

Movements at the joints

The movements of the body segments at the joints are given particular names. Now the reference axes of rotation and planes have been defined, these movements can be described (see Table 4.1). The movements are usually assumed to start with the segments of the body in the anatomical starting position (see chapter 1) with the individual standing upright, facing straight ahead with the feet parallel and close together and the palms facing forward.

MOTION IN THE SAGITTAL PLANE	
Flexion	Closing of the joint angle around the transverse axis at the joint.
Extension	Opening of the joint angle around the transverse axis at the joint.
MOTION IN THE FRONTAL PLANE	
Abduction	Opening of the joint angle around the anteroposterior axis at the joint.
Adduction	Closing of the joint angle around the anteroposterior axis at the joint.
MOTION IN THE TRANSVERSE PLANE	
Medial (inward) rotation	The anterior surface of the moving bone moves towards the medial (inside) aspect of the body.
Lateral (outward) rotation	The anterior surface of the moving bone moves towards the lateral (outside) aspect of the body.

↑ Table 4.1

These are the main fundamental movements that apply to all joints, as long as the structure permits movements around the appropriate axes. For example, the elbow joint *flexes* when it bends and *extends* when it straightens, but the structure of the joint does not permit abduction, adduction, medial or lateral rotation. Conversely, the shoulder joint flexes when the arm is raised, and extends when it is lowered (these two movements are the opposite to what might be expected), abducts when the arm is raised from the side and adducts when it is lowered again. The humerus (upper arm) also can undergo rotation around the transverse axis at the shoulder joint, demonstrated by the fact that when the elbow is kept fully extended, the hand can still go from facing anteriorly to posteriorly (medial rotation) and back again (lateral rotation).

When the word *hyper* (Greek for "beyond" or "more than") is added to any of these terms, this usually indicates that the action is beyond 180° or back past the starting position. It is also sometimes defined as movement of a body segment into the space posterior to the body when it is in the anatomical position. For example, hyperextension of the shoulder is when the arm extends in the sagittal plane and then continues past the anatomical position behind the body.

There are also some commonly used terms which apply to particular joints as listed in Table 4.2.

DORSIFLEXION	Flexion of the ankle joint.	These movements move the foot up and down in the sagittal plane.
PLANTAR FLEXION	Extension of the ankle joint.	
PRONATION	Medial rotation of the radioulnar joint (not the wrist joint).	These movements allow the forearm (and thus the hand as well) to rotate, even when the elbow is flexed. If the elbow is flexed to 90° from the anatomical position, pronation would take the hand from "palm upwards" to "palm downwards", and vice versa for supination.
SUPINATION	Lateral rotation of the radioulnar joint (not the wrist joint).	
EVERSION	Medial rotation of the ankle joint.	These movements involve "rolling" of the foot at the ankle. From the anatomical position, if the foot is moved so that the sole faces inwards, this is inversion. If the foot is moved so the sole faces outwards, this is eversion.
INVERSION	Lateral rotation of the ankle joint.	
HORIZONTAL ABDUCTION (ALSO CALLED HORIZONTAL EXTENSION)	Opening of the joint angle around the transverse plane when the body segment has already been flexed to 90°.	These actions are common at the shoulder. If the arm is flexed (raised in the sagittal plane) to 90° and then brought toward the midline of the body horizontal, this is horizontal adduction (horizontal flexion). If the arm is moved horizontally away from the midline when already flexed to 90°, this is horizontal abduction (horizontal extension).
HORIZONTAL ADDUCTION (ALSO CALLED HORIZONTAL FLEXION)	Closing of the joint angle around the transverse plane when the body segment has already been flexed to 90°.	

↑ Table 4.2

There are several movements that are actually combinations of the fundamental movements listed above, but which are given a single name for ease of understanding.

→ **Circumduction** This is the "circling" of a body segment at a joint, for example, moving the arm in a circle around the shoulder, such as in cricket bowling. This particular movement is actually a combination of hyperextension, abduction, extension and adduction. Circumduction may include other movements in the circling action depending on the direction, axes of rotation and the particular joint. Circumduction commonly occurs at the shoulder, hip, wrist, ankle and thumb, meaning it requires at least a biaxial joint.

→ **Pronation and supination of the foot** These movements are often used by sports medicine practitioners when describing motion of the foot at the ankle joint (combined with the other joints in the foot) during walking or running. Pronation combines dorsiflexion, eversion and abduction of the ankle and foot, and often occurs just after landing in walking or running as the body's weight is absorbed. Supination is plantarflexion, inversion and adduction and often occurs during push-off in walking and running as the ankle is used to propel the person forward and upward. Not all individuals demonstrate pronation on landing, however; it depends on their body structure and their movement technique.

Examples of some the movements are shown in Figures 4.6 to 4.8.

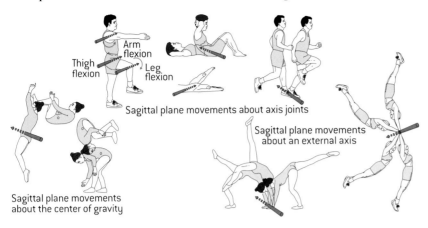

Thigh flexion

Arm flexion

Leg flexion

Sagittal plane movements about axis joints

Sagittal plane movements about an external axis

Sagittal plane movements about the center of gravity

↑ Figure 4.6

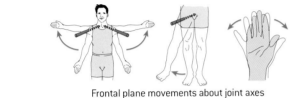
Frontal plane movements about joint axes

Frontal plane movements about the center of gravity

Frontal plane movements about external axis

↑ Figure 4.7

Transverse plane movements about joint axes

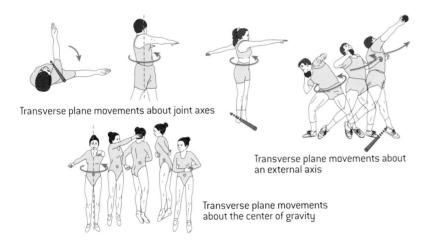
Transverse plane movements about an external axis

Transverse plane movements about the center of gravity

↑ Figure 4.8

Range of motion

The range of motion (usually abbreviated as ROM) at any particular joint depends on four factors:

→ the shape of the surfaces of the articulating bones in the joints
→ the position and length of the restraining ligaments (see chapter 1)
→ the effects of the muscles and tendons at the joint
→ the amount of soft tissue (skin, fat, muscle) at the joint.

A large range of motion is usually beneficial for sporting performance as it means forces can be applied over a greater distance. However, excessive range of motion is sometimes called *hypermobility* and can make joints susceptible to dislocation or damage. This can be a problem for performers in those sports and activities which require a large amount of flexibility such as gymnastics or ballet dancing.

Muscle contraction types

When muscles contract, the ends of the muscles are drawn towards the center of the body due to the sliding filaments. However, muscles can move the body segments by varying the force of contraction and where the muscle's line of action is relative to the joint.

→ **Concentric contraction** If the ends of the muscles are actually drawn together, this will result in the movement of one or more body segments. If the rotational effect of the force (known as torque or moment) from the muscle is greater than that of the resistance to be overcome (e.g. segment weight, external weight, other muscles, other person) then this is known as a concentric contraction.

→ **Isometric contraction** If the muscle contracts, but the rotational effect of the muscle force (muscle torque or moment) is *exactly equal* to that provided by the resistance, then the muscle will not physically shorten although it will be contracted. This is known as an isometric (or static) contraction.

→ **Eccentric contraction** If the muscle is contracting but the rotational effect of the muscle force (muscle torque or moment) is less than that of the resistance, then the ends of the muscles actually get further apart, even though the muscle is still contracting. This is because the muscle is *not* relaxed, but is not contracting strongly enough (and/or not in a suitable position) to overcome or balance the resistance. This type of contraction is known as an eccentric contraction. The lengthening of the muscle while still contracting is thought to break the actin-myosin bonds mechanically, and this means that greater muscle forces and torques can be produced than in concentric contraction. Fewer motor units are recruited for the same muscle force and there is also a lower oxygen cost for eccentric contractions than concentric contraction of the same muscle.

→ **Isotonic contraction** Eccentric and concentric contractions are sometimes known as isotonic contractions (meaning "same tension" or "same force") because the force remains constant during the movement of the body segment affected by the muscle. However, this is a misleading term, as the force in the muscle will usually change due to the change in joint angle (and therefore the angle of pull of the muscle relative to the joint will also change). This means that the force in the muscle will usually change throughout the range of motion, even if the external resistance is constant (for example, lifting a constant weight).

→ **Isokinetic motion** Isokinetic motion is when a muscle contracts so that the body segment to which it is attached moves at a constant speed around the joint. This type of movement is very rare in sport and exercise (most movements have an acceleration phase and a deceleration phase), and usually requires complex equipment to ensure the segment rotational speed is constant. This type of motion (regulated by equipment) is useful in rehabilitation when a therapist wants to make sure the speed of a limb is not excessive. However, as in isotonic contractions, just because the body segment moves at a constant rotational speed, it cannot be assumed that the muscle is contracting at a constant speed due to the different angles of pull through the range of motion.

Eccentric contraction and muscle soreness

Muscle soreness may be due to a variety of factors, but one of the most common is the sub-cellular damage (and the associated inflammation) that becomes apparent one or two days after exercise. This is called delayed onset muscle soreness (DOMS), and seems to be related to exercise which has large amounts of eccentric exercise (for example, running downhill, in which the quadriceps muscles contract eccentrically at the knee to control the body weight).

The mechanical breaking of the actin-myosin bonds that occurs in eccentric contraction combined with the large muscle forces that can be produced in this type of exercise result in various biochemical and mechanical changes in the muscle. These then cause inflammation, stiffness and pain which peaks 24 to 48 hours after exercise, although it can last up to 10 days. The muscle damage can be monitored by examining the levels of creatine kinase, an enzyme involved in the breakdown and synthesis of muscle proteins.

The most effective method of treating DOMS is light exercise, although some studies have suggested non-steroidal anti-inflammatory drugs (NSAIDs), massage or ice baths *may* help.

Have you ever experienced DOMS after intense exercise? Think about the activity that caused this—what muscles you were using and how were you using them?

→ **Muscle relaxation** The final way for a muscle to affect segment motion is to relax. This means that the contractile elements are not interlinked by the myosin heads, and that the ends of the muscle are not being drawn (or trying to be drawn) together. Therefore the muscle contraction force is zero. However, it should be noted that there still may be some resistance to movement (especially if the muscle is being moved beyond its relaxed length) due to the residual extensibility and elasticity of the muscle and tendon (see chapter 1).

Roles of muscle in joint movements

Muscles are used in various ways when joints are moved. These roles depend on the desired movement, the type of muscle used, the position of the muscles relative to the joint and the type of contraction.

→ **Agonist (mover)** In this role, the muscle contracts *concentrically* to move the bone relative to the joint. The muscle shortens and the muscle torque is greater than any resistance torque. There are different levels of agonist: prime, assistant or emergency. For example, when lifting a weight (elbow flexion) during a bicep curl, the prime mover or agonist would be the biceps brachii (the large muscle on the anterior surface of the upper arm), and the assistant movers would be the brachialis (a smaller muscle on the anterior surface of the elbow) and the brachoradialis (the muscle that runs from above the elbow to the wrist on the anterior surface of the forearm).

→ **Antagonist** If a muscle contracts *eccentrically*, then it is often acting as an antagonist for the joint action. This means it acts in the opposite direction to its usual concentric function, and gets longer even though it is contracting. For example, when *lowering* the weight during the bicep curl (elbow extension), the biceps brachii and the other two muscles act as antagonists to slow the descent (if the muscles relaxed, the weight would simply fall due to gravity). Note that the triceps brachii (the muscle on the posterior surface of the upper arm) does *not* contract in this action–this would simply 'throw' the weight to the floor as the elbow would be extended actively at speed, rather than under control.

→ **Fixator (stabilizer)** When muscles contract, both ends are drawn towards the middle of the muscle. However, if only one end of the muscle is required to move a body segment, then the body segment to which the other end of the muscle is attached (usually the other segment of the joint) must be kept stationary. Therefore, this will require at least one other muscle to contract (usually isometrically) to prevent this segment from moving so that the agonist may move the desired segment. These other muscles are called fixators or stabilizers and are very important. This is one of the main ideas behind the principle of core stability–the muscles of the core must be strong so they can hold the trunk of the body steady while the agonists or antagonists move the limbs.

→ **Synergist (neutralizer)** Most muscles have more than one action at a joint. For example, when the biceps brachii contracts, it not only flexes the elbow joint but also supinates the radioulnar joint. Therefore, if these extra actions are not required, other muscles must be used to prevent them. These muscles are named synergists or neutralizers and contract (usually isometrically) to prevent unwanted actions of the agonists or antagonists. In the example above, one or both of the pronator muscles would be used if supination was not desired when the biceps brachii was contracting.

It is very important to assess which type of contraction muscles (particularly the agonists) are undergoing in a movement. Generally, if a limb is being moved in the *opposite* direction to a resistance force (e.g. gravity) the agonists are undergoing concentric contraction. However, if a limb is moving in the *same* direction as the resistance force (but under control) an eccentric contraction is being performed by the antagonists.

If *no movement* is apparent, but the muscles are contracting, then isometric contraction is likely to be occurring.

→ **Reciprocal inhibition** When an agonist contracts to move a body segment, it is usual for the antagonist (the muscle with the opposite concentric contraction action) to relax. This means that the agonist is not being opposed by any muscle torque acting in the opposite direction to that of the motion. This is called *reciprocal inhibition reflex* and is an automatic action controlled by neurons. When the agonist motoneuron is stimulated, the motoneuron to the antagonist is inhibited, preventing it from contracting strongly. During sport and exercise, these signals are very important to ensure maximum torque around the joints when the agonist muscles contract.

It is a common misconception to think that when the agonist muscles contract concentrically, the antagonist muscles contract eccentrically. In most movements, this would be counterproductive as the antagonist muscles would be producing a torque in the opposite direction to motion, thus lowering the net torque around the joint. So, for example, during the upward phase of a biceps curl, the biceps brachii muscle contracts concentrically and the triceps brachii (the antagonist muscle) *relaxes*. During the downward phase (if slow and controlled), the biceps brachii muscle contracts eccentrically and the triceps brachii is *still relaxed*.

However, occasionally it is necessary for both agonist and antagonist to contract at the same time (for example, to control balance or to make a joint "stiffer" when learning a task). This is called co-activation and in this case reciprocal inhibition is overridden by the voluntary nervous system.

Fundamentals of biomechanics

Biomechanics can be defined as the "applications of mechanics to the human body and sporting implements, and studies the forces on (and caused by) the human body and the subsequent result of those forces" (Coleman1999).

This means that biomechanics examines the forces caused by the human body (for example, by the muscles) and forces on the body from outside (such as gravity or other players) and the effects they have on the body's motion.

Furthermore "biomechanics is the science underlying techniques" (Hay 1994). This means that if a coach or physical education teacher wishes to understand technique in order to improve performance or reduce injuries, he or she must have a good knowledge of biomechanics.

Biomechanics is divided into two areas: kinematics (dealing with the motion of bodies and objects) and kinetics (dealing with forces).

Kinematics

Kinematics is the study of motion, which is simply the change in position of a body or object. This might be a change in the position of the body's limbs, moving the body from one place to another or both together.

Motion can be:

→ **linear** motion in a straight line, such as an ice hockey puck sliding over the ice
→ **curvilinear** motion in a curve, such as a shot-put travelling through the air

- **angular** motion around an axis, sometimes known as rotational motion, such as a gymnast rotating around a high bar
- **general** (linear and angular motion together).

The most common type of movement of the human body in sport and exercise is general motion. This is because at almost all synovial joints in the body, one segment rotates around another. This means that even if we wish to run in a straight line, we must rotate our limbs while travelling linearly.

Measuring movement

A measurement that has both size and direction is known as a *vector*. One that only has size is known as a *scalar*.

The difference between scalars and vectors is important in biomechanics because it affects how measurements are combined (for example, by adding, subtracting, multiplying or dividing). If the direction of two vectors is the same, their sizes may be simply combined together, but if there are different directions, this must also be taken in account. Scalars can simply be added, subtracted, multiplied and divided.

Vectors in this chapter are given in bold characters while scalars appear in normal text.

Position

The position of an object or body is usually given by its coordinates. Linear coordinates are a linear measurement (e.g. metres) from an origin and are often given in two dimensions (horizontal and vertical) or three dimensions (horizontal, vertical and lateral). Two-dimensional coordinates are often named x and y (horizontal and vertical), while three-dimensional coordinates are usually called x, y and z. There are two systems for giving three-dimensional coordinates. In the first x is horizontal, y is vertical, z is lateral while in the second x is horizontal, y is lateral, z is vertical. The position of an object is sometimes given the symbol **r**.

Angular coordinates are given by the angles around one or more axes.

Linear kinematics

As mentioned above, linear kinematics looks at motion in a straight line.

Linear displacement and linear distance

If a body or object changes its position from one place to another it undergoes a displacement. This is given in terms of how far and in what direction the end position is from the start position. The displacement is often expressed as how far the body or object has moved horizontally, vertically and laterally. Therefore displacement is a vector quantity because it has size and direction. The size of linear displacement is named distance. Distance is a scalar quantity and has no direction, therefore it does not matter in which direction the object or body moves, only how far it goes.

Linear displacement is usually given by the symbol **s** (or sometimes δ**r** meaning change in position) and linear distance by the symbol **d**. The SI unit for the size of displacement is metres (m), and the direction may be specified in degrees (°) or radians (rad) from a particular direction, or may be along a coordinate axis (horizontal, vertical or lateral).

Linear velocity

Velocity is a change in displacement divided by the time taken for the change to take place. It has size (how fast) and direction and so is also a vector quantity. The size of linear velocity is called speed and is a scalar quantity as it does not have any direction.

> **Vector** a measurement that has both size and direction
>
> **Scalar** a measurement that only has size

Linear velocity is usually given by the symbol **v**. The SI unit for velocity is metres per second (m.s^{-1} or m/s) and again, the direction may be specified in degrees (°) or radians (rad) from a particular direction, or may be along a coordinate axis (horizontal, vertical or lateral).

Linear acceleration

Acceleration is a change in velocity divided by the time taken for the change to take place. It also can be linear or angular. It has size and direction and is a vector quantity.

As acceleration is a change in speed, a change in direction or both, if you are running around a bend at constant speed, you are accelerating. Acceleration should therefore not therefore just be used to indicate a change in speed, but also a change in direction.

Linear acceleration is usually given by the symbol **a**. The SI unit for acceleration is metres per second per second (m.s^{-2} or m/s/s) and the direction may be specified in degrees (°) or radians (rad) from a particular direction, or may be along a coordinate axis (horizontal, vertical or lateral).

KEY POINT

The symbols usually used for the different types of movement in linear kinematics and the SI units used are as follows.

Linear displacement	s	Metres
Linear distance	d	Metres
Linear velocity	v	Metres per second (m.s^{-1} or m/s)
Linear acceleration	a	Metres per second per second (m.s^{-2} or m/s/s)

Angular kinematics

Angular kinematics looks at motion around an axis.

Angular displacement

Angular displacement is the difference between start and end positions when a body moves around an axis with angular motion. Angular displacement is a vector quantity so has size and direction and is represented by the symbol θ (Greek theta). The SI unit for the size of angular displacement is usually degrees (°) or radians (rad) and the direction is anticlockwise or clockwise around the axis.

Angular velocity

Angular velocity is the change of angular displacement divided by the time taken. This is also a vector quantity. Angular velocity is given as the symbol ω (Greek omega). The SI unit for the size of the angular velocity is degrees per second (°.s^{-1} or °/s) or radians per second (rad.s^{-1} or rad/s) and the direction is usually clockwise or anticlockwise about an axis.

Angular acceleration

Angular acceleration is the change of angular velocity divided by the time taken for the change to take place. It is a vector and is given the symbol α (the Greek symbol alpha). The SI unit for the size of the angular velocity is degrees per second per second (°.s^{-2} or °/s/s) or radians per second per second (rad.s^{-2} or rad/s/s) and the direction is often clockwise or anticlockwise about an axis.

Instantaneous and average kinematics

As velocities and accelerations (linear and angular) involve division by time, the values obtained will depend on the duration over which the measurement is made. The time may be long (for example, over a whole race), or very short (fractions of a second). As the time gets shorter and shorter, it approaches zero. In mathematics, this is named calculus (invented by both Newton and Leibnitz separately in the 17th century).

The velocity or acceleration calculated over a long time is usually called average velocity or acceleration. The velocity or acceleration when the time is very nearly zero is called the instantaneous velocity or acceleration, and may be calculated in two ways. If the relationship between the displacement and time is known mathematically (i.e. by an equation), calculus allows the exact calculation of an equation for the velocity (and similarly, if the equation between the velocity and time is known, an equation for the acceleration can be found). Alternatively a graph of displacement against time can be drawn, and then the velocity is the *slope* of this graph at any point. This is usually found by drawing a *tangent* to the displacement-time graph. Similarly, the same method can be used to get acceleration from a velocity-time graph.

Average velocities and accelerations are much simpler to calculate. The change in displacement is simply divided by the time taken to get the velocity, and the change in velocity is divided by the time taken to get the acceleration.

Kinetics

Kinetics looks at the forces involved in the movement of an object or body. As with kinematics, we can look at linear kinetics for movements in a straight line or angular kinetics for movement around an axis.

Linear kinetics

Force

Force is sometimes described as a push or a pull. However, although correct, this is rather simple and so a better definition and understanding is needed. Force is simply the mechanical interaction that goes on between two objects or bodies. It may involve contact (such as friction) or it may act at a distance (such as gravity). A force changes or tries to change the motion of the objects.

Gravity

In 1687, Sir Isaac Newton published his *Principia* which set out to understand how objects changed their motions. Building on the work of previous scientists such as Galileo, Kepler and Halley, he realized that there is an attractive force between objects which is related to their masses (the amount of material in them) and inversely proportional to the square of the distance between them. This force causes the elliptical orbits of the planets around the sun, but also is the reason for the attraction between the earth and all bodies and objects near to it or on its surface.

It should be recognized that astronauts orbiting the earth are still subject to earth's gravity (that is why they are orbiting rather than travelling off into space) and so are not in "zero gravity". It is simply that their spacecraft is moving as fast as they are and so they are in "free fall" all of the time and thus have no force between them and the floor.

Mass and weight

Mass is the amount of material in a body or object. It is usually measured in kilograms, but is not its weight. Weight is the effect of the force of gravity on mass. This means that on the moon, the mass of an object is the same as on the earth, but its weight is less (because the moon's gravity is less than that of the earth). Because the force of gravity always acts between an object and the earth and is directed towards the center of the earth, there is always a force acting vertically on us.

Newton's laws of motion

In his *Principia*, Newton also stated the three laws that relate forces to the change of motion. Although today we know that Newton's laws of motion do not work well when considering motion near the speed of light or when looking at sub-atomic particles, they are very accurate when analysing the forces and motion on our bodies or everyday objects.

Newton's first law of motion

Newton's first law of motion can be stated as: "An object will remain at rest or continue with constant velocity unless acted on by an unbalanced force." This means that bodies or objects stay where they are or *keep moving* unless acted on by an unbalanced force. This law is sometimes known as the law of inertia.

For a body to be at rest (standing still) on the earth, there must be a force balancing the weight, acting in the opposite direction (upwards). This force often comes from supports or the ground and is called the reaction force. If an object is travelling at constant speed in a constant direction, the forces on it must also be balanced.

Thus, a true understanding of a force is that it is something that *changes* (or tries to change) a body or object's motion and *not* something that *causes* motion.

Newton's second law of motion

Newton's second law of motion relates the change in motion (acceleration) to the force causing that change. It can be stated as: "The acceleration (for a body/object of constant mass) is proportional to, and in the same direction as, the unbalanced force applied to it." This law is sometimes known as the law of acceleration.

This is sometimes written as: "Force is equal to mass multiplied by acceleration" ($\mathbf{F} = \mathbf{ma}$). Thus a body or object's change of motion is directly related to the size of the (unbalanced) force causing the change and will change motion in the direction of the applied force. The change in motion is also inversely related to the mass of the object. Therefore heavier objects will accelerate less for the same force, and to accelerate heavy objects, a large force is needed.

As we have seen, acceleration is change in velocity divided by the time taken. So Newton's second law of motion could be rewritten as $\mathbf{F} = m\,(\mathbf{v} - \mathbf{u})\,/\,t$, where v and u are final and initial velocities and t is the time for the velocity change.

Newton's third law of motion

The third law of motion explains the forces between two objects. It can be stated as: "When one body or object applies a force to another, the second body or object will apply a force equal in size but opposite in direction to the first body or object." This law is often called the law of reaction. This law is sometimes phrased as "for every action there is an equal and opposite reaction."

There are several important aspects to the understanding of this law: Firstly, the two forces are on two *different* bodies or objects (not on the same body/ object). Secondly, the forces on the objects are exactly the same size, regardless of the masses of the objects. The *effects* of those forces may be different if the bodies/objects are of different masses—this is due to Newton's second law of motion. Finally, the forces happen at exactly the same time—one does not occur later in response to the other.

TO THINK ABOUT

Example of Newton's laws of motion in sport

An example of Newton's first law of motion in sport is when an ice hockey puck is stationary on the ice. The force of the weight of the puck is balanced by the upward force from the ice and so it is at rest. However, when a player hits the puck, an unbalanced external force is applied to it so it accelerates in the direction of the hit. It then travels across the ice, being slowed slightly by friction, until another external force (another player's stick or the side walls of the arena) changes its motion again (for example, to stop it).

Newton's second law can be illustrated by considering the different forces required to accelerate a table tennis ball and a soccer ball. In order to give the soccer ball the same acceleration as a table tennis ball a much larger force must be applied by the player, as the soccer ball has a much greater mass than the table tennis ball.

Newton's third law is very important when a sprinter wishes to start a race from the blocks. He must push backwards and downwards with large forces onto the blocks. According to Newton's third law, the blocks will push back onto him with the same force, but in the opposite direction (forwards and upwards). As the blocks are connected to the ground (which has a much larger mass than the athlete), the ground will not move backwards, but the athlete will move forwards and upwards out of the blocks as soon as he raises his arms from the ground.

Linear momentum and linear impulse: the impulse—momentum relationship

Linear momentum is the property an object has due to its movement. It is calculated by the mass of the object multiplied by the velocity at which it is moving ($m\mathbf{v}$). It is usually given the symbol $\mathbf{p}$, and is a vector with size and direction.

Linear impulse is force multiplied by the time it acts for ($\mathbf{J} = \mathbf{F}t$) and is also a vector.

There is a very important relationship between linear impulse and linear momentum. Linear impulse is the change in linear momentum. This means that the size and direction of the change in momentum of a body or object depends on the force applied to it and the time for which that force acts. If the force is large and the time is also large, there will be a great change in momentum. As the mass of a body or object does not usually change, this will equate to a change in velocity.

TO THINK ABOUT

Impulse—momentum relationship in sport

During the high jump take-off, Annie must change her horizontal motion into vertical motion to jump over the bar. This means the horizontal linear momentum she has from the approach must be converted to vertical linear momentum. This is done by applying a large vertical force down on the ground, and thus, by Newton's third law, receiving the same ground reaction force acting upwards.

In order to gain the greatest vertical momentum, this force must be applied for as long a time as possible. Therefore Annie places her take-off leg in front of her, landing on the heel. The time taken for the body over the take-off foot, combined with the flexion and extension of the knee, means that the muscles can apply a very large force over a long period of time, thus maximizing the vertical linear impulse and gain a large vertical linear momentum.

Conservation of linear momentum

During collisions between two bodies or objects, the total linear momentum of the objects involved is conserved (stays the same). This is a direct result of Newton's second and third laws, as the forces between the objects will be the same, as will the time of the collision. Therefore, the linear momentum changes will be the same for the two objects.

However, some energy is lost in the collision due to heat and sound energy. There is an experimental law formulated by Newton that states that the difference in velocities of the two objects is directly related to the difference in velocities before the collision. The variable that quantifies this relationship is called the coefficient of restitution and is mainly dependent on what materials the objects colliding are made of (although it does depend slightly on the initial velocities of the objects—this is why it is an experimental law). The more elastic the objects in the collision, the closer to 1 the coefficient of restitution will be and the less energy will be lost in the collision.

> **TO THINK ABOUT**
>
> **Coefficient of restitution—cheating in ball games?**
> Because the coefficient of restitution depends on the material of the objects in the collision, it is sometimes possible to change this to your advantage in ball games. For example, the properties of many sports balls depends on their temperature (because the balls are made of rubber or may contain air). So by raising the temperature of the ball it may be possible to increase the coefficient of restitution, thus giving the ball a higher velocity after collision with racket or club.
>
> In some sports, such as squash, this is legal and a warm-up serves to increase the temperature of the ball. However, in some sports this is illegal. For example, in the 1950s some professional baseball teams kept baseballs in a freezer to cool them. This would reduce the coefficient of restitution and make them less elastic. If the home team were playing a visiting team who were renowned for hitting home runs, this could reduce the number of runs scored by the visitors. Therefore balls for baseball matches (and other sports such as tennis) are now kept in containers whose temperature is closely monitored by the governing authorities.
>
> In 2008, the governing bodies of golf (The Royal and Ancient and the US Golf Association) made particular designs of clubs illegal. Golf club manufacturers had been making clubs (particularly drivers) with contact surfaces that had a very high coefficient of restitution (sometimes called "trampoline club faces") and thus the ball could be hit faster and would travel further. The governing bodies therefore put an upper limit on the coefficient of restitution of the driver club face, to ensure fairness between players and to prevent golf courses from having to be lengthened to cope with the increased driving distances.

Angular kinetics

Torque (Moment)

If a force is applied to an object that is free to rotate around an axis, as long as the force is applied so that it does not act through the axis (center of rotation), it will create a *torque* (also sometimes called the *moment* of the force). The size of the torque created depends on three factors:

→ the size of the force
→ the direction of the force
→ how far it is applied from the axis of rotation.

Torque is measured in Nm and is a vector (has size and direction).

Understanding of torque is very important because almost all segments of the human body rotate about axes within the synovial joints. The way in which the muscles are anatomically arranged relative to the joints plays a large part in determining how much torque can be created around each joint. This is closely linked to the principle of levers—rigid rods (such as the bones) that are rotated about axes such as the joints.

Levers

Levers consist of a rigid rod, a fulcrum (axis), a resistance force and an effort force. The distance at which the resistance acts from the fulcrum is called the resistance arm, and the distance at which the effort acts from the fulcrum is called the effort arm.

A lever has a mechanical advantage. This is how much the effort force is multiplied by to overcome the resistance force and can be calculated as the effort arm divided by the resistance arm.

Levers can be classified into three types depending on the positions of the effort force and resistance force relative to the fulcrum.

→ **First class levers** have the effort force and the resistance force on opposite sides of the fulcrum. The effort arm may be smaller than, equal to or smaller than the resistance arm. These are fairly rare in the human body—an example would be the muscles of the neck providing the effort force to overcome the resistance force caused by the weight of the head.

→ **Second class levers** have the effort force and resistance force on the same side of the fulcrum, but with the effort arm longer than the resistance arm (i.e. the effort force is further away from the fulcrum than the resistance force). This means the mechanical advantage is greater than 1, and a small effort force can overcome a large resistance. This is common in machines such as wheelbarrows, in which larger loads can be carried close to the fulcrum (the wheel) by applying relatively small forces at the ends of the handles. However, this type of lever is very rare in the human body, and the only example that is commonly suggested is when the calf muscles contract to provide the effort force when standing on the toes in plantar flexion. This would suggest that the human body has not evolved to use its limbs as levers to overcome very large resistance forces.

→ **Third class levers** also have the effort and resistance forces on the same side of the fulcrum, but the effort arm is smaller than the resistance arm (the effort force is closer to the fulcrum than the resistance force). The mechanical advantage therefore is less than 1, and this might seem counterproductive as large effort forces are required to overcome small resistance forces. However, there is another advantage to this arrangement. A small movement of the lever near the fulcrum is magnified by the length of the lever, so that the end of the lever moves through a greater angle, and with a greater angular velocity. Thus the advantage is in range of motion and speed. This type of lever is very common in the human body, as shown in Figure 4.9 where the biceps brachii is providing the effort force at the elbow joint to hold a weight at the hand (the resistance force). Therefore, the lever systems in the human body seem to have evolved to favour range and speed of motion.

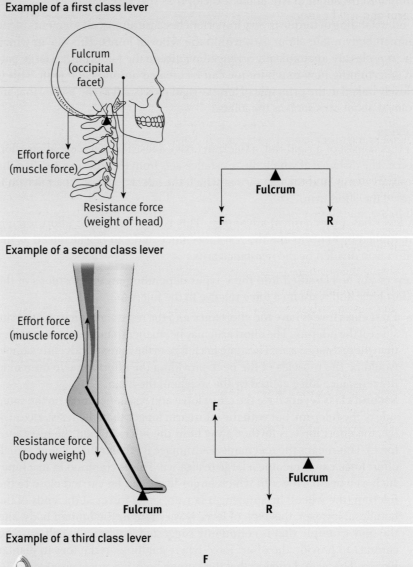

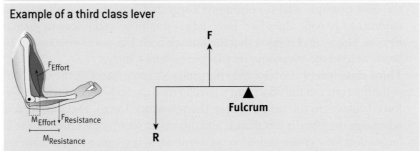

↑ Figure 4.9: Examples of the three classes of lever in the human body

Center of mass and center of gravity

The center of mass is the mathematical point around which the mass of a body or object is evenly distributed.

The center of gravity is the mathematical point of a body or object at which the force of gravity can be considered to be acting (although it acts throughout the body or object).

These two terms are often used interchangeably, and for bodies or objects in which the force of gravity does not vary (which is effectively true for human bodies and sporting implements), the two centers are in the same place. However, Hamill and Knutzen (2009) point out that the center of gravity refers to the effect of gravity and so is only in the vertical direction, and has no horizontal or lateral component. Therefore center of mass is the more general term and will be used in this text.

The center of mass depends on the distribution of the material in a body or object. This will be affected by the density of the body or object and also by its shape. In the human body, the density will depend on the different tissues in the body (muscle, fat, skin, air in the lungs), and the shape will depend on the position of the body segments and their different masses. Thus the center of mass will be in different place for individuals of different body types, ages, genders and other factors. Also, the positions of the body segments (particularly the limbs) will change the position of the center of mass.

As the center of mass is a mathematical, imaginary, point, it need not lie within the material of the body or object. For example the center of mass of a boomerang is in the space between the arms and not in the material. For the human body, this can also be true, particularly in sporting actions such as high jump or pole vault when clearing the bar.

Knowing the position of the center of mass is important for three reasons.

→ It determines the stability of static positions. If the vertical projection of a line downwards from the center of mass lies within the base of support (for example, between the feet when standing) then the position of the body or object is stable and, if disturbed by an external force, will return to its original position. This is the principle behind many balance activities.

→ It is the axis for all free airborne rotations of the body or object, for example, somersaulting in diving.

→ The center of mass acts as the reference point when considering whole body or object translation. For example, when performing the long jump in athletics the trajectory of the center of mass during take-off, flight and landing is crucial for understanding the distance jumped (see Figure 4.11).

↑ Figure 4.10: A picture of a high jumper with center of mass

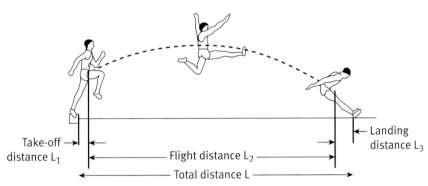

↑ Figure 4.11: Components of center of mass in the long jump

Hay et al. (1986) gave the following values for various long jumpers for L_1, L_2, L_3.

ATHLETE	L_1 (M)	L_2 (M)	L_3 (M)	TOTAL L (M)
Lewis	0.46	7.77	0.56	8.79
Grimes	0.37	7.80	0.22	8.39
Myricks	0.53	7.50	0.32	8.35
Williams	0.25	7.45	0.36	8.06

↑ Table 4.3: Components of center of mass distance in the long jump

The center of mass may be measured in several ways (for example, calculations from segmental positions and masses, reaction board, suspension of an object

↑ Figure 4.12: Moments of inertia with different axes of rotation and body positions

or model), but can probably only be measured to an accuracy of 1–2 millimetres for the human body, due to errors introduced by breathing, blood circulation and inaccuracies in segment densities and positions.

Moment of inertia

The moment of inertia is how difficult a body or object is to rotate about an axis and is measured in kg.m^2. It depends on the mass of the body or object, but also its mass distribution around the axis. More mass further away from the axis gives a greater moment of inertia and makes it more difficult to rotate. More mass nearer the axis of rotation makes it easier to rotate. The human body has different moments of inertia depending on the axis of rotation and the body position.

TO THINK ABOUT

Moment of inertia and sporting implements

When a sporting implement such as a golf club and a ball make impact, a force is applied to the ball, and so by Newton's third law the same force is applied back to the club or racket. If this force is off-centre, then it will create a torque (moment) that will try and rotate the club, which will then make the ball go in the wrong direction.

However, if the manufacturer can make the club with a larger moment of inertia, this torque will have less of an effect as it will be harder to turn. This can be done by designing the club so that more mass is distributed further from the center of the clubface. In golf, this is known as *peripheral weighting* and, in the last 20 or 30 years, putters and irons have had this design to minimize the effect of off-centre impacts, particularly for lower level golfers.

Projectile motion

An object that is thrown into the air or dropped and is acted upon by only the forces of gravity, air resistance and lift is known as a *projectile*. This might be a ball or javelin, or it might be the human body itself.

The most important principle to grasp about projectile motion is that once the object or body is in the air, there is no propelling force keeping it moving (unless it has a propeller or jet engine). The propelling force occurs only when the object or body is in contact with the thing that starts its motion (e.g. a hand or racket, or the ground for the body). As soon as contact is lost with thing propelling the object or body, the force no longer exists, and the object or body keeps moving only due to Newton's first law of motion (i.e. objects that are already in motion keep moving without the need for an external force).

This also means that the path of the object or body is determined mainly at the moment when it leaves the hand, racket or ground. Therefore the parameters at release or take-off are critical to the subsequent flight of the object or body.

The important parameters at release or take-off are:

→ the projection speed
→ the projection angle to the horizontal (these first two are often combined as the projection velocity)
→ the projection height.

These factors, combined with the forces experienced in flight (gravity, air resistance and lift) will determine how fast and how far the projectile will travel.

The most important factor in determining how far the object will go (the range) is usually the projection speed. The range is related to the square of the projection speed, so a small increase in projection speed will increase the range considerably.

The projection angle is also very important for the range, but is more important for the maximum height of the flight (for example, to get a volleyball serve over the net) or for accuracy (for example, in a basketball free throw).

The projection height might be important to beat an opponent (for example, a basketball jump shot or volleyball spike), or to maximize the range of values possible for the projection speed or angle.

The optimum projection angle for maximum range depends on the projection speed and, more importantly, the projection height. If the projection height is above the landing area or target (for example, in shot-put), the optimum projection angle is below 45 degrees. If the projection height is below the landing area or target (for example, in a basketball free throw), the optimum projection angle is above 45 degrees. If the projection height is the same as the landing height (for example, a goal kick in soccer), the optimum angle is 45 degrees. However, these optimum angles depend on the size of the air resistance in flight as well as other complex factors such as the strength and speed of contraction of human muscles. This is why long jumpers take off at 18-27 degrees, rather than 45 degrees.

Table 4.4 shows typical projection angles for some common sporting actions.

ACTION	PROJECTION SPEED	PROJECTION ANGLE	COMMENTS
Long jump take-off	10–11 m.s^{-1}	18–27°	Leg muscles are not strong enough or quick enough to produce 45° without losing projection speed.
High jump take-off	4–5 m.s^{-1}	40–48°	A lower speed, so jumpers have a higher angle of projection.
Shot-put	11–15 m.s^{-1}	35–42°	Lower than 45° as projection height is above landing area.
Basketball free throw	7.0–7.5 m.s^{-1}	50–60°	Depends on projection height. Above 45° as even tall athletes are below basketball hoop height.
Tennis first serve	50–60 m.s^{-1}	−3 to −15°	Angles are negative as ball is served down into court.
Golf drive	70–90 m.s^{-1}	10–20°	Angle is low because backspin causes a lift force to make the ball stay in the air longer.

↑ Table 4.4: Typical projection angles

Fluid dynamics

Drag force

As a body or object moves, it moves through a resistive medium such as air (e.g. projectile motion) or water (e.g. swimming). The effects of the medium on the motion of the object must therefore be considered. Air and water can both be considered fluids and so the same principles apply for movement through either medium.

When the body or object moves through the fluid, it experiences a force in the direction opposite to its motion. This force is called air (or water) resistance or drag. The reason for the force opposing the direction is that the motion of the body or object is trying to push apart the molecules of the fluid, and the forces between the molecules resist this and thus apply a force to the object or body.

There are several different types of drag.

→ **Surface drag** is caused by the interaction between the surface of the body or object and the fluid molecules. This type of drag is affected by: the velocity of the object relative to the fluid (a faster moving object has to push apart more molecules per second); the surface area of the body or object (a larger object will be contacting more fluid molecules); the nature of the surface of the body or object (a smoother surface will push apart molecules more easily) and the density of the fluid (denser fluids have more molecules to push apart).

→ **Form drag** is caused by the shape of the body or object. It is affected by: the frontal area of the body or object (a larger frontal area has to push apart more molecules); the shape of the object or body (a streamlined shape such as a rugby ball or American football travelling end-on experiences less drag than a spherical ball as the fluid molecules are parted more easily by the pointed end of the rugby ball) and also by the relative velocity to the fluid of the body or object.

→ **Wave drag** is the opposing force caused by the object making waves in the fluid. This is particularly important in motion through water, such as swimming, canoeing, rowing or sailing.

All of these factors combine into an equation for drag: $\mathbf{F} = -\frac{1}{2} C_d A \rho \mathbf{v}^2$

C_d is the drag coefficient, a variable affected mainly by the shape and surface roughness of the body or object.

A is the frontal area of the body or object.

ρ is fluid density.

$\mathbf{v}$ is the velocity of the body object relative to the fluid.

The drag force is negative because it resists the direction of motion of the body or object. Note that the drag force depends on the square of the velocity. At low speeds, there is little drag, but at higher speeds, the drag is very high. This is why drag has little effect on running (although reducing it can help performance slightly), but a very large effect in cycling (therefore cyclists must try and reduce it by their body positions and clothing).

Lift force

When fluid is moving (or a body or object is moving through it) the pressure it exerts reduces as its velocity increases. This is known as the Bernoulli principle (after the Dutch-Swiss scientist Daniel Bernoulli) and states that the pressure exerted by a fluid is inversely related to its velocity. When applied to a body or object, this means that faster fluid flow *reduces* the pressure on the body or object. If there is uneven speed flow on each side of the body or object, then there will be an uneven pressure on either side. This means the body or object will move from high to low pressure, thus changing its motion.

This principle is used to help generate a lift force. This is a force acting at right angles to the direction of motion, and explains why airplanes can fly. The aircraft wing is shaped differently on its top and bottom surfaces, thus leading to pressure differences above and below it. As the wing is shaped to speed up the flow over the top surface, the result is lower pressure above the wing and higher pressure below it, thus forcing the wing (and the airplane) upwards. The same effect happens to sails on a boat, but as the sail is vertical (rather than the horizontal wing), the force is directed sideways and forwards.

Unevenly shaped objects are rare in sport. However, it is also possible to gain lift force if the object is angled up or down relative to its motion through the fluid. For example, a javelin does not always fly best if it travels though its

KEY POINT

The Bernoulli principle states that the pressure exerted by a fluid is inversely related to its velocity.

point—it usually goes further if it is angled slightly upwards relative to its motion (although this is complicated by the effect of any wind).

If an object or body is experiencing a lift force it will rise or stay in the air longer than if there was no lift force. If it is experiencing negative lift, it will drop faster than with no force.

Magnus force

When a body or object is rotating while moving through the air (for example, a spinning ball), the air is dragged around by the rotation of the ball. This causes an increased velocity on one side of the object and a decreased velocity on the other. Therefore, by Bernoulli's principle, there are uneven pressures on the ball and the ball deviates from its motion. The lift force caused by this pressure difference (due to rotation) is called the Magnus force.

If the axis of rotation (spin) is horizontal and at right angles to the direction of travel, this will cause backspin or topspin and the ball will go up or down. However, if the axis of rotation (spin) is vertical and at right angles to the direction of travel, this will create sidespin and the ball will deviate left or right. The axis of rotation may be in a more complex direction and thus the spin maybe a combination of topspin and sidespin or backspin and sidespin.

TO THINK ABOUT

David Beckham's swerving free kicks in soccer

In soccer, when a free kick is awarded players often attempt to score a goal directly. Usually, the defensive team positions a wall to "cover" an area of the goal to prevent the player taking the kick from scoring there. However, some players such as David Beckham have perfected the skill of curving the ball around or over the wall to hit areas of the goal not covered by the goalkeeper. In order to do this, the kicker must create rotation of the ball at impact so that the Magnus force will bend its flight.

David Beckham has been so successful because he can generate sidespin *and* topspin so the ball not only swerves sideways in flight, but also "dips" and thus travels beyond the reach of the goalkeeper who cannot save it. Free kicks for England against Greece in the World Cup in 2002 and against Paraguay in the World Cup in 2006 showed Beckham's skills at their peak.

Golf clubs are designed to create backspin of the golf ball during impact. In the ball's subsequent flight this backspin will keep the ball in the air longer and thus the range will be further. Topspin is not required during golf (apart from possibly during putting) as this would bring the ball down quicker and thus decrease the distance travelled. The angled faces of golf clubs and the surface grooves mean that the ball gains backspin when it contacts the ball and thus ensures a longer flight.

In other sports, such as tennis and table tennis, topspin or backspin maybe applied to the ball by the path of the racket and the angle with which the face contacts the ball.

Boundary layers

The microscopic layers of fluid next to the body or object are called boundary layers. Normally, these layers have all the molecules moving in the same direction and are called *laminar* boundary layers. However, if the body or object is moving very fast or if the surface is rough enough, the molecules of the boundary layers get mixed up. Then they are called *turbulent*. Paradoxically, this causes less surface drag than would be expected so the body or object is not slowed down as much. This is why golf balls have dimples—they make the

TO DO

Bernoulli principle—try it yourself
In order to demonstrate the Bernoulli principle that generates the lift for airplane wings, you simply need a sheet of A4 or letter-size paper.

Hold the paper lightly at both of the short sides at about 3 centimetres from one of the long sides with the index finger and thumb of each hand. Then hold the long side about 1 centimetre below your bottom lip and let the paper hang down.

Now blow hard downward and forwards over the curve of the hanging paper. You should find that the loose end of the paper rises when you blow over the paper (it may require some practice to get right).

Because you have increased the velocity of the airflow over the top of the paper, the pressure decreases in line with the Bernoulli principle and thus the loose end of the paper moves upwards, from the higher pressure below the paper towards the lower pressure above it.

101

boundary layers turbulent and thus the ball is not slowed up as much and thus travels further.

Angular momentum

Angular momentum is a measure of the amount of (or potential for) rotation. It is calculated by multiplying moment of inertia by angular velocity: $\mathbf{L} = I\,\omega$

L is angular momentum (sometimes also represented by the symbol H).

I is moment of inertia.

ω is angular velocity.

Angular momentum is a vector quantity as it has size and direction. It is measured in $kg.m^2.s^{-1}$.

Generation of angular momentum

Angular momentum is generated by the application of torque (or moment) over a period of time to a body that is free to rotate. This means that a force must be applied some distance away from the axis of rotation and the force must not go through the axis of rotation. The force may come from another object (e.g. the ground or a sporting implement), another body or a segment of the body via the muscles.

Often angular momentum of the human body is generated by using the muscles and limbs to apply a torque to the ground, which applies the same torque back (by Newton's third law). As the body has a much smaller moment of inertia than the earth, the body will rotate much more. This is very important in sports such as gymnastics for creating the rotation necessary to perform somersaults, twists and other rotational movements. The angular momentum may also be created by applying and gaining a torque to apparatus such as a vaulting table or beam.

Often this will mean that a force must be applied to the ground or apparatus so that the reaction force does not travel through the individual's center of mass (the axis for airborne rotations).

Many other sports such as golf, throwing and kicking require rotational movements and so generation of angular momentum is an important principle here as well.

Conservation of angular momentum

Newton's first law of motion can be expressed angularly as: "A rotating body will continue to turn about its axis with constant angular momentum unless an external unbalanced torque (moment) is applied to it." Therefore, once the angular momentum has been generated, it will stay constant unless there is an interaction with another object or body which creates a torque to change it.

During human airborne flight in sports such as gymnastics, diving, long jump and high jump, the only forces acting are gravity and air resistance (drag). As the speed of the flight is fairly low (less than $15\ m.s^{-1}$ even in long jump) and the human body has considerable mass, the effect of air resistance (drag) will be very small. Therefore the only major force acting will be gravity acting through the center of gravity.

However, the axes of rotation in flight are also through the center of gravity, therefore the force of gravity does not create a torque as it goes through the axis of rotation (i.e. the distance of the force from the axis of rotation is zero). This means that there is no rotational effect of the force of gravity while the body is in flight. Therefore, according to Newton's first law above, the angular momentum must stay the same (it is *conserved*) during the flight.

Angular momentum comprises of moment of inertia multiplied by angular velocity. Therefore during flight, if the moment of inertia is reduced, the angular velocity must increase to keep the angular momentum constant. This is why when a gymnast "tucks" during a somersault (by bringing her arms and legs towards the center of gravity and reducing the moment of inertia), she will rotate faster. Similarly by the same principle, when the gymnast "opens out" prior to landing (increasing the moment of inertia) her rate of rotation will decrease.

A common misconception is that these changes in rotational speed (angular velocity) are due to decreases or increases in air resistance - this is untrue.

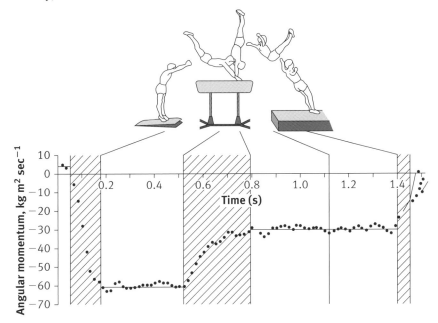

↑ Figure 4.14: Angular momentum in a Yamashita vault. Angular momentum only changes when the gymnast is in contact with the ground or the box and stays constant in the airborne phases. Angular momentum is negative due to a clockwise direction of rotation.

Transfer of angular momentum

As angular momentum cannot be created or destroyed unless there is an external torque, once an athlete is in the air, it is not possible to change the amount of angular momentum of the whole body.

This means that if one part of the body increases its angular velocity (for example, by muscle contraction), another part of the same body must slow down (reduce its angular velocity) to make sure the angular momentum of the whole body stays the same. However, when the first part then slows down, the second part will speed up again.

This is used in activities such as the piked dive (see Figure 4.15).

Trading angular momentum

As angular momentum is a vector quantity, if an athlete is rotating about one axis (e.g. somersaulting) and introduces rotation about another axis (e.g. tilting) by movements of body segments using the muscles, the combination of the two vectors is rotation around a third axis (twisting). In gymnastics, this is often used to create twisting in somersaults.

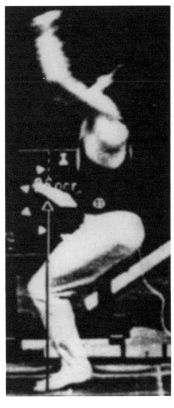

↑ Figure 4.13: Gymnast generating angular momentum in a backflip (top) and back somersault (bottom) by creating ground reaction forces (arrows) not directed through the center of mass (circle with cross).

This allows the trading of some of the somersault angular momentum for twisting (see Figure 4.16).

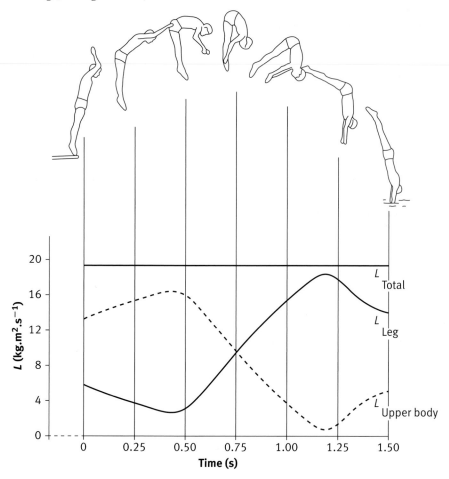

↑ Figure 4.15: Angular momentum in a piked dive

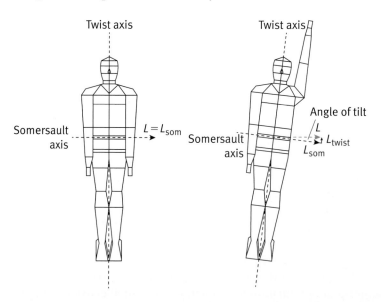

↑ Figure 4.16: Trading of angular momentum—creating twist by introducing tilt while somersaulting

→ Muscle are stimulated by nerves to contract
→ Motor units are made up of one motoneuron and the muscle fibers it innervates
→ Type I, Type IIa and Type IIb motor units have different speeds of contraction, forces of contraction and resistance to fatigue
→ Muscle contraction is due to actin filaments "sliding" relative to myosin filaments
→ Muscle activation can be measured using electromyography, but it is not always a precise method
→ Synovial joints can be non-axial, uniaxial, biaxial or triaxial depending on how many axes of rotation they have
→ There are three fundamental planes and three fundamental axes of rotation in the human body
→ Movements of body segments can be described accurately using correct terminology
→ Concentric, eccentric and isometric contractions are different ways the muscle contracts to move the body segments, and depend on the amount of force and torque the muscle can provide compared to the external force and torque being overcome
→ Eccentric contraction can cause delayed onset of muscle soreness (DOMS) and the best remedy is usually light exercise
→ Muscles can play different roles in different stages of movement depending on their contraction type and the requirements of the action
→ Kinematics is the study of motion and kinetics is the study of forces
→ Linear kinematics involves motion in a straight line and consists of linear displacement, linear velocity and linear acceleration
→ Angular kinematics is concerned with rotation and consists of angular displacement, angular velocity and angular acceleration
→ Newton's three laws of motion relate how forces change motion
→ The impulse-momentum relationship is important when understanding changes of motion
→ Torque is the angular effect of a force that does not act through the axes of a freely-rotating body or object
→ Center of mass and center of gravity are effectively the same for the human body
→ Projectile motion analyses how objects move when thrown into the air or dropped from a height
→ Drag forces oppose the motion of bodies or objects through air or water
→ Lift forces are caused by an object's shape and its orientation to the air and/or the spin imparted to it
→ Angular momentum measures the amount of rotation a body or object has.
→ In the absence of an external torque (for example in low speed flight such as jumping), angular momentum remains constant.

Self-study questions

1 Draw a diagram of a motoneuron.
2 Explain how the sliding filament theory accounts for muscle contraction.
3 What are the problems with using electromyography to measure muscle contraction?
4 Name the four classes of synovial joints.

5 What are the opposites of these joint movements: flexion, abduction, medial rotation?

6 Describe pronation of the forearm.

7 How do concentric, eccentric and isometric muscle contractions differ?

8 State Newton's three laws of motion and give examples of each in sport and exercise.

9 Which of these are vector quantities and which are scalars?

→ force

→ area

→ linear displacement

→ angular velocity

→ speed

→ temperature.

10 Explain how the impulse-momentum relationship can be illustrated by considering actions in the high jump take-off?

11 Describe the three different classes of levers. Which are most common in the human body and why?

12 What are the three factors that determine the motion of an object when it is thrown into the air?

13 Explain how the following factors affect the drag force on an object moving through the air:

→ shape

→ frontal area

→ velocity of the object

→ density of the air.

14 How can a gymnast generate enough angular momentum to allow him/her to perform a somersault?

DATA BASED QUESTION

Below is data taken from Usain Bolt's world record 100 m run in 2009 in Berlin.

Reaction	10 m	20 m	30 m	40 m	50 m	60 m	70 m	80 m	90 m	100 m
0.146s	1.89s	2.88s	3.78s	4.64s	5.47s	6.29s	7.10s	7.92s	8.75s	9.58s

More information can be found at:

http://berlin.iaaf.org/mm/document/development/research/05/31/54/20090817073528_httppostedfile_analysis100mmenfinal_bolt_13666.pdf

1 Calculate the average velocity for each 10 m interval using the displacement and time differences for each 10 m.

2 What was his maximum average velocity (in m.s^{-1}) and where in the race did he reach it?

3 How would you get the instantaneous velocities from a graph of displacement plotted against time?

4 Try and find out what his maximum instantaneous velocity was using a smooth displacement-time graph. How would you then find out the instantaneous acceleration at any time?

CHAPTER 5

Skill in sport

At the end of this chapter students should be able to:

→ define skill in sport

→ describe different types of skill

→ outline the role of ability in sport

→ describe information processing models

→ outline the role of memory in skill learning

→ describe motor programmes

→ describe the skill learning process

→ outline different types of practice

→ evaluate mental rehearsal and mental imagery

→ outline Mosston's spectrum of teaching styles

→ outline the role of motivation in skill learning.

Introduction

To all those individuals involved in sport, skillful performances can bring a great deal of pleasure, both as a performer and as a spectator. Usually we can appreciate and enjoy the performance of skill in our own sport but it is often just as pleasurable to observe a skillful performance in sports less familiar to us.

From another perspective, that of the teacher or the coach, seeing one of your athletes execute a skill that you have taught them is an extremely rewarding experience, especially when you know the hard work that has gone into achieving this level of performance. The purpose of this chapter is to develop further your knowledge and understanding of the key factors relating to skill, skill learning, theories of skill learning and practice.

The characteristics and classification of skill

The human capacity to perform skills is an important function of day-to-day living, they enable us to type words on a page, ride a bike to work or take part in physical activity. We begin to learn to perform skills from a very young age. We learn to crawl, to walk, and then to run. Some skills are very simple and can be mastered with a small amount of experience and maturation, for example, walking or lifting an object. Other skills, for example, swimming and driving a car, are much more complex. If proficiency is to be attained in performing these skills, then individuals have to engage in practice. This section will take you through a more detailed definition of the term "skill" before explaining the different ways in which skills can be described and categorized.

TO THINK ABOUT

What are the skills you perform from day to day? Why are they skills?

Identify the skills that are involved in a sport or activity you take part in. Why are they skills?

What is "skill"?

The term "skill" can either be used to describe a specific action or the level of performance of an individual. Skill infers that the movement has been learned and has a predetermined outcome or goal. It is not an action that a person can just naturally do; neither is it moving for the sake of moving. For example, idly swinging your legs while you sit on a park bench is not a skill. However, riding your bike in order to get to the park is a skill.

The main characteristics of skills, therefore, are the following:

→ They are goal oriented, using the skill will achieve an end result. For example, typing a letter, putting a golf ball in the hole or making a save in soccer.
→ They meet the performance goal with maximum certainty. For example, maintaining balance while riding a bike or making 90 per cent of shots in a basketball game.
→ They meet the performance goal with minimum outlay of energy. For example, steering a car, staying streamlined in the water during a freestyle race or skiing parallel down the slope.
→ They are learned through practice. They require some experience, repetition or feedback from a teacher or coach.

Types of skills

There are many different types of skills and they vary according to the different motor, cognitive, perceptual and perceptual-motor demands placed on the performer.

→ **Motor skill** Weightlifting, for example, is mostly a motor skill because it emphasizes movement and does not require much thinking. Other examples include sprint racing and wrestling.
→ **Cognitive skill** Playing chess requires mostly cognitive skill because it requires lots of thinking. Success in chess is not associated with the execution of the movements. In games such as soccer and field hockey, knowledge of the rules, game objectives and team tactics are cognitive in nature, and are associated with the decision-making element of game play.
→ **Perceptual skill** Reading the green in golf is a perceptual skill. The golfer receives information about the type of surface, the run of the green, the distance of the ball from the hole, and other environmental conditions through their perceptual senses. This enables golfers to make a decision about how to make the putt. Perceptual senses include vision, vestibular (senses that help you with balance closely related to your hearing), haptic (touch) and auditory. Another example would be in rock climbing when a rock climber assesses the rock face before a climb.
→ **Perceptual-motor skills** These skills involve the interpretation of environmental stimuli and the motor response to this sensory information.

Perceptual-motor skills depend on high perceptual ability and are very important in activities that require the performer to adapt to the environment. Another example would be dribbling with the ball in soccer to beat a defender. It is important to note that most sports involve perceptual-motor skills because they involve thought, interpretation and movement.

The characteristics and classifications of skill

Skills can be classified according to their characteristics and this helps us to understand the demands of the skill. This can help coaches or teachers to evaluate performance, plan sessions and provide the performer with feedback.

Skills cannot always be neatly placed in one class or another. To overcome this they are placed on a continuum; a line on which each skill can be placed depending on how much they match the characteristics within each classification.

Magill (1998) suggests three skill classification criteria based on:

→ the distinctiveness of the movement characteristics (*discrete* motor skills; *serial* motor skills; *continuous* motor skills)
→ the stability of the environment (*closed* motor skills; *open* motor skills)
→ the size of the musculature involved (*fine* motor skills; *gross* motor skills).

The distinctiveness of the movement

As mentioned above, skills can be classified as discrete, serial or continuous.

→ **Discrete skills** have a clear start and finish. They are usually brief and well defined. Examples of discrete skills are a forward roll in gymnastics, a golf swing or a penalty stroke in field hockey. Each of these skills are clearly defined and it is obvious when the movement starts and when it stops.

→ **Serial skills** involve the linking together of skills to form a longer, more complex movement. This takes place in gymnastics where the gymnast links together a series of flips and somersaults. This also takes place in the triple jump, where athletes bring together the hop, the skip and the jump to create one long movement in order to achieve maximum distance.

→ **Continuous skills** are where the end of one cycle of movement is the beginning of the next. They are repetitive, rhythmical and take place over a long period of time. A distance, a target or a set time usually governs the time that the skill is performed for. Continuous skills include swimming, running and cycling.

TO THINK ABOUT

Can you picture in your head the performance of a forward roll in gymnastics, a golf swing or a penalty stroke in field hockey? Can you clearly see the point when each movement starts, stops or links together? Can you think of other skills that fall into each category?

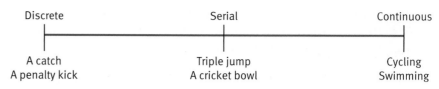

↑ Figure 5.1

The stability of the environment

This classification is related to the way in which the environmental conditions affect the skill. Environmental factors can be the weather, obstacles, boundaries, teammates and opponents.

Open skills are those skills that are significantly affected by the environmental conditions, to the extent that the conditions dictate the pace of the movement. The environment is largely variable and unpredictable and, as such, the performer has to adapt their movements accordingly. The performer has to pay close attention to external events to control the movement. Perceptual skills and perceptual-motor skills are critical for open skills.

Closed skills are skills that are performed in a more stable and predictable environment and, as such, can be internally paced by the performer. Closed skills follow set movement patterns and are performed in the same way each time.

↑ Figure 5.2

Size of the musculature involved

This classification of skills is related to the precision of the movement.

→ **Gross motor skills** are movements that involve large muscle groups such as arms and legs. They include skills such as walking, jumping, running and kicking.

→ **Fine motor skills** involve much smaller muscle groups and fine movements. They are more intricate, precise and often require high levels of hand-eye coordination. They include skills such as playing the piano, playing darts and catching a ball.

As with the other classifications described above, these skills are placed on a continuum. This is because while some skills may involve large muscle groups and therefore be mainly gross motor skills, they may also involve fine motor skills. An example of this is a bowl in cricket where the speed of the ball comes from the running (legs) and bowling (arm) actions, but the spin on the ball is generated by the fingers.

↑ Figure 5.3

TO DO

Can you think of activities that require open or closed skills?

TO DO

Can you think of an example of a skill from your own sport and place it along this continuum?

Skill classification task

Classify the following skills by placing up to three ticks in the appropriate column.

	DRIBBLING IN SOCCER TO BEAT AN OPPONENT	THE SHOT-PUT	A DANCE MOTIF
Open			
Closed			
Fine			
Gross			
Discrete			
Serial			
Continuous			

↑ Table 5.1

The interaction continuum

Different skills relating to different activities vary in the way and context in which they are performed. Sometimes they are performed alone and sometimes they are performed with or alongside others. We can characterize skills in this way by placing them on the interaction continuum. There are three main ways in which they can be categorized: individual, coactive and interactive.

→ **Individual skills** are those skills that are performed in isolation from others. Only one performer is involved at a particular time. For example, archery or the high jump.

→ **Coactive skills** are those skills that are performed with someone else, but with *no direct* confrontation. Coactive skills are performed in swimming and in track athletics such as the 100 meter or 200 meter sprints.

→ **Interactive skills** are where other performers are *directly* involved and can involve confrontation. This is because there is an active opposition and this directly influences the skill. Interactive skills are evident in games such as rugby, water polo and shinty.

Ability in sport

The term "ability" is often confused with the term skill, however, although they are related, they are not the same thing. As mentioned in the previous section, skills are largely defined by their purpose, goal or objective, and by the fact that they require practice. Abilities, however, are the traits that we are born with. They are the perceptual and motor attributes, inherited from our parents that enable us to perform skills. Abilities give us the capacity to perform skills.

Perceptual-motor abilities are abilities that enable the individual to process information about how and when to move. For example, in order to execute a skill such as a forehand groundstroke in tennis, the tennis player requires perceptual abilities such as multi-limb coordination and response orientation. Motor abilities are those abilities relating to the actual movement. For example, in order to perform a skill such as the 100 meter sprint individuals require motor abilities such as explosive strength and speed of limb movement.

KEY POINT

A skill is something we learn while an ability is something we are born with.

111

Abilities are the qualities that enable individuals to perform the skill and, compared to skills, they are much more stable and enduring. Further examples of the abilities that enable us to perform sports skills are muscular endurance, strength, flexibility, coordination and balance.

Individuals differ in the strength of their abilities. Those individuals who have strong abilities that underpin a specific skill or activity will appear to demonstrate competence in that activity with relative ease. However, it is only with practice that someone becomes truly skillful.

It is important to remember that ability is not the only factor that contributes to successful performance. Previous movement experiences, growth, body configuration and personal motivation all contribute to successful performance. Equally, someone with natural ability within a particular domain may not reach their full potential because they lack one or all of these qualities. Additionally, failure to invest in practice time may also result in a below-par performance.

Fleishman's taxonomy of abilities

One of the major researchers into abilities was Edwin Fleishman. Using a statistical method called factor analysis Fleishman identified a number of abilities (see Table 5.2).

PERCEPTUAL-MOTOR ABILITIES	PHYSICAL PROFICIENCY ABILITIES
Control precision (control over fast, accurate movements that use large areas of the body)	Extent (or static) flexibility
Multi-limb coordination	Dynamic flexibility
Response orientation (selection of the appropriate response)	Static strength
Reaction time	Dynamic strength
Speed of arm movement	Explosive strength
Rate control (coincidence-anticipation)	Trunk strength
Manual dexterity	Gross body coordination
Arm–hand steadiness	Gross body equilibrium
Wrist–finger speed (coordination of fast wrist and finger movements)	Stamina (cardiovascular fitness)
Aiming	
Postural discrimination (coordination when vision is occluded)	
Response integration (integration of sensory information to produce a movement)	

↑ Table 5.2: Fleishman's abilities

Fleishman sub-divided abilities into physical proficiency and perceptual-motor abilities. As you can see in Table 5.2, physical proficiency abilities are what you might expect to find in a chapter on exercise physiology. The perceptual-motor abilities may be less obvious to you but are a combination of how we make sense of our environment (perception) and how we act (motor control) within that environment. This is covered in some detail later in this chapter.

The ability–skill–technique interaction

Above we have used the words "motor control" to describe how we act or move. Another word that can be used to describe how we move is "technique". When physical educators and psychologists talk about technique they are commenting on the way the individual controls his or her limbs. It is a part of what we mean by skill but not the only part.

In order to perform skillfully the person must have the necessary technique or techniques and choose the correct one to use in any particular situation. In other words:

Skill = Ability + Selection of the correct technique

The difference between skilled and novice performers

Watching highly skilled performers is uplifting. Everything they do looks effortless. Their movements are fluent, they know what they want to achieve and how to achieve their goals. They are very efficient, energy is not wasted and there is great consistency in their performances. On the other hand, novices are inconsistent. They can and do sometimes produce a good performance but generally they do not. They are far from fluid and appear to lack coordination. Their movements are inefficient and often we cannot tell what they are trying to do. In fact, sometimes *they* do not know what they are trying to do.

TO DO

You can examine some of these expert–novice differences yourself. Get someone good at a skill and someone with little or no experience of that skill. Get them to have about 30 to 40 attempts at the skill. Devise some kind of scoring system. For example, if you choose the set shot in basketball you can have 3 points for a swish, 2 for hitting the rim or rebound board and going in, and 1 for hitting the rim or rebound board and not going in. Keep score for each shot.

Plot a graph of performance, with trial number on the x-axis and score on the y-axis. Look at how inconsistent the novice is compared to the experienced performer. Also notice the difference in accuracy. These differences do not occur by chance. The clue is in the word "experienced". The experienced performer has learned by practice and possibly also by being coached.

TO DO

Choose one or two skills similar to receiving a tennis serve and break them down. This will help you to understand how complex skills can be.

Information processing

When we perform skills we do so in environments of varying complexities. As we saw earlier, open skills in particular are performed in very complex environments. Just think about games like soccer and field hockey: 22 players, 1 referee and 2 assistants (soccer) or 2 referees (field hockey), the ball, the goals, the line markings, the spectators and the coaches. The players have to take all of this into account when performing. Even receiving a serve in tennis can be quite complex. The receiver has to take into account what kind of serve his or her opponent is making (this demands looking at all of their limbs and the general body position), the speed and direction of the serve, any spin on the serve, the wind speed and direction, and where they themselves are standing in relation to the service court. At the same time they have to decide what shot to play in order to return the ball and to where they are going to hit the return. Just how we humans can do this has puzzled psychologists for many years.

The Black Box Model of information processing

Information processing has been explained mainly by developing models which are depicted in the form of flow diagrams. Figure 5.4 shows the first of these models called the Black Box Model.

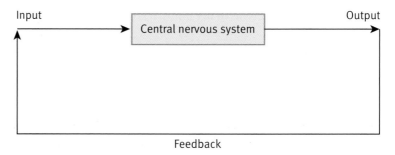

↑ Figure 5.4: The Black Box Model of information processing

The input refers to the environment that the performer can see, hear and feel. It is sometimes called the display and sometimes even the stimulus. In fact, in sport it is very rarely one stimulus but several stimuli, as we outlined above. The output is what the performer did. In the example of the tennis player it would be what shot they played in order to return the ball and whether or not this was successful. This is also often referred to as the response.

The box in the middle labeled Central Nervous System (CNS) refers to the person's brain and spinal cord. It is called the Black Box because early psychologists did not presume to know what went on in the CNS between experiencing the input and carrying out the response.

Welford's model of information processing

One of the first researchers to try to explain what actually happens in the CNS when processing information was AT Welford (1968). Figure 5.5 is based on Welford's model. In the following sub-sections we will elaborate on each of the boxes in Welford's model. We should note that although Welford presents his model linearly, he pointed out that many of the processes are being carried out simultaneously.

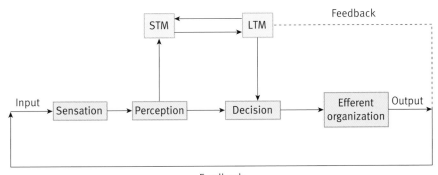

Note: STM = short-term memory
      LTM = long-term memory

↑　Figure 5.5: Welford's model of information processing

Sensation or sensory input

The senses are responsible for relaying information about the environment to the brain. This information is then interpreted by the brain based on past experience of similar situations, and is held in the long-term memory (LTM). The senses can be divided into exteroceptors and interoceptors.

→　**Exteroceptors** provide information from outside of the body. The main exteroceptors involved in sensation with regard to sport are vision and audition.

→　**Interoceptors** provide information from within the body, information about body position and the position of limbs. The main interoceptors involved in sport are the vestibular apparatus, which provides information about balance; and joint receptors, muscle spindles and Golgi tendon organs, which provide information about limb positions.

Signal detection

Swets (1964) reckoned that individuals receive over 100 000 pieces of information per second. This may be information from the environment and/or from within the person themselves. Thus actually perceiving an important piece of information, what he called a "signal", is problematic. In order to explain how we do this, Swets developed signal detection theory.

Swets termed the background, non-essential information "noise". This may mean actual noise, e.g. the sound of spectators, but covers all information that is not part of the signal. So noise can be visual or from within yourself such as worrying about failing. According to signal detection theory, the probability of detecting any given signal depends on the intensity of the signal compared to the intensity of the background noise.

There are numerous examples of the use of signal detection theory in everyday life. It is essential that traffic lights stand out from their background. Likewise signals on railways need to be very easy to see. Roadworkers in most countries wear bright clothing, normally yellow, which has been shown to contrast very well with most backgrounds. The use of flashing hazard warning lights on cars and trucks is also an example of signal detection theory in practice.

Of course, commercial enterprises also take advantage of this and we see the use of signal detection theory principles in billboards and neon lights on shops and theatres.

We also get the opposite with the use of clothing designed to blend in with the background in the military. Camouflage clothing is the use of signal detection theory in reverse. Nature also provides many examples of the use of signal detection principles with animals using camouflage or just the opposite, having brightly coloured skin that acts as a warning to their enemies.

The likelihood of detecting the signal would depend on the interaction between two variables, d-prime (d') and the criterion (C).

→ d' represents the individual's sensitivity to that particular signal. This sensitivity may depend on the efficiency of the person's sense organs, e.g. eyes, vestibular apparatus. It may also depend on experience, e.g. familiar signals are thought to be more readily detected than unfamiliar stimuli.

→ C represents the effect of a person's bias on detection. C is thought to be affected by arousal level, which in turn affects the probability of the detection of a signal. When arousal is low the signal is missed, what we call an error of omission. If, however, arousal is high and detection is considered to be a high priority, of too much importance in fact, the individual may perceive a signal when one does not exist, an error of commission.

Signal detection proficiency can be improved by ensuring that the performer is optimally aroused but can also be aided by good selective attention which is covered later in this chapter.

Memory

Tulving (1985) described memory as being the "capacity that permits organisms to benefit from their past experiences". In Welford's model he highlights short-term memory (STM) and long-term memory (LTM) but another stage of memory, the sensory information store (SIS) has also been described. All incoming information is held for a brief time in the SIS. Most of the information is lost within 0.5 seconds. It is only retained and processed if it is attended to. If this information is to pass to STM, it must be rehearsed. Rehearsal means being attended to, or processed mentally and/or physically.

Ninety per cent of all information entering the STM is lost within 10 seconds. Retention and passage to the LTM are dependent on rehearsal, mental, physical or both. Time is not the only limitation on the STM. Miller (1956) found that STM has a capacity or space limitation. He claimed that individuals could remember 7 ± 2 bits of information. This does not mean that if you read out a list of 12 words to a friend they would only be able to remember 9 of them. Later in this chapter, we explain how we overcome this limited capacity problem.

Unlike STM, LTM has no capacity limitations, although sometimes we have difficulty in retrieving memories. We have all experienced that infuriating situation where you cannot recall a person's name.

Selective attention–memory interaction

Given that our STM has a limited capacity, we have a problem when trying to deal with all of the information in our environment. The limitation is so great that some psychologists believe that we can only deal with one thing at a time; this is called single channel theory (Welford 1968). Others (such as Wickens 1980) have argued that we can deal with more than one piece of information at a time if the tasks are dissimilar, for example, running down the court bouncing a basketball while at the same time making a decision as to whether to pass or shoot. Running with the ball occupies a different part of the brain to making the decision therefore the two tasks will not affect one another.

The way we overcome this limited capacity is by the use of selective attention. Selective attention refers to the individual focusing on relevant information while ignoring irrelevant information. According to Broadbent (1956) all information enters the STM, but we only attend to the selected stimuli. Unselected stimuli are filtered out but selected stimuli are compared to information stored in LTM. This allows us to make decisions on what action to take.

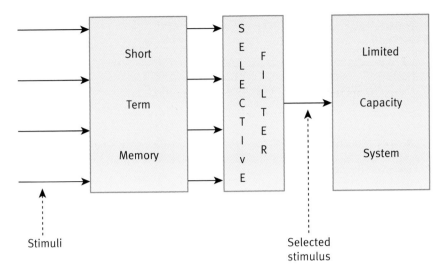

↑ Figure 5.6: Broadbent's filter model of selective attention

While selective attention takes place as described by Broadbent, i.e. stimuli being chosen for processing after entering STM, we can also make decisions on what to process before the information enters STM. Past experience of similar situations allows the performer to search the appropriate areas of the environment for relevant information. Sometimes attention is involuntary, however. A sudden loud noise or a flash of bright light will attract our attention probably as a subconscious safety factor.

TO DO

Aiding memory

Given that we have a limited STM capacity we must be careful when asking people to memorize information. What would happen if you give a list of 12 numbers to a friend and had them repeat them to you in order as soon as you finished? Try it with someone.

According to Miller (1956) we have a capacity of 7±2 bits of information, but I think that your friend will be likely to get more than 7, 8 or 9. If they really try they may get all 12.

Ask them what they did in order to remember the numbers. Most will say that they grouped the numbers together, in threes or fours normally. This process is called chunking. Each chunk makes up one bit of information. So 12 numbers will become 3 or 4 bits of information rather than 12.

TO RESEARCH

There are other strategies to help with retention and retrieval for improving learning, skill acquisition practice or teaching/coaching skills. Outline the following:
→ action words
→ brevity
→ clarity
→ organization
→ association
→ practice

Response time

Response time is the time from the introduction of a stimulus to the completion of the action required to deal with the problem (McMorris 2004). Response time is made up of reaction time and movement time. Reaction time is the time that elapses from the sudden onset of a stimulus to the beginning of an overt response (Oxendine 1968). Movement time is the time it takes to carry out the motor aspects of the performance.

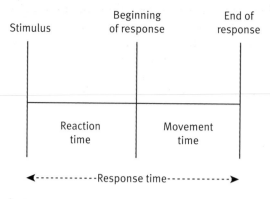

↑ Figure 5.7: Response time

Factors determining response time

Response time increases throughout childhood and adolescence, however, as we get older it gets slower. Movement time is affected by fitness, particularly power and speed of limb movement. Training can greatly affect movement time but reaction time is less easy to improve.

Figure 5.8 shows the stages of reaction time. As you can see it encompasses almost all of the information processing model.

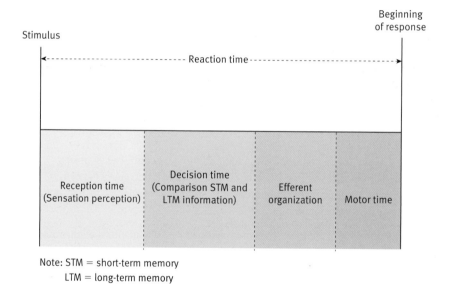

Note: STM = short-term memory
LTM = long-term memory

↑ Figure 5.8: Reaction time

The main factor affecting speed of reaction is the number of choices that the individual has to make. If there are no choices, what we call simple reaction time, the mean times range between 170 and 200 msecs. However, as we increase the number of choices, what is termed choice reaction time, the times increase. Hick (1952) found that as you doubled the number of stimulus-response couplings the reaction time increased. If the reaction time is plotted against the log of the stimulus-response couplings there is a linear increase. This is known as Hick's Law. Generally, reaction time increases by about 150 msecs every time the stimulus-response groupings are doubled.

The psychological refractory period

Earlier we examined single channel theory. In order to show the single channel at work, Welford (1968) undertook an experiment in which he had participants respond to a stimulus (S1). Reaction time to S1 was as Welford expected. However, when he introduced a second stimulus (S2) shortly after the introduction of S1, the participants demonstrated slower than normal reaction times to S2. Thus Welford stated that when two stimuli are presented close together the reaction time to the second stimulus is slower than normal reaction time. The time gap was called the psychological refractory period. Welford claimed that processing of S2 could not take place until processing of S1 had been completed.

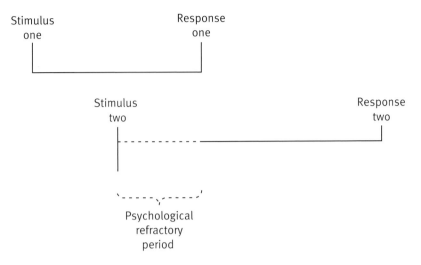

↑ Figure 5.9: Psychological refractory period

The effect of the psychological refractory period can be seen in many sports. Any example of a feint, dodge or dummy is an example of the use of the psychological refractory period. The feint is S1 and the actual movement is S2. If the timing is correct, the defender will be comparatively slow in reacting to the real movement. This is the skill of rugby players like Shane Williams, basketball players like Jason King and soccer players such as Cristiano Ronaldo. Similar feints can be seen in the drop shot in badminton or a dummy punch in boxing.

Motor programmes

Keele (1968) defined a motor programme as being a set of muscle commands that allow movements to be performed without any peripheral feedback. Examples of motor programmes are basically any skill that you can think of. Hitting a tennis ball, catching a netball and doing a somersault are all examples of motor programmes. A number of motor programmes can be put together to form an executive motor programme, e.g. an Arab spring and flick flack or the triple jump (hop, step and jump). Indeed the executive programme itself can become part of an even greater programme. Many gymnastics routines involve the completion of a number of executive motor programmes in quick succession. To the gymnast they have become one large executive programme.

Perhaps the best example of an executive programme outside of sport is playing the organ. The organist must put together movements from each hand, each of which are carrying out separate motor programmes, as well as the movement of both feet, which are also carrying out separate motor programmes to one another. To the organist however, he or she is playing one tune with "one" set of movements. We all know from games like tapping the head while rubbing the stomach that it is difficult to simultaneously make two separate movements with the hands, but think of adding two more separate movements with the feet!

Motor programmes: open and closed loop perspectives

Keele's (1968) model of motor programmes is what we call an open loop model. It accounts for the performance of a skill without recourse to feedback. It explains how we can carry out very fast movements. For example, a boxer throwing a straight left will do so at about 60–70 msecs. This is too fast for him to use feedback to alter the movement once it has begun. The same can be said for someone trying to hit a baseball pitched at over 100 kilometers per hour. Once the shot has begun, it cannot be changed.

However, not all movements take place this quickly. Many movements can be altered during their execution. We can alter our movements when hitting a baseball pitched at say 50 kilometers per hour or returning a slow serve in tennis. These movements are under what we term closed loop control.

The first to describe how we use closed loop control was Jack Adams (1971). He argued that as we learn a skill, we develop what he called the perceptual trace. The perceptual trace is memory for the feel of successful past movements. Once we have developed the perceptual trace, we can compare the trace with the feel of the ongoing movement. This allows us to correct inappropriate actions. While the perceptual trace controls an already ongoing movement, the selection and initiation of the movement is under the control of what Adams called the memory trace.

Schmidt's schema theory

Richard Schmidt (1975) set out to develop an explanation of motor programmes that included both open and closed loop control. This theory became known as schema theory. Schmidt described a schema as being a set of generalized rules or rules that are generic to a group of movements. Schmidt believed that we develop two kinds of memory for movements, which he called the recall and recognition schemas.

→ The *recall schema* is memory with regard to the choice and initiation of action.
→ The *recognition schema* is memory for the feel of a movement and it allows us to make appropriate changes in the action.

Both schemas require the individual to recall memory of similar past situations from LTM. These are then stored in STM and allow the person to decide the actual movement to be used. Remember the schema is a generalized set of rules but we must carry out a specific action. So comparing what I hold in STM about the past situations with what I hold with regard to the present situation allows me to decide on the specifics of the movement. Schmidt called this process deciding the *response specifications*.

Feedback and information processing

Feedback is the term we use to describe information resulting from an action or response. This feedback can be intrinsic or extrinsic.

→ **Intrinsic feedback** is available to the performer without outside help. We can see the results of our actions without anyone needing to tell us what happened. The feel of a movement is intrinsic by definition.
→ **Extrinsic feedback** is information that is provided for us by someone or something else. This can be a coach or teacher. Equally it could be a stopwatch or tape measure. This feedback can be concurrent, being given during performance, or terminal, given after completion of the performance.

There are two major forms of feedback, **knowledge of results (KR)** and **knowledge of performance (KP)**.

→ KR is post-response information concerning the outcome of the action.
→ KP, on the other hand, consists of post-response information concerning the nature of the movement.

The most obvious form of KR is visual. We see the end product of our action. In some cases, however, we need outside help to be able to make sense of our actions.

A long jumper needs to have the distance they jumped measured in order to have KR. Similarly, a track athlete will need to know the time that they ran.

The most obvious type of KP is the "feel" of the movement or, to be more technical, knowledge of the sensory consequences. Interestingly KP can be both concurrent, such as the feel of a movement while doing it, or terminal, feedback from a coach about how we moved. It can also be from video or film.

An issue that concerns the giving of feedback is whether it should be positive or negative.

Positive feedback can be telling someone that he or she has done well. It can, also, be what we call prescriptive feedback, i.e. the coach tells the learner how to improve performance by saying "Do it this way".

Negative feedback concentrates on errors. Sometimes coaches point out errors and then follow up with prescriptive feedback. Prescriptive feedback has been shown to be effective following either a negative or positive approach. However, negative feedback often includes "Don't do it like that" or "You got it wrong, you did this and shouldn't have". This latter type of feedback can be very demotivating and is also of little use to beginners, as they need prescriptive information.

Feedback and learning

All of the forms of feedback outlined above are involved in learning as well as information processing. In this section we will look at some specific issues involved in learning.

Feedback can be a great motivator. We all like praise, in particular praise from those whom we perceive as being important. The failure of coaches to praise good performance can have disastrous effects on the athlete's self-confidence. It can also give learners the false impression that they are not improving when in fact they are. However, overdoing the giving of praise can have negative effects. If all the athletes hear is "well done", "great" and "brilliant" then these words either come to mean nothing or become so familiar to the learner that, in fact, they are not perceived by them at all.

With regards to learning, the main factor is that the performer improves. As we saw above, beginners need prescriptive feedback. They need to be told what to do in order to improve performance. As they improve and increase their knowledge of the activity, all they require is KR. If they are making an error, they can resolve the problem themselves by comparing what is happening now with the store of knowledge they hold in their LTM. So we say that they now require descriptive feedback.

Principles of skill learning

In this section we examine a number of factors involved in skill learning. Some are common to everyone but some cover individual differences. We also examine an important factor, namely how we measure learning. Not as simple as you might think.

Learning versus performance

Although we measure learning by observing performance it is important that we know the difference between the two.

Kerr (1982) defined performance as being "a temporary occurrence fluctuating from time to time: something which is transitory". Figure 5.10a shows a learner's attempts to sink a putt in golf. Notice that one shot actually went in. Figure 5.10b shows the attempts by an experienced golfer. Notice the way the shots are

TO THINK ABOUT

What is your opinion about negative feedback. Does it motivate or demotivate you? The problem may be personal with personality type affecting how you feel, so talk to your friends about their feelings towards negative and positive feedback. An interesting exercise would be to debate the motion "This house believes that negative feedback is beneficial to learning".

Performance a temporary occurrence, fluctuating over time

Learning a relatively permanent change in performance resulting from practice or past experience

clustered around one point. Even the beginner can produce *one* good shot but we are not thought to have fully learned a skill until we can perform it with some consistency. The process of acquiring this consistency is what we mean by learning. Kerr described learning as "a relatively permanent change in performance resulting from practice or past experience."

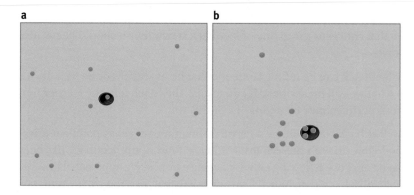

↑ Figure 5.10: **a** shows a learner's attempts to sink a putt in golf while **b** shows the attempts by an experienced golfer.

Stages of learning

One of the most widely held theories of learning is that of Fitts and Posner (1967). They claimed that learning takes place in three stages, the *cognitive, associative and autonomous* stages.

In the cognitive stage the individual tries to make sense of instructions. They use lots of verbal labels. This does not mean that instruction needs to be verbal, but simply that the individual uses verbalization to aid memory. In skills requiring perception and decision-making, there are often mistakes made and the individual attends to irrelevant as well as relevant stimuli. The motor component is characterized by crude, uncoordinated movement.

With practice the individual develops the knowledge of what to do. When someone is at this stage they are said to be in the associative stage (sometimes called the intermediate stage). At this stage, practice is required to perfect the skill and develop the consistent, coordinative movement that demonstrates learning.

When the individual can perform consistently and with little overt cognitive activity, they are said to have reached the autonomous stage.

Learning curves

When we learn an easy-to-perform skill we can often demonstrate what we call a *linear* learning curve (see Figure 5.11a). It is rare that learning is as easy as this, however.

Many skills are difficult to learn at first. Progress is slow but then we reach a point where performance improves more quickly. This is called a *positively accelerated* curve (see Figure 5.11b).

Sometimes, however, the opposite happens. We learn quickly at first but then slow down. This is a *negatively accelerated* curve (see Figure 5.11c).

A fourth type of curve is demonstrated in Figure 5.11d. Learning is positive and probably fairly quick at first but then there is a period when we show no improvement in performance. This is called a *plateau* effect. However, if we keep on practising, there is a breakthrough and more learning is demonstrated. We are, in fact, probably still learning during the plateau phase but it is not being shown in our performance. Remember performance is not the same as learning.

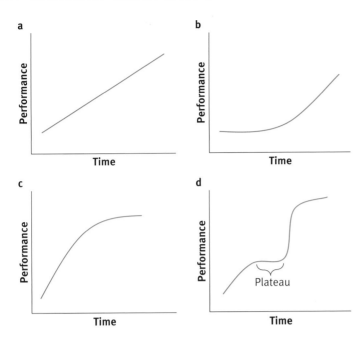

↑ Figure 5.11: Examples of typical performance curves: **a** linear, **b** positively accelerated, **c** negatively accelerated, while **d** shows a plateau effect.

Factors contributing to inter- and intra-individual differences in the rate of learning

Before beginning this section we should note that there are far more factors that will affect learning than those we cover here. In this section we are focusing on physical maturation, physical fitness and motivation.

We cannot expect an individual to learn a skill that has physical demands which they are not yet capable of meeting. Sometimes, however, the individual has the physical maturation but is simply not fit enough to do the task. In such cases physical training is necessary. The most important factor affecting learning, however, is motivation. The learner needs to want to learn. This is often closely linked to physical maturation. The learner is good at knowing when he or she is ready to acquire a skill.

TO THINK ABOUT

Children provide many examples of the link between physical maturation and motivation in learning. Babies often learn to crawl because they are motivated to get something which is out of their reach. Of course they cannot do this unless they are sufficiently physically developed.

It is not unusual for children to be motivated to copy older siblings in carrying out skills but wanting to do so before they are physically capable. When the physical catches up with the desire they will successfully attempt the skill.

Sometimes the child is physically capable but is not motivated to carry out the skill. So we have to wait until they do become motivated.

When motivation, and physical and indeed mental maturation are coordinated we say that the child has reached the optimal or critical stage of learning. This is surprisingly young for many skills. If we miss the optimal period we can have difficulty in catching up with those who did learn at the usual time. In the animal kingdom failure to learn at the correct time can mean that the skill is never learned. Given that most animal skills are involved in survival this can be fatal.

Transfer of training

Transfer of training refers to the effect that practice on one task has on the learning or performance of another task. Transfer of training can be positive, negative or zero.

→ **Positive transfer** is when the practice of one task has a facilitating effect on the learning or performance of another.

→ **Negative transfer** is when the practice of one task has an inhibiting effect on the learning or performance of another.

→ **Zero transfer** represents no effect.

Table 5.3 gives a list of examples of different types of transfer, with some examples from sport.

TYPE OF TRANSFER	EXAMPLE
Skill to skill	Throwing a ball to throwing a javelin
Practice to performance	Batting in cricket or baseball against a bowling/pitching machine
Abilities to skills	Improving dynamic strength in order to start races better
Bilateral	A soccer player learning to kick with his or her weaker foot
Stage to stage	From three-on-three basketball to the full game
Principles to skills	From learning that long levers aid throwing to throwing a javelin.

↑   Table 5.3: Types of transfer

Practice

The next section of this chapter will help you to understand what is meant by the term "practice", the different forms practice can take, how they impact on performance and how this knowledge can support teachers and coaches as they work to enhance their athletes' performance.

Practice is essential in acquiring motor skills. Practice and learning are said to be monotonic, that is, as the amount of practice increases, so does the rate of learning. However, the rate of learning is said to level off over time even as practice continues. It is important to note that the type of practice an individual engages in also affects learning. This seems logical when you consider that learning may be negatively affected by over-practice, or when an individual practices an incorrect or ineffectual technique.

From an information processing perspective, practice provides individuals with opportunities to gather information about the movement. This information is used to develop the motor programmes for that movement which are stored in the long-term memory. During practice, the individual gathers key pieces of information (or cues) to develop the motor programme and to compare the motor programme to the model, usually provided to the learner by the teacher, coach or peer. When the motor programme does not match the model, corrections are made through further practice until the motor programme matches the model.

Before the information can be used to develop the motor programme, it must firstly be interpreted. Consequently, perception and memory play important roles during practice. Through practice, individuals learn to interpret the cues from the environment by comparing the information that is held in the short-term memory to information that is held in the long-term memory (past experiences). The more past experiences an individual has, or the more they have practised, the more accurate the movement should be. However, as indicated above, the amount of practice may not be the only factor that affects learning. The way in which the practice is organized may also affect their learning of a motor task.

Types of practice

Intervals between practice

Types of practice can differ according to the intervals between the trials of a task. The two types of practice that differ in this respect are called massed practice and distributed practice.

→ Massed practice is when there are little or no gaps in practice. For example, a field hockey team practises shooting techniques non-stop for 40 minutes, or a judo player practises a particular move for an entire session. Massed practice is described as having intervals between the trials of a task that are shorter than the time it takes to perform one compete trial.

→ Distributed practice is when the practice is interspersed with rest or a different activity. For example, a shooting practice in basketball that is punctuated at regular points with opportunities for a short scrimmage game. Distributed practice is described as having intervals between the trials that are greater than the time it takes to complete one trial. Distributed practice can often lead to better performances because it reduces the levels of fatigue and boredom experienced by the performer.

Although performance may be positively influenced by distributed practice, there is little evidence to suggest that there are differences between the two types of practice with regards to how we learn. Additionally, it may be that the coach or teacher wants to develop the individual's performance while fatigued as this may represent more accurately a specific stage of the competitive environment.

Ultimately, when organizing practice, the coach needs to take into account the needs of the individual and the nature of the task being performed. For example, if a task is very simple or is very tiring, it may not be fruitful to practise this task for long, uninterrupted periods of time. However, if the task is more complex, or if the individual is a novice performer, then it may be of greater benefit for the practice to be prolonged. However, this may not be the case for very young children as their ability to concentrate for long periods of time is limited.

Order of practice

Another way to think about the structuring of practice is the order in which the practice of skills takes place. Generally, there are three ways practice can be ordered: blocked, random or serial.

→ **Blocked practice** is when one movement is repeated over and over again in a drill-like fashion. For example, a tennis player practises forehand ground strokes in 5 sets of 10 strokes with a few minutes rest in-between each set. As with massed practice, this can lead to quick improvements in performance, however, such almost immediate improvements can lead the individual to believe that they have learned the skill when really they have not.

→ **Random practice** is when the practice of one movement is randomly interspersed with the practice of other movements. For example, a learner golfer may randomly vary the club and the type of shot they play during practice. They may begin with a small chip shot, followed by a full swing with a six-iron, followed by a half-swing with an eight-iron and so on.

→ **Serial practice** is when different movements are practised, but in a structured and consistent order. For example, a volleyball player may practise the dig, the overhead pass and the spike in the same order each time.

The diagram below can help you to picture these three scenarios.

BLOCKED	aaa	bbb	ccc
RANDOM	cab	bca	acb
SERIAL	abc	abc	abc

Research shows that random practice is more effective than blocked practice for learning. Shea and Morgan (1979) used the elaboration hypothesis to explain this. This hypothesis explains that when two different tasks are presented side by side, the differences between the tasks are amplified. Presenting the learner with different types of information in this way, encourages them to apply more cognitive effort to learning the tasks and results in more distinct and meaningful storage of information to memory. This in turn, strengthens the motor programme for these tasks.

The action plan hypothesis (Lee, Magill 1983) suggests that in order to move on to a different task the individual must forget the previous task so that they have enough space in the working memory to engage in the new task. This means that each time they are faced with a new task they have to re-develop an action plan for learning the task. This requires more cognitive effort and they become more competent at creating action plans for learning. Consequently, they should become more efficient at problem-solving when they are faced with a new situation or task. This goes some way to explain why research shows that retention and transfer are enhanced when practice is ordered in a random fashion.

Task presentation

It is very important that teachers, coaches and performers understand how different forms of practice can impact on performance. However, it is also important that they understand the different ways in which practice tasks can be presented. Teachers and coaches have to decide whether to present the whole task or skill, part of the task or skill or a combination of the two. In other words, should the movement be practised in its entirety (whole) or should it be broken down into its parts and then presented whole–part–whole, or part–whole?

The key factor in deciding how the task should be presented is the nature of the task itself. Generally speaking, the whole task should be presented when its component parts are performed simultaneously, for example, the serve in tennis or volleyball. However, when the component parts of the skill are performed consecutively, then this skill can be broken down into those parts, for example, a lay-up in basketball.

Teachers or coaches may also present the whole skill when all of the component parts are highly integrated, interdependent and when the parts on their own do not have any meaning in relation to the whole skills. Conversely, when the component parts of the movement are highly dependent or even made up of individual skills, the coach or teacher may organize part practice.

In an effort to simplify the learning of the tennis serve or reduce its dimensionality, coaches often decompose the service action or, in other words, they break it down and practice it in its component parts. This is done to improve the consistency of the component parts, so that when reassembled, this consistency is carried over to the serve itself. In context, this type of practice is typified by the rehearsal of the ball toss independent of the swing and vice versa. Interestingly, recent research has challenged the utility of these approaches, suggesting that so important is the information-movement couple formed by the swing and toss, their independent practice is in fact counterproductive.

Consequently, this study aimed to report the kinematics of the hand, ball and racket in the flat serve (FS) of elite junior players. The authors of this study also compared those kinematics to their kinematic equivalent when the serve was decomposed: when the toss was rehearsed independent of the swing or contact (BT) and when the swing was rehearsed independent of the toss (SW).

The authors found that the vertical displacement of the ball at its zenith increased significantly during BT compared with the FS and temporal associations between racket and ball motion during the FS were affected during task decomposition. The results from this study show that consistency in swing and toss kinematics characterize the performance of the FS at a young age. This consistency decreases when the serve is decomposed, as is routinely done by coaches in practice while key characteristics of the serve, like ball zenith, change significantly when the ball toss is practiced in isolation. In conclusion, the authors question the efficacy of the routine or unconditional use of skill decomposition in the development of the tennis serve.

Reference

Reid, M., Whiteside, D., and Elliot, B. 2010. Effect of skill decomposition on racket and ball kinematics of the elite junior tennis serve. *Sports Biomechanics*, vol 9, number 4, pp. 296–303

An alternative perspective

One of the criticisms of using part practice during learning, particularly in team games, is that by taking the skill out of context, the learner concentrates only on technique and ignores the decision-making aspect of the task. However, to place a beginner straight into a game may be overwhelming. To overcome this, teachers or coaches could apply the concept of simplification. They do this by manipulating the task constraints such as the size of the playing area, the number of opponents and the object of play. This makes it easier to perform the skill, whilst retaining the key features of the environment that are critical in developing the player's decision-making skills.

Example

In soccer, a small-sided game could be organized with passive defenders to develop the players' ability to make a pass and know when and where to pass in a game environment. The players could be supported further by playing with a "Futbol de Salao", a smaller, heavier ball with less bounce that was developed in South America, used by players like Pele, Rivelino, Zico, Juninho, Ronaldo and Rivaldo before they moved on to conventional football.

Variable practice

What is perfection and is this really what we want? Is it effective, or even desirable, to practice the same movement over and over again until you have eradicated all errors in performance? This section will highlight that practicing the perfect movement may be detrimental to overall performance. It will show that varying the way you practice a skill is not only effective in learning a skill, but is a necessary requirement of successful performance, even at elite levels of performance.

"Practice makes perfect."

Variable practice is when the demands placed on the performance of a skill are altered, for example, throwing a ball towards different targets at different distances, angles or heights. When organizing variable practice, it is important for the coach or the teacher to note that practice variations should not be so great that the movement's form changes completely. With variable practice, the fundamental movement form remains the same, but variety is created with the task (different size of balls) and/or within the environment (different targets) to produce different versions of the movement.

Research suggests that variable practice results in better consistency and accuracy compared with repeating the same movement over and over again. This is particularly the case with children, since it has been suggested that variable practice helps them to develop schema for a particular movement. Indeed, if skill learning is associated with the development of rules, or schema, to be applied in a variety of contexts, it makes sense to suggest that the more diverse the context for learning is, the stronger the schema will become.

Variable practice and schema theory

According to schema theory, we store information about the specific invariant features of a movement (for example, relative timing and organization of limb parts in coordination). These are known as generalized movement programmes (GMPs). Variability of practice develops the learner's ability to control the GMP in a number of different ways.

This is because when we perform we gather information about:

→ the initial conditions
→ the response specifications
→ the sensory consequences
→ the outcome.

This information creates and strengthens schema that are applied to our GMPs and enables us to control or apply the skill in different situations (transfer).

Some level of variability in practice is necessary for all skills, however, it is particularly important for skills that are performed in more open environments. By varying the demands on the task, performers learn to parameterize the movements. When future, different demands are placed on the movement, the performer can generate the new parameter values based on their previous attempts.

Functional variability

Research suggests that even highly skilled performers show variations in the performances of a task. Importantly, variations are greater at the start of the movement and reduce at the end of the movement, or the point of contact or release. For example, during practice of a forehand ground stroke shot in tennis, the player will show greater amounts of variability in the performance during the preparation phase of the swing and reduce the variations as they move towards the point of contact. This allows the performer to adapt to any variation in ball speed, spin, bounce and trajectory, yet maintain accuracy and consistency at the point of contact. This is known as functional variability.

To attempt to reduce variability through practice, therefore, may have a detrimental effect on skill learning and performance, especially in activities that are performed within a more open environment.

Mental practice

Mental practice, sometimes known as mental rehearsal, is when a performer thinks about specific components of the movement without actually performing the movement. For example, the dancer who thinks about a complex footwork sequence, or the golfer who thinks about the point at which the wrists break at the top of the backswing. This type of mental practice aids performance because it helps the performer to understand and practise the cognitive components of the movement, where sequence, timing or strategy might be critical to successful performance.

However, most researchers believe that, as a learning tool, mental rehearsal only works *in conjunction with physical rehearsal*. Research has shown that individuals who use mental rehearsal, as well as physical rehearsal, learn more quickly than those using physical practice only. One theory put forward to explain the advantages of mental rehearsal is that, by thinking about the skill, we build up a picture or model in our Central Nervous System (CNS) of how the skill should be performed. The CNS, which includes the brain, reacts to this mental process in a very similar way as to when we actually practise physically. Thus, if we think about doing something, the CNS learns in the same way, or almost the same way, as when we actually carry out the task.

Bruce Hale (1982) provided some experimental support for this. He had people mentally rehearse doing a task. While they were mentally rehearsing, he had electromyographs (EMGs) fitted to the muscles that would be used if they were physically performing the skill. He showed that there was some neural activity even though the person never overtly moved.

Mosston's spectrum of teaching

The physical educationist Muska Mosston identified 11 teaching styles, A to K, used in physical education. However, these styles are also used in coaching and, when used appropriately, can facilitate the development of cognitive, affective and motor skills. The governing principle that underpins the teaching styles is that *decision-making* is the unifying element that connects the teaching and learning experience. By identifying specific sets of decisions made by the teacher and the learner, significantly different learning conditions are produced.

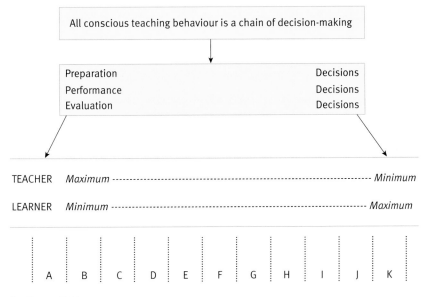

↑ Figure 5.12

Styles A through to K can be divided into two clusters, the reproductive cluster and the productive cluster.

The reproductive cluster (A to E) is more akin to direct, didactic teacher-centered approaches. A teacher or coach would choose to use these styles when the objective is to replicate specific known skills and knowledge. The teacher specifies the subject matter, the learning conditions (style) and defines the criteria for correct task completion. The task climate is one of performing the model, repeating the task and reducing error. Feedback is specific, often corrective and there is an acceptable way to perform the selected tasks.

The productive cluster (F to K) involves the discovery of new information by the learner. The learner is engaged in cognitive operations such as problem-solving, inventing, comparing, contrasting and synthesizing; the climate favours patience and tolerance, and individual, cognitive and emotional differences. Feedback refers to the production of new ideas.

The command style (Style A)

When adopting the command style, the coach or teacher is very much in charge. They select the content for the session as well as the methods of practice and training. There is no ambiguity in the role of the coach/teacher or the learners. This style can be particularly useful when working with a large group or when the activity involves an element of danger, e.g. coaching the javelin or discus. It is also useful when teaching very technical skills, or closed skills, where accuracy of performance is paramount. However, this style has major limits if the learners are at different levels of ability and development; it is much more suitable for homogenous groups.

For teachers or coaches to use this style successfully they need to be particularly well respected for their knowledge of the activity, of the teaching style and the learners. For example, teachers or coaches have to be aware that some learners may experience boredom in this style, and many will not experience success. This highlights the importance of constantly monitoring performance and altering practices, or even aborting them, when it is necessary.

The reality is that not many teachers or coaches use this style in its purest form. Effective teachers and coaches are flexible with their use of styles according to the needs of their learners and the demands of the activity or task.

The reciprocal style (Style C)

The reciprocal style is sometimes called peer teaching or coaching. As with the command style, the teacher or coach sets the agenda, i.e. chooses the topic or topics to be learned. They then encourage the learners to work in pairs so that they can provide each other with feedback about their performance in the task. To facilitate this process, the teacher or coach can provide the learners with a task card with the criteria for a successful performance.

An example of a task card appears in Table 5.4 below.

Performer: Perform six forward rolls. After the third, receive feedback from the observer.

Observer: Observe the performer against the criteria. After three forward rolls, provide them with feedback that describes their performance and then suggest one area for improvement. Discuss the same issues, and any improvements in performance, again after the final forward roll.

CRITERIA	X OR √	SUGGESTIONS FOR IMPROVEMENT	X OR √	SUGGESTIONS FOR IMPROVEMENT
Crouch position, straight back, arms reaching out straight in front of the body.				
Take weight on hands, shoulder width apart.				
Tuck head between the arms so that contact with the ground is made with the back of the head.				
Strong push through the legs, arms bend to create forward rolling movement.				
Body remains in a tucked position with a rounded back.				
Put feet on floor close to hips.				
Reach forward with arms and straighten legs to come up to a standing position.				

↑ Table 5.4

The teacher or the coach may have to spend some time with the learners to develop their ability to observe and provide feedback, however, this style is useful when the learners know the tasks well and are willing and able to help one another. Some individuals like this style because they feel that making mistakes will not lead to them being seen as being poor performers. They can progress at their own rate and can work on the specific aspects of their own performance. Some care may have to be taken when pairing learners, as not everyone is able to work cooperatively.

The divergent style (Style H)

The divergent style is also known as the problem-solving approach. The coach or teacher sets a problem or task and lets the learner work out a solution or solutions for themselves. This style can lead to some great moments of innovation by the learners. It also allows for an increase in independence and self-esteem in the individual. Additionally, when games players have developed a solution of their own, they are more likely to want to implement it during the game than one which has been forced upon them. In team sports different parts of the team can be working on different problems.

The main issue for the teacher or coach is to set realistic problems and to explain the scenario succinctly to the learner. Learners do need a lot of experience to use this method successfully.

Factors affecting skill learning

This section will highlight some of the other factors that impact on skill learning. Primarily, this section will look at how the coach's or teacher's preferred

<aside>
TO THINK ABOUT

Which of Mosston's styles do you tend to use when coaching?

Are you capable of moving between styles during a practice session?

If not, why do you think that is? If yes, are there any styles that you have not yet used?
</aside>

Case studies

In each of the case studies below, how would you manipulate the task so that the learner has to explore the learning environment to discover solutions to the task or problem (rather than giving specific instructions/information about how to perform the task)?

Case 1

Johnny "Jojo" Johnson is an 18-year-old basketball player. He is tall and has a good lay-up and free throw technique. He has good tactical insight and is always on the right spot at the right time. Johnny has one problem: his dribbling is clumsy and is not as smooth as you would like it to be.

How would you manipulate a dribbling task to facilitate his learning?

Case 2

Sheila is a promising young golfer. The one weakness in her game is in her chipping. She is unable to get any height on the ball when she plays this shot.

How would you manipulate a task to facilitate her learning?

Case 3

You are faced with a team of under-12 soccer players. They are enthusiastic, but have no clue about tactics. They all run after the ball from one end of the field to the other. They don't look around to other players; they only focus on the ball. When a player has possession of the ball, they run with it across the field and try to score the winning goal.

How would you manipulate the game to facilitate learning?

instructional style might impact on performance, before explaining some of the key considerations relating to the learner that must be addressed during each training session or lesson.

The coach/teacher

Every coach or teacher varies in the approach they adopt in developing their athletes' performance. The approach they take is largely based on their prior experiences as a performer and instructor, as well as the coaching knowledge they have gained through coach education programmes. Traditionally, both coaching and teaching have been informed by information processing theories of learning. Thus many teachers and coaches adopt an approach that can generally be described as coach/teacher-centered. Here, their role is to set the task and present the information that will facilitate the development and strengthening of the motor programme. In the early stages of learning, this means reducing the amount of information the learner has to attend to by applying strategies such as part practice or providing specific learning cues. As the learner develops and progresses, the coach increases contextual interference by adopting strategies such as randomization of practice.

These more traditional approaches to coaching/teaching closely reflect Mosston's reproductive teaching styles, in which the teacher plays an autocratic and central role in the learning process. With this approach, the teacher directly shapes the learning while the learner makes only a few (or no) decisions in the learning process. The main goal is for the learner to reproduce and refine movements through practice, repetition and feedback. One of the problems with this approach is that often skills are practiced outside the context of the activity. When this happens learners often become efficient at performing the technique in practice but are unable to transfer this technique into the activity context.

An alternative approach is one where the coach or the teacher views themselves as a facilitator of learning, rather than the source of learning. This type of approach can be linked to Mosston's productive cluster, a democratic style in which the teacher facilitates or guides the learning. In the cluster of productive approaches, the responsibility for learning shifts towards the learner. One of the ways in which a coach or teacher can achieve this is by manipulating the task so that the learner has to explore the learning environment to discover solutions to the task or problem.

For example, rather than giving specific instructions about how to dribble with the ball in field hockey (how to hold the stick, how to turn the stick to change direction, when to turn the stick, body position, etc.), the teacher may provide the learner with different types of field hockey sticks (different lengths, grips, weight, etc.) and ask the performer to move in an area without making contact with the other performers. The different type of sticks will encourage the performer to explore different ways of holding the stick, while the other performers within the learning environment encourage the player to keep their head up and move away from them, changing direction, in order to avoid collision. Thus, although the teacher sets up the initial learning environment, it is the performer's explorations and interactions with the environment that shapes their movements.

The learner

Regardless of the preferred coaching or teaching style, good coaches or teachers should always take the needs of their learners into account when planning their sessions. Understanding the performer in terms of their age, stage of development, past experiences and motivation level is critical to successful coaching or teaching.

"The reasons for modification are usually twofold: first, to enhance the skill acquisition of the learner; and second, to increase the fun/motivation of the learner and in turn maximize the chance of continued participation in the sport."

Farrow and Reid, 2010

Farrow and Reid conducted an experiment that attempted to identify the differences in the performance of beginner tennis players when scaled equipment was used in a five-week intervention compared to the use of standard equipment. Following a pre-test, where all participants (n=23, 8.0 ± 0.4) performed a rally in each of the four conditions (standard ball/scaled court; modified ball/scaled court; standard ball/standard court and modified ball/standard court), each condition group took part in one 30-minute practice session per week for five weeks. Each practice group used the same tennis racquet and completed identical tasks, largely consisting of game play, where players were presented with a combination of cooperative rally situations and competitive playing opportunities. One week after the final practice session, a post-test identical to the pre-test was completed.

The authors hypothesized that the completely scaled intervention (modified ball and court) would lead to more favourable skill acquisition, as evidenced by greater hitting success and volume than the standard court and ball condition as used in the adult game. The main finding from this experiment was that the standard ball/standard court practice condition (or the group that practiced under adult game constraints) recorded significantly less hitting opportunities on the forehand and backhand side than the scaled-court intervention conditions. The decreased hitting opportunities experienced within the standardized adult condition then flowed into significantly poorer hitting success relative to the scaled court groups. This study highlights the negative influence of teaching children to learn to play tennis in adult conditions. The authors conclude by stating that scaling was a useful technique for simplifying the task for beginners, so that they could successfully develop appropriate movements within an environment that retained key information sources for movement.

Reference

Farrow, D., Reid, M. 2011. "The effect of equipment scaling on the skill acquisition of beginning tennis players." *Journal of Sports Sciences*. Vol 28, number 7. Pp 723–32.

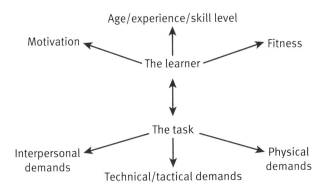

↑ Figure 5.13

TO THINK ABOUT

Why is the growth spurt an important consideration for a gymnastics coach?

Why is the growth spurt an important consideration for a tennis coach?

Why is the growth spurt an important consideration for a hurdles coach?

How can any problems be overcome?

Children grow and develop at different rates and this determines what they can and cannot cope with in learning. When working with young children, for example, age 8 to 10 years, it is inappropriate to teach them to play the same activities as an adult. Consequently, games and equipment have been adapted, or scaled, to suit the developmental needs of younger children. An example of this is the game of short tennis. In this game, the court dimensions are smaller than a regular tennis court, the racquets are smaller, the net is lower and the ball is lighter so that it flies more slowly through the air to give the performer more time to play the shot. This game enables younger children to develop movements that are more like the "adult" movement (rather than adapted and inappropriate movements), scaled to suit their size and strength. This is much more beneficial to their learning and development as they progress, and reduces the likelihood that they will develop bad habits or even injuries.

Puberty can also have a major impact on learning, particularly in co-educational settings. Girls, for example, begin adolescence on average two years before boys at about nine years old. This causes a growth spurt that can peak about two years after it starts.

The increase in height, particularly for boys, can be quite dramatic, even as much as 15-20 centimetres (6-8 inches) in a year. Weight increases in boys tend to occur almost simultaneously with height, mostly due to increases in height and muscle mass. Increases in girls' weight, however, are due to increases in adipose tissue as well as height and muscle mass. Indeed, muscle mass in girls increases less than in boys. Developing longer limbs, bigger feet and with an initial lack of muscular structure over a relatively short period of time can often lead to a loss in coordination. Clumsiness is often unavoidable and this can have a negative impact on both performance and motivation.

Motivation

It is generally accepted that there can be little learning unless the individual concerned is motivated to learn. Motivation is what influences our decisions to participate in sport and physical activity. It enables us to maintain interest and continued involvement. Consequently, it is a key consideration for the coach/teacher. They need to understand what motivates the learner and ways in which they can increase motivation. Motivation is described as the direction, intensity and persistence of behaviour. *Direction* is concerned with our choice of activity, *intensity* is how hard we work at these activities and *persistence* is the length of time that we are willing to work at the task.

There are two general forms of motivation, intrinsic and extrinsic. Intrinsic motivation is when the performer's behaviours are highly autonomous and based on an inherent interest and enjoyment in the activity. This form of motivation involves making a judgment about the value of the task and then accepting it as being personally important. It is closely related to our inherent need to demonstrate self-competence or self-efficacy. We enjoy performing the activity because, through it, we can demonstrate our self-worth. Research suggests that intrinsic motivation is better than extrinsic for learning and performance, and it leads to more satisfaction with performance. Most children rate intrinsic factors such as fun, excitement and skill improvement as more important than extrinsic factors such as trophies and praise.

Research also suggests that, in learning, individuals with high levels of intrinsic motivation are more likely to select more challenging tasks, engage in the task for longer periods of time and apply more effort in learning. Moreover, coaches and teachers can influence intrinsic motivation by creating a learning environment that reduces external incentives, encourages individual goal setting and provides choice and relevance. The concept of relevance is particularly important when considering how to present the learning task. Coaches who use part practice, or massed skill practice in isolation from the context of the activity run the risk of rendering the task meaningless to the learner. When this happens, learners quickly become disengaged and apply less effort to learning, which can have a negative impact on their performance.

Learners have to understand why they are engaging in practice and how it will affect their overall performance. This was the key point made by Bunker and Thorpe (1982) in their development of the "Teaching Games for Understanding" approach (TGfU). They recognized that pupils were not able to transfer the skills they learned during practice to the game because they did not understand the relationship (or the relevance) between the practice environment and the game. As such, they developed an approach to teaching games that emphasizes the game context before the technical skills of the game. Among other things, they suggested that this would make learning more meaningful and that this would increase motivation and learning in games lessons. Additionally, TGfU categorized games (invasion, net and striking and fielding) so that players could recognize the similarities between games from within the same category. This meant that teachers could draw upon pupils' previous experiences of other games from within the same games category to enhance their learning.

In contrast, extrinsic motivation is associated with the performer's need for social recognition. Individuals, for example, may use peer comparisons in order to experience positive feelings of competence or self-worth. This can be beneficial for those learners who thrive on competition for their own learning, or in some activities where competition between performers is critical. Coaches or teachers, therefore, can use material or social rewards in order to reinforce extrinsic motivation. They do this by praising their athletes' learning, performance or effort. Moreover, in sports such as gymnastics, swimming and athletics, it is not uncommon for athletes to receive badges as a reward for reaching a specific level of performance. However, one of the problems with this type of motivation is that it can result in more negative behaviours to avoid feelings of, for example, incompetence or shame. Additionally, over time, extrinsic rewards can lose their power and when this happens, enjoyment of the activity can be lost. More importantly, this means that intrinsic motivation will not be developed. In order to persist in an activity, intrinsic motivation needs to be encouraged.

To ensure high levels of motivation for all performers, coaches or teachers have to develop strategies that develop performers' intrinsic motivation. This can be achieved by providing challenging, fun, interesting and relevant activities, as well as opportunities for performers to receive feedback about their performance, particularly improvements in their performance.

SUMMARY

- → The term "skill" can either be used to describe a specific action or the level of performance of an individual. Skill infers that the movement has been learned and has a predetermined outcome or goal.
- → Skills can be classified according to their characteristics.
  - ▶ the distinctiveness of the movement (discrete motor skills, serial motor skills, continuous motor skills)
  - ▶ the stability of the environment (closed motor skills, open motor skills)
  - ▶ the size of the musculature involved (fine motor skills, gross motor skills).
- → Abilities are the traits that we are born with. They are the perceptual and motor attributes inherited from our parents that enable us to perform skills.
- → Information processing models depict input as the environment that the performer can see, hear and feel. The output is what the performer does. The box in the middle is labeled Central Nervous System (CNS), which is the person's brain and spinal cord.
- → The senses are responsible for relaying information about the environment to the brain. This information is then interpreted by the brain based on past experience of similar situations, which is held in long-term memory.
- → Memory is the "capacity that permits organisms to benefit from their past experiences". In Welford's model he highlights short-term memory (STM) and long-term memory (LTM) but another stage of memory, the sensory information store (SIS), has also been described.

→ Ninety per cent of all information entering the STM is lost within 10 seconds. Retention and passage to the LTM are dependent on rehearsal—mental or physical or both.

→ Selective attention refers to the individual's ability to focus on relevant information while ignoring irrelevant information.

→ Response time is the time from the introduction of a stimulus to the completion of the action required to deal with the problem. Response time is made up of reaction time and movement time.

→ Open loop motor programmes account for the performance of a skill without recourse to feedback. It explains how we can carry out very fast movements. Closed loop programmes describe how, as we learn a skill, we develop a perceptual trace. The perceptual trace is memory for the feel of successful past movements. Once we have developed the perceptual trace, we can compare the trace with the feel of the ongoing movement. This allows us to correct inappropriate actions.

→ Schmidt's schema theory is a motor programme theory that includes both open and closed loop control. Schmidt described a schema as being a set of generalized rules or rules that are generic to a group of movements. Schmidt believed that we develop two kinds of memory for movements, which he called the recall and recognition schemas. The *recall schema* is memory with regard to the choice and initiation of action. While the *recognition schema* is memory for the feel of a movement and it allows us to make appropriate changes in the action.

→ One of the most widely held theories of learning is that of Fitts and Posner (1967). They claimed that learning takes place in three stages, the *cognitive, associative and autonomous* stages.

→ Many skills are difficult to learn at first. Progress is slow but then we reach a point where performance improves more quickly. This is called a positively accelerated curve. Sometimes, however, the opposite happens. We learn quickly at first but then slow down. This is a negatively accelerated curve. When learning is positive and fairly quick at first but then there is a period when we show no improvement in performance, this is called a plateau effect. There is also a linear learning curve for skills that are learned easily and quickly.

→ Practice is essential in acquiring a motor skill. The amount of learning is directly related to the amount of practice.

→ Massed and distributed practice relate to the spacing of practice within or between sessions.

→ Blocked, random and serial practice relate to the order in which the practice of skills takes place.

→ Variable practice is when the demands placed on the performance of a skill are altered, for example, throwing a ball towards different targets at different distances, angles or heights.

→ Mental practice, sometimes known as mental rehearsal, is when a performer thinks about specific components of the movement without actually performing the movement.

→ Muska Mosston developed a spectrum of teaching styles that can facilitate the development of cognitive, affective and motor skills. The governing principle that underpins the teaching styles is that decision-making is the unifying element that connects the teaching and learning experience.

→ It is generally accepted that there can be little learning unless the individual concerned is motivated to learn. Motivation is what influences our decisions to participate in sport and physical activity. It enables us to maintain interest and continued involvement.

Self-study questions

1 Explain the difference between skill and ability.

2 List three characteristics of a skilled performance.

3 State three abilities that are beneficial for learning.

4 Describe what is meant by each of the following terms and give an example for each from a sport of your choice:
   → cognitive skill
   → perceptual skill
   → perceptual-motor skill.

5 Outline why "whole-practice" is more beneficial for learning one of the following skills:
   → a drop-kick in rugby
   → a serve in tennis
   → a spike in volleyball.

6 Explain why variability is an important feature of skill learning.

7 Distinguish between teaching style A and teaching style G.

8 Explain why selective attention is important in sports performance.

9 Describe the psychological refractory period, and outline two examples from sport.

10 Discuss how knowledge of results and knowledge of performance aid skill acquisition.

DATA BASED QUESTION

Electromyography (EMG) is the electrical recording of muscle activity. The figure below shows an EMG profile from one of the quadriceps muscle group of a basketball player recorded during a reaction time task.

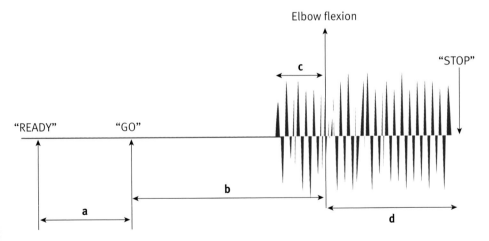

↑ Figure 5.14

1 Identify **a**, **b**, **c** and **d**.
2 Explain the psychological refractory period using an example from a sport of your choice.

CHAPTER 6

Measurement and evaluation of human performance

By the end of this chapter students should be able to:

→ calculate mean and standard deviation using a graphic display calculator or computer program

→ understand what the standard deviation and coefficient of variation tell us about the distribution of the data

→ understand what *t*-tests tell us about differences between two sets of data

→ understand what a correlation is

→ outline the importance of specificity, accuracy, reliability and validity in a fitness test

→ discuss the importance of good study design in experiments

→ outline the importance of the PAR-Q

→ evaluate the advantages and disadvantages of field, laboratory, sub-maximal and maximal tests when examining human performance

→ describe the components of fitness

→ outline why and how fitness is assessed

→ introduce the principles of training programme design

→ suggest ways of monitoring exercise intensity.

Introduction

There are many different ways we can measure the performance of an athlete. In this chapter we will look at different techniques for gathering data including how to design a fitness test and how to assess different studies. This information can then be used to compare the performance of individuals, develop training strategies or measure improvement.

Statistical analysis

Standard deviation

The standard deviation is the spread of scores around the mean or average. As an example we will look at an individual's performances, measured by distance from the hole, on a golf putting test over a period of five lessons.

The person had 30 test putts at the end of each lesson. In order to show how the learner was progressing, the coach plotted the graph shown in Figure 6.1. The coach calculated the mean or average of each set of 30 trials. These can be seen clearly in the diagram, represented by the red diamonds. However, means provide only very limited information about how a person has performed. On the graph, we can see that the coach has added error bars. Error bars are a graphical representation of the variability of the data. They depict the standard deviation from the mean and can add much valuable information for the coach and learner.

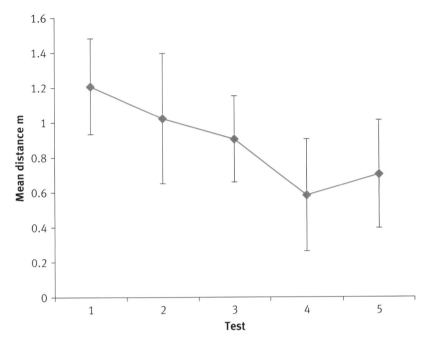

↑ Figure 6.1: Mean (SD) distance from hole of a learner golfer's putts over 5 sets of 30 trials

As you can imagine, our learner golfer will not be consistent when making their putts and the standard deviations can tell us something about that inconsistency. Figure 6.2 shows the means and standard deviations of two sets of 30 trials on a test of putting for two beginner golfers.

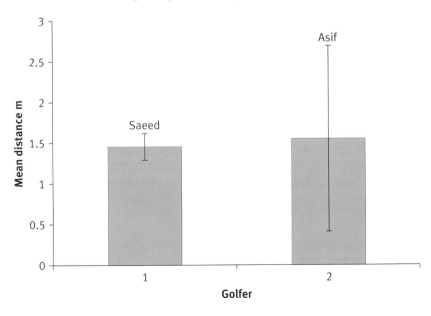

↑ Figure 6.2: Mean (SD) distance from the hole of two learner golfers' putts over 30 trials

KEY POINT

The standard deviation is the spread of scores around the mean. When the data are normally distributed, about 68% of all values will lie within ±1 standard deviation, while 95% will be within ±2 standard deviations.

TRIAL	ERROR (m)
1	1.23
2	2.03
3	0.97
4	1.67
5	2.00
6	1.89
7	1.58
8	0.67
9	1.88
10	2.01
11	4.01
12	0.59
Mean	1.71
SD	0.89

↑ Table 6.1: Caterina's mean (SD) error

As you can see the means are very similar but the standard deviations differ greatly. If we only knew the means we might think that both were equally as good as one another but Saeed's standard deviation is much smaller than Asif's, meaning that he is much more consistent than Asif. Each of Saeed's attempts was not far from his mean but Asif's varied greatly. This would affect the way in which the coach would train each of the two golfers.

The standard deviation is calculated from the spread of scores around the mean. The terms s and SD are often used for standard deviation, as is the Greek letter σ (sigma). Using a graphic display or scientific calculator we can compute the mean and standard deviation for another beginner, Caterina. Caterina's performance on one set of 12 trials on the golf putting test can be seen in Table 6.1.

While the terms s, SD and σ are used for standard deviations we also sometimes simply see the mean given with the symbols ± followed by the standard deviation. So Mean = 1.71, SD = 0.89 is the same as Mean = 1.71 ± 0.89. The use of ± is because the standard deviation is the spread *around* the mean.

In Table 6.1 we can see that the distance from the hole in some of Caterina's putts were more than the mean but others were less than the mean. Statisticians have found that when the data are what they term normally distributed (see Figure 6.3) about 68% of all values will lie within ±1 standard deviation, while 95% will be within ±2 standard deviations.

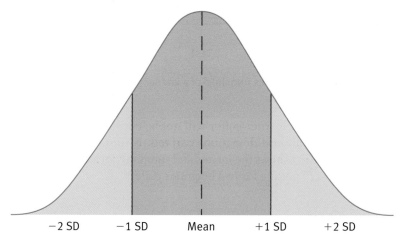

−2 SD   −1 SD   Mean   +1 SD   +2 SD

Note: SD = Standard deviation

↑ Figure 6.3: Typical bell curve for normally distributed data

Coefficient of variation

Another useful measure of variation is to calculate the coefficient of variation, which is denoted by the letter V. The coefficient of variation is the ratio of the standard deviation to the mean expressed as a percentage. The formula for the coefficient of variation is:

$$V = \frac{100 \times SD}{Mean}\%$$

So the coefficient of variation for Caterina would be:

$$V \quad \frac{100 \times 0.89}{1.71}\%$$

$$V = 52.05\%$$

KEY POINT

The coefficient of variation is the ratio of the standard deviation to the mean expressed as a percentage.

This, of course, provides very similar information to the standard deviation but the use of percentages allows many people to understand it better.

Using t-tests

Means, standard deviations and coefficients of variation can be very useful when we are comparing differences in performance between individuals and groups or by the same individual or group but at different times.

Table 6.2 shows the distances covered in 60 seconds by a group of 12 soccer players who undertook a running with the ball test following rest, and then again after 20 minutes' exercise at 70% of their individual maximum volume of oxygen uptakes ($\dot{V}O_2$max).

PARTICIPANT	AFTER REST	AFTER 20 MINUTES AT 70% $\dot{V}O_2$MAX
1	450	390
2	345	455
3	389	378
4	327	405
5	401	366
6	387	388
7	397	400
8	400	405
9	359	401
10	395	432
11	333	411
12	412	399
Mean	382.92	402.5
SD	35.66	23.42
V	9.31%	5.82%
t	1.194	
p	0.21	

Note: SD = standard deviation; V = coefficient of variation

↑ Table 6.2: Distances (metres) covered in 60 seconds by soccer players following rest and after exercise at 70% maximum volume of oxygen uptake ($\dot{V}O_2$max)

The key issue is the question of whether the difference in mean distances is due to the exercise or is it simply due to chance? In order to test whether or not there is a real difference we can carry out an inferential statistical test called a t-test. This can be calculated using a graphic display or scientific calculator, or a computer program.

Using a graphic display calculator we find that $t_{11} = 1.194$. By itself this means little. We need to use it to calculate the probability (p) of finding this difference between the times. Our graphic display calculator does this for us and it shows that $p = 0.205$. The p-value can also be found using probability tables for t-tests; these can be found in most statistics texts. In order to use the tables you need to know what the statisticians call the degrees of freedom. These are represented by the number 11 in our example. This number is normally written in subscript but sometimes in brackets, e.g. $t(11)$.

To understand degrees of freedom think of the following example. You are the coach of a soccer team and you have a team sheet with 11 blank spaces relating to the positions on the soccer team. When the first player arrives for the match you have a choice of 11 positions in which to place this player. You give him a position (e.g. goalkeeper) and this means that one position on your team sheet is now occupied. When the next player arrives you have a choice of 10 positions but you still have the freedom to choose which position this player is now allocated. As more players arrive you will reach the point at which 10 positions have been filled and then the final player arrives. With this player you have no freedom to choose their position because there is only one position left. Therefore, for 10 of the players you had some degree of choice over the position they played, but for one player you had no choice. The degree of freedom is one less than the number of players.

The important thing to note in our example of a *t*-test is that the *p*-value we obtained is greater than 0.05. This means that there is more than 5 per cent possibility that our results are by chance rather than being caused by the exercise. We therefore say that these results are non-significant. For a result to be significant we must show that $p < 0.05$.

THEORY OF KNOWLEDGE

Scientists use *r* as a measure of the strength of the relationship between two variables.

The use of $p < 0.05$ to denote a significant difference or indeed a significant correlation when determining *r* is used by the whole of the scientific community. By using an objective value we can guard against, for example, unscrupulous makers of drugs who might claim that their product has significant effects when in fact it does not.

We must be very careful when describing results that fail to show $p < 0.05$. They are not *statistically* significant but we must not call them insignificant. They are non-significant. Non-significant results can be very significant scientifically. For example, if a pharmacologist finds that using a particular drug has a non-significant effect on the patients then that is a very important finding as it tells him that this drug does not work.

The *t*-test described above is what we call a paired *t*-test. It is called this because it was the same people tested following rest and exercise. For a test to be paired it does not need to be the same people, it can be people who are paired for reasons such as height or weight, or experience.

The other kind of *t*-test that is of interest to us is the independent *t*-test or unpaired *t*-test. McMorris and Beazeley (1997) compared the speed of decision-making of 10 experienced and 10 inexperienced soccer players on a soccer-specific test. The experienced group had a mean decision time of 1.242 s, SD = 0.01, while the inexperienced had a mean time of 1.599 s, SD = 0.02. This was significantly different ($t_{18} = 9.50, p < 0.001$). The *p*-value shows that there was only a 0.1 per cent possibility of this result being by chance.

Note also that the degrees of freedom for this test were 18 when the total number of participants was 20. In the paired *t*-test the degrees of freedom were 11 when the total was 12. One of the differences between the calculation of paired and unpaired *t*-tests is the degrees of freedom, therefore it is important to choose the correct test.

The experiment of McMorris and Beazeley is one of many that have shown that experience affects decision-making in team sports and is a type of cause and

---

TO RESEARCH

How do you overcome the problem of dependence on the measurement scale?

For example, if you wanted to measure the relationship between attitude to climbing every 1000 meters during a climb of Mount Everest, you cannot measure attitudes in meters!

KEY POINT

Probability tells us the likelihood of the differences between two sets of data being statistically significant.

effect experiment. In the next section, we will examine the design of cause and effect experiments more fully but before we do so we need to look briefly at another type of measurement, namely a correlation.

Correlation

We may want to know if there is a *relationship* between two things, e.g. we might want to know if there is a correlation between athletes' ages and times for the 5 000 meters. We do this by calculating the r- and r^2-values.

A common criterion for interpreting the meaningfulness of the correlation is r^2. This is called the coefficient of determination (r^2) and is simply the square of the correlation. Usually the coefficient of determination is expressed as a percentage. For example, for a correlation of 0.70 between standing long jump and vertical jump score, only 49 per cent of the variance (or influence) in one test is associated with the other.

If we multiply r^2 by 100 we get the percentage of overlap between the two measures. Even if this is high it does not mean that age causes the athlete to run the 5 000 meters faster. It simply means that age and speed are related.

Study design

We begin this section by examining some of the main factors involved in ensuring that when measuring individual's fitness levels we do so correctly. There are four very important factors that we must take into account: specificity, accuracy, reliability and validity.

→ **Specificity** If we were asked to measure the fitness of a volleyball player we would want to know something about how high they could jump as that is an important factor in volleyball. We could use the Sergeant Jump Test which measures the height that the individual can jump from a standing position. This is definitely very similar to the skill required in volleyball, so we could say that it is specific. But just how specific is it? Do you only jump for the ball *once* in a volleyball game? Of course not. You have to repeatedly jump to block a spike or to make one yourself. So for our test to be really specific we would need to test the people on several jumps. We could have two measures of fitness: one would be how high could they jump on a single jump and the second would be how well they can maintain that height over several repeated jumps.

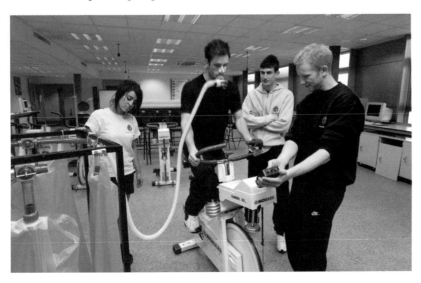

↑ Courtesy of Graham Clark (Photographer: University of Edinburgh)

→ **Accuracy** We must make sure that the instruments with which we measure the fitness component are accurate. Taking a very simple example, we can look at measures of weight. We all know that if we do not look after weighing machines properly they will provide inaccurate information. The same is true for most measures of fitness, so we need to make sure that our equipment is working properly.

→ **Reliability** Reliability is the "degree to which a measure would produce the same result from one occasion to another" (Clark-Carter 2000). If we want to know whether someone has become fitter, we need to be sure that any improvement we see from our testing is due to fitness and not because there is something wrong with the reliability of the test. Tests can be unreliable when there is a learning or habituation effect. If there are such effects we might need to have a series of practice sessions to allow the participants to learn the task fully, i.e. reach a point where they can get no better. McMorris et al. (2005) found that it took their participants 160 trials on a non-compatible choice reaction time test before they had fully learned the task. So they had participants undertake 160 practice trials before carrying out their experiment.

→ **Validity** This simply means that the test actually measures what it claims to measure. We have already seen an example of this with our jumping in volleyball test described above. One jump is an invalid way of measuring jumping ability for volleyball. We need repeated jumps. Similarly having soccer players run 100 meters will not tell us how quick they are in a soccer game, where sprints are much shorter and are repeated many times.

Designing sport and exercise science experiments

In this section we examine the factors that you need to take into account when designing sport and exercise science experiments. Here we are interested in cause and effect experiments. We might want to know if taking caffeine tablets has an effect on starting time in a 100 meters race. Figure 6.4 shows an experimental design that might be used in such an experiment.

↑ Figure 6.4: A weak experimental design

What is wrong with the design in Figure 6.4? Can we be sure that any changes in reaction time are due to caffeine intake? Could it simply be that there has been a learning or habituation effect? What do you think that we could do to solve this problem?

Figure 6.5 shows the most common way of overcoming the learning/habituation problem—the use of a control group.

Experimental group	Pre-Test	→	Treatment (caffeine ingestion)	→	Post-Test
Control group	Pre-Test	→	No treatment	→	Post-Test

↑ Figure 6.5: An experimental design using a control group

The inclusion of a control group, in itself, does not ensure that our experiment is well-designed. Our experimental group were given caffeine tablets and probably expect these to have some effect on their performance. Our control group got nothing and therefore probably expected to see no improvement in their performance. Thus our results could be due to the expectations of the participants (those doing the experiment) rather than the caffeine. What could we do to overcome this? Figure 6.6 shows a possible method—the use of a placebo.

TO DO

Choose a sport or a physical activity and devise a specific, accurate and valid test of either overall performance or of one aspect of performance. How would you test reliability?

Experimental group	Pre-Test	→	Treatment (caffeine ingestion)	→	Post-Test
Control group	Pre-Test	→	Treatment (placebo ingestion)	→	Post-Test

↑ Figure 6.6: An experimental design using a control group with a placebo

The placebo will taste like the real thing but is in fact a harmless substance which will not affect performance. If we tell the participants which group they are in then we are defeating the object, so all participants have to think that they may be getting the caffeine. We call this blinding the participants. Often we will see that an experiment is called a double-blind experiment. In these experiments not only are the participants blind to which treatment they have but so are the experimenters (another person issues the tablets). This is to make sure that the experimenters do not accidently influence the participants.

In the caffeine study we must also be careful not to bias the results by, for example, choosing all the conscientious individuals in the caffeine group and those less likely to try hard in the control group. To guard against this we use a process called randomization, i.e. we randomly allocate individuals to the groups.

In some studies we may want to ensure that at the start the groups are fairly evenly matched. To do this we can pair them based on results from the pre-test. In other studies, like the McMorris and Beazeley (1997) study for example, we will place people into groups based on their experience.

Physical Activity Readiness Questionnaire (PAR-Q)

The types of test used to measure the components of fitness require the individual to undertake physical activity, often strenuous physical activity. Before asking someone to take part in a physical test you must make sure that taking part in the test will not put their health, indeed possibly even their life, at risk. It is recommended that before asking someone to undertake physical activity they complete the Physical Activity Readiness Questionnaire (PAR-Q). People should also be asked to complete this form when asking for training advice or joining a sports and/or exercise club.

Physical Activity Readiness Questionnaire (PAR-Q)

		YES	NO
1	Has your doctor ever said that you have a heart condition and that you should only do physical activity recommended by a doctor?		
2	Do you feel pain in your chest when you do physical activity?		
3	In the past month, have you had chest pain when you were not doing physical activity?		
4	Do you lose your balance because of dizziness or do you ever lose consciousness?		
5	Do you have a bone or joint problem that could be made worse by a change in your physical activity?		
6	Is your doctor currently prescribing drugs (for example, water pills) for your blood pressure or heart condition?		
7	Do you know of any other reason why you should not do physical activity?		

TO RESEARCH

Use the following website to find and describe an effect size and explain why it is important.

http://www.sportsci.org/resource/stats/index.html

Double blind experiment an experiment in which neither the participants nor the experimenters know who has been given the placebo.

TO DO

Choose a research question that you would like answered and design a study that will allow you to answer the question.

TO THINK ABOUT

In the McMorris and Beazeley (1997) study they measured decision-making performance in soccer using laboratory tests. These were accurate and reliable but they are not specific and it could be argued that they have limited validity. The authors claimed that they had to use these as the only alternative was to have coaches watch the players in games and give them a mark out of 10. McMorris and Beazeley believed that this might be specific and valid but it would be open to bias and would depend on the coaches' abilities as much as the players' thus accuracy and reliability would be very weak. What do you think? Were McMorris and Beazeley justified or does the fact that they used a laboratory test make their test totally invalid?

If the person answers "No" to all questions then there should be no problem with them undertaking physical activity. However, if the person answers "Yes" to one or more questions they must see their doctor before undertaking any physical tests, training programmes or playing sport.

Use of field tests versus laboratory tests

Once we have ascertained that the person is healthy enough to undertake testing using the PAR-Q, we have to decide which test or tests of fitness to use. In doing this we must remember the criteria outlined earlier with regard to testing. Are the tests specific, accurate, reliable and valid?

The first thing we must decide is what is it that we want to test. If we want to know what someone's $\dot{V}O_2$max is there are laboratory tests that meet the criteria and measure $\dot{V}O_2$max accurately. However, we do not all have access to laboratories so we may need to use a field test such as the bleep test or Cooper's 12-minute run test. These are not as accurate nor as reliable but they may be what we have available to us.

Maximal tests versus sub-maximal tests

Given the criteria–specificity, accuracy, reliability and validity–it would appear that if we want to know the maximum amount a person can do, e.g. $\dot{V}O_2$max or the maximal weight they can lift, carrying out a maximal test meets all of the criteria. However, if someone is not used to undertaking maximal exercise they are likely to stop before actually reaching their maximum because they become anxious about causing themselves injury.

As a result some sub-maximal tests have been devised and from these we can calculate what the person's maximum would be. These tests are particularly useful with groups such as children who are not used to working to their maximum or with the elderly who may feel concerned about going to the maximum.

Components of fitness

Physical fitness is a complex and challenging term to define, but essentially it relates to an individual's physical ability to perform a specific activity. It is also important to acknowledge that there are other important types of fitness and the term fitness can be used in a range of contexts, e.g. "fit for purpose", "mental fitness". This section will focus on physical fitness, emphasising that there are many different components and furthermore that for each of these components there are often a variety of ways to try and assess an individual's fitness.

Historically, physical fitness has been considered more in the context of sports performance, with athletes demonstrating superior levels of fitness that contribute to outstanding sporting performances. Different sports are naturally characterised by varying physical demands, with factors such as exercise intensity and duration contributing to the determinants of performance. This means that being fit for performance in one sport will not necessarily mean being fit for a very different sport. This concept will be discussed shortly as an important principle of training programme design, to ensure that the correct components of physical fitness are being trained. In summary, there are a range of physical factors that determine an individual's **performance-related physical fitness**, i.e. an individual's physical ability to perform in a specific sport.

More recently, however, we are becoming increasingly aware that the concept of physical fitness also has an important role in non-sporting contexts. The relationship between physical activity and health is complex and this topic

TO RESEARCH

Using the internet see if you can find examples of field and laboratory tests that claim to test the same thing. Also can you find sub-maximal and maximal tests that claim to measure the same things. Which do you prefer?

> 66 **We want to try to prove without a shadow of a doubt the relationship between physical fitness and health, not just physical fitness and ability to perform.** 99
> Kenneth H Cooper, designer of the Cooper test

is further discussed in Chapter 15. The main point is that in contrast to physical fitness for sport, in different populations it is the physical fitness to perform activities of daily living that is crucial. In elderly populations and those with chronic disease, a proportion of the world's population that is getting progressively larger, sporting performance is clearly irrelevant. However, the physical ability to get out of a chair, bathe and walk is extremely important for the health and well-being of these individuals. Indeed, when such tasks become impossible then the decline in fitness and health will become even faster, emphasising that a clear goal for individuals in these populations is to maintain their physical fitness. In this context it is **health-related physical fitness** that is important. This can be defined as an individual's physical ability to maintain health and perform activities of daily living.

The major components of physical fitness

Given the wide range of physical activities performed in both the health and sport domains, it is not surprising that there are many different components of physical fitness and many of these are inter-related in terms of mechanisms and outcomes. The following is a brief outline of some of these most important components, with other chapters going into more detail.

Body composition relates to the proportion of an individual's total body mass that is made up of fat and fat-free mass (see Chapters 1 and 17). Although total body mass itself is easy to assess, and is therefore often measured and interpreted in relation to health and sports performance, in both contexts what makes up this total body mass is actually more important. Body fat mass (FM) includes *essential* fat found in the tissues and organs and *stored* fat, which is essentially an energy reserve. In contrast, fat-free mass (FFM) refers to what makes up the rest of the total body mass, including muscle, water and bone. The following examples illustrate why body composition may be important for health and sport:

→ High levels of body fat are associated with many pathological disorders and so maintenance or attainment of low body fat mass is important for health-related physical fitness. In contrast, a body mass that is too low will typically have a fat mass that is also too low (e.g. *anorexia*) and/or muscle mass that is too low (e.g. *sarcopenia*).

→ There are many sporting activities where total body mass and body composition are very important. In almost all of these the body fat is kept low (Sumo wrestling being an extreme opposite example). Instead it is the FFM that is more important, whether it be an advantage to have a large FFM (e.g. in many collision sports such as American football or rugby union) or a low FFM (e.g. in weight-restricted sports such as boxing, or more aesthetic sports such as gymnastics).

KEY POINT
The ability to perform physical activities has a very important functional role, whether this is for everyday activities and health (health-related physical fitness) or high performance sport (performance-related physical fitness).

→ Bone density is another important aspect of body composition. A low bone density underpins osteoporosis and exercise can play an important role in maintaining bone density.

It is very clear that body composition has a functional role in both health-related and performance-related physical fitness.

Cardio-respiratory fitness refers to the ability to take in, deliver and use oxygen for use by the aerobic or oxidative energy system (see Chapter 2). It is most commonly characterised by an individual's maximal oxygen uptake ($\dot{V}O_2$max), which is the maximal rate that oxygen can be used during maximal exercise. It is often also referred to as **aerobic capacity**, although it should be recognised that there are other functional markers of aerobic performance. Cardio-respiratory fitness is underpinned by the limits of the cardiovascular and ventilatory systems to extract oxygen from the atmosphere, deliver it to respiring tissues and use it. The following examples illustrate why cardio-respiratory fitness is important for health and sport:

→ Low levels of cardio-respiratory fitness are associated with many diseased states and epidemiological research has shown an association with a shorter lifespan.

→ In conditions where cardiovascular or ventilatory function is impaired (e.g. heart disease, chronic lung disease), cardio-respiratory fitness is reduced. Functionally, this means that only very low intensities of physical activity can be tolerated before anaerobic energy systems need to be relied on and these are less sustainable. The result is that even simple physical tasks become unachievable and this worsens the physical deconditioning.

→ In contrast, very high levels of cardio-respiratory fitness are observed in endurance trained athletes, enabling them to tolerate much higher intensities and durations of physical activity.

Strength is defined as the ability to generate force by a muscle or muscle group (see Chapters 1 and 4). Strength is underpinned by the muscle mass that is available (volume and muscle fiber-type), the ability to activate that muscle mass and the co-ordination of this muscle activity. It is therefore dependent on both the neural and muscular systems and their successful interaction.

Speed is defined as the change of distance with respect to time when movement occurs (see Chapter 4). This could refer to whole-body speed or speed of a particular joint or muscle group, depending on the context in sport and exercise. Speed is determined by the complex interaction of biomechanics and physiology, although maximum speed performance is also dependent on psychology. Physiologically, speed is dependent on similar factors as strength, however, the rate at which force is being applied and the coordination of the subsequent movement are the key determinants of the outcome.

→ In many sporting competitions the time that it takes to complete a given activity is what determines the outcome. For example, in a 100 meters running sprint strength is important, especially at the start when ground contacts are longer. But the ability to apply that strength quickly is more important in determining running speed.

→ Explosive sporting activities such as jumping and throwing rely on the speed of movement.

In contrast to the previous examples, speed has much more relevance for performance-related fitness than health-related fitness, where the speed at which actions are completed is of less importance.

Power is defined as the rate of doing work. Functionally, it represents the combination of force and velocity, or **strength** and **speed**. Therefore, it is underpinned by the same factors as strength and speed, the relative importance of these factors dependent on the activity. Where high forces are required the emphasis will be more on strength, whereas with lower forces the emphasis will be more on speed. Muscular power is often seen as one of the most important determinants of sporting performance.

Muscular endurance is the ability of a muscle or muscle group to maintain force or power (see Chapters 1, 3 and 4). It is also sometimes described as *fatigue-resistance* at a local muscular level. The underpinning physiology is a complex interaction of a number of factors and their relative importance depends on the relative intensity of the muscular contractions. Typically, local muscular endurance is mostly related to the availability of substrates, enzyme activity and build-up of metabolites, although the nervous system also has a very important role.

Flexibility refers to the ability to move through the full range of movement around a joint (see Chapter 1). Flexibility is underpinned by a range of factors, such as: the capacity of muscles and tendons to stretch; ligament condition; joint mechanics; size and shape of bones. There is a wide range of flexibility observed across populations. Joints may have impaired range of movement, yet, for some individuals, some movement of joints can go beyond what is the accepted normal range of motion (called *hypermobility*). Therefore, flexibility can be both advantageous and possibly detrimental in the extreme.

Agility can be defined as the ability to rapidly change direction or speed. This may or may not be in response to a stimulus, meaning that it can be separated into the physical ability to change direction or speed and the perceptual and decision-making component of responding to a stimulus (see reaction time below). Despite performance of agility being very short in duration, the underpinning factors are many and complex. Briefly, they include similar underpinning factors of strength (both to decelerate the body and accelerate the body), power, speed, flexibility, balance, peripheral vision, anticipation and experience.

Balance refers to the stability of the body. To maintain balance the center of gravity needs to be maintained above the supporting base of the body and this is achieved through coordinated contraction and relaxation of postural muscles in response to positional changes. Positional changes are detected by visual, vestibular and proprioceptive processes and this stimulates the coordinated muscular responses in order to maintain balance. Therefore, successful balance depends on the ability to sense position and respond to the sensory information in a coordinated fashion, with integration of neuromuscular systems.

Reaction time is described as the duration between the presentation of a stimulus and the associated response. Therefore, similar to balance, this depends on the integration of neuromuscular systems. The reaction time reflects the combination of detecting sensory information, processing this information, sending a response and effecting this response. The reaction time is very dependent on the interaction of the stimulus type and environment. For example, there may be a single stimulus and single response in the simplest tasks, compared to highly complex tasks with multiple stimuli and multiple responses with distracting information.

TO DO

Does each of the following have a functional role for both health-related and performance-related fitness? Provide examples for each which illustrate why.
- → Strength
- → Power
- → Muscle endurance
- → Flexibility
- → Agility
- → Balance
- → Reaction time

KEY POINT

There is a very wide range of physical fitness components and the underpinning determinants depend entirely on the specific components. Interestingly, many components are relevant for health- and performance-related physical fitness, although those components which are more time-dependent tend to be more important for sports performance than heath.

TO RESEARCH

HOW FAST A REACTION TIME IS PHYSICALLY POSSIBLE?

The reaction time at the start of many sporting events can significantly contribute to performance outcome, especially when the total duration is short. The 100 meters sprint is commonly considered to be the flagship event in athletics and the ability to get away from the blocks quickly is very important. Therefore, athletes will often attempt to predict when the starting signal will be delivered and instigate their own movement to coincide with this prediction, rather than wait for the reaction time in response to the signal itself.

Moving too soon, however, will result in what is classified as a "false start". Historically, this was judged by eye and a warning would be given before a restart of the race, with repeat offenders being disqualified. More recently, where technology enables exact measurement of movement initiation in relation to the starting signal, false starts result in immediate disqualification. Which raises the question of how fast is too fast?

Research the measurement and estimation of the fastest possible reaction times and evaluate how they relate to the ruling regarding what is deemed a "false start" in the 100 meters sprint.

Why is fitness assessed?

Testing fitness is important for both health and performance reasons. Health-related fitness assessment is primarily used to evaluate health and identify any weaknesses, relative to healthy "norms", as this can assist with diagnosis, assessment of severity and in some cases even prognosis. However, testing will also be used to monitor progress as a result of interventions (e.g. exercise training, medication), to assist with education of participants/patients and design individual exercise training programs. These same reasons also apply in the performance sport context, with a few additional purposes: to provide feedback to athletes; to try and predict performance potential; to establish goals for athletes to work towards.

How is fitness assessed?

KEY POINT

Before assessing an individual's physical fitness, it is important to ensure they have medical/ health clearance, as well as the requirement to sign an informed consent, prior to participating.

In section 6.2, the important concepts of specificity, accuracy, reliability and validity were introduced. These concepts form important principles when deciding what fitness tests to use, as there are already an enormous number of different fitness tests in use, with more being developed all of the time. The relative value of the test will be determined by a number of factors in addition to these general principles, many of these of a practical nature. These include, but are not limited to: the safety of the participants; ethical considerations; the number of participants to be tested; the resources and facilities available; the accuracy that is required; the order of tests. Therefore, the practitioner must decide on the appropriateness of a fitness test based on the balance between the optimum, often called the *gold-standard* test, and what is actually practical. Accordingly, there will then be associated limitations that must be taken into consideration when interpreting and applying the results.

In many situations it is not possible to directly assess a fitness component. This does not necessarily preclude fitness assessment, but may require either an indirect assessment of fitness or prediction of fitness using a field or laboratory test. In such circumstances the tester will need to consider the suitability and accuracy of the prediction. For example, what data are the prediction equations based on? This might mean that one equation is suitable for one population, but not for another. Another suitable question may relate to how accurate and valid the prediction is, relative to whatever the criterion measure is. Such questions will enable the tester to evaluate how much bias may have been introduced due to the known limitations.

Testing aerobic capacity

As discussed in Chapter 2, the gold-standard assessment of cardio-respiratory fitness is the direct assessment of $\dot{V}O_2$max. This requires a progressive (gradually increasing exercise intensity) maximal test to exhaustion, including measurement of gas exchange. While this is routinely carried out in sport and medical laboratories around the world, the requirement for expertise and equipment to run the test, the maximal nature of the test, as well as only being able to test one participant at a time, make this test unfeasible in many sport and health situations. Therefore, there are a large number of field-based tests that have been designed to enable estimation of $\dot{V}O_2$max. The following 3 examples are only some of the more commonly-used tests.

Multistage Fitness Test (MSFT)

The Multistage Fitness Test (also known as the Beep or Bleep Test) was originally devised by Leger and Lambert (1982) and was then validated and commercialized by the National Coaching Foundation (Ramsbottom et al. 1988). The test requires participants to perform repeated 20-meter shuttles at progressively increasing speeds until exhaustion is reached. The running speed is indicated by an audio-sound (the "beep") that indicates that the next shuttle should start at this point, i.e. the turn at each end of the 20-meter course should coincide with the sound. The first level of the test is of low intensity (fast walk or light jog) and then approximately each minute the frequency of the sounds increases to the next level, causing an increase in running speed for that level. Performance in the test is described as the level reached and the number of completed shuttles in that level before the participant either voluntarily stops or fails to keep pace with the sound and was disqualified from continuing. For example, a score of Level 10-6 would imply 6 shuttles were completed in level 10. This score is then compared against a reference table where an estimate of $\dot{V}O_2$max can be obtained based on the number of shuttles. An increased score corresponds to a higher $\dot{V}O_2$max.

The evaluation of this test requires consideration of advantages and limitations compared to the gold-standard test. The following table lists a few of these.

ADVANTAGES	LIMITATIONS
Limited expertise and equipment needed	Prediction based on performance and not direct measurement
Maximal test (not a sub-maximal prediction), so similar to gold standard	Maximal test (safety and ethical considerations, as well as importance of motivation)
Easy to score	Environmental factors influence performance as not in a laboratory
Large numbers can be tested at once in a short time	Score is known by participants and previous scores or target scores may impact on performance
	The protocol is stop-start in nature, compared to continuous in the gold standard

KEY POINT

Physical fitness testing can play an important role in health and sport. However, for the assessment to be meaningful the appropriateness of a test must be assessed relative to a wide range of factors. Where a gold-standard test is not possible, the tester must assess the relative value against the associated limitations of the test, in the specific context of the participant and environment.

THEORY OF KNOWLEDGE

The placebo effect, with its central role in clinical trials, is acknowledged as a factor in sports medicine. Placebo effects of varying magnitudes are reported in studies addressing sports from weightlifting to endurance cycling. Findings suggest that psychological variables such as motivation, expectancy and conditioning, and the interaction of these variables with physiological variables, might be significant factors in driving both positive and negative outcomes. Research involving the triangulation of data, and investigation of contextual and personality factors in the mediation of placebo responses may help to advance knowledge in this area.

(Source: Beedie, C.J., Foad, A.J. 2009. *Sports Medicine*. Vol 39, number 4. Pp 313–329.)

→ Explain how motivation might be a significant factor in driving both positive and negative outcomes of a placebo.

→ Discuss whether placebo responsiveness is a generalized trait.

→ If placebo responsiveness were a generalized trait does this represent a desirable or an undesirable characteristic in terms of athletic personality.

This test is widely used with healthy adults in sports teams as it has been shown to be reliable, provided the test is carefully standardised, and reasonably accurate for the estimation of $\dot{V}O_2$max. It is also sensitive to training improvements, so although the value of $\dot{V}O_2$max obtained will not be fully accurate, improvements in score will still indicate improvements in aerobic fitness. However, for other populations alternative data are required to improve the accuracy of the estimation. For example, as the tables have been developed with adults free of disease it is not possible to use the same tables to estimate $\dot{V}O_2$max in children. Therefore, alternative equations have been developed for use with children. Note that due to the maximal nature of the test, it will not be suitable for people with pre-existing medical conditions who are not permitted to take part in maximal exercise.

Cooper's 12-minute run

There are a number of field-based tests where performance is assessed by the distance covered in a fixed period of time, or the time to complete a fixed distance. One such example was developed by Dr Ken Cooper (Dallas, Texas). This test simply requires participants to run/walk as far as they can in a period of 12 minutes, the total distance then entered into an equation to estimate $\dot{V}O_2$max.

ADVANTAGES	LIMITATIONS
Limited expertise and equipment needed	Prediction based on performance and not direct measurement
Maximal test (not a sub-maximal prediction) with continuous exercise	Maximal test (safety and ethical considerations, as well as importance of motivation)
Easy to score	Environmental factors influence performance as not in a laboratory
Large numbers can be tested at once in a short time	The protocol is not progressive in nature and therefore pacing will be a key factor

Similar to the MSFT the test is widely used in non-clinical populations and the same limitations do apply. As the protocol is continuous and self-paced, many performers are more comfortable with the test and may perform better than in the MSFT.

Harvard step test

In contrast to the two previous examples, many tests for estimation of $\dot{V}O_2$max do not involve maximal exercise. One of the oldest such tests is known as the Harvard step test developed as early as the 1940s, although there are other commonly used step tests such as the Queens or McArdle step test. The outcome measure for this test is not performance, but based on the recovery of heart rate after performing a fixed amount of work. Participants are required to step on and off a step (45 cm high) at a rate of 30 steps each minute for five minutes, making a total of 150 steps completed. The heart rate of the participant is then measured at the end of the first, second and third minutes of recovery following completion of the test. An equation then uses the total of these three heart rate values to estimate $\dot{V}O_2$max, based on the association of a lower heart rate (and faster recovery) at a fixed intensity with higher $\dot{V}O_2$max.

ADVANTAGES	LIMITATIONS
Limited expertise and equipment needed	Prediction based on heart rate values
Sub-maximal test (suitable for more participants) with continuous exercise	Does not account for individual variation in heart rate (not training-related)
The test is based on physiological findings and not performance (pacing and motivation will not affect the results)	Heart rate needs to be measured accurately, as small differences will impact on the result

The main advantage of such a test is clearly that it does not require participants to exercise maximally, making it safer to conduct on a wide variety of participants. However, the test is less accurate unless alternative equations are used for differing populations. This test is more suitable for assessment of health-related fitness than sport-related fitness.

Evaluation of other fitness tests

TO DO

The above examples illustrate how to evaluate the suitability of fitness tests for use in assessing performance- and health-related fitness. For the following fitness tests related to the components of fitness, please research what the test involves and evaluate the strengths and limitations of the test. Deduce the contexts in which you would (or would not) use the test.

→ Body composition: body mass index (BMI), anthropometry and underwater weighing
→ Flexibility: the Sit-and-reach test
→ Muscle endurance: maximum sit-ups, maximum push-ups, flexed arm hang
→ Agility: the Illinois agility test
→ Strength: the handgrip test using a handgrip dynamometer
→ Speed: the 40-meter sprint
→ Balance: the standing stork test
→ Reaction time: the ruler drop test and also look at computer-based tests of reaction time
→ Power: vertical jump and standing broad jump

THEORY OF KNOWLEDGE

When assessing an individual's physical fitness, there is often a comparison made between a recorded or estimated score and reference normative data. Care must be taken to ensure that this comparison is fair and that the normative data are applicable to the individual being tested, as differences in fitness are not the only factors to contribute to individual differences.

An interesting example of this is what is "normal" for acceptable or healthy body composition. Chapter 16 discusses this in more detail, but for now please research regional and cultural differences regarding norms for body composition. This is not restricted to only physiological factors, but should also include perceptions and acceptance as well.

Principles of training programme design

Training theory encompasses all aspects of fitness knowledge, and there are a number of essential elements and basic training principles that apply to all types of exercise programmes. Designing an actual training session demands an understanding of the essential elements to put principles into practice, whether the planned outcome is to improve cardio-respiratory fitness, musculo-skeletal fitness, body composition, or flexibility. The following activities are the essential elements of a general training programme:

→ warm-up and stretching activities
→ cardio-respiratory endurance training
→ cool-down and stretching activities
→ flexibility activities
→ resistance training
→ recreational activities.

Every training/exercise/competition session should begin with low-intensity physical activity of a similar mode that you will be performing. This is to increase your body temperature, heart rate and breathing rate, and safely prepare your cardiovascular respiratory system to function more effectively during the more rigorous training/exercise/competition that follows. A good warm-up also decreases the amount of muscle or joint soreness during the early stages of beginning a training programme. Warm-up before dynamic stretching to reduce your risk of injury, and then progress to the cardio-respiratory endurance training element. Activities such as walking, jogging, running, cycling, swimming, rowing and aerobic dancing are designed to improve your cardiovascular, respiratory and metabolic systems.

Every training session should include cool-down and stretching immediately after finishing your cardio-respiratory exercise. It is important that the cool-down is done by slowly reducing the intensity of the cardio-respiratory activity for several minutes. After this cool-down period is an especially good time to engage in stretching activities, to improve flexibility and lower the risk of joint or muscle injury.

Resistance exercise can be defined as *exercise specifically designed to enhance muscular strength and endurance.* This method of training involves the progressive use of a wide range of resistance loads, including:

→ specific body mass exercises (e.g. curl-ups)
→ weight and load bearing exercise (e.g. climbing)
→ the use of resistance equipment (e.g. free weights).

Resistance training has grown in popularity over the past 25 to 30 years and research has demonstrated many health, fitness and performance related benefits. The British Association of Sport and Exercise Sciences (BASES, 2004) have recommended that:

→ all young people should be encouraged to participate in safe and effective resistance exercise at least twice a week
→ resistance exercise should be part of a balanced exercise and physical education programme.

Recreational activities such as squash, basketball and kayaking are social, enjoyable and relatively inexpensive. Recreational activities can also include cardiovascular and resistance training exercise. They contribute to improving health and fitness, and are sufficiently varied to sustain life-long interest and can involve the whole family.

To plan/design an effective exercise programme, it is necessary to understand and apply training principles. A number of basic principles of training apply to all types of exercise programmes, including:

TO RESEARCH

Explain the difference between passive and dynamic stretching.

TO RESEARCH

From the research literature on resistance training, give an example of:

1 a health benefit
2 a fitness benefit
3 a performance benefit.

- → progression
- → overload (frequency, intensity and duration)
- → specificity
- → reversibility
- → variety.

Monitoring exercise intensity using cardiovascular exercise as an example: heart rate and rate of perceived exertion

Intensity refers to the level of stress achieved during an exercise session, and intensity and duration of exercise are indirectly related. Exercise intensity can be expressed in many different ways, such as a percentage of maximal aerobic capacity ($\dot{V}O_2$max) or peak oxygen consumption, or by calculating the percent $\dot{V}O_2$ reserve i.e. the difference between $\dot{V}O_2$max and resting oxygen consumption. These and similar gas analysis methods require graded exercise testing and the use of fairly expensive laboratory equipment (e.g. metabolic carts) to determine $\dot{V}O_2$max. Other indirect methods of quantifying exercise intensity that are easier to administer "in the field" as well as having additional benefits, such as being relatively inexpensive, include:

- → the training heart rate concept
- → the Karvonen method
- → the training heart rate zone
- → ratings of perceived exertion.

The **training heart rate** (THR) is based on the linear relationship between heart rate and $\dot{V}O_2$ with increasing rates of work. The THR is calculated by using the heart rate that is equivalent to a set percentage of your $\dot{V}O_2$max. There can be various classifications of exercise intensity using percent heart rate maximum (%HRmax), for example:

- → "light" exercise is 35-54%HRmax
- → "moderate" exercise is 55-69%HRmax
- → "heavy" exercise is 70-89%HRmax.

The **Karvonen** or percent heart rate reserve method (HRR) takes into account the difference between resting heart rate (HRrest) and maximal heart rate (HRmax). The training heart rate is calculated by taking a percentage of HRR and adding it to the HRrest. It is important to select an exercise intensity appropriate to the health needs and fitness status of the individual. For example, a sedentary individual about to begin an aerobic exercise programme might be well advised to target a "light" (say 35%HRmax) THR for the first few sessions (and gradually increase intensity over time) as follows:

$$\text{THR}_{35\%} = \text{HRrest} + 0.35(\text{HRmax} - \text{HRrest})$$

Technological advances allow heart rate monitors to measure exercise intensity as well as time in a target heart rate zone, and the Karvonen method can also be used to establish a THR zone rather than a single THR value. For example, a recent study investigated time spent in the target heart rate zone and cognitive performance of nine-year-old children as part of the FIT kids programme. The Fitness Improves Thinking (FIT) programme is designed to improve the physical fitness of children and enhance their cognitive performance and the THR zone for the children was set to 55-80%HRmax. This study also used the children's OMNI scale to collect a child's ratings of perceived exertion (RPE). This involved using the range of numbers 1-10 and child-like pictures to quantify how tired the child was during exercise testing.

TO DO

From your favourite sport select one fitness component and give an example of how each of the first three basic training principles (above) can be applied to this component.

TO RESEARCH

Distinguish between absolute and relative exercise intensity.

TO RESEARCH

1. Distinguish between the following RPE scales:
   a. Borg
   b. OMNI
   c. CERT
2. Outline two reasons as to why it may be a more sensible approach to establish an exercise intensity THR zone rather than a single THR value.

SUMMARY

→ The standard deviation is calculated from the spread of scores around the mean.

→ The terms s, SD and the Greek letter σ (sigma) are often used for standard deviation.

→ When the data are normally distributed, about 68 per cent of all values will lie within ± 1 standard deviation, while 95 per cent will be within ± 2 standard deviations.

→ The coefficient of variation is the ratio of the standard deviation to the mean expressed as a percentage.

→ Whether differences between group means is due to the exercise or is simply due to chance can be examined by a t-test.

→ If the probability (p) is less than 0.05 or 5 per cent, we say that the results are significant.

→ Paired t-tests are carried out if scores by the same people are being compared or the individuals have been paired for height or weight, or for experience.

→ If participants are not paired then we use an independent or unpaired t-test.

→ If we wish to know whether there is a relationship between two things, we calculate their correlation. We do this by calculating the r- and r^2-values.

→ If we multiply r^2 by 100 we get the percentage of overlap between the two measures.

→ Performance tests should be specific, accurate, reliable and valid.

→ Reliability is the "degree to which a measure would produce the same result from one occasion to another".

→ Validity simply means that the test actually measures what it claims to measure.

→ Experimental designs can be improved by the inclusion of a control group.

→ Where appropriate the control group can take a placebo.

→ The Physical Activity Readiness Questionnaire (PAR-Q) should be completed before individuals take part in an experiment.

→ Performance-related physical fitness is an individual's physical ability to perform in a specific sport.

→ Health-related physical fitness is an individual's ability to maintain health and perform activities of daily living.

→ Major components of physical fitness include: body composition; cardio-respiratory fitness; strength; speed; power; muscular endurance; flexibility; agility; balance; reaction time.

→ Factors that must be taken into account when measuring an individual's fitness level are: specificity; accuracy; reliability; validity.

→ The MSFT and the Cooper 12-minute run are field-based tests designed to estimate $\dot{V}O_2$max.

→ There are six essential elements of a general training programme.

→ Monitoring exercise intensity can be quantified on the basis of the training heart rate or the rating of perceived exertion.

Self-study questions

1 Distinguish between *standard deviation* and *coefficient of variation*.

2 Outline what is meant by *degrees of freedom*.

3 Describe **four** important factors that we must take into account for study design.

4 Discuss the placebo effect.

5 Outline why a PAR-Q is used before fitness testing.

6 Evaluate the use of field tests versus laboratory tests.

7 Outline two components of physical fitness.

8 Discuss the advantages and disadvantages of the multistage fitness test.

9 Outline **one** method used to monitor exercise intensity during cardiovascular exercise.

10 List **six** essential elements of a general training programme.

DATA BASED QUESTION

Below is a table showing the raw data (time in seconds) for two field hockey players, Roisin and Mary, on a ball dribbling test. They had to dribble through a slalom course as quickly as possible. Using a graphic display calculator or computer program, calculate the means and standard deviations for each of them.

Trial	Roisin	Mary
1	10.1	8
2	10.4	9.2
3	13	7.9
4	11.1	10
5	14.6	9.9
6	9	8.1
7	11.8	10
8	9.2	7.5
9	8.8	9.5
10	11	10.3
Mean		
SD		

What can you say about their consistency? Do you think that there is much difference between them? What time would Roisin have when she dribbled at 1 SD? What time would Mary have when she dribbled at 1 SD? Do the answers to the last two questions change your opinion as to whether there is much difference between them?

CHAPTER 7

Training to optimize physiological performance

OBJECTIVES

By the end of this chapter students should be able to:

→ define the terms training, undertraining, overreaching and overtraining

→ explain the impact of frequency, intensity and duration of training on the athlete's training response

→ describe some of the common methods of training

→ discuss the overtraining syndrome, its impact on an athlete, how it may occur, the tools used for its diagnosis and the issues associated with those tools

→ explain the concept behind periodization of training

→ describe the key components of a periodized training programme and how they fit together.

↑ Figure 7.1: Athletes come in all shapes, sizes and genders

Introduction

Sport is played by athletes of different shapes, sizes, ages and genders (Figure 7.1). These athletes all have different physical requirements based on the nature and demands of their chosen sport. For example, a javelin thrower requires a large amount of explosive muscle power, but does not need the aerobic endurance that would be extremely important to a 5 000 meter runner. It may appear, therefore, that across different sports athletes do not have much in common with one another. However, there is one thing that unites all athletes, regardless of their chosen sport: the need to improve and maximize their physical performance.

Maximizing physical performance is achieved in many ways. For example, appropriate diet, adequate sleep and rest, and reduced stress levels will all help the athlete to improve performance. However, appropriate training is, undoubtedly, one of the most important methods that an athlete can use to maximize physical performance.

Training

Training is the systematic, repeated performance of structured exercise sessions over a period of time, with the achievement of a specific goal in mind. The type, duration, intensity and frequency of training will vary depending on what this goal is. While training is crucial for improving and maximizing sports performance, unsuitable training prescriptions can actually be detrimental to performance.

Undertraining is a failure to provide adequate stimulation to the body by training too infrequently, for too short a period of time, or at an insufficient intensity that will not generate the physical adaptations that are required for enhanced performance.

Overtraining occurs if an athlete attempts to do more training than he or she is able to physically and/or mentally tolerate over a prolonged period. The performance and even the health of the athlete can deteriorate significantly. If this is allowed to continue, it can become a career-threatening problem (further discussed later in this chapter). However, athletes do need to stress their bodies sufficiently for a training response to be generated (chapter 14 explores overtraining in more detail.)

Overreaching is when an athlete places stress on their body that is beyond their current limit of tolerance, but only for a short period of time. Short-term decrements in performance may be observed, with full recovery of performance taking from several days to several weeks (Meeusen et al. 2006). Therefore, overreaching can be thought of as transient overtraining.

Coupled with appropriate recovery, overreaching can be a useful tool in maximizing the training response, although the consensus on its efficacy is inconsistent (Brittenham et al. 1998). When using the method of overreaching, if appropriate recovery is not provided, overtraining can develop.

The interaction of the different concepts of training discussed above can be viewed as a training continuum. The diagram in Figure 7.2 shows the progression of training states from undertraining through to overtraining (boxes), with the associated outcomes for each training state (circles). It also demonstrates the fine degree of difference between developing minor performance enhancements or no enhancements at all (a), and between optimizing physiological adaptations and performance enhancement or reaching a state of overtraining (b).

> **Training** the systematic repeated performance of structured exercise sessions over a period of time
>
> **Undertraining** not providing the body enough stimulation for performance to improve by training too infrequently or at too low an intensity
>
> **Overtraining** training too often or at too high an intensity over a prolonged period of time
>
> **Overreaching** pushing the body beyond its limits for a short period of time to stimulate a training response

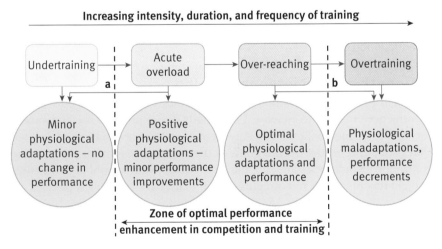

↑ Figure 7.2: A schematic of the training continuum

Types of training

There are different types of training, each placing different stresses on the body, therefore stimulating different adaptations. As a result, athletes use a number of these types of training, depending on the demands of their sport and the goals of their specific training programmes and cycles (see the section on periodization). The following summarizes some common types of training.

Flexibility training

Flexibility training is the systematic stretching of the muscles, tendons and other connective tissues of the body, resulting in an increased range of motion (i.e. flexibility) of the affected body parts. This may be done to correct abnormally small flexibility, to increase flexibility in order to improve the performance of a sporting technique, or to reduce the risk of, or aid recovery from, injury. Flexibility training uses different forms of stretching.

→ **Static stretching** The target muscle is stretched until mild discomfort is felt and then held in this position.

→ **Active stretching** A muscle is held statically in a stretched position via contraction of the opposing muscle. For example, the quadriceps muscles are stretched by contracting the hamstring muscles, thereby flexing the knee joint.

→ **Dynamic stretching** The target muscles are moved in a controlled fashion using repeated dynamic movements through their full range of motion with gradually increasing reach and/or speed of movement. For example, the muscles at the front and back of the hip and thigh are stretched by swinging the straight leg backwards and forwards in a kicking motion.

→ **Ballistic stretching** A repeated bouncing motion at the point of peak stretch in an attempt to force the tissue beyond its normal range of motion. This form of stretching is discouraged as it can increase the risk of injury to the affected area.

→ **Proprioceptive neuromuscular facilitation (PNF) stretching** While this form of stretching can be undertaken in different ways, the most common method is to begin with a static stretch followed by an isometric contraction of the target muscle for approximately 10 seconds. This is immediately followed by a brief relaxation of the muscle and then another static stretch where the muscle is stretched further than the initial static stretch. The muscle is then allowed to relax before another cycle of stretching begins.

The type of stretching undertaken will depend on many factors including the type of athlete, the age, gender and physical abilities or restrictions of the individual athlete, and the goal of the stretching (warm-up, cool-down, rehabilitation etc).

Strength and resistance training

Strength and resistance training is the application of resistance against muscle contractions in order to increase the strength, size or power of skeletal muscle, or to alter its metabolic profile. Any form of resistance can be used, but will likely depend on the overall goals of the training session or programme. Common forms of resistance include gravity, body weight, rubber bands, fixed weight machines and free weights (dumb-bells, bars and weight plates).

Strength and resistance training has the potential to change the musculoskeletal system in different ways, depending on how it is carried out. The most common adaptations from a general strength and resistance training programme can include increased bone, muscle, tendon and ligament strength, improved joint function, reduced risk of injury, increased bone density and improved neuromuscular and cardiovascular function.

Increasing muscle strength, tone and power all require different approaches, therefore the prescription of a strength and resistance training programme must be specifically tailored to the goals of the athlete. The methods of structuring training programmes are discussed in the periodization section of this chapter.

Circuit training

Circuit training combines strength and resistance training exercises with aerobic/cardiovascular exercises to achieve an overall increase in conditioning. These exercises are structured into an easy to follow sequence, with each exercise completed for a set amount of time or number of repetitions followed by a short recovery before moving on to the next exercise in the sequence. Completion of all exercises in the sequence is termed a circuit. A circuit can be repeated more than once, or more than one sequence of exercises can be structured for the completion of multiple circuits.

Figure 7.3 describes a basic eight-exercise circuit training programme for general conditioning. Each exercise would be completed maximally for 30 seconds, followed by a 10-second period to move to the next station and prepare to begin the exercise. Participants could begin the circuit on any exercise they wish, and successful completion of all eight exercises would represent one completed circuit.

TO THINK ABOUT

What types of training are best suited to the sports you play?

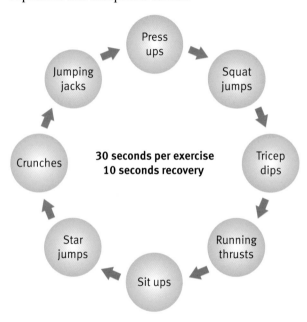

↑ Figure 7.3: An example of a basic circuit training session

Interval training

Interval training involves bouts of high or maximal intensity work interspersed with low intensity "recovery" exercise. This type of training can be used in any form of cardiovascular exercise (running, cycling, rowing, swimming etc) and is widely used by athletes of all levels.

Interval training sessions are structured by altering key variables including the intensity and duration of the work and rest components and the number of interval repetitions performed. The ability to change these variables makes interval training a flexible tool that can be used by a variety of athletes, from 100-meter sprinters to Tour de France cyclists.

Plyometrics training

Plyometrics training is composed of extremely fast, powerful, short-duration movements designed to increase the speed and the force of muscle contractions. Therefore, plyometrics is used predominantly to improve explosive, forceful sporting activities, such as running speed in a 100-meter sprint, jump height in a high jump, distance in a javelin throw or the power of a boxer's punch.

Plyometrics movements involve rapid stretching of a muscle followed immediately by a forceful shortening of the same muscle. The stretching movement activates a stretch reflex within the muscle which causes it to contract in order to prevent damage to the muscle tissue from excess stretching. When this is combined with the forceful contraction initiated by the athlete, a large force is produced by the muscle, which should initiate improvements in muscle strength and power.

The effectiveness of plyometrics training is greatly reduced if the athlete is unable to contract their muscles as forcefully as possible. Therefore, short bursts of plyometrics exercise are interspersed with comparatively long periods of recovery to prevent the athlete from becoming fatigued.

Continuous training

Unlike interval or plyometrics training, continuous training, as the name suggests, involves a period of exercise completed without rest. However, this form of exercise can still be completed at a range of intensities from low to near maximal. Continuous exercise at lower intensities may continue for several hours, whereas at high or near maximal intensities it may be completed only for a few minutes. However, continuous training must be completed at a minimum threshold intensity to ensure aerobic adaptations (McArdle et al. 2010).

In non-athletes, continuous training represents a relatively comfortable, accessible form of exercise, particularly for individuals with health issues, compared to the challenges of, for example, interval training. For athletes, the requirement for, and duration and intensity of, continuous training will depend in part on the individual athlete and their sporting goals and requirements.

Continuous exercise was historically believed to be the most effective form of exercise for burning fat stores and improving aerobic endurance and $\dot{V}O_2$max. However, recent research has suggested that other forms of training, such as interval training, may be at least as effective, perhaps more so, than continuous training for improving variables such as these.

Fartlek training

Fartlek (Swedish for "speed play") training involves a combination of interval and continuous training. However, unlike those other forms of training, Fartlek training does not employ regimented exercise intensities, durations or rest periods. Instead, the athlete regulates the intensities of the training session based on how they feel at any given time. Fartlek training can tax all energy systems, provide good overall conditioning and make for a varied and enjoyable workout. However, its random, spontaneous nature makes it extremely difficult to quantify its efficacy and to adequately replicate Fartlek sessions within a training programme.

Cross-training

Cross-training involves training using different techniques with the goal of making general improvements in overall performance. Individuals involved in cross-training may make use of some, or perhaps all, of the training methods discussed above. However, a goal of cross-training is to use the strengths of one training method to attenuate the weaknesses of another. For example, a marathon runner may use interval training to improve their ability to complete the race at a faster pace, but also use continuous training to develop the mental strength and focus required to complete an endurance running event; something that interval training cannot provide.

TEST YOURSELF

1 Define the following training terms:
   a Training
   b Undertraining
   c Overreaching
   d Overtraining

2 For each athlete noted below, choose the type(s) of training you think would be beneficial to the athlete's performance. Justify how each method you choose would benefit the athlete.
   a High jumper
   b Triathlete
   c Boxer

Most athletes will use multiple forms of training at various stages of a training programme to ensure peak overall performance, and also to reduce the risk of encountering overtraining.

Overtraining

As discussed earlier in this chapter, undertaking a prolonged period of training that exceeds what the athlete can physically and/or mentally tolerate is called overtraining. This process, usually accompanied by insufficient recovery, can lead to the development of overtraining syndrome (OTS). This is an important differentiation. Overtraining and OTS are not one and the same thing; overtraining is the process, whereas OTS is the eventual outcome of that process.

Athletes suffering from OTS can struggle to train hard or compete at their previous levels, struggle or fail completely to adapt to training and find it increasingly difficult to fully recover from a workout (McArdle et al. 2010). It is also important to note that stressors on the athlete outside of training or competition, for example, family concerns, financial worries etc, can also contribute to the development of OTS (Smith, Norris 2002).

Figure 7.4 shows the five aspects of performance that impact the overall athletic performance of an athlete. An excess of one or more of these aspects or their constituents could contribute to development of OTS.

Overtraining syndrome (OTS)

Overtraining syndrome is a highly variable condition that can affect athletes differently and induce different symptoms—over 80 have been identified. It can take weeks or months to recover from (Slivka et al. 2010; Urhausen, Kindermann 2002).

Symptoms of OTS are often the same as those from a multitude of other illnesses and conditions, meaning that OTS can go undiagnosed for some time. To compound this, no diagnostic tool exists to conclusively identify an athlete as suffering from OTS (Halson, Jeukendrup 2004). Indeed, OTS is termed a "syndrome of exclusion", meaning that it is diagnosed only when all other possible causes of an athlete's symptoms have been ruled out. Potential causes

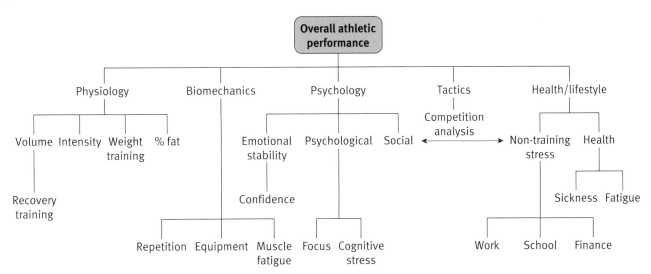

↑ Figure 7.4: A conceptual model of five aspects of performance that impact the overall athletic performance of an athlete

KEY POINT

Overtraining is the process, whereas OTS is the eventual outcome of that process. They are not one and the same thing.

for many symptoms of OTS that must be ruled out include anemia, magnesium deficiency, viral infections, muscle damage, hormone disorders, eating disorders, depression, allergies, cardiovascular disease and asthma (Purvis et al. 2010). Furthermore, the causative mechanism(s) behind OTS are currently unknown (Armstrong, VanHeest 2002), and the only known "cure" for the condition is prolonged rest from training and competition.

For these reasons, OTS represents one of the most feared conditions for competitive athletes (Urhausen, Kindermann 2002). Despite this, the prevalence of OTS in athletes can be high, although it appears to be influenced by factors including the performance level of the athlete, the type of sport undertaken, the length of time that the athlete has been competing and the amount of time that the study of OTS was conducted (Matos et al. 2010). Table 7.1 gives examples of research studies that have been conducted to investigate the prevalence of OTS across a range of different athletes and sports.

STUDY	SPORT AND ATHLETE INFORMATION	PREVALENCE OF OTS SYMPTOMS
Gustafsson et al. (2007)	908 adolescent athletes (mean age 17.1 years) across a variety of sports	1–9%
Koutedakis, Sharp (1998)	257 elite athletes (variety of sports)	15% over a 12-month training period (50% of these developed OTS symptoms in the 3-month competition phase)
Matos et al. (2010)	376 non-elite and elite athletes (mean age 15.1 years) across a variety of sports	29% at least once in their careers
Raglin et al. (2000)	231 competitive adolescent swimmers (mean age 14.8 years)	35% at least once in their careers

↑ Table 7.1: Some of the recent research studies investigating the prevalence of overtraining syndrome across a range of different athletes and sports

The lack of a clear, defining diagnostic measure of OTS, coupled with the variability of symptoms, makes the scientific study of OTS very difficult. The fact that it is unethical to induce a state of overtraining in athletes increases this difficulty. As a result, most research has used athletes deemed to already be suffering from OTS (which is subject to the inherent difficulties in diagnosis that have been previously described), or has induced a state of overreaching in research subjects as a model for studying OTS.

Females appear less susceptible to OTS than males (Shephard 2000). Additionally, more than one form of OTS has been proposed to exist, dependent in part on the type of athlete involved.

→ The **sympathetic** form of OTS is purported to affect athletes involved in short duration, explosive sports such as sprinting, jumping and throwing events (Armstrong, VanHeest 2002). This form of OTS is rare.

→ The more prevalent **parasympathetic** form of OTS is suggested to affect endurance athletes involved in lower intensity but longer duration events.

Insufficient research has been carried out to document the physiological and biochemical features of each of these forms of OTS (Lehman et al. 1992); therefore, the understanding of them is limited. However, existing work does shed light on various aspects of the condition, including the proposed key symptomatic markers of OTS. These markers are discussed below.

TEST YOURSELF

Explain why OTS is hard to diagnose.

Sudden, unexplained and persistent performance decrement

The critical, gold-standard criterion for the diagnosis of OTS is a rapid onset, persistent decrement in the exercise performance of an athlete that is not rectified even when modifications are made to training. This underperformance will persist despite a recovery period lasting from several weeks to months (Urhausen, Kindermann 2002). Of course, there are numerous factors other than excessive training demands that could cause a sudden and prolonged performance decrement. These factors must all be excluded prior to a tentative diagnosis of OTS being made. This is why, as discussed earlier, OTS is a condition of exclusion.

Chronic performance decrement is the gold-standard OTS diagnostic tool as it is the only potential marker of OTS present in all diagnosed cases. Unfortunately, detection of performance decrement is too late for any preventative action as OTS has already developed, and therefore underperformance is useless as a predictor or warning sign of the onset of OTS. It is therefore important that future research continues to strive to identify accurate, reliable prediction criteria for OTS in order to halt the development of the condition before it is too late.

While underperformance can be used as a criterion for the diagnosis of OTS, the obvious question is what causes the underperformance that is characteristic of OTS? Unfortunately, this is a difficult question to answer as it appears that OTS, as well as being a condition of exclusion, is also a very variable condition that presents differently from athlete to athlete, with the search for a uniform and reliable marker of the condition proving elusive. This may be a factor in why, once OTS has developed, it can prove extremely difficult to eradicate or overcome.

KEY POINT

The main indicator that an athlete has OTS is a decrease in their performance level. This means OTS is not spotted until it has already developed, making it impossible to predict or prevent.

The following sections detail some of the other common potential markers of OTS, which may contribute to the commonly observed underperformance associated with the condition.

Resting heart rate

An increase in resting heart rate is commonly cited as a sign of OTS and has been reported as such in some studies (Kindermann 1986; Stone et al. 1991). However, more recent work has failed to find significant alterations in resting heart rate in overreached individuals (Jeukendrup et al. 1992; Halson et al. 2002; Lehmann et al. 1992; Urhausen et al. 1998). While perhaps not a strong direct indicator of OTS, increased resting heart rate may indicate the presence of illness or disease. This may indicate an acutely reduced exercise tolerance, which if not accounted for could lead to development of OTS (Urhausen, Kindermann 2002).

Sleeping heart rate appears to be increased when individuals are overreached (Jeukendrup et al. 1992; Stray-Gundersen et al. 1986). This may be a more reliable measure of OTS than resting heart rate while awake, as it is less likely to be affected by confounding variables.

Chronic muscle soreness

Muscle soreness is a common, normal response to an acute bout of hard exercise, particularly unfamiliar exercise (for example, a session of weightlifting for someone who has not performed resistance training for a long period of time). This type of muscle soreness is termed delayed onset muscle soreness or DOMS. With appropriate recovery, this soreness usually dissipates 24-72 hours after the exercise bout.

Delayed onset muscle soreness has a number of causes including:

→ minute tears in the muscle tissue
→ pressure changes that produce fluid retention in the tissues surrounding the muscle
→ muscle spasms
→ overstretching and tearing of the connective tissue attached to the muscle
→ acute inflammation
→ a combination of these factors.

This acute muscle damage is widely believed to be a necessary occurrence for adaptations to training, as the response to healing this damage is to adapt the muscle, bone and/or connective tissue to ensure that greater stress is required in order to produce the same degree of damage (Smith 2000). In other words, these structures become "stronger".

However, some athletes suffering from OTS report muscle soreness that is not alleviated by rest or recovery. It appears that this may relate to the common short-term muscle damage discussed above. Trauma to the muscle or its associated structures, as occurs during high intensity, high volume and/or unaccustomed exercise, produces proteins that regulate the process of inflammation which is common in all forms of tissue damage and is an important part of the healing process for damaged tissue. These proteins are called cytokines. If tissue-damaging exercise continues without adequate rest and recovery, the local inflammation of the damaged tissues can last for much longer than normal, i.e. it can become chronic (Smith 2000). In this situation, a cascade effect can occur where the circulating cytokines produce even more cytokines and the tissue inflammation becomes systemic, i.e. it spreads to other organs and tissues of the body not affected by the initial trauma. This systemic inflammation can cause a collection of symptoms commonly encountered when a person is unwell, such as reduced appetite, feelings of lethargy or tiredness, sleep disturbances and altered mood state (Smith 2000).

As you read the rest of this section, you will see that these symptoms are also potential indicators of OTS. Therefore, this potential cause of chronic muscle soreness in OTS may occur at the early stage of the development of the condition, and may even be a prevalent causative factor of OTS (Smith 2000). However, chronic muscle soreness is a subjective measurement, i.e. the severity of muscle soreness can be perceived differently by different people. Therefore, the usefulness of it as a measure of OTS is restricted as a clear reference scale/value would be difficult to find (Urhausen, Kindermann 2002). Also, chronic muscle soreness is not consistently reported in all cases of OTS.

Reduced immune function

Reduced immune function has been proposed as a marker of OTS, probably due to the observation of an increased risk of upper respiratory tract infections (colds, sore throats) in overtrained athletes (Armstrong, VanHeest 2002).

Cytokines proteins that regulate the process of inflammation which is common in all forms of tissue damage and is an important part of the healing process for damaged tissue

However, upper respiratory tract infections can appear with the same frequency in both appropriately trained and overtrained athletes (Pyne et al. 2000). Furthermore, immunosuppression has been observed in overtrained athletes with and without the presence of upper respiratory tract infections (Fry et al. 1994; Nieman 1994). It therefore appears that attenuated immune function is not a reliable marker of OTS.

Indeed, reviews of the literature around overtraining and immune system function have concluded that overtrained athletes are not clinically immune deficient, but do have an increased risk of upper respiratory tract infections during periods of heavy training and for a one- to two-week period following this training (Mackinnon 1997). However, the key word here is "clinically". It is possible that immune function during overtraining may be compromised by relatively small changes in factors that are crucial for immune defences (Armstrong, VanHeest 2002).

More research is required into the potential influence of overtraining on immune function, preferably focusing on the development of mechanisms or models for the relationship between OTS and immune deficiency (Armstrong, VanHeest 2002), which may further our understanding of whether immunosuppression is a valid marker of OTS.

Sleep disturbance

Disturbances to normal sleep patterns are one of the few tools available to diagnose OTS under resting (i.e. non-exercising) conditions (Urhausen, Kindermann 2002). Sleep disturbances may be an early indicator of OTS (Urhausen et al. 1998) with the term "sleep disturbance" relating not only to an increased amount of time spent in an awake state, but also encompassing increased rates of movement during sleep which can compromise sleep quality (Taylor et al. 1997).

The exact causes of these proposed sleep disturbances with OTS are not clear, and may be due to factors such as increased muscle fatigue and soreness (Taylor et al. 1997), and altered immune system function and hormone regulation (Fry et al. 1994). However, as with many other proposed markers of OTS, sleep disturbances are not consistently observed (Taylor et al. 1997). Therefore, the usefulness of this as a marker of OTS should be questioned.

Sleep disturbances not only fewer hours spent sleeping but also increased movement during sleep that reduces the quality of sleep

Fatigue

Overtraining syndrome is characterized by persistent fatigue, particularly in endurance athletes (Armstrong, VanHeest 2002). The nature of this fatigue has not been well explored and can be attributed to central components (alterations in brain chemistry and function) and peripheral components such as alterations in circulating hormone levels, changes in muscle energy, metabolism etc. (Armstrong, VanHeest 2002; Purvis et al. 2010).

It is extremely difficult to pinpoint the exact cause and nature of fatigue. Questions about fatigue include the following:

→ Is fatigue psychological or physiological? (Purvis et al. 2010)
→ Does it stem from chronic fatigue associated with overreaching or OTS, or is it simply tiredness as a result of an isolated training session? (Purvis et al. 2010)
→ Is the fatigue a result of another diagnosed or undiagnosed condition?

It is also known that conditions such as depression, anemia, hypoglycemia and hypothyroidism can all cause fatigue (Kaltsas et al. 2010; Matza et al. 2011; Smith 2010). Furthermore, reductions in athletic performance can be related to protracted upper respiratory tract infections (Nieman 1998), rather than clinical fatigue associated with OTS.

The branched-chain amino acid hypothesis of overtraining states that excessive endurance training can lead to alterations in the blood transport of free fatty acids and amino acids, leading to an increase in the blood concentration of an essential amino acid called tryptophan (Tanaka et al. 1997). Increased blood concentrations of tryptophan will facilitate an increased movement of this amino acid into the brain, where it is converted to a neurotransmitter called serotonin (Petibois et al. 2002). One of the main functions of serotonin is to induce a feeling of sleepiness (Blomstrand et al. 1997). Therefore, it is possible that this could contribute to the sensation of fatigue reported by some athletes deemed to be suffering from OTS. However, the link between this hypothesis and OTS is not sufficiently strong to support this suggestion (Petibois et al. 2002). Therefore, many questions remain about the nature of fatigue during OTS and whether it is directly related to, or caused by, OTS.

Decreased appetite

Alterations in brain chemistry can affect a wide array of regulatory functions, one of which is appetite. As discussed in the section above, increased levels of serotonin in the brain can cause a feeling of sleepiness. Additionally, high serotonin levels can reduce a person's appetite. Therefore, potential alterations in neurotransmitter and/or hormone levels and function in OTS may contribute to reductions in appetite. However, as with other markers of OTS discussed above alterations in appetite levels are not consistently observed in individuals believed to be suffering from OTS.

The implications of decreased appetite in an overtrained state should be considered important in light of the potential for an exercising individual to become energy deficient (i.e. not consume sufficient calories to replenish those they use during exercise) when consuming a less than normal amount of food. This would be particularly relevant to carbohydrate availability, as carbohydrates are the body's main fuel source during exercise. If this energy-deficient state were to continue, the body would be forced to generate its energy by other means, for example by an increased use of amino acids as fuel. This may lead to increased production of serotonin, which could elicit appetite disregulation and sensations of fatigue as already discussed. Therefore, prolonged periods of exercise in the presence of an inadequate diet could exacerbate the overtraining state or contribute to the initiation of OTS (Armstrong, VanHeest 2002). However, this does require further study.

From the discussions in this section, it is clear that OTS is a real concern for any athlete. Once the condition has developed, it can be debilitating to the athlete's health and performance. Furthermore, the somewhat mysterious nature of the condition means that once it has developed, it cannot be easily dealt with or "cured". Therefore, the focus of an athlete and their coach and support team must surely be to optimize the athlete's training and competition performance while avoiding the development of OTS altogether. One of the ways in which they can accomplish this is to appropriately plan the athlete's training load.

KEY POINT

One of the difficulties in diagnosing OTS is that not all the symptoms are experienced by all athletes suffering from OTS and many of the symptoms can be put down to other causes.

TO THINK ABOUT

If you were planning to study OTS further, which of the symptoms would you choose to investigate? How might you go about this?

Mark is a 23-year-old triathlete. Six months ago he moved up to national level competition, and is hoping to represent his country at the European Championships next year. Before moving up to national level, Mark was a competitive triathlete for six years and won numerous local and regional competitions. Mark is generally healthy, although he suffers from mild asthma and has a tendency to develop anemia for which he regularly takes iron supplement tablets.

Since moving up to the national level, Mark has a new coach. He has redesigned Mark's training programme, as he believed the old programme would not have allowed Mark to reach his goal of competing at the European Championships. The new training programme is more intense, and has notably increased the volume of training compared with that Mark used to do. His coach is also entering him into more competitions, as he believes this will give Mark an advantage in the future.

One month into this new training regime, Mark suffered a close family bereavement. Two months into the new training regime, Mark's coach noticed that his performance in training was decreasing. Mark was finding it more difficult to do the same amount of training. He also noticed a difference in Mark's mood: he became less motivated and willing to train, and was prone to developing angry mood swings. His performance in competitions also worsened: his average finishing position fell from 4th to 11th. Mark noticed that he was feeling tired and sluggish; he would wake up in the morning still feeling exhausted, and for the rest of the day would feel like he wanted to go to sleep. Mark's appetite decreased and he lost several kilograms in weight.

Mark's coach is concerned and believes that Mark is at risk of having to stop training altogether. He thinks that Mark may be suffering from OTS.

Questions:
1. How would you respond to Mark's coach asking you: "Does Mark have OTS?" Justify your answer to the question.
2. What information would you get from Mark and his coach in order to be more confident in your diagnosis of whether or not Mark has OTS? Think about possible physical and medical tests or measurements, personal information from conversations etc. that you could use to get this information.
3. Based on your answers to the first two questions, do you think that Mark is suffering from OTS? Justify your response.
4. What would you recommend Mark and his coach do to try to solve the problem?

As discussed in the above section, knowledge of OTS is limited in part by ethical restrictions, namely the inability to induce OTS in research participants. The scientific study of OTS is beneficial for athletes as it enables the development of strategies to combat and prevent the syndrome. Therefore, the restriction on inducing a state of overtraining appears to be a conflict of interest.
1. Investigate the ethical implications of inducing OTS in research studies designed to understand and combat this syndrome.
2. Using the results of your investigations, provide a consensus statement on whether or not you believe it would be appropriate to enable the inducement of OTS in research studies. Justify your statement.

Periodization

Periodization is a structured, organized approach to training. This approach revolves around the completion of certain "phases" of training within a given time frame, with the aim of ensuring the athlete is in peak physical condition for the most important events of their sport. In the case of a track athlete, this may involve peaking for several competitions within a single year or season. For a soccer player, it may mean ensuring a high level of performance for the beginning of the season, and attempting to maintain that performance level for the duration of the season.

Structure of periodization

The exact structure of periodization will depend largely on the specific sport the athlete is involved in, the performance level and experience of the athlete, their performance potential and the sporting calendar they are working to. However, the overall theory of periodization contains broadly similar concepts. Generally, periodization is split into three phases: transition (usually post-season), preparation (pre-season) and competition. These phases are cyclical, i.e. one follows the other (see Figure 7.5).

Transition (post-season)

Following a competitive season, athletes will probably be mentally and physically fatigued. This fatigue can take some time to dissipate therefore it would be unwise to place an athlete directly into a new training phase. The main goal of the transition phase is to allow the athlete to recover and become refreshed before beginning the new pre-season phase of training. To do this, an effective transition phase should provide opportunities for the athlete to rest and relax, physically and mentally, while maintaining an acceptable level of physical fitness (Bompa 1999).

The approximate duration of the transition phase is three to four weeks, usually no longer than five weeks (Bompa 1999). An inappropriate approach to the transition phase is to encourage the athlete to rest completely with no exercise or physical activity undertaken at all as this will lead to detraining and lack of conditioning, losing gains made in the previous training cycle and placing greater stress on the subsequent cycle in order to regain this lost conditioning. A more effective approach is to encourage the athlete to take part in exercises and activities that are different to their normal training activities and in different environments. This will maintain fitness levels while providing the athlete with active rest and relaxation. For example, a 400-meter runner who normally trains on an athletic track may take part in off-road cycling or swimming in their transition phase.

↑ Figure 7.5: The cyclical nature of the main phases of periodization

Preparation (Pre-season)

As the name suggests, this periodization phase prepares the athlete with the physical, psychological, technical and tactical tools necessary to maximize their performance in the competitive phase of the season. As a result, it is crucial that this phase is constructed and executed appropriately, as failure here will mean an under-prepared athlete entering the competition phase. The preparation phase lasts approximately three to six months, depending on factors such as the athlete, whether it is an individual or a team sport and the structure of the sport's competitive season. Bompa (1999) recommends dividing the preparation phase into two distinct, but related, sub-phases.

→ **General preparatory phase** Here, the main focus is on developing the athlete's basic fitness/physical conditioning. This will enable the athlete to tolerate the greater volume and/or intensity of training as the preparatory phase progresses. Also, the development of technical and tactical skills will be focused on.

→ **Specific preparatory phase** In this second sub-phase of preparation, focus shifts to preparing the athlete for the competitive season. Training objectives do not differ significantly from the general preparatory phase, but training becomes more specific to the skills and technical requirements of the athlete's specific sport. This phase may involve taking part in competitions of lower importance than those undertaken during the competition season, such as friendly or exhibition competitions. This will provide the athlete and coach with feedback as to the athlete's competition "readiness".

Competition phase

As the name suggests, this is the phase of periodization that takes place during the athlete's competitive season. Clearly, it would not be appropriate for the athlete to be attempting to make large gains in fitness/technique during this phase, as the effort to do this would likely be detrimental to their competitive performance. Therefore, in this phase the goals for the athlete are to maintain general physical condition, continue improving sport-specific skills and technique, perfect their tactical approach to competition and gain competition experience (Bompa 1999). To achieve this, the athlete's training volume is reduced, and the focus shifts to working predominantly on breaking down and improving sport-specific skills.

Breaking down training phases

The phases of training discussed above can range from several weeks to several months in duration. Obviously, training must be structured and monitored during these periods, as waiting until the end of the phase to see if the desired training effects have been achieved would be very risky. Coaches can use three sub-phases of training, each of which can be applied within the three phases discussed above, to enable a structured, periodized training programme to occur throughout an athlete's season. These sub-phases are called microcycles, mesocycles and macrocycles. The organization of these sub-phases is shown in Figure 7.6.

Microcycles

A microcycle is a weekly training programme that forms an important foundation of the athlete's longer-term training programme. The microcycle includes all of the athlete's training and recovery sessions in that week. Within a microcycle, each training session will have a specific goal, and each of those goals will contribute to the overall goal of the training phase that the athlete is in. In other words, each microcycle will be specifically structured to achieve the overall goals of the athlete's training phase. Therefore, microcycles are very important to the overall success of an athlete's training programme.

Mesocycles

A mesocycle is a specific block of training designed to achieve a specific goal that fits within one of the training phases described in Figure 7.5. Each of these phases will contain a number of mesocycles; this is another way that the athlete's training is broken down and focused.

An example of a mesocycle is as follows. At some point within a four-month long preparation phase of an athlete's training, the coach may want the athlete to focus on improving his aerobic fitness (endurance). Therefore, the coach would construct a three-week block of training designed to focus on improving the athlete's endurance. This three-week block of training is a mesocycle.

Mesocycles are made up of microcycles. In this example, as the mesocycle lasted three weeks, it would have consisted of three microcycles (one week = one microcycle). Mesocycles allow the athlete to accomplish specific training goals, which also allow them to achieve the overall goal or goals of the whole training programme.

Macrocycle

Macrocycle is the name for the training programme of an athlete for the entire year or season. The macrocycle includes all of the main phases of training in Figure 7.6, as well as every mesocycle and microcycle. In this chapter, microcycles and mesocycles are discussed before the macrocycle. However, it is likely that a coach and athlete would initially identify the overall aims of the training programme by planning the macrocycle (usually by starting at the main competition point of the athlete's season and working backwards), and then work out the more specific goals or requirements of the programme (planning mesocycles and microcycles). Of course, the training programme would be flexible and subject to change as time goes on to account for unforeseen issues like athlete illness and injury that could affect training.

Figure 7.6 shows the organization of a periodized training programme. The macrocycle incorporates every training phase, mesocycle and microcycle. Each phase of training is made up of several mesocycles. Each mesocycle is subsequently composed of microcycles. As one microcycle is equal to one week of training, the number of microcycles will always correspond to the number of weeks that the mesocycle lasts.

Macrocycle the name of the athlete's training programme for an entire year or season

Mesocycle a block of training composed of several week-long microcycles

Microcycle a weekly training programme

TO DO

Choose one of the three phases, transition, pre-season or competition. Design your own training in a specific sport, thinking about the goals for each mesocycle and for each microcycle.

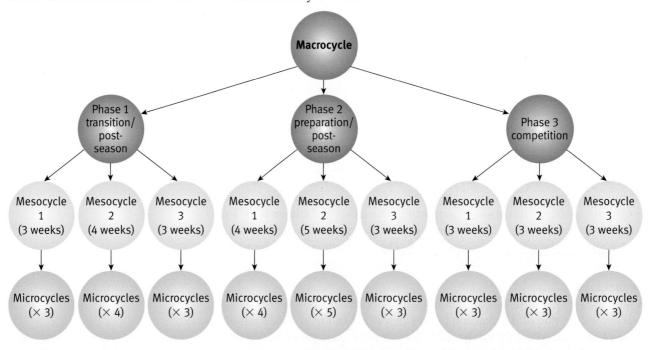

↑ Figure 7.6: The organization of the macrocycle, mesocycles and microcycles within a periodized training programme

THEORY OF KNOWLEDGE

Various concepts of periodization have been researched extensively. However, most research studies have only investigated small, short-duration sections of a periodization training programme, rather than the whole annual programme. The main reason for this is the logistical difficulties in conducting a year-long training study. This means that athletes and coaches are designing and implementing periodized training programmes without full supporting evidence that they are effective. This is contrary to the predominant research methodology of sports science, where a theory is developed and objectively tested, with the results supporting or refuting the stated theory. Evaluate the relative merits of two primary research approaches, deductive research and inductive research, within sports science research.

SUMMARY

- → Training is the systematic, repeated performance of structured exercise sessions with a specific goal in mind.
- → Appropriately structured training is crucial for optimizing an athlete's physical performance.
- → Many types of training are available for the athlete to choose from, based on individual sporting goals and requirements.
- → Failure to appropriately structure training can lead to undertraining or, more seriously, overtraining.
- → Prolonged, excessive training can lead to development of overtraining syndrome (OTS).
- → OTS affects athletes differently and has no clear diagnostic tool, therefore it is a condition of exclusion.
- → The exact cause(s) of OTS are not known and, once developed, OTS can last for several weeks or months.
- → OTS is characterized by persistent underperformance and failure to adapt to training, therefore it is a serious condition for any athlete.
- → Various markers of OTS have been proposed, but all are open to debate.
- → Once developed, the only potential method of alleviating OTS is to drastically reduce, or completely stop, training and competition.
- → OTS can be avoided by the use of periodization to appropriately plan and structure training loads.
- → The athlete's annual training plan (macrocycle) is broken down into key phases, each of which has its own more specific sub-phases (mesocycles and microcycles).
- → The exact structure of a periodized training programme will depend on the specific sport, performance level and experience of the athlete, their performance potential and the sporting calendar.

Self-study questions

1   Define the terms training, undertraining, overreaching and overtraining
2   List the **eight** types of training introduced in this chapter.
3   Describe cross-training.
4   Distinguish between overtraining and the overtraining syndrome.
5   Outline the primary symptom of the overtraining syndrome.
6   Explain why the overtraining syndrome is a "syndrome of exclusion".

7   Outline how you would determine whether an athlete you were working with was suffering from the overtraining syndrome.

8   Discuss the benefits of a periodized training programme.

9   Outline the three main phases of a periodized training programme.

10 Describe the terms *microcycle, mesocycle* and *macrocycle.*

DATA BASED QUESTION

A study was conducted comparing the effects of two different four-week training programmes on 5 000 meter running performance. One group was prescribed cardiovascular (CV) training, and one group was prescribed CV training plus inspiratory muscle training. All participants completed a 5 000 meter run as fast as possible before and after the training programme. The results of the study are described in the graph below.

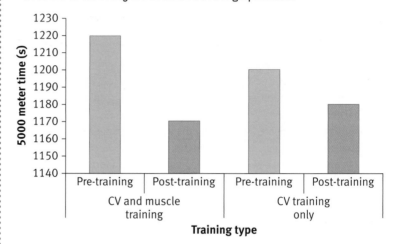

(Source: Edwards, A.M., Wells, C., and Butterly, R. 2008. "Concurrent inspiratory muscle and cardiovascular training differentially improves both perceptions of effort and 5000 m running performance compared with cardiovascular training alone." *British Journal of Sports Medicine.* Vol 42. Pp 823–7.)

1   Compare the pre-training running performance of the two groups.

2   Identify which training programme improved 5 000 meter running performance the most.

3   Would it have been beneficial to the above data to include an additional control group who completed a 5 000 meter run before and after the four-week period, but did not perform any structured training?

4   Evaluate the benefits of using multiple types of training to enhance sporting performance.

CHAPTER 8

Environmental factors and performance

By the end of this chapter students should be able to:

→ describe the production of heat in the body

→ state the role of the hypothalamus in body temperature regulation

→ outline the four physical processes of body heat loss

→ explain some aspects of the acclimatization process

→ identify some of the factors that affect individual heat stress

→ outline heat illness

→ introduce the challenge of exercise in cold environments

→ outline wind chill

→ introduce the clo unit and suggest implications for clothing during exercise.

Introduction

Hot and humid or cold environments add to the challenge that sport, exercise and health-related physical activity places on human thermoregulation. The added environmental stressors of extremes in ambient temperature and humidity can have a negative effect on performance. This can increase the risk of either heat illness or cold injury, and both can be life threatening. This chapter attempts to improve knowledge and understanding of environmental physiology and the implications for sport, exercise and health.

The production of heat in the human body

All energy originates from the sun as light energy (see Figure 8.1). Chemical reactions in plants convert light into stored chemical energy. In turn, we obtain energy by eating plants or eating animals that feed on plants. Energy is stored in food in the form of carbohydrates, fats and proteins, and we use this energy for muscle contraction. Foods are primarily composed of carbon, hydrogen, oxygen and nitrogen. The energy in food molecule bonds is chemically released within our cells. This energy is then stored in the form

66 **Earth, third planet from the sun, contains an awesome array of surface environments, ranging from Antarctica to the Sahara Desert. ... Although each locale presents danger to human life, we attempt to explore, work in, or inhabit these extreme environments. Physical training and athletic competition are no different.** 99

Lawrence Armstrong, 2000

66 **Life is an example of the way in which an energy system in its give and take with the energy-system around the earth can continue to maintain itself.** 99

Sir Charles Sherrington, 1940

of adenosine triphosphate – a high-energy compound for storing and conserving energy for muscles to contract and provide movement. Muscle contraction is about 20 per cent efficient, with around 80 per cent of this energy released as heat that must be removed from the body to avoid heat storage and too much of an increase in body temperature. For heat loss to occur, excess heat must be transported from the core of the body to the skin where the heat can be lost to the environment.

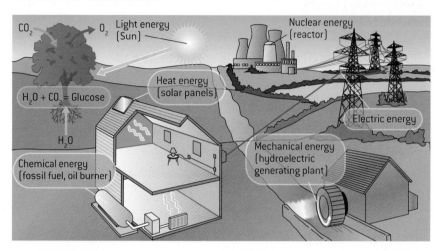

↑ Figure 8.1: Interconversions of forms of energy

TO THINK ABOUT

Energy from food is stored in adenosine triphosphate (ATP), and the splitting of ATP provides energy for muscle contraction. Energy can be measured in kilocalories (kcal). One kcal equals the amount of heat energy needed to raise 1 kg of water 1°C at 15°C. Carbohydrate and protein each provide about 4.1 kcal of energy per gram, compared to about 9 kcal per gram for fat. When energy is converted to heat during exercise this heat production can be measured in watts (W), where 1 W = 1 joule per second. In adults, this can range from around 70 W when resting, to more than 1 000 W during heavy exercise.

There are limited stores of ATP in muscle tissue. The average person will only have about 40–50g in total. This is enough to enable high-intensity activity for around 2 to 4 seconds. Hence the importance of resynthesis of ATP – see chapter 3.

KEY POINT

With globalization of sporting events, adventure tourism, oil exploration in the arctic, space travel etc., environmental stressors are more than simply the daily variation in local weather.

Temperature regulation

Knowledge of temperature regulation is important because of the impact of globalization that has led to increased participation in activities such as adventure tourism in extreme environments. Although performance is the main interest for athletes, safety must be pivotal when planning training programmes, events (such as the Marathon Des Sables: www.darbaroud.com/index-gb) and policies for sport and exercise. For example, a rise in body temperature of only a few degrees Celsius can result in your body proteins beginning to break apart at the molecular level.

Normal physiological range for core temperature

Humans are able to maintain a reasonably constant core body temperature (T_c) throughout their lives despite a wide range of ambient temperatures.

Common methods used for measuring core body temperature during exercise testing include:

→ a basic mercury thermometer (held in the mouth to measure oral temperature)
→ an ear thermistor (measures tympanic membrane temperature)
→ the use of a rectal probe (considered one of the most accurate methods)
→ a gastrointestinal radio pill (expensive; a small single use pill is swallowed and gives off a radio signal).

Core body temperature (T_C) is the temperature deep within the body. Shell temperature is the temperature near the body surface (e.g. around the skin). Depending on the environmental temperature, shell temperature is 1-6°C lower than T_c. We detect that our bodies are under thermal stress with the help of temperature sensors located throughout the body, such as the skin. The control center that functions as the body's thermostat is the hypothalamus located in the brain.

TO RESEARCH

Why is there no one true core body temperature?

When thinking about this, consider:
→ heat production in muscles in different parts of the body
→ blood flow
→ temperature difference between inside the body and near the body's surface.

The temperature of inactive skeletal muscle is between 33°C and 35°C.

KEY POINT

Under normal resting conditions in a temperate environment, body temperature is usually within ±1.0°C of average core body temperature.

TEST YOURSELF

1 State normal core body temperature.
2 At rest, how does the difference between core body temperature and skeletal muscle temperature help transfer heat?
3 When does the heat transfer gradient flow from the body?

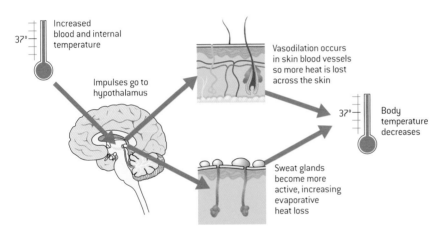

Increased blood and internal temperature

Impulses go to hypothalamus

Vasodilation occurs in skin blood vessels so more heat is lost across the skin

Body temperature decreases

Sweat glands become more active, increasing evaporative heat loss

↑ Figure 8.2: The hypothalamus and temperature control

Thermoregulation

Body temperature reflects a careful balance between heat production and heat loss. When we start to exercise there is an increase an heat production within the skeletal muscles, i.e. skeletal muscle temperature rises. Sometimes there is an imbalance such as too much heat production and too little heat loss, and this leads to a medical condition called hyperthermia.

Environmental heat stress increases the need for sweating and circulatory responses to remove body heat. The heat from deep in your body (the core) is moved by the blood to your skin, and transferred to the environment by any of four mechanisms.

→ **Conduction** Heat generated deep in your body can be conducted through tissue to the body's surface and to the clothing or air (or water) that is in direct contact with your skin. The rate of conductive heat loss depends on the temperature gradient between the skin and surrounding surfaces. However, in most hot and humid situations, conduction accounts for less than 2 per cent of heat loss.

Hyperthermia an elevated body temperature, usually above 39°C (102°F)

KEY POINT

Evaporation of sweat is potentially the most important mechanism of heat dissipation, dependent upon the relative humidity of the environment.

→ **Convection** Convection involves moving heat from one place to another by the motion of air (or water) movement. For example, blood transfers heat by convection from the deep body tissues to the skin. If air movement is minimal, the air next to the skin warms and heat loss slows down. Conversely, if cooler air continually replaces warmer air around the body, such as on a windy day, heat loss increases.

→ **Radiation** Radiation is the transfer of energy waves that are sent out from one object and absorbed by another. For example, solar energy from direct sunlight can be reflected from snow, sand or water to help warm a person. The body absorbs radiant heat energy when the temperature of the environment is higher than skin temperature.

→ **Evaporation** As the environmental (ambient) temperature increases, conduction, convection and radiation decrease their effectiveness for helping body heat loss. When this happens evaporative cooling (conversion of sweat from liquid to water vapour) is the main way for the body to lose heat during exercise.

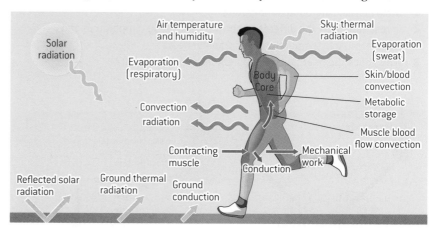

↑ Figure 8.3: The potential avenues for heat exchange during exercise

Water vaporizing from the respiratory passages and skin surface (referred to as insensible water loss) continually transfers heat from the body to the environment (580 kilocalories of heat for each litre of water vaporized). This accounts for about 80 per cent of total heat loss when you are physically active, but only about 20 per cent of body heat loss at rest.

The body's surface contains between two and four million sweat glands. Sweat production over a given/particular area of the skin is dependent on both the density of sweat glands (i.e. the number per cm^2 of skin surface) and the amount of sweat per gland. In most people, the back and chest have the greatest sweating rates. The limbs have relatively high sweating rates *only* after a substantial elevation in core temperature.

Heat production increases almost immediately at the onset of exercise, causing the core temperature to rise. The increase in sweating during exercise reflects this increase in body temperature. However, sweating is not 100 per cent efficient, because some sweat can drip from the body and not be evaporated.

Maximal evaporative heat loss from the body occurs when sweat is vaporized from the skin. Sweat that either drips off the skin, or is towelled off, does not provide any evaporative cooling. Sweat evaporation is also influenced by the amount of moisture in the air. For example, dry air receives vaporized sweat readily, whereas wet air receives little evaporated sweat because it is already heavily laden with moisture. The relative humidity provides an index of the amount of water in the air, and represents the most important factor in determining the effectiveness of evaporative heat loss.

KEY POINT

When the environmental temperature is above skin temperature, evaporative heat exchange will account for almost all heat loss.

KEY POINT

The respiratory system is important for conductive, convective and/or evaporative heat exchange. Inspired air, that is air that is breathed in, is warmed (and humidified) by the respiratory tract and even air below 0°C is near body temperature by the time it reaches the alveoli.

Unlike most animals, in humans, respiratory evaporative cooling is much less efficient.

KEY POINT

Dehydration is a significant concern when losing body fluid through increased sweating in the heat.

THEORY OF KNOWLEDGE

The 27th Sultan Marathon des Sables came to an end on Saturday 21 April 2012 in Merzouga. For a week, over 800 runners and nearly 400 organization members have been walking, running or driving through the Moroccan desert. Yet their mark on the six bivouac sites or on the race track is not so easy to spot, even a caravan of that size must leave a print, especially a carbon footprint. "The Earth doesn't belong to us" says Patrick Bauer, race director. "It's very important for us that we erase all traces of our passage." And this is carried out in many ways. "Each water bottle given to a competitor bears his or her number, both on the cap and on the actual bottle. If we find either lying around, there's a penalty attached. Pocket ash-trays are given to all members of staff: we don't want any cigarette ends lying around either. Scandinavian toilets have been made available to the whole caravan, both for runners and staff members. For several years now, we've added an incinerator truck to the caravan so as to burn all our waste."

The environment team of the Sultan Marathon des Sables has ten members. "We must leave each site as we found it" says Morad, who has been on the race for 12 years and who is responsible, among other things, for the protection of the environment. "In my everyday life, I work in the tourism industry. I like open spaces and I must leave them intact for the generations to come. Out of respect for the Earth and for our land. Of all the competitions organized in Morocco, the Sultan Marathon des Sables is by far the most exemplary."

(Source: www.darbaroud.com)

Identify a sporting event that is taking place outdoors in your own country. Try to find out how the participants and organizers protect the environment and "leave them intact for the generations to come."

THEORY OF KNOWLEDGE

In 2012 the Green School in Bali (Indonesia) was voted the greenest school on earth: www.greenschool.org

1. Discuss what a "green" school is and why this might be important.
2. Compare the Green School in Bali with your own school.
3. Suggest what a "green" physical education curriculum might be.

Hot environments

Heat acclimatization

Homeostasis is the condition in which the body's internal environment remains relatively constant, within physiological limits. Adaptations are the body's attempts to counteract stressors, such as heat, humidity, and cold, and maintain homeostasis. There are at least 31 climatic zones around the world ranging from year-round freezing conditions to daily hot temperatures of around 45°C. Each zone is inhabited by people who have acclimatized to accommodate the environmental conditions.

Acclimatization is a natural adaptation, for example, to improve exercise performance and heat tolerance in a hot climate. Heat acclimatization requires exercise in a hot environment, not merely exposure to heat, and usually requires 10 to 14 days. It results in better matching of thirst to the body's water needs and increased total body water (by as much as 5 per cent).

Your total exercise-heat exposure time each day should work towards 90-100 minutes. However, you should reach this gradually by increasing duration and intensity. Important signs of heat acclimatization during sub-maximal exercise in the heat are a lower heart rate and core temperature, and a higher sweat rate. Chronic adaptations to exercise that can improve exercise performance in the heat include:

→ increased plasma volume
→ earlier onset of sweating (and at a lower core temperature)

Homeostasis the condition in which the body's internal environment remains relatively constant, within physiological limits

KEY POINT

Heat stress depends upon the environmental conditions (ambient temperature and humidity), clothing, exercise intensity and acclimatization.

TO RESEARCH

Distinguish between the terms acclimatization and acclimation.

KEY POINT

The acute acclimatization
response, such as changes in
core temperature and heart rate
response, occurs in the first
five days of exposure to heat.
Whereas the chronic acclimatization
response, such as changes in the
onset of sweating and the rate
of sweat production takes about
9–14 days to be about 80 per cent
complete. However, the degree of
acclimatization is highly variable
between individuals and some who
engage in sports competitions in
the heat never fully adapt.

→ a more dilute sweat composition (i.e. electrolyte loss reduced)
→ reduced rate of muscle glycogen use
→ decreased psychological perception of effort.

Heat stress during a single exercise bout increases the metabolic rate (including increased muscle glycogen use) to perform sub-maximal exercise. With acclimatization there is a reduced rate of muscle glycogen use when performing at the same relative sub-maximal exercise intensity. This may help improve endurance performance.

Sub-maximal exercise refers to the intensity of an exercise session and means exercising below maximum effort. With acclimatization you are able to maintain sub-maximal exercise for longer periods of time. For example, classification of exercise intensity could be based on a percentage of maximal heart rate (HRmax), such as:

→ 35–50% of HRmax = light exercise intensity (i.e. sub-maximal light)
→ 60–79% of HRmax = moderate exercise intensity (i.e. sub-maximal moderate)
→ 80–89% of HRmax = heavy exercise intensity (i.e. sub-maximal heavy).

Higher levels of aerobic fitness decrease the intensity and duration needed to maintain acclimatization (or to re-acclimate) to heat. The major benefits of heat acclimatization gradually disappear if not maintained by continued heat exposure. The benefits of heat acclimatization are retained for about a week after returning to a cooler environment, but approximately 75 per cent of the benefits will be lost after about three weeks away from the heat exposure.

Heat illness

The hyperthermia that accompanies exercise in the heat can lead to increased risk of heat illness. This is because more people are participating in extreme sports and ultra-endurance events worldwide, such as the Marathon des Sables.

Hyperthermia, heat exhaustion, and heatstroke are recognized as major risks during exercise in hot or hot and humid environments. Such problems can even occur in cool conditions with intense or prolonged exercise such as marathons or triathlons. Heat exposure can also be a significant clinical problem for non-exercising populations. For example, the 2011 summer heat wave in the USA was blamed for at least 24 deaths, including an 18-year-old landscape gardener. This can happen even where summers are traditionally very hot and the population is heat acclimatized (Yip et al. 2008).

For most people, a higher level of aerobic fitness can provide protection from heat stress during exercise in the heat, similar to that observed with acclimatization to hot environments. These benefits include:

→ greater evaporative heat loss through improved sweating response
→ initiation of sweating at a lower core temperature
→ greater sensitivity of sweating response to increasing core temperatures
→ an elevated plasma volume and cardiac output, minimizing the competition for blood distribution between skeletal muscle and skin.

Individual variability in heat tolerance

Some of the major factors that may predispose individuals to heat intolerance during exercise in hot environments are:

→ lack of acclimatization
→ low fitness
→ large body mass

KEY POINT

Competing in sport, exercising or
participating in physical activity
in the heat can physiologically
challenge individuals to maintain
effective temperature regulation.
This is dependent upon a range of
factors including your age, fitness
level and acclimatized status.

→ dehydration

→ age (the elderly or pre-pubertal children).

The range and severity of heat illness is shown in Table 8.1.

Heat illness: Causes, signs and symptoms, and prevention			
CONDITION	CAUSES	SIGNS AND SYMPTOMS	PREVENTION
Heat cramps	Intense, prolonged exercise in the heat Muscle fatigue Sodium loss in sweat	Pain Involuntary spasms of active muscles Low serum Na$^+$	Stop exercise; rehydrate Massage/light stretching
Heat syncope	Peripheral vasodilation and pooling of venous blood Hypotension Hypohydration	Light-headedness Partial/complete loss of consciousness Person looks pale High core temperature	Acclimatize Rehydrate Reduce exertion on hot days Avoid standing still in the heat
Heat exhaustion	Increasing negative water balance	Fatigue/exhaustion Loss of movement coordination/dizziness Flushed skin Reduced sweating High core temperature	Remove subject to shaded/air-conditioned area Hydrate before and during exercise Acclimatize
Heat stroke	Thermoregulatory failure Dehydration	Core temperature >41°C Lack of sweating Disorientation/twitching/seizures/coma	Immediate whole body cooling Acclimatize Adapt activities to climatic constraints

↑ Table 8.1: Heat illness

Exercise capacity and performance in hot conditions

Fatigue and reduced exercise capacity in the heat can have many underlying causes, ranging from direct temperature effects on the brain's cognitive functioning through to changes in the muscular and cardiovascular systems. For example, in the cardiovascular system, this is likely due to competition for blood flow to both active muscles and the skin for conductive heat exchange. The loss of plasma volume through sweating and dehydration adds to the cardiovascular strain.

While mild muscle warming or warm ambient temperatures help muscle force generation, hyperthermia has a negative effect and impairs the level of maximal muscle force generation and muscle activation. Impaired mental activity associated with hyperthermia may be connected to decreases in brain blood flow. For example, the feeling of lethargy during exercise is often reported with people experiencing hyperthermia. This may reflect a reduced state of arousal and is commonly associated with higher ratings of perceived exertion during exercise. Thus, exercise in the heat increases thermal strain, such as during a game of tennis in a hot and humid environment, and can result in hyperthermia.

The development of hyperthermia impairs exercise capacity and performance in hot environments, and often can result in an earlier than planned reduction in intensity during exercise. One of the reasons for this is that the temperature of the brain is dependent on the temperature of the blood that supplies it. Some studies have shown benefits of cooling the head and neck during exercise in hot environments. This knowledge has been used to good effect by

TO RESEARCH

Some matches of the 2022 soccer World Cup will take place in Qatar during the month of July. Research the typical July weather in Qatar and explain how you would plan an acclimatization training programme to try to prevent heat illness and optimize the performance of a participating national soccer team.

181

Novak Djokovic (world number 1 tennis player in 2011-12) when using a towel packed with ice and placed around his neck between games during the 2011 Australian Tennis Open in the hot summer conditions of Melbourne.

Minimizing exercise-related increases in core body temperature *before* exercise (pre-cooling) in hot environments is more frequently being used to try to lessen the effects of heat stress on performance. Wearing ice vests during warm-up seems to reduce the physiological and perceptual results of exercise in the heat. For example, the Australian rowing team at the 1996 Atlanta Olympics used vests containing ice packs during warm-ups before competition.

There is some good evidence that pre-cooling interventions such as ice baths and ice vests may act to improve performance in events that rely on a high and sustained aerobic effort (e.g. running, rowing, long distance cycling) by delaying heat build-up during the warm-up. Pre-cooling can also decrease perceptions of heat stress and thereby possibly promote an up-regulation of work intensity, i.e. a faster running pace/cycling speed or higher stroke rate in rowing. Thus, practical strategies, such as wearing an ice vest during the warm-up (pre-cooling) and using an ice packed towel (during breaks in the event), seem to be effective in reducing heat stress to help performance in hot environments (Skein et al. 2011).

TO RESEARCH

There is wide inter-individual variability in response to a set environment and exercise load. Intra-individual response can also vary based on acclimatization, hydration, drugs (e.g. caffeine) and so on.

Moran et al. (1998, 1999) have developed an individual heat strain index from a combination of heart rate and core body temperature, as well as a cold strain index based on core and skin temperatures.

Find out more about this index and how it is measured.

Hypothermia low body temperature that has different clinical categories depending on the severity

THEORY OF KNOWLEDGE

Initial concern about the possible effects of global warming on infections has declined with the realization that the spread of tropical diseases is likely to be limited and controllable. However, the direct effects of heat already cause substantial numbers of deaths among vulnerable people in the summer. Action to prevent these deaths from rising is the most obvious medical challenge presented by a global rise in temperature. Strategies to prevent such deaths are in place to some extent, and they differ between the United States and Europe. Air conditioning has reduced them in the United States, and older technologies such as fans, shade, and buildings designed to keep cool on hot days have generally done so in Europe. Since the energy requirements of air conditioning accelerate global warming, a combination of the older methods, backed up by use of air conditioning when necessary, can provide the ideal solution. Despite the availability of these technologies, occasional record high temperatures still cause sharp rises in heat-related deaths as the climate warms. The most important single piece of advice at the time a heat wave strikes is that people having dangerous heat stress need immediate cooling, e.g. by a cool bath. Such action at home can be more effective than transporting the patient to hospital. Meanwhile, it must not be forgotten that cold weather in winter causes many more deaths than heat in summer, even in most subtropical regions, and measures to control cold-related deaths need to continue.

(Source: www.ncbi.nlm.nih.gov/pubmed/15586600 November 2004. *Southern Medical Journal*. Vol 97, number 11. Pp 1093–9.)

Climate change with global warming may affect health, as reflected in the article above. Discuss the potential impact that global warming may have on training heart rate to monitor exercise intensity (chapter 6).

Cold environments

The main factors for environmental cold stress during outdoor activities in cold weather are air temperature and wind speed. Normally we dress ourselves to decrease sensations of cold when exposed to a cold environment, to prevent dangerous drops in core body temperature, and to avoid cold injury including hypothermia. Hypothermia can be defined simply as low body temperature, but there are different clinical categories (mild, moderate, severe, profound).

It is not uncommon to experience mild hypothermia, and the most commonly cited core body temperatures for mild hypothermia are around 34 to 35°C. The warning signals for hypothermia include uncontrollable shivering, slurred speech, stumbling, drowsiness, and inability to stand and move after a rest. Ironically, although wearing clothing helps ensure exposure to cold is minimized, this can reduce the potential for heat loss from evaporative cooling, radiation and convection. In fact, you need to be careful during exercise in the cold because too much body insulation from clothing could lead to exercise-induced hyperthermia, as well as exercise-induced dehydration!

There is a large potential for heat loss from the head. The head represents only about 8 per cent of the body's total surface area, but nearly 30 to 40 per cent of body heat is lost through the head region. This is because vasoconstriction does not seem to occur in the brain circulation during exercise in cold weather.

Humans possess much less capacity for adaptation to long-term cold exposure than to prolonged heat exposure. Nowadays, there are many recreational, competitive and occupational activities in cold environments, and increased participation in winter sports such as cross-country skiing, hiking and snowboarding all expose the body to cold air and wind chill. When the ambient temperature is colder than body temperature heat loss occurs, and wind increases heat loss by convection.

The British Antarctic Survey (BAS) team, as an occupational example, carry out research and surveys in the Antarctic and surrounding regions. For instance, they use observations from polar regions to improve our understanding of how natural and human-induced factors contribute to climate change.

Acute response

With cold exposure skin and core temperature decreases, and this stimulates the hypothalamus. The peripheral response to cold involves vasoconstriction of the skin and skeletal muscle circulations, decreasing blood flow and therefore convective heat transfer between the body's core and shell (skin, subcutaneous fat and skeletal muscle). Cold exposure results in the stimulation of shivering. The characteristics of shivering include the following:

→ involuntary, repeated, rhythmic muscle contractions
→ can start immediately or after several minutes of exposure to the cold
→ there is minimal movement
→ highly effective method of heat production from metabolic energy
→ usually begins in the torso and then spreads to limbs
→ as shivering intensity increases, more muscles are used
→ intense shivering can equate to more than 1 L.min^{-1} of oxygen consumption.

> **" A man in the cold is not necessarily a cold man. "**
>
> Bass, 1960

TO RESEARCH

Galloway and Maughan (1997) found that endurance cycling performance is optimal in an ambient temperature of 11°C, and there was a 13% decline in endurance cycling performance at 4°C.

Can you find out the optimal temperature for other sporting activities?

TO THINK ABOUT

During cold exposure there can be a reduction in muscle efficiency associated with:
→ decrease in muscle contractility
→ decrease in the velocity and power of muscle contraction
→ change in the pattern of muscle fiber recruitment.

KEY POINT

Body composition (ratio of body fat mass to lean muscle mass), body size (ratio of skin surface area to body volume) and training status influence ability to cope with cold exposure.

TO RESEARCH

During the same relative sub-maximal exercise intensity in a cold compared to a temperate environment, explain what happens to economy (the rate of oxygen uptake).

Exercise in cold environments

If heat production from sub-maximal exercise during cold exposure is not enough to balance heat loss from the body to the cold environment, there will be an increase in oxygen uptake from shivering because of the added oxygen requirement for metabolism in the shivering muscles. Cold exposure can also affect cardiovascular responses to sub-maximal exercise. Compared to exercise at the same intensity in a temperate climate, exercise in the cold results in lower heart rates and increased stroke volume to maintain cardiac output. One explanation for the lower heart rates and stroke volume increase during exercise in the cold is increased central blood volume resulting from peripheral vasoconstriction.

During cold exposure the amount of clothing required to maintain thermal balance will depend upon the exercise intensity. It is good advice to dress in layers during exercise in the cold and remove layers as exercise intensity increases to prevent too much net body heat gain (because of too much clothing insulation).

Fuel utilization during cold exposure

Prolonged exercise is marked by the eventual depletion of carbohydrate stores and inability to maintain blood glucose. In cold environments, it is thought that the added energy requirements of shivering increase glycogen breakdown during exercise. There is good evidence that shivering, like low intensity exercise, relies on fat (lipids) as the main energy source, and blood glucose, muscle glycogen and even protein can be used as well. The relative contribution of fats, carbohydrates and proteins to heat production during cold exposure depends on whether glycogen levels are low or high, shivering intensity, and the severity and type of cold exposure. Recent thinking is that more carbohydrate intake may be required for prolonged exposure or exercise in the cold (Haman 2002, 2006).

Body composition and size, exercise and cold stress

Cold stress depends on environmental temperature and exercise intensity (metabolic rate) as well as the resistance to heat flow provided by body fat. Fat is an effective insulator because its capacity for transferring heat is relatively low, helping to slow down heat transfer from the inside of the body to the body's surface. This enables individuals with greater amounts of body fat to retain more of their heat and reduce the effects of cold environments (by increasing the effectiveness of skin vasoconstriction). Thus, as the amount of fat increases, the rate of heat loss decreases, that is, heat loss is inversely related to the amount of (subcutaneous) fat. This partly explains why people with more fat can generally tolerate a lower water or air temperature than lean people before shivering begins.

The ratio of body surface area to body mass affects the rate of heat loss. A larger surface area to body mass ratio makes heat loss easier, and this can be advantageous in a warm environment. In adult males and females with the same body mass and similar surface areas, the females have better insulation because of their greater fat content. However, females tend to have a relatively smaller total muscle mass than males. This reduces their capacity for heat production from shivering compared to men.

Children are smaller and lighter than adults and, therefore, tend to have a large area to mass ratio compared to generally taller, heavier adults. This helps explain why children find it more difficult to maintain normal body temperature in cold environments, making them more at risk of hypothermia. During exercise in the cold children can partly compensate for their relatively large body to body mass ratio by being more active (increasing energy metabolism) and having a more effective constriction of the blood vessels supplying the skin and the skeletal muscles (i.e. increased insulation of the shell of the body).

Human adaptation to chronic cold exposure

Individuals can adapt to cold environments, but have less physiological adaptation to chronic cold stress than to prolonged heat exposure. The cold adaptation, which is slower to develop than heat acclimatization, results in less discomfort, enhances dexterity, helps prevent cold illnesses and injuries and improves survival in a cold environment. There are three main adaptive responses by which your body regulates its core temperature from chronic exposure to a cold environment:

→ **Habituation** is a desensitisation of the normal response to cold
→ **Metabolic acclimatization** for example, greater shivering response to increase heat production
→ **Insulative acclimatization** increased vasoconstriction to enhance heat conservation.

> **KEY POINT**
>
> The human body is less able to adapt to the stress of cold environments than it is to hot environments. To protect against cold exposure, humans depend upon behavioural change, such as moving to shelter and wearing more clothes and/or more appropriate clothing.

Wind chill

When exercising outdoors the air temperature is not the only factor in the amount of thermal stress from cold that you experience. Both air temperature and wind influence the coldness of an environment experienced by an individual. Therefore, there is a large difference in how cold we feel on a cold but calm day as opposed to a cold plus windy day. Wind increases the rate of heat loss (via convection and conduction) because the warmer insulating air layer surrounding the body continually exchanges with the cooler ambient air.

Windproof clothing and/or doing strenuous exercise reduces wind chill effects. The wind chill index illustrates the cooling effect of wind on exposed skin for different temperatures and wind velocities. The effects of increasing wind speed with decreasing air temperature, including values for dangerous exposure to frostbite, are shown in Figure 8.4.

TEST YOURSELF

1 When running outdoors in an air temperature of −10°F on a windy day (wind speed = 25 mph):
   i   what is the wind chill index?
   ii how long before frostbite could occur?

Wind direction is important. For example, when running at 8 mph *into* a 12 mph headwind, this creates a relative wind speed of 20 mph. When running at 8 mph with 12 mph wind at one's back, this creates a relative wind speed of 4 mph.

2 When running at 10 mph into a 20 mph headwind, what is the relative wind speed?
3 When running at 10 mph into a 20 mph headwind in an air temperature of −25°F:
   i   what is the wind chill index?
   ii how long before frostbite could occur?

Wind Chill Chart

Temperature (°F)

Calm	40	35	30	25	20	15	10	5	0	−5	−10	−15	−20	−25	−30	−35	−40	−45
5	36	31	25	19	13	7	1	−5	−11	−16	−22	−28	−34	−40	−46	−52	−57	−63
10	34	27	21	15	9	3	−4	−10	−16	−22	−28	−35	−41	−47	−53	−59	−66	−72
15	32	25	19	13	6	0	−7	−13	−19	−26	−32	−39	−45	−51	−58	−64	−71	−77
20	30	24	17	11	4	−2	−9	−15	−22	−29	−35	−42	−48	−55	−61	−68	−74	−81
25	29	23	16	9	3	−4	−11	−17	−24	−31	−37	−44	−51	−58	−64	−71	−78	−84
30	28	22	15	8	1	−5	−12	−19	−26	−33	−39	−46	−53	−60	−67	−73	−80	−87
35	28	21	14	7	0	−7	−14	−21	−27	−34	−41	−48	−55	−62	−69	−76	−82	−89
40	27	20	13	6	−1	−8	−15	−22	−29	−36	−43	−50	−57	−64	−71	−78	−84	−91
45	26	19	12	5	−2	−9	−16	−23	−30	−37	−44	−51	−58	−65	−72	−79	−86	−93
50	26	19	12	4	−3	−10	−17	−24	−31	−38	−45	−52	−60	−67	−74	−81	−88	−95
55	25	18	11	4	−3	−11	−18	−25	−32	−39	−46	−54	−61	−68	−75	−82	−89	−97
60	25	17	10	3	−4	−11	−19	−26	−33	−40	−48	−55	−62	−69	−76	−84	−91	−98

(Left axis: Wind (mph))

Frostbite times   ▢ 30 minutes   ▢ 10 minutes   ▢ 5 minutes

↑ Figure 8.4: The wind-chill index

Frostnip the initial freezing of the superficial skin tissue

Frostbite the continued cooling and freezing of cells

Cold air exposure, hypothermia and frostbite

In cold climates of the earth, the main environmental stressors that disturb homeostasis are:

→ air temperature below skin and core body temperature
→ air movement across the body (accelerating loss of body heat)
→ cold, dry air
→ cold water immersion (which causes faster cooling of skin and core body temperature compared to cold air at the same temperature).

The main life-threatening cold injury is a dangerous loss of body heat leading to hypothermia as discussed above. The risk for hypothermia on land increases during cold, moist and windy conditions.

The fingers and toes are poorly designed for holding heat, both in their anatomical arrangement and in their pattern of circulatory control. Long and narrow digits result in a relatively high ratio of surface area to volume for convective heat loss. Also, the low muscle mass and low amount of fat in the feet and hands provide minimal heat-generating capacity and insulation against heat loss. Additionally, upon initial exposure to cold, vasoconstriction can very rapidly decrease distribution of blood flow to the extremities and divert blood and heat to the core and vital organs such as the heart and brain. Thus freezing cold injuries like frostnip and frostbite are more likely to happen in the feet, hands and exposed parts such as the nose and ears. Factors that are associated with getting frostbite include alcohol use, low physical fitness, fatigue, dehydration, and poor peripheral circulation, but it can happen to anyone. However, frostbite cannot occur if the air temperature is above 0°C (32°F).

The rate of local heat loss and cell damage from (convective) heat loss are the main determinants of frostnip and frostbite. Frostnip is the initial freezing of the superficial skin tissue. It is painful but typically does not produce long-term damage. Frostbite is continued cooling and freezing of cells. This can lead to the destruction of cells, with the damaged regions becoming insensitive to touch. Due to the risk of infection and gangrene, it is recommended that re-warming and frostbite treatment occur in a medical setting if possible.

Cold–wet injuries

Radiation and sweat evaporation are the primary mechanisms for heat loss in air. However, heat conduction away from the body is greater during exposure to a given cold air temperature when skin and clothing are wet. The body loses heat more quickly in water than it does in air of the same temperature. Further increases in heat loss occur in water when there is water movement over the body because of the increased contribution of convective heat loss. However, individuals vary greatly with respect to the water temperature they can tolerate.

Body heat loss from conduction is greatest during immersion in cold water. The most important predictors for the onset of cold–wet injuries are the water temperature and duration of exposure.

Too cold to exercise?

The direct effect of exercise in the cold is the breathing of cold (and dry) air. As alveolus tissue is thin, moist and fragile, the inhaled air must be warmed (and humidified) before entering the lungs. Therefore, one potential hazard is the possibility of asthma attacks. For asthmatic individuals and those with exercise-induced asthma, the breathing of cold air can trigger shortness of breath and reduced exercise capacity.

Stenstrud et al. (2007) compared exercise in a 20°C versus a -18°C air temperature environment. They found that individuals with exercise-induced asthma had a lower maximum oxygen uptake and slower running speeds in the cold air environment (-18°C) compared to the 20°C environment. For all athletes, high breathing (ventilation) rates during exercise in cold air temperatures can result in significant heat loss and potentially dehydration. Therefore, ensuring adequate hydration is important during exercise in the cold. However, even for people with respiratory issues aggravated by cold air inhalation, the health benefits of physical activity likely outweigh any potential health risks if appropriate precautions are taken.

Castellina et al. (2006) highlighted some important preventative measures to consider when exercising in the cold.

→ Clothing insulation requirement is dependent on the exercise intensity and environment, and too much clothing insulation can lead to heat stress.
→ In high wind chill conditions, people should ensure that exposed skin is kept to a minimum.
→ The feet, hands, face and ears are the locations at highest risk for frostbite and other cold injuries. Therefore, care must be taken to provide insulation or supplemental heating to the feet, hands, face and ears.
→ A higher core body temperature promotes blood flow to the extremities, so it is important to ensure that core body temperature is preserved.
→ Carbohydrate ingestion is recommended to allow for increased glucose metabolism during exercise in the cold.

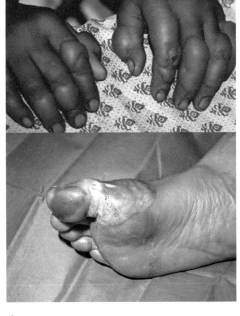
↑ Frostbite of the fingers and toes

Cold water immersion

The initial respiratory and cardiac responses to cold water immersion are thought to be responsible for a significant number of open water deaths each year. The initial responses to cold water immersion include tachycardia, a reflex inspiratory gasp and uncontrollable hyperventilation, causing difficulty for individuals trying to hold their breath if submerged.

Tachycardia is an abnormally rapid resting heartbeat or pulse rate (over 100 beats per min) and hyperventilation is a rate of respiration higher than that required to maintain a normal partial pressure of carbon dioxide in the blood. For example, going from average resting adult values of 12 breaths and 6 litres in ventilation per minute to more than 30 breaths and 80 litres in ventilation per minute when immersed in 10°C cold water (Tipton et al. 1998).

The main stimulus for the cold shock response described above appears to be the rapid drop in skin temperature upon immersion in the cold water. Swimming in cold water results in significant redistribution of blood to the core, intense peripheral vasoconstriction and reduced muscle blood flow through the limbs. Additionally, sudden immersion in cold water can result in a reflex contraction of skeletal muscles making proper neural coordination difficult.

↑ Many people enjoy swimming outdoors in winter environments!

Effects of clothing

Various types of specialist clothing are available to provide protection during physical activity, exercise, sport, recreational and occupational activity in cold conditions. The amount of clothing insulation required to maintain body temperature (and comfort) by insulating against excessive body heat loss during cold weather activity will depend upon the ambient temperature and the exercise intensity. The standard unit of clothing insulation is known as the clo.

The clo unit is a measure of the insulatory capacity provided by any layer of trapped air between the skin and clothing. The clo unit requirement is affected by an individual's metabolic rate at a given ambient temperature, i.e. more clo units are required as ambient temperature decreases and/or metabolic intensity reduces and vice versa.

A clo unit of 1 is defined as maintaining a sedentary person at 1 MET (a unit of resting metabolism or energy expenditure at rest) indefinitely in an environment of 21°C (68.8°F), and 50 per cent relative humidity.

The wearing of suitable clothing can significantly decrease evaporative heat loss by slowing down the movement of water vapour across the clothing layers. In hot, humid environments the majority of sweat either drips from the body or is trapped within the fabric layers of clothing. When this happens there is a significant reduction in the capacity of evaporation to remove heat energy. In cold weather environments this can create even more body heat loss during exercise because clothing loses much of its insulating qualities when it becomes wet.

However, often during exercise in cold air the challenge is not from inadequate clothing insulation, but from the clothing barrier preventing the loss of heat that is being created by the exercise itself. Cross-country skiers, for example, overcome this problem by removing layers of clothing as the body warms up, and this removal of layers of clothing helps maintain core temperature without reliance on evaporative cooling. Thus, the ideal winter clothing in cold, dry weather insulates the body while allowing water vapour to escape through the clothing if sweating occurs.

TO RESEARCH

Arms have a greater ratio of surface area to mass and thinner subcutaneous fat compared with legs. How might this influence the design of cold weather athletic clothing?

SUMMARY

→ Muscle contraction is only about 20 per cent efficient, with about 80 per cent of energy released as heat. This heat must be lost from the body to avoid overheating.

→ Core body temperature increases during exercise, and the intensity of the exercise determines the size of the increase.

→ The control center for temperature regulation is the hypothalamus, located in the brain.

→ Four factors contribute to heat loss:
  ▶ radiation
  ▶ conduction
  ▶ convection
  ▶ evaporation.

→ Evaporation accounts for almost all heat loss
  ▶ during exercise
  ▶ at high ambient temperatures.

→ The effectiveness of evaporative heat loss is reduced significantly in warm, humid environments.

→ The three factors that influence sweat vaporization from the skin are:
  ▶ the amount of body surface exposed to the air
  ▶ the ambient air temperature
  ▶ the relative humidity.

→ Too much sweating without fluid replacement can lead to dehydration.

→ Heat acclimatization produces a lower resting core temperature, greater plasma volume and an increased sweating rate that improves exercise capacity and reduces discomfort during heat exposure.

- → Heat cramps, heat exhaustion and heat stroke are the main heat illness risks during exercise in hot (and humid) environments.
- → During cold stress the body:
  - ▶ initially constricts blood vessels in the outer part of the body to prevent heat loss
  - ▶ begins the shivering response to produce heat, if there has been too much heat loss.
- → In cold air environments intense exercise can produce enough heat to maintain core body temperature.
- → Fat provides an extremely good insulation against cold stress.
- → Both ambient temperature and wind influence the coldness of an environment.
- → The clo index reflects thermal resistance from clothing, and the clo unit is a measure of the insulatory capacity provided by any layer of trapped air between the skin and clothing.
- → Water conducts heat faster than air and this has serious effects if clothing is wet during exercise in cold air or if immersed in cold water.
- → Ideal winter clothing for exercise is lightweight, layered and insulates the body while allowing water vapour to escape if sweating occurs.

Self-study questions

1 List the four major avenues for loss of body heat.

2 State which avenue for loss of body heat is most important for controlling body temperature during exercise.

3 Outline the role of the shivering response to cold exposure as a mechanism for helping to generate body heat.

4 Distinguish between heat cramps and heat stroke.

5 Outline how an individual can best prepare to limit dehydration during prolonged exercise in a hot environment.

6 Describe the physiological adaptations that allow a person to acclimatize to exercise in the heat.

7 Outline how the body minimizes excessive heat loss during exposure to cold environments.

8 Explain the body weight loss–dehydration relationship during exercise.

9 Discuss how you would prepare your national soccer team to compete in the hot environment ($\geq 40°C$) of the 2022 Qatar soccer World Cup.

10 Explain why high humidity is an important factor when performing in hot environments.

11 Sweating rates of up to 3.5 L.hour^{-1} have been reported in trained athletes. For every ml of water that evaporates from the body surface, 2.43 kJ of heat is lost.
   a How much heat is lost for one L of sweat that evaporates?
   b Describe the role of sweating in thermoregulation.
   c Outline how dehydration may compromise exercise performance.

12 If an unacclimatized person secretes sweat with a sodium concentration of $\geq 60 mEq.L^{-1}$, will sodium concentration in sweat increase or decrease with acclimatization? Why?

13 What is hydromeiosis?

14 What impact does exercise in a hot environment ($\geq 30°$) have on the metabolism of carbohydrate?

15 Distinguish between shivering thermogenesis and non-shivering thermogenesis.

16 Outline why vasoconstriction in the skin capillaries during cold exposure is likely to have a detrimental effect on performance (i.e. an earlier onset of fatigue).

17 Explain why elderly people might be less tolerant of the cold than young people. In your answer consider the following:

- ▶ vasoconstriction
- ▶ heat conservation
- ▶ physical fitness
- ▶ heat production
- ▶ absolute exercise intensity and time to fatigue
- ▶ sensitivity to cold.

DATA BASED QUESTION

The performance of two groups of trained cyclists was studied in a hot environment (40°C). Group A was tested before and after a 10-day acclimation training programme in a hot environment (40°C). Group B (control) was tested before and after an identical 10-day training programme that took place in a cool environment (13°C).

The mean $\dot{V}O_2$max and the amount of work done during a 60-minute cycling time trial in a hot environment (40°C) for both groups are shown in the table below.

	Group A		Group B	
	Before	**After**	**Before**	**After**
$\dot{V}O_2$max (ml kg^{-1} min^{-1})	53	59	53	54
Time trial work done (kJ)	709	762	735	714

Source: Adapted from Lorenzo et al 2010. *Journal of Applied Physiology*. Vol 109. Pp 1140–7.

1 State which group had the highest $\dot{V}O_2$max:
   i   before the 10-day training programme.   (1 mark)
   ii after the 10-day training programme.   (1 mark)
2 Identify which group shows the greatest change in the results of their time trial work before and after the 10-day training programme.   (1 mark)
3 Discuss the physiological adaptations that occur with heat acclimation.   (3 marks)

CHAPTER 9

Non-nutritional ergogenic aids

OBJECTIVES

By the end of this chapter students should be able to:

→ define the term ergogenic aid and provide examples of different classifications of ergogenic aid

→ explain the placebo effect and provide a sporting example of this effect

→ differentiate between nutritional and non-nutritional ergogenic aids

→ describe the following key non-nutritional ergogenic aids: anabolic steroids, hormones, diuretics and masking agents, beta blockers, caffeine

→ discuss the proposed benefits of the above ergogenic aids to athletes and say which athletes may be expected to benefit from which ergogenic aid

→ discuss the possible risks to the health of athletes using the above ergogenic aids

→ gain an understanding of the reasons why some non-nutritional ergogenic aids are banned in sport, as well as the complexity of the issue of substance use/abuse in sport.

Introduction

Maximizing sporting performance is a goal that all athletes share, regardless of their chosen sport. Many factors come together to determine the level of sporting performance that an athlete can produce. Some of these factors are fixed, i.e. they cannot be changed by outside influences. For example, the genetic make-up of an athlete will influence their sporting ability. Other factors that influence sports performance can be manipulated in such a way as to maximize the influence of that factor on an athlete's performance. These factors include physical training, psychological training, diet, medical care and injury rehabilitation.

However, at the elite level of sport, most coaches will be aware of the different forms of training and dietary practices used by other athletes in the same sport, and most athletes will have access to similar standards of medical and rehabilitation services. Therefore, the influence of changes to these factors on the success of an elite athlete may be comparatively small, as all of the athlete's competitors will also be making similar changes to the same factors.

The difference between winning and losing in elite sport can be very small. For example, in the 2004 Olympic 100 meter sprint final, the difference between the gold medal time and fourth place (no medal) was just 0.04 seconds. This is put in perspective when you consider that it takes between 0.3 and 0.4 seconds to blink your eyes. Therefore, the difference between success and failure in

> "… building a peaceful and better world by educating youth through sport … without discrimination of any kind and in the Olympic spirit, which requires mutual understanding with a spirit of friendship, solidarity and fair play. … Olympism is a philosophy of life, exalting and combining in a balanced whole the qualities of body will and mind. … Olympism seeks to create a way of life based on the joy of effort, the educational value of good example, social responsibility and respect for universal fundamental ethical principles."
>
> Excerpts from the International Olympic Committee "Fundamental Principles", Olympic Charter

> "The overwhelming majority of athletes I know would do anything, and take anything, short of killing themselves to improve athletic performance."
>
> Harold Connolly, former Olympic hammer-throwing champion

sport can be less than the blink of an eye! Because of this, athletes and their coaches are always seeking ways to gain a performance advantage over their rivals. One way this can be achieved is through the use of ergogenic aids.

Ergogenic aids

An ergogenic aid is any substance, phenomenon or device that improves an athlete's performance. There are a large number of potential ergogenic aids available, and they are classified into different types. A very important distinction between ergogenic aids is that some are deemed acceptable for use by athletes while others are banned by the World Anti-Doping Agency (WADA). An athlete caught using a banned ergogenic aid can be punished in a variety of ways, ranging from a fine up to a lifelong ban from their sport. Despite this, some athletes still use, knowingly and/or unknowingly, illegal ergogenic aids.

Table 9.1 lists some of these ergogenic aids that athletes may use to improve performance. This is not an exhaustive list. The ergogenic aids highlighted in red are banned by WADA and/or sports governing bodies.

TO DO

Look at the WADA website at www.wada-ama.org to find out more about what substances are banned and why.

MECHANICAL AIDS	PHARMACOLOGICAL AIDS	PHYSIOLOGICAL AIDS	NUTRITIONAL AIDS	PSYCHOLOGICAL AIDS
Altitude training	Anabolic steroids	Blood doping	Sodium bicarbonate	Centering
Water training	Caffeine	Acupuncture	Carbohydrate	Cheering
Heart rate monitors	Creatine	Erythropoietin	Protein	Hypnosis
Computer analysis of training or competition data	Sodium bicarbonate	Homeopathy	Fat	Imagery
Hypoxic tents	Protein supplements	Herbal medicines	Sports drinks	Meditation
Nasal strips	Beta blockers*	Physiotherapy	Sports gels	Music
Sharkskin swimsuits	Ephedrine**	Sports massage	Dietary changes	Relaxation
Weighted vests	Amphetamine	Human growth hormone	Water	Yoga
Compression socks	Cocaine	Sauna	Carbohydrate loading	T'ai chi
Vibration training	Non-steroidal anti-inflammatory drugs (NSAIDs)	Creatine	Vitamin supplements	Breathing techniques

* Beta blockers are only illegal in specific sports such as archery, snooker, shooting and golf.

** Ephedrine has a threshold limit applied to it. This means that it only becomes an illegal substance when the amount of the substance found in an athlete's body exceeds this limit.

↑ Table 9.1 Some ergogenic aids that athletes may use to enhance sports performance

Caffeine is a substance that has been consistently proven to improve endurance exercise performance (this will be discussed later in the chapter). Caffeine used to be on the WADA list of banned substances. However, it is not currently on the WADA list of banned substances, in part because it is such a widely consumed substance in daily life that it would be very hard for athletes to avoid. This would make it difficult for officials to prove intentional use of caffeine as an ergogenic aid. This means that athletes can use caffeine in any way they see fit, and could perhaps gain a performance advantage from use of this substance. Interestingly, although not on the WADA list of banned substances now, caffeine is presently being monitored again.

Think about the quotes at the beginning of this chapter.

With these quotes in mind, do you think that caffeine should be banned? Does the fact that all athletes are able to use it make it acceptable for it not to be a banned substance? If it is acceptable because all athletes are able to use it, surely this would apply to all other banned substances too? Therefore, would it be easier to legalize all potential ergogenic aids and let the athletes make their own choice of whether to use them?

Do all ergogenic aids work?

While there are an abundance of substances, techniques and pieces of equipment that claim to be ergogenic aids, not all of them have definitive proof to back up this claim.

Examples of ergogenic aids that are proven to work include the following:

→ Ingestion of appropriate amounts of carbohydrate before and/or during exercise can improve the exercise performance of young people and adults during continuous and intermittent exercise lasting approximately 45 minutes or longer (Nicholas et al. 1995; Phillips et al. 2010).

→ The practice of living at high altitude and training at sea level, one form of "altitude training", is frequently reported to increase sea-level endurance exercise performance (Millet et al. 2010).

→ One of the most successful ergogenic aids of recent times was the "sharkskin" swimsuit. This type of swimsuit enabled swimmers to swim significantly faster, cover a set distance significantly quicker, swim with reduced drag, cover a greater distance per swim stroke and do all this while expending less energy (Chatard et al. 2008).

However, there are examples of ergogenic aids that have become popular despite a lack of supporting evidence. In the last 10 to 20 years, the use of "external nasal dilators" (Figure 9.1) became a popular method of "improving" exercise performance. The theory behind these pieces of equipment was that the strips placed across the nose pull the nostrils up, thereby increasing the size of the nasal passages and helping the athlete to exercise more efficiently by reducing the metabolic demand of breathing. However, only one research study has ever associated these nasal dilators with improvements in exercise responses (Griffin et al. 1997). The vast majority of research has found no significant influence on exercise performance or the physiological responses to exercise (Boggs et al. 2008; Bourdin et al. 2002; Chinevere et al. 1999; O'Kroy et al. 2001).

KEY POINT

The ergogenic aids available to athletes have different levels of evidence and support. Some are well established in improving exercise performance; others have been consistently shown not to improve exercise performance; and others have not been sufficiently tested to form an opinion. However, the individual athlete's perception of the benefits they may receive can also influence the effect of an ergogenic aid, regardless of what the research says.

Placebo effect a positive effect that cannot be attributed to the properties of the placebo itself but must be due simply to the person's belief that the placebo works

Despite this, many athletes still use nasal dilators. One of the reasons for this is that they may believe they are receiving some form of benefit from the product, despite the evidence to the contrary. This relates to a phenomenon called the *placebo effect*.

↑ Figure 9.1: External nasal dilators worn by two professional sportsmen. Despite their popularity, the evidence to show that these dilators improve exercise performance is weak. But could a placebo effect be at work?

An example of the placebo effect is as follows. An athlete comes to a laboratory to volunteer in a study testing the benefit of a new energy drink (Drink X) on 10 kilometer running performance. Drink X is being tested against a drink that looks and tastes the same, but does not have the "special" new ingredient that will improve exercise performance. Therefore, this is the placebo drink. Before the athlete begins his first 10 kilometer run, he is told that he will be drinking the placebo drink.

On the second visit to the laboratory, the athlete is told that he will be drinking Drink X, and that it is expected he will run faster than he did on his first visit. The athlete completes the run, and indeed does run the 10 kilometer distance notably faster than on his first attempt. However, what the researcher did not tell the athlete was that the drinks he received during both runs were, in fact, identical and neither had any ingredients that would improve his exercise performance.

So, what caused the athlete to run significantly faster on his second attempt? Quite simply, he believed that the drink he was consuming would help him run faster, therefore he ran faster. This is the placebo effect; a person's belief in the benefit of a particular substance, procedure or piece of equipment that can cause them to perform better, even when there is no performance advantage to be had by using the "aid".

TEST YOURSELF

Which of the following is an example of the placebo effect? Justify your answer.

1 A football team play poorly in the first half of a match and concede two goals. At half-time, the coach uses some imagery techniques on the players, and in the second half they score three goals to win the game.

2 A racing driver is told by his team manager that he must pull away from his nearest rival by 20 seconds in order to win the race. However, the manager is being cautious and in reality, the driver only needed to pull away by 10 seconds. However, the manager did not tell his driver this, and the driver manages to pull out the 20 second lead.

3 A 1500 meter runner and his coach believe that the runner has anemia, as he is feeling tired and sluggish during training. They decide to try iron supplements while waiting for a decision from the doctor, as they have both heard that iron supplements can help you recover from anemia. After taking the supplements for a short while the athlete is performing back to his best, and reports feeling very good in training. Subsequently, the athlete receives information from the doctor confirming that he never had anemia, and all blood parameters were normal.

The following is an excerpt from a 2008 editorial called *Record breaking or rule breaking?* by Jonathan Wood.

"It's all getting heated down at the swimming pool in the run up to the Olympics. A total of 37 world records have been broken so far this year. And of the 29 records to fall since Speedo introduced its latest high-tech swimsuit, 28 have gone to swimmers wearing their new LZR Racer outfit. This has caused controversy about a possible unfair advantage for athletes using Speedo's kit, questions on whether the suits break the rules, and whether this is a kind of 'technological doping'. The US head swimming coach has even said he feels sorry for swimmers at the Beijing Games sponsored by other manufacturers: 'Do you go for the money or go for the gold?'

Speedo's swimsuit is designed to reduce a swimmer's drag on moving through the water. The suits are made out of lightweight water-repellent material, bonded rather than stitched together. Textured patches are added at points of high friction on the swimmer's body, and the whole suit is designed to shape, girdle, and compress the athlete's body as ideally as possible. In developing the suit, Speedo have worked with NASA on the fabric, the University of Otago, New Zealand in flume tests, made use of the University of Nottingham's expertise in computational fluid dynamics, and gone to Australia to measure the suit's performance.

Speedo's Italian competitor Arena issued an open letter to the sport's governing body in protest. 'The credibility of sports competitions is at stake,' they claim. The reason? 'A firestorm of publicly expressed concern has ensued about the alleged buoyancy advantage provided by Speedo LZR Racer and Tyr Tracer Light swimsuits.' Buoyancy aids are strictly against the rules, but FINA (the international governing body of swimming) has now issued a simple statement confirming that all swimsuits approved so far comply with regulations."

Questions

1 Do you agree that the use of equipment that allows athletes to perform to a level they would not otherwise be able to attain is "technological doping"? Justify your answer.

2 What impact do performance aids such as these swimsuits have on the public credibility of sport? Is it positive or negative?

3 Should these "technological ergogenic aids" be treated or controlled differently to other forms of ergogenic aids, such as nutritional or psychological aids? Why?

4 Compare and contrast the use of these swimsuits in swimming with the use of spiked shoes in track running. What are the differences and similarities? Are spiked running shoes an ergogenic aid that should be controlled or banned?

Olympic swimming gold: the suit or the swimmer in the suit? Discuss.

↑ Medal ceremony for the men's 400 m swim at the 1924 Paris Olympics. 'Boy' Charleton (Australia), Johnny Weissmuller (USA), and, in a lower-cut suit, Arne Borg of Sweden. Photo: Official Report of the Paris Organizing Committee, with permission of the IOC

Speedo's LZR Racer

The Speedo LZR Racer swimsuit was launched on 13 February 2008 as the focus of Speedo's campaign for the Beijing Olympics. Marketed as "the world's fastest swimsuit", it was launched with a holographic video of Michael Phelps at events in London, Sydney, New York and Tokyo, with Phelps exclaiming: "When I hit the water [in the Speedo LZR swimsuit], I feel like a rocket". Among other effects, the suit compressed the body into a more hydrodynamic shape, while revolutionary LZR Pulse fabric and ultrasonically welded seams reduced drag in the water.

Within a week of its launch three world records had been broken by swimmers wearing the suit. It led a Japanese coach to say: "If swimmers don't wear the LZR Racer, they won't be able to compete in Beijing Olympics". At those Olympics 94 per cent of all swimming events were won by swimmers wearing the Speedo LZR Racer, an achievement which included the unprecedented eight gold medals won by Phelps.

↑   Michael Phelps poses in his LZR Racer suit.

↑   (Source: The Royal Statistics Society 2012. *Significance*. April. Pp 13–17.)

Non-nutritional ergogenic aids

Look again at the classifications of ergogenic aids in Table 9.1. These five different classifications would fit into two further, more general classifications. The ergogenic aids under the classification "nutritional aids" all contain substances that are either found naturally in the body, and/or can be ingested as part of a natural, balanced diet. Therefore, these ergogenic aids can be called "nutritional ergogenic aids".

Now look at the ergogenic aids under the other four classifications of Table 9.1. None of these are a necessary component of a person's diet or nutritional intake. Therefore, all of these could be classified as "non-nutritional ergogenic aids". It is this classification of ergogenic aid that will be the focus of this chapter.

Of course, the possible list of non-nutritional ergogenic aids is very long, and it is not possible to address all of them here. Therefore, focus will be kept on five classes of non-nutritional ergogenic aid. This section will simply introduce the substances; subsequent sections will discuss their possible benefits, risks, and side effects. These classes are discussed as they represent some of the most commonly used ergogenic aids in world sport.

Anabolic steroids

Anabolism is the metabolic process of creating, or building, more of a certain substance or tissue. For example, with regard to the muscles of the body, anabolic processes result in an increase in the size of the muscle tissue. Steroids are a general class of chemical substances that can be found in the body (for example, some hormones are steroids), and can also be synthesized (many drugs are steroids). Therefore, anabolic steroids are a class of substances that initiate or assist the process of building up the amount and/or size of certain substances/tissues in the body.

As already mentioned, anabolic steroids can be synthesized outside of the body or occur naturally within the body. For example, the primary male sex hormone testosterone is an anabolic steroid, as it helps to stimulate the development of various male characteristics such as increased muscle and bone mass, body hair, height, and overall body size compared to females. All of these processes require an increase in the amount and, therefore, size of various tissues (i.e. muscle and bone). This hormone is naturally occurring up to a certain concentration in the bodies of males and females (although men have on average 10 times the amount of testosterone that females have).

Anabolic steroids is the general term for drugs that mimic the effects of the male sex hormone testosterone. Anabolic steroids can be used legitimately to help certain medical conditions, including stimulation of body growth in young people who are not growing normally, stimulation of appetite and muscle mass in individuals with chronic illnesses such as AIDS and cancer, and as a hormone replacement therapy for men with low endogenous testosterone levels.

However, in otherwise healthy athletes they are primarily used to increase one or more of the following: muscle mass, muscle strength, muscle power, and speed. Anabolic steroids achieve this in two main ways: firstly, they increase the production of proteins, which are required to form muscle tissue; the more protein produced, the more muscle tissue can develop. Secondly, they allow an athlete to recover faster from exercise by blocking the effects of stress hormones such as cortisol. In this scenario, the muscle tissue is not broken down as much following exercise. Further discussion of the potential risks and benefits of anabolic steroids, and why these substances are banned in sport, is included later in the chapter.

Hormones

Pharmacological versions of naturally occurring hormones are another class of non-nutritional ergogenic aid. Many hormones associated with processes such as the development of muscle tissue, tendon and ligament strength, and the regulation of energy metabolism are potential ergogenic aids. However, two of the most prevalent ones are **human growth hormone (HGH)** and **erythropoietin (EPO)**.

Human growth hormone is a naturally occurring protein-based hormone that stimulates body tissue growth, cell reproduction and regeneration. Human growth hormone concentrations are greater in children than adults, due to the greater requirement for growth and development in children. A number of pharmaceutical companies now manufacture and sell artificially synthesized human growth hormone (called recombinant human growth hormone or rHGH). This form of HGH can be used medically as a replacement for naturally occurring HGH in adults with HGH deficiency and to treat various conditions that inhibit normal growth and development.

Erythropoietin is another protein-based hormone that is naturally found in the body. The primary function of EPO is to regulate the production of red blood cells which transport oxygen to all areas of the body. It does this in two ways: by protecting red blood cells from becoming damaged/destroyed, and by stimulating the production of new red blood cells in the bone marrow. Erythropoietin is produced by the kidneys and the liver. As with HGH, EPO

Anabolism the metabolic process of creating more of a certain substance or tissue

Steroids a class of chemical substances that can be found in the body and can also be synthesized

KEY POINT

Anabolic steroids is the general term for drugs that mimic the effects of the male sex hormone testosterone and have lots of legitimate uses in medicine. In athletes they can be used to increase performance through increased muscle mass and strength.

Diuretics substances that increase removal of water from the body

Masking agents a substance or agent that hides the presence of another substance or agent

can be artificially manufactured, called recombinant EPO or rEPO. The synthesized version of the hormone can be used to treat anemia that occurs as a result of a variety of different complications, illnesses and diseases.

Diuretics and masking agents

Diuretics are substances that increase the removal of water from the body, usually by increasing the frequency and/or volume of urination (Figure 9.2). Different classes of diuretic exert their effects in different ways. Some suppress hormones that regulate urine formation, some increase blood flow to the kidneys, leading to greater filtration of water from the blood, some inhibit the reabsorption of sodium from the kidneys, which leads to greater water removal from the circulation, and some promote water loss via osmosis.

Most diuretic agents are chemically synthesized and are purposefully introduced into the body. However, there are naturally occurring diuretics that may form part of a normal diet, including caffeine (a mild diuretic), alcohol and certain fruits and vegetables. Medical uses for diuretics (particularly synthesized ones) include the treatment of conditions such as heart failure, liver cirrhosis, hypertension, and some diseases of the kidneys. Diuretics can also be used to facilitate the removal of certain substances from the body, for example, aspirin, following an overdose.

Diuretics are also known as masking agents. A masking agent is any substance or agent that interferes with the detection of, or "hides", another substance or agent. For example, diuretics can be used as masking agents when urine analysis is being undertaken to detect the level of a certain drug in a person's urine. Taking a diuretic will increase the volume of urine produced, thereby making the urine more dilute and reducing the amount of the drug present in the urine. This may make the amount of drug present in the individual appear lower, or even make the drug impossible to detect.

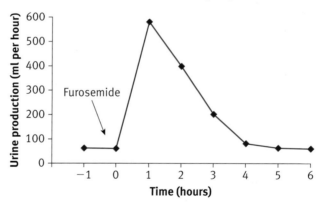

Figure 9.2: Typical changes in the rate of urine production following oral ingestion of furosemide (a diuretic)

Beta blockers

Beta blocker is the collective term for a class of drugs that are termed "beta-adrenergic antagonists". Essentially this means that beta blockers reduce, or "block", the influence of adrenaline on various tissues of the body. In a clinical/health setting, beta blockers are commonly used to treat and control conditions such as heart arrhythmias (irregular heart beat/unusually high or low heart rate), angina (lack of blood flow to heart tissue) and hypertension (high blood pressure), and as a protective measure following a heart attack.

Beta blockers exert their effect by blocking the influence of adrenaline on the heart tissue. This decreases the heart rate and the amount of work the heart is doing, therefore reducing the stress placed on the heart. Because of this decrease in heart rate and the amount of work the heart can perform, beta blockers can affect the response of the heart to exercise and may influence exercise performance.

Beta blockers can also be used in the treatment of anxiety. A number of the symptoms of anxiety (elevated heart rate, sweating, trembling muscles, dizziness, shaking hands) are caused by production of the stress hormones adrenaline and noradrenaline. As beta blockers reduce the influence of these hormones, they can help to alleviate the symptoms of anxiety. However, they do not affect the emotional symptoms of anxiety. Therefore, beta blockers are not a cure for anxiety and are most often used to treat symptoms of social anxiety (e.g. giving a speech in front of a large audience) or performance anxiety.

Beta blockers drugs that reduce the influence of adrenaline on the body

Stimulants

Stimulants are psychoactive drugs. Psychoactive drugs are substances that enter the brain and exert their effects on the central nervous system (the brain and the spinal nerves). These effects lead to various alterations in the way a person feels. This can include greater levels of alertness, a sharper perception of what is occurring in the immediate environment, a more positive mood state, greater levels of motivation, greater vigilance and feelings of greater physical and mental "power".

Stimulants come in various forms. For example, many substances we consume in our daily lives, such as caffeine, sugar and vitamin supplements can be classed as stimulants. There are also chemical stimulants, including substances such as amphetamines and cocaine. In a clinical setting, amphetamines can be used to treat a variety of mental disorders, particularly depressive disorders, narcolepsy (a condition where the sufferer is unable to prevent themselves from falling asleep), Parkinson's disease and attention deficit disorder in children. However, amphetamines can become addictive, likely due to the positive and pleasant sensations they generate. Medically, cocaine can be used as a local anaesthetic and vasoconstrictor during surgery in areas such as the nose, throat and mouth. In many countries, both amphetamines and cocaine are classed as illegal substances for non-clinical (i.e. recreational) use.

TO THINK ABOUT

Why do you think beta blockers are banned in sports such as archery, snooker and shooting, but not in sports such as sprinting or swimming?

THEORY OF KNOWLEDGE

Our understanding of the benefits and dangers of many banned substances, for example, anabolic steroids, has been hindered by the ethical concerns about conducting experimental studies on these substances in healthy individuals.

1 Why is there an ethical concern here? Surely if individuals are informed of the potential risks of the research and still wish to continue, then the researcher should go ahead with the experiment? Discuss your point of view regarding this statement. Do some research of your own into the ethics of research experiments in order to support your discussion.

2 Imagine that you work for the World Anti-Doping Agency, and are in charge of compiling the list of banned substances in sport. A group of Olympic-level athletes present you with a signed petition asking for a response to the following: "There is a lack of specific evidence to show that 'Steroid X', a new form of anabolic steroid, can significantly improve sports performance, yet it has still been banned. We believe that it is inappropriate to ban a substance with no conclusive prove of its performance-enhancing effects or its health risks, and ask the World Anti-Doping Agency to review its decision to ban Steroid X."

   What would be your response to these athletes?

   What arguments would you employ to support your decision, and justify why you believe it is the right decision?

Potential benefits of non-nutritional ergogenic aids

Anabolic steroids

Findings regarding the effects of anabolic steroid administration in humans are inconsistent for many reasons (Table 9.2). The available evidence suggests that the potential benefits of anabolic steroid use would be more applicable to athletes involved in strength or power events (sprinting, shot-put, powerlifting etc) or those engaged in sports such as bodybuilding. The following is a summary of the main proposed benefits of anabolic steroid use.

Weight gain

Regular anabolic steroid use is reported to induce rapid weight gain in athletes, healthy non-athletes, and individuals with chronic health conditions (Casner et al. 1971; Loughton et al. 1977; Schols et al. 1995; Yeh et al. 2002). This weight gain can range from 2–5 kg as a result of short-term (less than 10 weeks) anabolic steroid use (Hartgens, Kuipers 2004). Weight gain could be of benefit to particular athletes, for example, a full back in American football or a forward in rugby.

However, some research has shown that the increase in weight gain with anabolic steroid use is not always accompanied by increased muscle strength or power (Casner et al. 1971; Loughton et al. 1977). Indeed, it is not fully clear what causes the increased weight gain with anabolic steroid use, particularly when increased muscle size is not reported. Increased weight gain without concomitant increases in muscle strength/power would be undesirable for any athlete, as it would negatively affect factors that would influence performance, such as power to weight ratio.

Ability to train more frequently and more intensely

Anabolic steroid use has been associated with a faster recovery/healing time of damaged muscle tissue (Beiner et al. 1999). This probably relates to their anabolic, i.e. tissue-building, abilities, which would facilitate development of new tissue to replace that which was damaged. However, anabolic steroids also have a potent "anti-catabolic" property. Essentially, this means that they prevent tissue such as muscle from being broken down or damaged as much as it normally would be during exercise. They achieve this by improving the way in which the body utilizes dietary protein and by improving the synthesis (making) of protein within the body (Haupt et al. 1984; Kadi et al. 1999).

Catabolism the breaking down of molecules

As catabolism of muscle tissue is one of the potential causes of injury, this suggests that anabolic steroid use may reduce the risk of injury to muscle tissue during exercise, or increase the stress that the muscles can be placed under before they become injured. Put together, these effects of anabolic steroids may enable an athlete to train longer and harder, and therefore improve their performance to a greater extent than they could without using steroids. Clearly, this would be of great benefit to all athletes, regardless of their sport.

Increased muscle mass, strength and power

Perhaps the most common perceived benefit of anabolic steroid use is an increase in muscle mass and/or strength and power. Indeed, evidence in humans does show a significant increase in muscle mass and muscle strength with anabolic steroid administration (Bhasin et al. 1996; Bhasin et al. 2001). It appears that this effect may demonstrate a dose-response relationship, i.e. the more anabolic steroid used, the greater the effect on muscle mass and strength (Bhasin et al. 2001). However, this dose-response relationship may only exist for certain muscles (Kutscher et al. 2002). It also appears that steroid use without exercise can increase muscle mass and strength, but that steroid use combined with exercise produces the greatest increases in these variables, more than either one individually (Bhasin et al. 1996).

However, it is important to note that not everyone would gain the same increases in muscle mass and strength with anabolic steroid use. It has been shown that individuals who are experienced in weight training increase muscle mass and strength with anabolic steroid use above that which would be expected with training alone. But for individuals who are not experienced weight trainers, using anabolic steroids will not result in them gaining any more strength or muscle mass than would be expected from exercise alone (Bahrke, Yesalis 2002). The main way in which anabolic steroids increase muscle mass and strength is by increasing the rate of protein synthesis (Kutscher et al. 2002).

The majority of research into anabolic steroids has focused on changes in muscle size and strength (how much resistance the muscle can overcome). Comparatively little work has focused on the influence of anabolic steroids on muscle power (the speed at which a muscle can generate force). It appears that anabolic steroids do not induce increases in muscle power in the same way that they do muscle size and strength. However, the comparative lack of research makes a consensus regarding anabolic steroids and muscle power difficult.

Lower body fat

It is important to note that anabolic steroid use does not reduce fat mass, that is, the absolute amount of fat that your body contains (Hartgens, Kuipers 2004). However, as has already been discussed, anabolic steroids can significantly increase muscle mass. It is this increase in muscle mass (or fat-free mass) that causes an apparent visual decrease in fat mass (the athlete looks more muscular and less fat), and causes a reduction in the percentage of the athlete's total body mass that is attributed to fat. This is highlighted in the following example:

Before steroid use	Total body mass: 95 kg	Muscle mass: 76 kg (80% of total body mass) Fat mass: 19 kg (20% of total body mass)
After steroid use	Total body mass: 102 kg	Muscle mass: 83 kg (80% of total body mass) Fat mass: 19 kg (18% of total body mass)

Here, you can see that before steroid use the athlete had 19 kilograms of fat, which meant that 20 per cent of his total body mass was fat. After steroid use, the athlete gained 7 kilograms, all of which was muscle mass, but his fat mass stayed the same (19 kg). Therefore, as a percentage of his new body mass, his fat content appears to be lower. However, in absolute terms, the amount of body fat is the same (19 kg).

Endurance performance

Long-term use of anabolic steroids can increase concentrations of hemoglobin (Hinterberger, Vierhapper 1993), the protein in red blood cells that oxygen binds with in order to be transported around the body. Increasing hemoglobin concentration can increase the oxygen-carrying capacity of the blood, and has been shown to improve endurance exercise performance. As a result, anabolic steroids have been used by endurance athletes as a means of improving exercise performance (Hartgens, Kuipers 2003).

However, the vast majority of research demonstrates that anabolic steroids do not increase endurance exercise performance (Bowers, Reardon 1972; Johnson et al. 1972; Johnson et al. 1975). Anabolic steroids have now largely been abandoned by endurance athletes as a means of improving exercise performance due to more stringent anti-doping controls, a greater ability to detect steroid use and the development of rEPO (Hartgens, Kuipers 2003).

KEY POINT

The potential benefits of using anabolic steroids are weight gain, being able to train more, increased muscle mass, strength and power.

VARIABLE	REASON
Dosage	Studies use varied dosages. Only a few studies have used dosages approximating those used by competing strength athletes.
Testing methods	Strength is often not measured in the training mode. Body composition is often assessed from skinfold estimates, reducing the accuracy of the data.
Training methods	Volumes and intensities of training vary between studies.
Drugs	Studies used a variety of different anabolic steroid(s). Few studies have reported the self-administration of anabolic steroids by athletes.
Study participants	The number of participants, their experience in weight training, and their physical condition at the start of the studies varies.
Diet	Mostly diet was not controlled or recorded.
Study design	Some studies are crossover, some single-blind, some double-blind, some not blind; some had no controls.
Mechanisms of action	There are unknown and varying degrees of anabolic and anti-catabolic action and of interaction with motivational effects.
Length of study	Studies vary in length and are generally short; reports on prolonged training and self-administration of steroids is lacking.
Placebo effect	It is difficult to assess placebo effect due to easy detection of steroid administration by athletes; consequently blind studies are lacking.
Data interpretation	Interpreters had different backgrounds (scientific, clinical, athletic, administrative), perspectives and goals.
Legal and ethical factors	These considerations preclude design and execution of well-controlled studies using doses and patterns of administration of drugs with unknown long-term effects in healthy volunteers in a manner comparable to that of many steroid users.

↑ Table 9.2: Reasons for the lack of consensus on the effects of anabolic steroid use on performance variables in humans

Erythropoietin

The following discussion of the proposed benefits of EPO use refers to the administration of rEPO in healthy people.

Increased oxygen carrying capacity of blood

The primary mechanism by which EPO exerts its effects on exercise is via an increase in the maximal oxygen transport capacity of the blood. Regular injections of rEPO for 4-14 weeks have shown significant increases in the hemoglobin concentration of healthy individuals (Lundby, Olsen 2011).

It has long been thought that the increase in hemoglobin concentration with rEPO use was due to significant increases in red blood cell number, as this is a primary function of naturally produced EPO. Indeed, increased red blood cell count is a crucial function of EPO use. However, EPO also decreases plasma volume, the liquid portion of blood (Lundby et al. 2007). This would also have the effect of increasing the volume of red blood cells, as the volume of red cells as a percentage of total blood volume would be greater in much the same way as the relationship between fat mass and total body mass in the previous anabolic steroid example. Therefore, physical increases in the number of red blood cells and a decrease in the plasma volume both serve to increase red cell number and therefore the oxygen carrying capacity of the blood.

As a result of this increased blood oxygen carrying capacity, significant increases in $\dot{V}O_2$max (the maximum rate at which the body can consume oxygen) of 8–12% with administration of rEPO have been reported (Lundby et al. 2008; Robach et al. 2008; Thomsen et al. 2007).

Increased exercise capacity and performance

The main way in which EPO use has directly improved exercise performance is by allowing the athlete to work at a higher intensity, or to work at a lower relative intensity at any given workload, due to their increased $\dot{V}O_2$max. The metabolic cost (i.e. oxygen requirement) at a given exercise intensity is not altered with rEPO use, therefore the oxygen requirement of any given exercise intensity will represent a lower percentage of an EPO-using athlete's maximum oxygen carrying and consumption capacity. Essentially, exercising at any given workload becomes relatively easier compared to before EPO was used.

Using rEPO can also allow athletes to exercise for longer at a given exercise intensity before they become fatigued (Thomsen et al. 2007). Clearly, these potential influences of rEPO would be of benefit to endurance athletes across many different sports. Improvements in exercise capacity and performance are almost solely due to the EPO-induced increase in the oxygen carrying capacity of the blood (Lundby, Olsen 2011).

Figure 9.3 demonstrates this effect on relative exercise intensity. The cyclist at the top is exercising at an intensity that requires an oxygen consumption of 3.75 liters per minute. This represents 75 per cent of his maximum oxygen uptake, which is 5 liters per minute. The cyclist then takes EPO regularly for 10 weeks, which increases his maximum oxygen uptake to 5.5 liters per minute. As a result, cycling at the same exercise intensity (3.75 liters per minute) only requires 68 per cent of his maximum oxygen uptake. Therefore, the exercise has become easier. For clarity, the exercise intensity corresponding to 75 per cent of the cyclist's post-EPO maximum oxygen uptake has been included. You can see that exercising at that relative intensity would require a greater workload than before EPO was used.

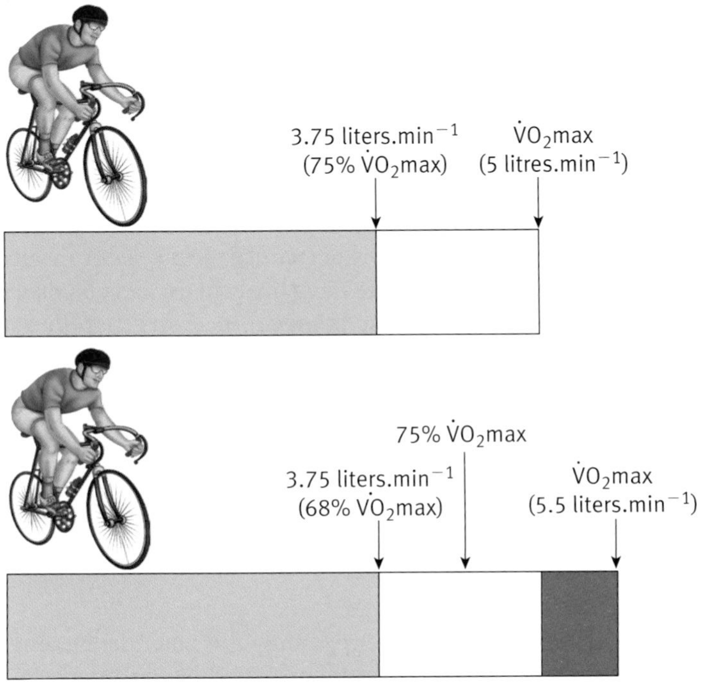

3.75 liters.min^{-1} $\dot{V}O_2$max
(75% $\dot{V}O_2$max)   (5 litres.min^{-1})

75% $\dot{V}O_2$max

3.75 liters.min^{-1} $\dot{V}O_2$max
(68% $\dot{V}O_2$max)   (5.5 liters.min^{-1})

↑ Figure 9.3: The influence of erythropoietin use on relative exercise intensity

Alterations in cognitive function

Some recent evidence suggests that EPO use may also have an effect on cognitive function (awareness, thought processes, ideas etc). The role of the brain in controlling and influencing exercise performance is becoming more obvious and it has been shown that interventions that alter certain cognitive brain functions can have a profound effect on exercise performance. Therefore, EPO may have a role to play in improving exercise performance by altering brain function. However, available data focuses on the influence of EPO on the brain function of healthy people in non-exercising situations (Miskowiak et al. 2008), or on the brain function of individuals with mental health issues (Ehrenreich et al. 2007). More work needs to be done in an exercise setting before the influence of EPO on cognitive function during exercise can be fully understood.

Beta blockers

As mentioned earlier in this chapter, beta blockers are used in a therapeutic setting for treating various diseases associated with the cardiovascular system and for treating symptoms of anxiety. There has not been much research conducted on the effect of beta blockers in sport-specific settings.

Improved precision and accuracy and reduced symptoms of anxiety

The ability of beta blockers to decrease heart rate and reduce hand tremors and other symptoms of anxiety means their administration could improve performance in sports that require a state of calm, steadiness and accuracy, for example shooting and archery (Davis et al. 2008). The small amount of sport-specific research that is available supports this notion. Kruse et al. (1986) demonstrated that beta blocker use significantly improved shooting performance and attributed the increased performance to decreased hand tremors. Other work has found improved performance in sport shooting and bobsled with beta blocker use (Schmid 1990).

In contrast to those sports that require high levels of accuracy and fine muscle control, beta blockers are highly unlikely to improve performance in endurance sports or any sport that requires high levels of exercise intensity. This would include running events ranging from 400 meters to the marathon, almost all cycling disciplines, team games such as soccer and rugby, swimming events of 100 meters or longer, and any other sporting events of this nature. This is because, as discussed previously, beta blockers limit heart rate, reduce the amount of work that the heart can accomplish, and reduce the metabolic response to exercise (Davis et al. 2008). As a result, the athlete would be unable to push their body to the same level that they would if they were not using beta blockers. In other words, beta blockers reduce the physical capacity of an individual. Therefore, athletes that are most likely to use beta blockers to gain a competitive advantage are those involved in sports that do not require a high aerobic or anaerobic capacity, but do require high levels of accuracy, precision and mental focus.

Endurance capacity how long a person can continue to exercise before they become exhausted

Endurance performance how much distance/work can be completed in a given time, or how quickly a given distance/amount of work can be completed

Caffeine

Caffeine is one of the most widely used ergogenic aids (Astorino, Roberson 2010) and has been researched in a variety of different exercise situations.

Improved endurance capacity

Below is a summary of current knowledge regarding the potential benefits caffeine could afford an athlete in exercise of different durations and intensities.

Type of exercise	Duration	Effects of caffeine
Endurance exercise	Longer than 40 minutes	Many research studies have consistently shown that ingestion of caffeine before and during endurance exercise can improve both endurance capacity and endurance performance (Tarnopolsky 2010). Endurance capacity is defined as how long a person can continue to exercise before they become exhausted, and endurance performance is how much distance/work can be completed in a given time, or how quickly a given distance/amount of work can be completed. Therefore, athletes involved in endurance running, cycling, cross-country skiing and other sports could benefit from caffeine ingestion.
Short exercise	20 to 40 minutes	It was originally thought that caffeine only exerted an ergogenic effect during prolonged endurance exercise. However, there are a number of research studies that now demonstrate that caffeine is able to improve both endurance capacity and performance during exercise lasting approximately 20 to 40 minutes (Graham et al. 1998; MacIntosh, Wright 1995). This means that many more athletes across a wider range of sports may be able to access the ergogenic benefits of caffeine. The exact reasons for how caffeine exerts its benefits during exercise of this duration are not fully known, but it is likely that the reasons relate less to metabolic causes and more to the potential influence of caffeine on the central nervous system.
Very short exercise	4 to 8 minutes	Again, research now indicates that caffeine intake can improve endurance capacity and performance during high intensity exercise lasting only approximately four to eight minutes (Anderson et al. 2000; Bruce et al. 2000; Jackman et al. 1996). As above, these findings suggest that caffeine could be used as an ergogenic aid in an even wider range of athletes and sports. The exact mechanisms behind caffeine's effect during exercise of this nature is not known, but may be a combination of effects on metabolism, muscle contraction and the central nervous system.
Sprint exercise	30 to 90 seconds	In a recent review, it was found that of 12 studies investigating the effect of caffeine intake during high intensity exercise lasting approximately 30–90 seconds, 6 found a benefit of caffeine and 6 did not (Astorino, Roberson 2010). Therefore, current knowledge makes it difficult to answer the question of whether caffeine intake would be beneficial for athletes involved in sports lasting 30–90 seconds. Also, the mechanisms for caffeine's possible benefit during this form of exercise have not been confirmed. The differing findings in the research may be due to the inherent difficulties associated with researching caffeine during exercise (see "Difficulties when studying caffeine intake and exercise").
Resistance exercise	Any	Current knowledge regarding the ergogenic effect of caffeine intake on the parameters of resistance exercise such as the number of repetitions that can be performed before fatigue, the maximum load that can be lifted for one repetition, peak power and peak torque is similar to that for sprint exercise. Approximately half the research supports that caffeine improves aspects of resistance exercise performance and approximately half fails to show a benefit of caffeine intake on these parameters (Astorino, Roberson 2010). Once again, specific mechanisms of caffeine's potential enhancement of resistance exercise performance have not been fully confirmed.

↑ Table 9.3: Effects of caffeine on performance

How caffeine enables improvements in endurance capacity and performance is still not fully known. However, there are three overriding theories.

→ Caffeine exerts a "metabolic effect" whereby it promotes a greater use of fat by the body during exercise, and enables "sparing" of the finite stores of carbohydrate, therefore allowing the athlete to exercise for longer

TO DO

Can you think of other sports that could benefit from caffeine ingestion?

TO THINK ABOUT

It is likely that you ingest caffeine in your food and drink. Have you ever noticed an effect on your performance in any sport?

(Essig et al. 1980; Spriet et al. 1992). However, more recent research has shown very little evidence for a sparing of carbohydrate stores during exercise with caffeine ingestion (Graham 2008).

→ Caffeine enables the muscles to contract with more force due to a greater release of calcium within the muscle fibers (calcium plays an important role in allowing the muscle fibers to contract). This hypothesis does have some supportive research (Tarnopolsky, Cupido 2000).

→ Caffeine may be able to increase performance by its actions on the central nervous system. It is well known that caffeine is a central nervous system stimulant, and elicits increased feelings of alertness, vigilance and wakefulness. However, many research studies have shown that caffeine can also reduce the perceived exertion an individual feels during exercise, i.e. caffeine makes the exercise feel easier (Tarnopolsky 2010). Also, a reduction in pain has been reported when caffeine is consumed during exercise (Tarnopolsky 2008). This could certainly contribute to improved endurance capacity and performance.

Difficulties when studying caffeine intake and exercise

The overall body of research investigating caffeine ingestion before and during exercise shows a wide variability in the response to caffeine. This means that there are factors present that can alter a person's response to caffeine ingestion, so that giving different people the same amount of caffeine at the same time during the same exercise protocol will not necessarily generate comparable results. Some of these potential factors have been identified.

→ The amount of caffeine that a person habitually consumes in their diet can influence the relative effect of a caffeine supplement before and during exercise. People who generally consume less caffeine in their diet may receive a greater ergogenic effect from a caffeine supplement then someone who habitually consumes large amounts of caffeine (Kalmar, Cafarelli 1999).

→ People may fall into "responder" or "non-responder" groups regarding caffeine intake during exercise, particularly of short duration (Astorino, Roberson 2010). This means that some people simply do not respond to caffeine intake during exercise for as yet unknown reasons. These first two points are important, as they suggest that caffeine is not a universal ergogenic aid, i.e. it will not necessarily work for all athletes, or even different athletes within the same sport or team.

→ The training status of an individual may affect caffeine study data. Well-trained athletes are likely to be more motivated to perform maximal or fatiguing exercise (Astorino, Roberson 2010). As most research studies into caffeine require maximal and/or fatiguing exercise to be performed, it could be that those studies using well-trained athletes produce more reliable data than those using less well trained or untrained individuals. This difference in study samples could contribute to the variability in research findings.

Is caffeine a suitable ergogenic aid for all sports?

It is unlikely that caffeine would be an appropriate ergogenic aid for athletes engaged in sports that require high levels of accuracy, precision and fine muscle control. The reason for this is that one of the side effects of caffeine supplementation is the "jitters", an uncontrollable shaking or tremor, particularly in the hands. Obviously, this would place the performance of athletes such as archers, shooters, golfers etc. at risk. The side effects of caffeine are further discussed later in the chapter.

Diuretics

Weight control

Many sports structure levels of competition according to weight categories or classes. Examples of these sports include boxing, wrestling, and powerlifting. Often, athletes will desire to be as close to the upper weight limit of their class as possible, in order to gain a potential weight advantage over their rival(s). This will often require the athlete to rapidly lose weight just prior to competition, to ensure that they qualify for the correct category. Athletes can do this by using starvation diets and/or drugs to induce diarrhoea or vomiting. However, they can also lose weight by losing body water, as the loss of one liter of body water is equivalent to about one kilogram of body weight. This can be accomplished by using dehydration techniques such as exercising in hot conditions, wearing suits that do not permit the body to evaporate sweat, therefore leading to greater sweat production, and the use of saunas. They can also invoke dehydration by using diuretic agents. Often, an athlete will use a diuretic in combination with some of the above techniques in order to achieve the desired outcome.

There are also sporting situations where being as light as possible may confer a competitive advantage. Jockeys may attempt to be as light as possible prior to a race to reduce the load that the horse must carry and therefore enable the horse to run faster for longer. Indeed, the use of diuretics by jockeys is commonplace (Bahrke, Yesalis 2002).

Physical appearance

Success in some sports is, at least partly, dependent on the physical appearance of the competitor. For example, female gymnasts have emphasis placed on a slender, lean physical appearance. Conversely, bodybuilders require excellent muscle definition in order to be successful. Diuretics can, and have, been used to help gymnasts get a slender, lean appearance, and to help bodybuilders get a "cut" look and maximize muscular appearance and definition before competition (Bahrke, Yesalis 2002).

Hiding illicit substance use

As was briefly mentioned earlier, diuretics can be used by athletes in an attempt to hide, or mask, the use of other illegal substances that can be detected via urine analysis. This is primarily achieved by increasing the volume of urine output, thereby diluting the illicit substance so that it appears that less is present in the athlete's body, or by making detection of the substance altogether impossible. The first athlete to be disqualified at an Olympic Games for the illicit use of diuretics was a Bulgarian powerlifter in Sydney in 2000 (Bahrke, Yesalis 2002). It was reported in the media that the athlete was using diuretics in order to mask the use of anabolic steroids, however this was not conclusively proven.

Health issues associated with use of non-nutritional ergogenic aids

Most, if not all, non-nutritional ergogenic aids will cause changes in the physiological and/or mental function of the individuals who use them. That is how many exert their beneficial effect. However, prolonged and/or excessive use of some can cause potentially serious, even fatal, conditions.

Anabolic steroids

Prolonged use of anabolic steroids can potentially affect the body in many ways. The common adverse effects of prolonged anabolic steroid administration are summarized in Table 9.4.

TO DO

Can you find examples of other sports where weight is a key factor?

TO RESEARCH

Find three other examples of high profile sportspeople being disqualified from world class competition for using banned substances.

Heart problems

Prolonged anabolic steroid use can cause disease of the heart muscle (termed cardiomyopathy). Additionally, anabolic steroid use can significantly reduce the concentrations of a particular form of cholesterol called high density lipoprotein (HDL) cholesterol. This form of cholesterol helps to protect the arteries of the heart from clogging up, and therefore lowers the risk of developing coronary artery disease or of suffering a heart attack. Low levels of this form of cholesterol significantly increase the risk of encountering these conditions.

Liver problems

The liver is closely involved in the metabolism of chemicals that compose anabolic steroids. Long-term use of steroids can cause liver toxicity and can also cause liver disease (hepatitis). Prolonged steroid use can lead to the development of liver tumours which can be cancerous.

Hormone problems

Prolonged use of anabolic steroids reduces the production of gonadotropic hormones, a group of hormones that control the function of the testes in males and the ovaries in females. Reduced production of these hormones in males can cause testicular atrophy (a reduction in size, or shrinkage, of the testicles), a reduction in testosterone concentration and a reduced sperm count, therefore affecting fertility. It can also lead to an enlargement of male breast tissue.

Reductions in gonadotropic hormone production in females can significantly disturb the menstrual process, again affecting fertility, and can reduce the production of estrogen. This can lead to "masculinization" effects in females (i.e. the development of male characteristics). These include a reduction in breast size, enlargement of the clitoris, deepening of the voice and the development of facial and body hair.

Skin problems

Anabolic steroids increase the amount of free fatty acids and cholesterol present in the skin. This can cause oily hair and skin, increased acne, alopecia (hair loss) and hypertrophy of the sebaceous glands.

Mental problems

The potentially damaging effects of anabolic steroids are not limited to physical issues. Prolonged steroid use can significantly alter an individual's mental state. It is commonly reported that individuals using steroids demonstrate a marked increase in aggressive and/or violent behaviour. Increased feelings of depression are also reported. There is also evidence to show that anabolic steroid use can become addictive. However, it should be noted that, mainly for ethical reasons, well-controlled studies into the psychiatric effects of steroid use in humans are lacking. Furthermore, the effects of steroids on psychiatric variables can be individual and overall conclusions are difficult to make (Kutscher et al. 2002).

It is very important to note that the potential long-term (i.e. lifelong) effects of anabolic steroid use in humans are unknown. It is known, however, that long-term intake of anabolic steroids can significantly reduce the lifespan of mice (Bronson et al. 1997).

KEY POINT

Using anabolic steroids can affect both physical and mental health, with problems ranging from greasy skin and hair to heart disease.

Liver	Reproductive and hormonal
Liver toxicity	Males:
Liver cancer	Decreased sperm count
	Abnormal sperm structure
Cardiovascular	Increased breast size
Decreased HDL cholesterol	Shrinkage of testicles
Increased LDL cholesterol	Females
Decreased triglycerides	Voice deepening
Fluid retention (increased blood pressure)	Enlargement of clitoris
	Decreased breast size
Cardiac hypertrophy	Disruption to menstrual cycle
Increased risk of coronary heart disease	Male pattern baldness
	Increased facial and body hair
Increased risk of heart attack	
	Dermatologic
Psychiatric	Oily hair
Mood changes	Oily skin
Increased aggression	Alopecia
Increased hostility	Increased occurrence of acne
Depression	Increased size of sebaceous glands
Dependence/addiction	

↑ Table 9.4: Possible physical and mental adverse effects associated with anabolic steroid use

Erythropoietin

It is impossible to predict how many new red blood cells will be produced with rEPO use. Therefore, there is always a risk of increasing blood viscosity due to the production of a large number of new red blood cells. This increased blood viscosity can increase the risk of blood clots, which could lead to a number of health problems including stroke, heart failure and heart attack. The risk of blood clots is also increased as EPO initiates activities associated with platelets and the inner lining of blood vessels that increase the likelihood of developing blood clots.

Athletes who use rEPO may also combine this with injections of iron in an attempt to further boost the oxygen carrying capacity of the blood (Bahrke, Yesalis 2002). Excess iron in the body can cause a number of serious problems in many organs, most notably the liver.

Blood pressure during submaximal exercise after rEPO administration is higher than before its use. This is not solely due to increased blood viscosity, and the exact cause is currently unknown. This elevation in blood pressure infers a greater stress on the heart during exercise, despite the lower exercising heart rate, and may contribute to the unexpected deaths of some athletes that have used rEPO (Bahrke, Yesalis 2002). In cycling alone, the use of rEPO is strongly thought to have caused the deaths of more than 20 athletes (Szygula 2010).

Beta blockers

The main health concerns result from prolonged use of beta blockers. Beta blockers can cause bronchospasms in people suffering from asthma. They can also cause cardiac failure in people with underlying cardiovascular issues. Beta blockers increase the secretion of insulin in the blood and can therefore cause hypoglycemia, especially in people with type II (non-insulin dependent) diabetes. Some of the most common side effects with beta blockers are brachycardia (abnormally low heart rate), orthostatic hypotension (a drop in blood pressure), a feeling of dizziness or light-headedness due to reduced blood pressure, and potentially life-threatening heart arrhythmias. Beta blockers can also cause feelings of fatigue, obviously not beneficial for optimal sports performance.

Caffeine

Many people are familiar with some of the common side effects of caffeine ingestion. They include nervousness, restlessness, insomnia, and tremors. These side effects are exacerbated in people who are not familiar with caffeine ingestion, who are sensitive to caffeine or who consume high doses. Disturbed sleep caused by caffeine ingestion can lead to fatigue. Some people also suffer gastrointestinal upset. Caffeine acts as a diuretic and can lead to dehydration, particularly during exercise in hot and/or humid conditions. Clearly, all of these issues could negatively influence sports performance, but are not of serious danger to health.

Caffeine is an addictive substance, and people who rapidly stop taking it can suffer withdrawal symptoms including headaches, irritability, fatigue and gastrointestinal upset. High doses of caffeine can also be associated with more serious health risks, such as heart arrhythmias and mild hallucinations. There is also a possible link between continued ingestion of caffeine and problems in pregnancy, risks of cancer, problems with calcium levels and with bone health (Bahrke, Yesalis 2002).

Diuretics

The use of diuretics can hinder the ability of the body to thermoregulate. During exercise, a greater skin blood flow is required so that heat can be lost from the body to the environment. However, diuretics reduce plasma volume (the liquid portion of the blood). In this situation, more blood is required in the central/core areas of the body in order to maintain an adequate blood pressure. Therefore, less blood would be available to travel to the skin, reducing the potential for body heat loss.

Diuretic use is associated with a number of potentially performance-affecting issues such as fatigue, drowsiness, muscle cramps and soreness, a feeling of numbness/tingling in limbs/extremities, nausea and vomiting, diarrhoea, mood changes and blurred vision.

Increased sensitivity of the skin to light is also a possible side effect, likely due to an allergic reaction or sensitivity to a specific type of diuretic. Use of diuretics can increase electrolyte loss, particularly sodium and potassium, and it is thought that many of the above issues are caused by this loss of electrolytes, especially potassium. Excess loss of potassium can also contribute to life-threatening conditions such as heart arrhythmias and cardiac arrest. Loss of potassium can also cause changes to metabolism such as a reduced ability to synthesize glycogen. Clearly, this would be an issue affecting sporting performance.

THEORY OF KNOWLEDGE

It is widely accepted that modern athletics is blighted by the use of performance-enhancing substances that can give athletes a better physical condition and can help them win an important sports competition. A number of well-known athletes have been caught cheating and others, by refusing to undergo tests, raise suspicions about their use of such substances. In recent decades, a number of athletes have had to give back Olympic medals and, generally, the scale of concerns over doping is ruining sports. The World Anti-Doping Agency (WADA) was established in 1999 with the mission *"to promote, coordinate and monitor the fight against doping in sport in all its forms"*. WADA regularly publishes updates of the list of prohibited substances, some of which can be detected by blood tests. However, most anti-doping agents are detected by urine analysis. Recently, a very interesting study by Schroeder et al. reported for the first time the occurrence of a large number of anabolic doping substances and other drugs (steroids, diuretic agents) and selected metabolites in wastewaters. As a part of their study, they monitored wastewaters from a fitness centre where the concentrations of these substances were particularly high, but also municipal wastewaters, where the concentrations were diluted yet still detectable. The link of the aforementioned study with the sports community is that, for the first time, environmental monitoring strategies can help anti-doping authorities enhance their targeted testing of athletes before and during major athletic events.

(Source: Katsoyiannis, A., Jones, K.C. 2011. *Environ. Sci. Technol*. Vol 45, number 2. Pp 362–363.)

In groups of three, discuss how you would plan and design a research study to investigate the use of prohibited substances by athletes, utilizing the sewerage systems of sport villages.

Why are some non-nutritional ergogenic aids banned in sport?

Ethical and moral obligation

All athletes competing at the Olympic games are sworn to an oath, taken by a representative athlete, to perform and abide by the rules of their sport and to abstain from doping and drug-enhanced performance. This represents a non-legal binding agreement between the athletes, the sporting governing bodies and, indirectly, the spectators and fans of the sport to compete to a certain ethical and moral standard. However, this standard is not always maintained, for a variety of reasons (Table 9.5).

We know from earlier sections of this chapter than some non-nutritional ergogenic aids have the potential to improve sporting performance. We also know that these same ergogenic aids can contribute to, or directly cause, significant health issues, some of which can prove fatal. If athletes decide to use a banned non-nutritional erogogenic aid (anabolic steroids, EPO etc.), they are not only compromising their own ethical and moral participation, but could also be compromising that of other athletes who may feel great pressure to also

> **In the name of all competitors I promise that we shall take part in these Olympic Games, respecting and abiding by the rules which govern them, committing ourselves to a sport without doping and without drugs, in the true spirit of sportsmanship, for the glory of sport and the honour of our teams.**

The Olympic Oath sworn by Chinese table tennis player Zhang Yining on behalf of all competing athletes prior to the Olympic Games in Beijing, 2008

TO THINK ABOUT

If an athlete decides to take a banned substance because they believe their opponent is doing likewise, does that athlete have any right to "blame" their opponent for pressurizing them into taking the substance? Or, as a legal adult, does the responsibility lie solely with the individual athlete?

employ the use of banned substances in order to remain competitive. Not only that, they may also be endangering the health of fellow athletes by applying indirect pressure to use banned and potentially dangerous ergogenic aids.

Having said that, elite athletes, certainly Olympic athletes, tend to be fully grown, legally recognized adults. Therefore, they are deemed to have certain social responsibilities, one of which is taking responsibility for their own actions.

→ Pressure to win
→ Attitude that doping is necessary to success
→ Public expectations about national success
→ Financial rewards of winning
→ Desire to be the best in the world
→ Grants and fees to athletes from governments and sponsors, linked to performance
→ Coaching that focuses upon winning as the only goal
→ Psychological belief that performance is assisted by a "magic pill"
→ Expectations of the spectators, friends and family
→ Pressure of the competitive calendar

↑ Table 9.5: Possible reasons for the ethical dilemma regarding the use of banned ergogenic substances in sport

Another perspective is this: some athletes are still taking banned substances, despite knowledge of the health risks and the illegality of these substances in their sport. Despite improvements in drug testing and detection, it is still not possible to catch 100 per cent of athletes using banned substances. Therefore, rather than spending large amounts of time, effort and money in trying to detect "cheating" athletes, why not legalize the substances? Indeed, there is a school of thought that argues that legalization of drugs in sport may be the most effective way of levelling the playing field and ensuring the safety of athletes (Savulescu et al. 2004).

However, in this situation it is plausible that factors such as performance pressure, desire to succeed, and suspicion of drug use by competitors may drive athletes who normally would not consider using potentially dangerous performance-enhancing substances to use them. Should an athlete who does not wish to risk their career, health, even their life, by taking a banned substance on the grounds of personal morals, ethics, or safety concerns be penalized or hampered in their ability to succeed in their chosen sport, or be forced into engaging in this unwanted behaviour/practice, by the legalization of these substances, or by their fellow athletes being willing to take that risk?

It is likely that some athletes who have used banned substances in sport see this as a positive example of their competitive spirit and unbreakable will to do anything necessary to succeed and win. Whether this is seen as a valid view or an attempt to distort the facts and provide an excuse for their behaviour is probably going to depend on the personal beliefs of the individual observer. However, the view of the International Olympic Committee is unequivocal:

> **The use of doping agents in sport is both unhealthy and contrary to the ethics of sport. It is necessary to protect the physical and spiritual health of athletes, the values of fair play and of competition, the integrity and unity of sport, and the rights of those who take part in it at whatever level.**
>
> International Olympic Charter against Doping in Sport

It is therefore clear that the use of potentially dangerous substances in sport that enable athletes to perform to a level they would not naturally be able to achieve is a moral and ethical minefield and will be seen differently by different people/athletes/coaches, depending on their own personal moral and ethical perspectives. It is precisely for this reason that an independent, objective consensus is required as to the use of certain ergogenic substances in sport, and that it is not left to the ethical and moral compass of individuals, as these values are exactly that, individual, and subject to widely different interpretation.

Current perspective

The discussion and debate regarding the status and level of acceptance of the use of banned ergogenic aids in sport has continued for many years and is an extremely complex area. Currently, most of the rationale for excluding certain ergogenic agents revolves around two key areas.

→ The ethical and moral dilemma and incompatibility between the values of sport and the use of illegal, dangerous substances with the sole aim of gaining a competitive advantage.

→ Safeguarding the health of athletes.

Despite this, the intentional use of banned substances by athletes continues. Additionally, there are calls from some to legalize currently banned substances, in the belief that this will provide a more level playing field on which athletes can compete. Clearly this is an area for debate, with moral, ethical, medical, philosophical, idealistic and personal perspectives, that will no doubt continue for many years to come.

THEORY OF KNOWLEDGE

This is the current Olympic oath that all athletes are obliged to abide by:

"In the name of all competitors I promise that we shall take part in these Olympic Games, respecting and abiding by the rules which govern them, committing ourselves to a sport without doping and without drugs, in the true spirit of sportsmanship, for the glory of sport and the honour of our teams."

A specific phrase in the oath has been highlighted. Think of this oath, and this phrase in particular, from an ethical perspective while you consider your responses to the following statements/questions:

→ The highlighted phrase specifically states "doping" and "drugs". Does this imply to the athlete that any other method of performance enhancement, regardless of how dangerous or socially unacceptable it may be to themselves or others, is therefore ethical, as long as it is not a "drug"?

→ Why are doping and drugs specifically highlighted, but not other performance enhancement methods? Some non-nutritional ergogenic aids, such as analysis of performance using sophisticated laboratory equipment and expertise, is not within the reach of smaller, less well-funded nations who complete at the Olympic Games. Therefore, if doping and drugs are banned in order to achieve a level playing field in sport, has this been achieved?

"Drug use in sport is contrary to the very principles upon which sport is based. Sport is considered as character building, teaching the virtues of dedication, perseverance, endurance and self-discipline."

"... sport helps us to learn from defeat as much as from victory, and team sports foster a spirit of co-operation and interdependence ... import(ing) something of moral and social values and ... integrating us as individuals, to bring about a healthy, integrated society."

Commission of inquiry into the use of drugs and banned practices intended to increase athletic performance, 1990

Now think of the oath and the highlighted phrase from a legal perspective. Consider the following:

The aim of the International Olympic Committee and other sports governing bodies is to prevent the use of banned ergogenic aids in order to protect athletes' health and provide a level playing field. Therefore, should the Olympic oath be made into a legally binding contract, where criminal charges can be brought against an athlete found guilty of breaking the oath? How would this affect the opinion/perspective of an outsider to elite sport?

Provide a balanced argument to these questions, analysing them from both possible perspectives.

SUMMARY

→ One of the key ways in which an athlete can improve their performance and gain a competitive advantage is by the use of ergogenic aids.

→ Ergogenic aids come under different classifications, but can be classed as "nutritional" and "non-nutritional".

→ Some non-nutritional ergogenic aids are legal in certain sports but banned in others, while some are banned in all sports.

→ Not all proposed ergogenic aids have been proven to be beneficial to sports performance. Some may exert a benefit due to the placebo effect.

→ Non-nutritional ergogenic aids exert their benefits in different ways. Some act on physiological responses such as metabolism, the breakdown or synthesis of body tissues, regulation of fluid levels, the production and function of hormones, cells and other substances in the body, the central nervous system or a combination of these factors.

→ Not all non-nutritional ergogenic aids will be suitable for all athletes. Some would be more suitable for strength athletes (anabolic steroids), some for athletes involved in precision and accuracy sports (beta blockers) and some for endurance athletes (EPO).

→ Individual responses may occur to non-nutritional ergogenic aids, meaning the responses to their use will not be uniform, even within a similar group of athletes.

→ Many non-nutritional ergogenic aids have risks and side effects that range from mild to potentially fatal.

→ Some non-nutritional ergogenic aids are banned in sport as they contravene the moral and ethical basis of sporting participation, do not allow a level playing field of competition and are potentially hazardous to athletes' health. However, debate in this area continues.

Self-study questions

1 Define the term "ergogenic aid".

2 What are the five classifications of ergogenic aid? List as many specific ergogenic aids in each classification as you can.

3 What is meant by the term "placebo effect"?

4 Why is it important to include a placebo when researching the ergogenic effect of a substance/piece of equipment/technique?

5 List the five main classes of non-nutritional ergogenic aid.

6   For each non-nutritional ergogenic aid listed in the previous question, identify two potential benefits and two potential health risks.

7   Explain why caffeine is a legal non-nutritional ergogenic aid, despite its proven performance benefits and potential negative health effects.

8   Outline why our understanding of the effects of anabolic steroid and erythropoietin use is limited.

9   Discuss the moral and ethical debate regarding the use of non-nutritional ergogenic aids in sport.

DATA BASED QUESTION

A study was carried out investigating the influence of creatine (CR) supplementation, creatine combined with caffeine (CR + CAF) supplementation, or a placebo (PLA) on repeated sprint performance. Participants completed six 10-second cycle sprints, with 60 seconds rest between each sprint. Every participant completed all three trials. Peak power output for each sprint in all three trials is in the graph below.

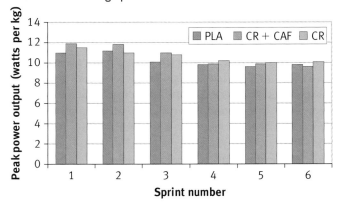

(Source: Lee, C., Lin, L. and Cheng, C. 2011. "Effect of caffeine ingestion after creatine supplementation on intermittent, high-intensity sprint performance." *European Journal of Applied Physiology*. Vol 111. Pp 1669–77.)

1   State which of the three supplements (PLA, CR + CAF, CR) is more beneficial for peak power output during sprint number 3.

2   Compare and contrast performance across the three supplement groups in sprint 2 and sprint 4.

3   Analyse the general response of peak power output from sprint 1 through to sprint 6 and draw a conclusion as to whether one supplement group generated better sprint performance compared to the other groups.

Individual differences in sport

Introduction

On British television in December each year the BBC screens a two-hour show entitled *BBC Sports Personality of the Year*. The programme is a review of domestic and international sport and is watched by millions of sports fans. The awards ceremony culminates in the presentation of a trophy to the "Sports Personality of the Year". Think carefully about how the word "personality" is being used in this context. The award winner is clearly successful, and popular, but the use of the term personality, as we will discover, is not accurate. Perhaps a more apt title for the programme should be "Most Popular Sportsperson of the Year".

Personality in psychology

To understand what the term "personality" really means we need to consider how it is has been developed. Psychology is a new science—it is barely 120 years old. Since the birth of psychology, the only constant seems to be the continual scientific advances as psychologists seek to understand, predict and modify human behaviour. In so doing, psychologists are continually refining scientific techniques to investigate who we are as individuals and why we think and behave in the ways that we do.

As advances in our understanding of how we think and behave are made, new knowledge adds to or conflicts with previous understanding. In order to get to the forefront of current thinking, psychology students have to consider the contribution and limitations of work carried out as far back as the 19th century. Therefore, it is important to appreciate what each theory concerning personality adds to our understanding of the way that human beings think and behave—this chapter seeks to do just that.

If psychologists are going to realize the goal of helping people to help themselves, it is important that the views of the individuals are taken into consideration. Therefore, theories of human personality are necessarily accompanied by techniques of collecting information about human personality.

Unsurprisingly, sport and exercise psychology is a comparatively recent branch of psychology. It has been endorsed by mainstream psychologists such as the British Psychological Society (www.bps.org.uk), the American Psychological Association (www.apa.org), the European Federation of Psychologists' Associations (www.efpa.eu), and the Australian Psychological Society (www.psychology.org.au), alongside other important areas of practice and inquiry, such as clinical psychology.

There are two broad functions that a sport and exercise psychologist performs.
→ The first is to research, create and evaluate knowledge.
→ The second is to improve human performance and health.

Applied sport psychology can be subdivided into two roles.
→ The first is to help performers from the novice/learner to top level sportsmen and sportswomen achieve their potential in sport.
→ The second is to guide individuals in the use of exercise as a means of coping with, or reducing the risk of acquiring, a physical and/or psychological illness.

Therefore, the interest in theories of personality for sport and exercise psychologists tends to differ depending on what they are seeking to understand or achieve. In this chapter, theories of personality are reviewed, and the implications for those who play sport will be outlined.

In a brief review such as this, the list of theories related to personality is necessarily incomplete. A further note of caution: just because a theory of personality is widely accepted and endorsed, it does not mean that it can be applied uncritically to performers and exercisers. There is an important rule that is observed by applied psychologists that is relevant here: test before you try. It simply means that a psychologist needs to understand what factors are influencing a performer's personality before an intervention can be attempted. (MacPherson 2009. Doctoral Thesis, University of Edinburgh.) The uncritical application of mainstream psychology theories related to the study of personality has led some sport and exercise psychologists to take a negative view of the potential impact of personality theory on sport and exercise. However, after reading this chapter it is important that you make up your own mind as to what is and what is not important for sports scientists to understand as they seek to assist performers and exercisers alike.

Defining personality

Personality has been defined as "those relatively stable and enduring aspects of individuals which distinguish them from other people, making them unique but at the same time permit a comparison between individuals" (Gross 1992). The implications of this quotation are important: if aspects of personality were not stable or enduring they would be very difficult to study. After all, we need to be able to predict others' behaviour, and other people need to be able to predict how we are going to respond to all kinds of interpersonal behaviours.

Our respective personalities define in our own eyes and in other peoples' opinions who we are and what we are likely to think and feel. Having relatively stable and enduring patterns of behaviour allow us to develop, forge and maintain relationships. Children learn from a very young age to predict what their parents or guardians will be angry about. Imagine growing up in an environment where you could not predict what your parent or guardian would get angry about because that adult had an unstable personality. Living with someone like this can do a lot of emotional damage to the people for whom they are responsible.

One way of understanding the functions of human personality is to consider what happens to people when they are experiencing mental illness, for example, bipolar or manic depression. This form of depression results in swings between manias—bursts of energy and fantastical notions of self are followed by feelings of low self-worth and, in some cases, accompanied by suicidal thoughts. Famous sportspeople such as the Great Britain boxing legend Frank Bruno, the American John Daly, Open Golf champion, John Kirwan, the great All Blacks rugby union winger and the very tragic case of Robert Enke, the national soccer goalkeeper for Germany, have experienced periods of mental illness: it is not uncommon and it does affect how these individuals see themselves and how other people, some of them misinformed, see them.

Aside from the serious stigma associated with mental illness, one of the main reasons that people with bipolar depression report feelings of isolation is the difficulty for friends and family to predict and make allowances for changes in their patterns of behaviour. This inconsistent pattern of behaviour inhibits the development and maintenance of close relationships, but can the study of personality make us healthier and perform better in sport?

Personality in sport psychology

Personality theory in mainstream psychology is dominated by researchers and thinkers who have developed psychometric tools to measure personality in a reliable and consistent fashion. These tools include questionnaires such as Eysenck's extrovert personality questionnaire (EPQ), or Cattell's five factor model. Despite the fact that they accurately measure **traits** (relatively enduring patterns of attitudes and patterns of behaviour), and despite a substantial amount of research, psychologists have yet to determine what types of personality characteristics are associated with elite performance.

At the conclusion of the Florida Conference on Personality and Sport in 1975, Robert Singer, an eminent sport psychologist, observed: "We have tried to fish for minnows with a net designed for whales; we cannot really complain about the size of the catch."

The crucial point appears to be that general personality factors, and the instruments which are used to measure them, are just not sensitive to the more subtle differences that determine sport performance. For many, this comment seemed an effective epilogue to a long debate on the role of personality theories in sport, an area of study which was a dominant topic in the early days of sport psychology. An earlier comment by Rushall (1970), another eminent sport psychologist, was even more explicit: "Personality is not a significant factor in sport performance", a statement that will be considered at the end of this chapter.

Set against this critical backdrop, the main aim of this chapter is to identify theories of personality that have the potential to deepen our understanding of human performance in sport and exercise, and to enable us to prepare athletes to perform beyond what they consider to be their potential. The aim is not to classify aspects of peoples' personalities into being high in one factor and low in another. Rather, it is concerned with change: how can psychologists maximize an individual's performance in a specific activity? The answer lies in possessing a thorough appreciation of social learning theory and by considering what an interactionist view of personality holds for psychologists and the people they work with.

An interactionist view of personality

In the 1930s, a group of psychologists based in Germany developed the principle of interactionism in human personality. One of the main supporters of this principle was Kurt Lewin who became one of the most influential social psychologists of the 20th century. Lewin suggested that neither nature (inborn tendencies) nor nurture (life experiences) can account for an individual's behaviour and personality. Instead, he proposed that our personalities are developed through a constant interaction between the person and their environment.

To neatly summarize this contention, Lewin formulated the following equation:

$$B = f(P, E)$$

In essence, **B**ehaviour is a function of the **P**erson and their **E**nvironment.

This has important ramifications for the way we not only think about improving human performance, but also how, as psychologists, we think of and treat illness associated with poor lifestyle choices. Therefore, exercise psychologists, if they are going to succeed in their goal to promote a healthier lifestyle, need to be aware of the effect the environment is having on the individual.

An interactionist view of personality holds that the individual's experiences cannot be understood if personal and situational factors are separated (Mischel, Shoda, Smith 2003). While the interactionist view of personality is still a matter of some debate among certain psychologists, the principle of interactionism, that organisms and environment interact to determine behaviour, is widely recognized, particularly in the fields of biology and genetics. Lewontin (2000) states that genetic and environmental influences are intertwined making development "contingent on the sequence of environments in which it occurs".

Yet, a fundamental part of who we are is dependent on our genes. If Lewin's equation is correct, then our genetic profile will interact with the environment in which we work and live. In terms of understanding why people behave and think in the way that they do, there are two distinct ways of describing the function and effect of genes on human personality.

→ Emergenesis is the first scientific principle that has a bearing on our understanding of personality. A trait is called emergenic if a specific combination of several genes interact. Emergenic traits will not run in families, but identical twins will share them (Lykken et al. 1992). Certain forms of mental illness, aspects of leadership and genius may, according to Lykken et al. be emergenic. If emergenesis can be substantiated then it has the potential to undermine part of the premise upon which Lewin's equation and, therefore, interactionism is based.

→ Epigenesis is the second scientific principle that informs our understanding of personality. The study of why and how genes interact with the environment and, in turn, shape human behaviour is termed as epigenetics. The field of epigenetics has emerged to bridge the gap between "nature" and "nurture" and is therefore "interactive" in its focus. If genes are epigenetic then this lends substantial support to Lewin's equation.

Using scientific techniques at the forefront of medical science, further support for the interactionist perspective can be derived from the work of Srvakic and Cloninger (2010), who state that: "DNA (deoxyribonucleic acid) is no more considered to be the master blueprint for physical and behavioral features that operates in an ecological vacuum. Rather, DNA outlines the overall adaptive potential of an organism." Therefore the person and their genome respond to the environment—they interact.

In terms of understanding why mental illness occurs, Srvakic and Cloninger believe that strong biogenetic dispositions interact with environmental factors (e.g. factors that cause chronic physical and psychological stress) which then act as a tipping point where an individual's adaptive potential to negative life events becomes compromised, which in turn negatively influences their psychological well-being. Therefore, as we are concerned with optimizing human performance, we need to think carefully about how sources of negative stress affect different performers in different situations.

A more contemporary model of interactionist theory than that provided by Lewin can be found in the work of the psychologist Walter Mischel who takes what is known as a social-cognitive approach. He is interested in four personality variables (Beneckson 2011):

→ competencies—our skills and knowledge
→ encoding strategies—our particular style and the schemas we use in processing information
→ expectancies—what we expect from our own behaviour and our anticipations of our performance levels
→ plans—what we intend to do.

The interaction of these cognitive factors with environmental situations results in the expression of personality (Mischel et al. 2003).

Essential to understanding personality from an interactionist standpoint is that you consider how an individual's personality unfolds, or develops, across a number of social situations. Behavioural instances, if repeated, have the potential to demonstrate the inner workings of a meaningful characteristic, or what may be considered a behavioural signature, of an individual's personality (Mischel et al. 2003). Mischel's work, as it is epigenetic in nature, has much in common with the research conducted by Albert Bandura (to be discussed in the next section).

In summary, it is important to get an insight into an interactionist approach to personality because as psychologists, and sports scientists, we need to understand the role that emergenic and epigenetic factors can play in athletes' behaviour, particularly, for example, when we consider the central role that talent development plays in human performance.

Social learning theory and personality

One of the most influential theories in psychology is social learning theory (SLT) (Bandura 1977; 1997; 2001). One of its most remarkable features concerns our capacity to learn without reinforcement (either rewards or punishments). According to the principles derived from extensive research, SLT states that we have a capacity to learn by observation, even in the absence of rewards (Pervin, Cervone, John 2005). It further emphasizes our individual capacity to influence our destiny and to try to achieve our potential.

The personality structures of SLT are mainly cognitive: that is, they are related to the processes of knowing, being aware, thinking, learning and judging. According to Pervin et al. to get a full understanding of SLT and how it relates to personality there are four constructs that must be taken into account:

→ competencies and skills
→ beliefs and expectancies
→ behavioural (evaluative) standards
→ personal goals.

Competencies and skills

How someone speaks or looks is noticed and is often used to make judgments about their personality, for example, whether they are sad or outgoing. Bandura (1982) argues that how we are perceived by others is influenced by our own feelings of competence. Therefore, an individual can appear shy and introverted because they are not confident at carrying out a particular task or role, not because

TO THINK ABOUT

All countries that send athletes to the Olympic Games want their athletes to perform well. However, if you were in charge of your country's athlete development budget, before you allocate funds to athletes or teams, you need to decide whether you think athletic talent is emergenic or epigenetic.

that is how they behave all the time. In summary, how you behave depends on the actual skills you have and whether you expect to be good at something.

According to Pervin et al. (2005) there are two important implications relating to competency. The first involves context specificity and the second relates to psychological change.

→ Context specificity means that certain psychological structures that are relevant in one situation are not relevant in another. For example, an individual may be a confident and enthusiastic surfer but might not be a conscientious pupil in art classes. Albert Bandura has demonstrated that we can work on our weaknesses and in some cases cope with, and even improve at, the tasks that we struggled with previously.

→ Psychological change refers to the manner in which competencies are acquired. Bandura (1986) states that competencies are acquired through observation and social interaction; therefore, a person who lacks particular skills in an area of their life, for example, sporting performance, *can* learn to improve them.

While this may seem obvious and something most people recognize in the behaviour of others, Bandura has developed ways to effect change in behaviour which in turn influences personality.

Beliefs and expectancies

A crucial component of psychological change and self-improvement is concerned with beliefs and expectancies. In very general terms, beliefs relate to how the world is, while expectancies concern what an individual thinks will happen in the future.

A sub-category of these two concepts is what the world *should* be like. According to Bandura (1986) and Pervin et al. (2005) this sub-category of thinking concerns evaluating the worth and quality of a particular event. For self-improvement to occur a person needs to hold a belief about an action they perform, have expectations as to the outcome of that action and think about what the execution of that action *should* be like. According to social learning theory, these are the three factors that create the dynamic necessary for change to occur in the personalities of humans.

Behavioural standards

A mental "standard" is a criterion for judging the goodness or worth of a person, thing or event. Behavioural (evaluative) standards are standards concerning one's self or personal standards, and personal standards are fundamental to human motivation and performance. Thus, you use behavioural (evaluative) standards to judge the goodness or worth of your own behaviour.

According to Bandura (1986) we evaluate our own actions and then respond in an emotionally satisfied way (e.g. we meet our standards for performance) or dissatisfied way (e.g. we fail to meet our standards for performance). It is a kind of "internal guidance/psychological system" through which people consider their own actions, and contrasts with behaviourist theory which argues that ongoing behaviour is determined by forces in the environment.

Goals

A key concept that relates to influencing change in our personalities is the identification and realization of goals. (Towards the end of this section of the chapter, goals and goal-setting will be revisited.)

THEORY OF KNOWLEDGE

Moral emotions represent a key element of our moral apparatus, influencing the link between moral standards and moral behaviour. People do, on occasion, lie, cheat, and steal, even though they know such behaviour is deemed wrong by moral and societal norms. Individual differences in people's anticipation of and experience of moral emotions likely play key roles in determining actual moral choices and behaviour in real-life contexts.

(Tangey et al. 2007. "Moral emotions and moral behaviour." *Annu. Rev. Psychol.* Vol 58. Pp 345–72.)

TO DO

In groups of four, discuss how behavioural (evaluative) standards could be used:

→ as a theoretical tool to study moral behaviour and violations of moral standards
→ to influence behaviour among criminal offenders.

KEY POINT

The main components of social cognitive theory as it relates to personality are competencies and skills, beliefs and expectancies, behavioural (evaluative) standards and goals.

Social cognitive theory: self-efficacy

Before we examine athlete case studies of performance profiling and goal setting, it is necessary to understand how performance can be improved on an individual basis. Self-efficacy refers to the expectation that people have of their own capabilities for performance.

TO THINK ABOUT

At the start of a match or competition do you already have an idea of how well you or your team will do? Does it affect your actual performance?

Research conducted by Baumeister et al. (2003) and Bandura and Locke (2003), demonstrated that the relationship between self-efficacy and physical performance was robust. If you can increase feelings of self-efficacy then a consequent increase in physical performance can be observed. Self-efficacy has been defined as confidence towards learning. There is a famous quote by Henry Ford who said, "If you think you can do it or think you can't do it, you're right." While it is an extreme viewpoint, the essence of what Henry Ford said is correct. However, the important difference between what he said and where SLT is of great value to everyone, is that SLT, as we are about to discover, demonstrates how meaningful change that is personal to an individual can be achieved.

KEY POINT

Self-esteem is how someone feels they are valued overall whereas self-efficacy is how they feel they can perform in a specific setting.

It is important to understand that self-efficacy is distinct from self-esteem. The latter refers to a person's global evaluation of their personal worth, whereas self-efficacy refers to what someone feels that they are able to achieve in a given setting.

TO THINK ABOUT

Consider the example below that illustrates the difference between self-efficacy and self-esteem. Ian Woosnam is a former world number one golfer and has won 48 professional tournaments including the Masters. Read carefully what he states about his performance.

"I had a bit of the twitches in the last couple of rounds here last year but I've got the long putter this week and hopefully I'll be able to knock the short ones in.

I've been working with Bob Torrance recently and getting my swing near where it used to be. I've put on a bit of distance as well and feel I've actually got a chance of winning this week. It's been a long time since I thought that.

I feel I haven't had a good putting week for as long as I can remember. I can have two good putting days and then two poor ones and shoot 74 or 75. I still feel I can win and I want to win again before I'm 50.

Fifteen years ago I would come in and say I was going to win the tournament. If my putting was good I knew I was going to win certain tournaments. These days my putting isn't strong enough to say that but I am working on it."

June 2006

This example outlines why it is important to understand the important difference between self-efficacy and self-esteem. Consider how Woosnam evaluates himself as a putter, but

not a golfer. He knows what he needs to do to win. He also knows that most of his golf game is in great shape, but not his putting. If you were to measure his self-esteem as opposed to examining his self-efficacy, the result you would get would be imprecise and would not enable a sport and exercise psychologist to design a tailored performance solution.

Importantly, self-efficacy can be manipulated because it refers to specific competencies and expectations; self-esteem is far more cumbersome because it includes many facets of a person's life. With regard to Woosnam's putting, using techniques discussed below it may in fact be possible to increase his self-efficacy by influencing his view of what can be achieved and thereby increasing his confidence towards learning (i.e. self-efficacy).

In order to measure perceived self-efficacy, Bandura states that a micro-analytic research strategy be used. What he means by this is that an individual be measured immediately before the performance of specific behaviours in specific situations (i.e. putting not golfing). Now, recall what Singer (1975) was quoted as saying earlier in this chapter regarding fishing for minnows with nets designed to catch whales and the relative imprecision with which personality has been investigated in relation to sports performance. If we extrapolate from social learning theory, taking into account individuals' beliefs and expectations regarding their future performance, human personality should be studied in relation to specific areas of a person's life, and not examined as a whole.

TO THINK ABOUT

Can you think of examples from your own sporting experiences where a change in mindset, believing you could improve, actually led to an improvement in your performance?

How can self-efficacy be manipulated?

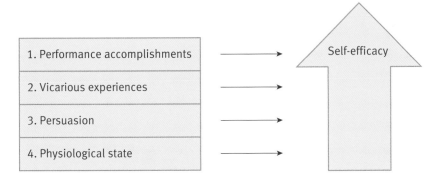

↑ Figure 10.1: Antecedents of self-efficacy

An antecedent is defined as previous or pre-existing factors that are known to increase self-efficacy. To improve performance the four factors shown in Figure 10.1 can be used in isolation or in combination to increase self-efficacy.

Performance accomplishments

Performance accomplishments are described by Morriss and Summers (1995) as the most potent antecedent of self-efficacy. Before we discuss this particular type of antecedent it is important to recognize what is perceived by a particular athlete to be a performance accomplishment.

A technique commonly used by psychologists to ascertain how athletes see themselves is termed "performance profiling" (Butler, Hardy 1992), originally introduced to sport and exercise psychologists some twenty years ago (Butler 1989; 1991). It stems from Kelly's work on personal construct psychology (PCP) which emphasizes that psychologists need to try and understand the ways in which athletes perceive the world in which they train, live and perform (Gucciardi, Gordon 2009). The performance profile encourages practitioners and researchers to regard an individual's perception or meaning of their performance as a vital source of information to optimize performance.

The information that is being elicited from an athlete concerns *their* view of *their* performance. It is their opinion about what makes them effective, and also how they could improve aspects of their performance in relation to the best performer they can think of. You may be thinking that what is being described does not sound very different from a questionnaire that you may have had experience of filling in. However, questionnaires impose constructs on performers (i.e. they tell you whether you are an extrovert or an introvert) whereas a performance profile allows an athlete to create a personalized profile that gives them a central role in its construction.

Once the categories are generated by an athlete, and in some cases compared to a profile completed by a coach, the performer is encouraged to take ownership of their profile. This gives the performer a central role in how to close the gap between their current performance self and their ideal performance self.

CASE STUDY

Butler, Smith and Irwin (1993) used the performance profile to assess the beliefs of boxers and their coaches about the technical, tactical and physical qualities they possessed before boxing at the Olympic Games in Barcelona in 1992 (see Figure 10.2). In total, sixteen boxers and three coaches took part.

The boxers were divided into three groups and asked to brainstorm what they believed the characteristics of a champion or elite boxer to be. After this, each group shared their vision of the characteristics of a champion/elite boxer, i.e. the common characteristics. Against each common characteristic generated by the three groups, the boxers assessed themselves. If there was a difference in the assessment between the ideal champion and the boxer, then goals were set to try and reduce any discrepancy. Immediately before the Games the coaches then reviewed each boxer's profile. It was shown that where the athletes and the coaches were in overall agreement regarding the respective strengths and weaknesses of a performer's profile, the boxer's performance was closely associated with the attainment of a medal.

Where the beliefs and the expectations of the coach and the performer were closely matched, the accurate use of performance profiles could be used to gauge performance

accomplishments. In three out of four cases where the mean discrepancy in the performance profile was low between the coach and the boxer, a medal was attained. According to the work of Butler et al. (1993) using the performance profile to accurately gauge the perception of strengths and weaknesses is associated with achievement at the highest level.

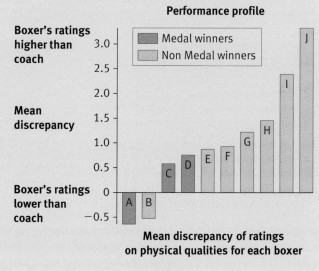

↑ Figure 10.2: Performance profile

Antecedent previous or pre-existing factor known to increase self-efficacy

Goal setting

Another powerful tool to improve self-efficacy with regard to physical accomplishments is goal setting, also looked at in chapter 13 on psychological skills training. In 1990, Locke and Latham published their book entitled *A Theory of Goal Setting and Task Performance*, in which they outlined the characteristics of purposeful and accurate goal setting practices. Most of us are familiar with the acronym SMARTER goals (Specific, Measurable, Attainable, Realistic, Time-locked, Exciting, Review). However, Locke and Latham (1990) also stated that goals needed to be perceived as moderately difficult. If the goal was perceived as being too easy then it did not engage the individual in question.

Furthermore, a goal setting programme should include *negative* and *positive* goals. An example of a negative goal is to stop conceding fouls close to the penalty area, whereas a positive goal might encourage a soccer player to look for an outlet to pass to before they receive the ball.

A further component of goal setting is goal proximity. This refers to using both short-term and long-term goals. Most of us find it harder to work towards something that we will enjoy the benefits of at a later date. Therefore, the solution to this is to include goals that can be achieved quickly but form the path to reaching a goal that is distant. Distant goals, often termed outcome goals, are important because they direct attention towards an objective, but they need to be used in conjunction with performance and process goals, the former providing individuals with updates regarding their progress towards the outcome goal (e.g. a lap time in an 800 meter race), whereas a process goal is an action that, if realized, aids in the acquisition of the outcome goal. An example of this type of goal might be for a rugby union prop forward to engage his opposite number on his terms, to "get the hit in first", thereby obtaining an advantage for his team in an important aspect of the overall game.

While it may be the job of a sport and exercise psychologist to increase an individual's self-efficacy in order to increase the amount they exercise, or to improve their sporting performance, it is important to be mindful of the context in which the original research on goal setting was conducted. Goal setting research was conducted by psychologists who wanted to understand how to maximize productivity in the workplace. It was determined that if goal setting was applied correctly, managers and executives could expect an improvement in productivity of between 8.4 and 16 per cent. However, if goal setting is applied to someone who is already close to their performance potential, such as an elite sportsperson, then it is unlikely such an improvement will be feasible.

Vicarious experience

The second of the four antecedents is vicarious experience (VE). A straightforward way to understand it is to consider how you would feel if you observed one of your peer group successfully completing a task you were expected to perform. VE is sometimes described as modelling and is so-called because seeing an example of how to complete a task by a peer can act as a stimulus to attempt an activity you might not have considered otherwise, but there are positive and negative aspects to modelling.

From a positive standpoint, training with a group of people who are striving to be better at a task, whether academic or sporting, has the potential to spur you on to achieve feats that you did not think possible, provided you are not in awe of the people completing the task in the first place: In essence, for VE to influence self-efficacy you have to think or believe it is possible that you can attempt to complete the target activity.

From a negative standpoint, Bandura demonstrated that acts of aggression, if viewed by impressionable people, can then be unthinkingly repeated in similar social situations. The negative aspect of modelling has obvious implications for the repetition of socially undesirable behaviours, such as bullying.

It is important that we understand how and when to use VE positively, but we should also be aware of the benefits of VE for skill acquisition. In summary, VE has been shown to have a powerful change-provoking effect on the subsequent behaviour of the individual observing the target behaviour (Bandura, 1982).

Persuasion

Bandura uses the term persuasion, but he is specifically referring to verbal persuasion (Morriss, Summers 1995). However, persuasion can also come in the form of an act. Persuasion often comes from a high-status individual and is designed to encourage you to act in a particular way. It can be inspirational to be persuaded by someone you hold in high regard.

THEORY OF KNOWLEDGE

Albert Bandura is the original proponent of social cognitive theory. His theory has had a profound effect across a number of academic disciplines. As you have already discovered Bandura (2001) developed the concept of self-efficacy: self-efficacy falls under the auspices of social cognition. His research has led to the view of people as their own agents of social change. This agentic perspective allows humans being to shape their destiny and has significant ramifications as to how we view human personality. In Bandura's article (2001), he states that,

"Gould (1987) builds a strong case that biology sets constraints that vary in nature, degree, and strength in different activity domains, but in most spheres of human functioning biology permits a broad range of cultural possibilities. He argues cogently that evidence favors a potentialist view over a determinist view. In this insightful analysis, the major explanatory battle is not between nature and nurture as commonly framed, but whether nature operates as a determinist or as a potentialist." (Bandura, 2001, p.20)

(Source: Bandura, A. (2001). "Social cognitive theory: An agentic perspective." *Annual Review of Psychology*. Vol 52. Pp 1–26.

In groups of four, discuss how your understanding of social cognitive theory influences the following:
→ your personality
→ your competence in the physical domain.

Consider the effect of Nelson Mandela's presence in the changing room before the Rugby World Cup Final in 1995. Joost van der Westhuizen, the Springbok scrum-half, said the following.

"There was a lot of stress in the changing room. … It was dead quiet and suddenly the door opened and there was Nelson Mandela walking in. … I think the best thing was to see him in a Springbok jersey, that was the best thing for us—it was a total surprise. Then we realized that the whole country was behind us, and for this man to wear a Springbok jersey was a sign, not just for us, but for the whole of South Africa, that we have to unite, and we have to unite today."

Not only did Mandela wear a sporting shirt that was previously considered to be an emblem that upheld apartheid, but the shirt he wore had a number 6 on the back—the number that Francois Pienaar, the captain, would wear that day. The persuasion that took place was in word and in deed. It came from one of the

most inspirational figures of our time and he did not just say, "You can win this", his actions went beyond sport. It was about demonstrating the potential of healing cultural rifts and saying to the players "we have a future together—we all wish you well".

TO DO

Think how you would like to be persuaded, and who you would like to be persuaded by? Discuss this with your classmates. Would you all have chosen the same source, repeating the same message?

We have seen the potential impact of persuasion when used by a high-status individual, used at the right time, in the right place, but can you persuade yourself to enact a difficult task? A specialism among psychologists concerns the use of imagery and evidence has shown that emotionally charged images personal to the performer can be used to motivate in training, or form part of a pre-performance routine designed to adjust the level of arousal (Morriss, Summers, 1995).

Like vicarious experience and modelling, persuasion must come from a credible source. As with all the antecedents of self-efficacy, the factors in the model presented need to be used in a way that is not perceived as critical, but in a positive fashion.

Physiological state

The final antecedent of increased self-efficacy concerns the interpretation a performer makes of their physiological state before a performance. Preparing to perform in front of an audience or trying a new but challenging activity often results in heightened levels of arousal.

In term of cognitive processes, arousal often results in attentional narrowing and selecting the most relevant cues upon which to focus. The construct of attention has three dimensions:

→ **Concentration (or effortful awareness)** For example, listening intently to your sports coach during a timeout in basketball.
→ **Selective attention** That is, the ability to focus ("zoom in") on relevant information and ignore distractors that compete for our attention, for example, ignoring the hostile crowd of spectators and listening intently to your sports coach during a timeout in basketball.
→ **The ability to coordinate two or more actions at the same time** For example, checking the score on the scoreboard while at the same time listening intently to your sports coach during a timeout in basketball.

Also it is important to note that attentional narrowing can have a negative effect on performance, for example, if you focus your attention on the hostile crowd rather than listening intently to your sports coach during a timeout in basketball.

From a somatic standpoint (the physical sensations experienced), increased arousal can result in, for example, elevated heart rate, breathlessness, a dry mouth, a churning stomach ("butterflies") and sweaty hands (Morriss, Summers 1995). If you are not familiar with these sensations you would be forgiven for thinking you are having a panic attack. However, as you prepare for action, your body automatically enables hormones to enter the bloodstream which have a corresponding effect on how you feel.

Understanding the changes your body is making before physical exertion helps to reassure the performer and as a result increases self-efficacy. Therefore, a key antecedent to increased self-efficacy lies in understanding how and why your body works in the way that it does.

However, not all physical activities require us to experience high levels of cognitive and somatic anxiety. In fact, in some sports you may want low levels of somatic anxiety but require high levels of focus, for example, in self-paced target sports like archery, whereas in sports like weightlifting, experienced performers have learned to realize that high levels of arousal accompanied by somatic anxiety can reassure the performer that they are going to exceed, or perform close to, their personal best.

Almost 2000 years ago, philosopher and Roman Emperor Marcus Aurelius wrote that: "Everything is but what your opinion makes it; and that opinion lies within yourself." Therefore the capacity to change established traits in our personalities lies within us.

Reflecting upon what was discussed earlier in this chapter, by taking the interactionist approach advocated by Lewin, we have come to understand that the environment influences our genetic make-up throughout our lives. Studies of the causes of mental illness have illustrated the importance of understanding human behaviour from an epigenetic viewpoint. With regard to social learning theory, Bandura has demonstrated the effect of four powerful antecedents (performance accomplishments, persuasion, vicarious experience, and physiological states) that can influence our confidence in approaching learning (i.e. self-efficacy).

Therefore, the role of psychologists working in the realm of human performance is to show clients that the power to determine their future really does lie in their own hands. People can, with the right tools, focused on specific factors, influence and alter their own personality. However, before change occurs psychologists need to collect reliable information.

> **KEY POINT**
>
> The four antecedents of self-efficacy according to Bandura are performance accomplishments, vicarious experiences, persuasion and physiological state.

Measuring aspects of personality

There are LOTS of ways to gather scientific data regarding personality but there are four main ways. Psychologists working in the field of personality have developed an acronym, LOTS (Block 1993), to make it easy to remember what these four categories of data are.

LOTS stands for:

→ L-data—lifetime history
→ O-data—observations from knowledgeable others including parents and friends
→ T-data—experimental procedures and standardized tests
→ S-data—information provided by the client.

To develop an understanding of how to measure personality it is important to consider how a psychologist might use the information gathered from these different sources. The goal of a psychologist working with personality data is to consider how these factors are influenced by the environment in which that individual lives, and therefore how personalities alter over time and according to experiences.

To be confident in the assertions they make, psychologists need to know the information they are collecting about someone's personality is reliable. To do so they need to understand the confidence limits of the data they are working with and consider what might be reliable and unreliable information.

L-data

Firstly, consider how L-data (lifetime history) might be used. This data might include IQ (intelligence quotient) tests, academic performance at school or at university. It might also include other personal performance data such as achievements in other hobbies or sports. L-data could also include information about where somebody grew up, who raised them, whether any family members had any criminal convictions or used illegal substances, and if they have/had a spouse and any children or dependents. More positively, it might also focus on an individual's career aspirations and history of employment (Pervin et al. 2005).

Clearly, there is a large volume of information that comprises L-data and it is vital that a psychologist understands what information is relevant and what data is misleading. For example, if someone has a high IQ it doesn't necessarily mean they are going to be successful when they leave school. L-data needs to be considered very carefully in order to build up a pattern of behaviour over an extended period of time so as to determine why individuals behave in the way they do, and why they have made certain choices that affected outcomes in their lives and the lives of those they are related to.

O-data

O-data concerns the observations and insights of knowledgeable others, such as friends, teachers, peers and family members. According to Pervin et al. (2005), O-data is often collected using questionnaires that are designed to focus on a specific facet of the target individual's personality, for example, extroversion (Michaelis, Eysenck 1971), or conscientiousness (Pervin et al. 2005).

O-data can also be collected by trained observers who might use Davies and West's (1991) multi-modal approach for gathering information on an individual which they call BASIC-ID. This is another acronym, which stands for **B**ehaviour, **A**ffect, **S**ensations, **I**magery, **C**ognition, **I**nterpersonal functioning, and **D**iet and drugs. Briefly, trained observers consider and collect data on:

→ how someone is behaving (B)
→ their emotional state (A)
→ what bodily sensations they experience (S)
→ what mental pictures they are aware of (I)
→ what they are thinking (C)
→ how they interact with other people and peers (I)
→ whether they are eating properly and/or using medication or drugs (D).

This allows a researcher to develop a considered picture of how an individual is functioning in a particular setting.

There are a number of important factors to consider when evaluating the worth and accuracy of O-data. In the case of questionnaires, how reliable is the questionnaire? Furthermore, what are the biases of the people providing this information—what do they really think the psychologist wants to find out? Finally, if observers are being used what are they being instructed to monitor, and is there a risk of them confirming their own biases?

There are a quite a number of data collection and measurement techniques that fall into the category of O-data which may yield varying degrees of accuracy. The important factors for psychologists to be aware of are the limitations and flaws in the measures themselves and in the expectations of those administering them.

T-data

T-data refers to specific tests that might be used to assess someone. These can be used to assess someone's suitability for a specific occupational role, but the use of this type of data by sports scientists, particularly sport psychologists, is comparatively rare.

S-data

S-data, information provided by the individual, is widely used. The problem with self-report data is that it may be inaccurate for two reasons. Firstly, an individual may want you to evaluate them in a favourable light and present a more flattering, though inaccurate, picture of what they are and what they do. It is described by psychologists as self-presentation. The second reason this form of data may be inaccurate relates to a tendency among certain individuals referred to as denial. Individuals with substance abuse problems or mounting financial debts can erect mental barriers that prevent them from consciously assessing their true emotional and behavioural state.

In summary, personality data can be collected in different ways, in different circumstances. While error and bias will always be present in any assessment of personality, the important factor for psychologists to be aware of is the sources of bias. Finally, consider the nature of the assessment of personality that is being advocated in relation to sport and exercise: it is situation specific, it is individually oriented and it is micro-analytic.

SUMMARY

- → The uncritical export of mainstream personality theory into sport and exercise psychology has met with mixed success. As yet psychologists have not been able to identify personality characteristics that predict sporting success.
- → Our personalities are influenced by the interactions we have with the environment in which we live.
- → It is fortunate that personality is a relatively stable construct because other people need to predict how we will react to changing social circumstances.
- → If our personalities were fixed we would not be able to adapt to changes in our social circumstances.
- → As students of sport and exercise psychology we need to be aware of the environment that athletes and exercisers are training and, in some cases, performing in and the effect that this may have on their respective personalities.
- → A major factor in determining how well we adapt and learn is self-efficacy. At certain times in our lives we need to learn new skills and adapt to different environments. In this regard, self-efficacy is a key attribute.
- → As psychologists we need to be able to gather LOTS of meaningful, reliable data before we decide what antecedents of self-efficacy may increase an individual's confidence towards learning.
- → Psychologists have developed techniques that enable us to approach difficult tasks with increased confidence so individuals can shape their destiny.

Self-study questions

1 List the four factors that allow psychologists to collect "LOTS" of data.

2 State the component parts of Lewin's Interactionist Equation.

3 According to epigenesists, what two principal factors interact?

4 Identify the four antecedent factors in Social Learning Theory.

5 In relation to human personality, identify the four factors that interest Walter Mischel.

6 Describe why it is important for a performer or exerciser to have an awareness of the following facets related to effective goal-setting practices:

> ▶ outcome
>
> ▶ process
>
> ▶ performance goals.

7 Applied sport psychology is often concerned with bringing about change in order to optimize human performance. According to Social Learning Theory, explain how the four antecedents outlined in this chapter have the potential to increase an individual's self-efficacy.

8 What are the implications of epigenetics for the way young athletes are trained and subsequently developed?

9 Social Learning Theory states that we have a capacity to learn by observation, *even in the absence of rewards*. In your own words, explain why this research finding provides us with an important insight into an individual's motivation for performing or taking part in physical activity.

DATA BASED QUESTION

The Type D personality (individuals who frequently experience negative emotions) was developed to identify cardiac patients at risk of developing emotional and inter-personal difficulties. A 2012 study of Icelandic cardiac patients used a questionnaire to investigate the relationship of Type D personality with anxiety, depression, stress and health-related behaviour. Following analysis the cardiac patients were divided into two groups: Type D and non-Type D personality (do not frequently experience negative emotions). The differences in average (± SD) anxiety, depression and perceived stress are shown in the figure below (lower scores = "less"). Additionally, the average prevalence of some health-related behaviour practices is shown in the table (right).

	Eat fruit & vegetables every day (%)	Smoke cigarettes (%)	Use anxiety-reducing medication regularly (%)
Type-D personality	70	17	15
Non Type-D personality	81	8	11

(Source: Adapted from Svansdottir et al. 2012. *BMC Public Health*. Vol 12. p 42)

1 State which group had:
   i) less depression (1 mark)
   ii) more perceived stress. (1 mark)
2 Distinguish between groups for health-related behaviour practices. (3 marks)
3 Discuss social learning theory and personality. (5 marks)

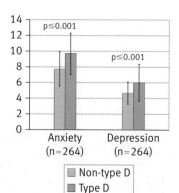

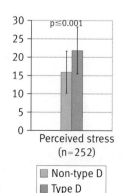

CHAPTER 11

Motivation in sport and exercise

OBJECTIVES

By the end of this chapter, students should be able to:

→ define motivation

→ discuss intrinsic and extrinsic motives for participation

→ understand the self determination continuum of motivation

→ describe the McClelland–Atkinson Theory of Achievement Motivation

→ describe attribution theory

→ describe achievement goal theory

→ understand and use a Task and Ego Orientation in Sport Questionnaire

→ develop an understanding of how motivational climate impacts upon sports performance and participation in physical activities.

Introduction

Sport and exercise offer opportunities to participate in physical activities that enhance cardiovascular health, relieve stress and help maintain healthy minds and bodies. In order to gain these potential health benefits, individuals need to be motivated to participate. It is, therefore, important for sport psychologists, coaches, teachers, parents and participants to understand motivation, its impact on sports performance and how it influences physical activity levels. This chapter will begin by defining motivation and then go on to outline some of the most influential motivational theories including intrinsic and extrinsic motivation, self-determination theory, achievement motivation, attribution theory, achievement goal theory and motivational climate.

Definitions of motivation

In simple terms, motivation can be defined as the direction and intensity of one's effort (Sage 1977). The direction of effort refers to whether an individual is attracted to, seeks out, or approaches certain situations. For example, a student may be motivated to try and gain a place on the school soccer team but not on the gymnastics team. The intensity refers to how much effort a person exerts in a particular situation. For instance, an athlete may attend a training session but not put much effort in. Alternatively, athletes can sometimes become too intense and consequently perform poorly in competitions. Individuals, therefore, differ in the direction and intensity of their behaviours. Two different people may be motivated to play tennis, but one of them may be more strongly motivated (have greater intensity) than the other. Or one person may be interested (directed) in participating in sport for social reasons, whereas another may be more interested in exercising for health benefits. Gage and Berliner (1984) use the analogy of a motor car, where the engine is the intensity and the steering is the direction of motivation. For the majority

TO THINK ABOUT

Think about your own direction and intensity of effort in different sports or physical activities that you participate in. Which sports or physical activities are you directed towards and does your intensity vary for these different activities?

of people, however, direction and intensity of behaviour are closely related and are difficult to separate. For example, athletes who regularly and punctually attend training typically expend good effort during participation.

Others define motivation as an internal process that activates, guides and maintains behaviour over time. In other words, motivation is "what gets you going, keeps you going and determines where you're trying to go" (Slavin 2003). According to Roberts (2001) "the study of motivation is the investigation of the energization, direction and regulation of behaviour" and motivational theories need to address all three aspects in order to be recognized as a theory. Goal setting is an example of a theory that addresses the direction and/or regulation of behaviour, but not why the behaviour was energized and is, therefore, not a true theory of motivation according to Roberts' criteria. Motivational theories ask why we do things and the history of motivational research has been a search for the "right" theory.

Types of motivation

TO THINK ABOUT

Think about the sports or physical activities that you participate in and consider whether your motives are more intrinsic or extrinsic.

An important distinction in the types of motives for human behaviour is between intrinsic and extrinsic motivation. Intrinsic motivation comes from within the person and is associated with doing an activity for itself and for the pleasure and satisfaction derived from participation. Intrinsic motives for taking part in sport and physical activity include excitement, fun, enjoyment and the chance to improve skills (Deci, Ryan, 1985). Extrinsic motivation results from external rewards such as money, trophies and prizes, and less tangible rewards such as praise and status.

Combining intrinsic and extrinsic motivators

The "additive principle" suggests that intrinsic motivation can be boosted by extrinsic motivators. However, contrary to popular belief, this is not always a good idea. In fact, in some situations where the task is being performed because of intrinsic motivation, extrinsic rewards can lower the person's intrinsic motivation.

Deci and Ryan (1985) developed cognitive evaluation theory to explain this phenomenon. This theory states that rewards can be divided into two types: controlling rewards and informational rewards. Controlling rewards include praise and trophies and are given to influence (control) an individual's behaviour. Informational rewards on the other hand convey information about an individual's competence at a particular task. According to Deci and Ryan, rewards perceived by the recipient as controlling decrease intrinsic motivation, whereas rewards viewed as informational increase intrinsic motivation.

KEY POINT

Intrinsic motivation comes from within the person and is associated with doing an activity for itself and for the pleasure and satisfaction derived from participation. Extrinsic motivation results from external rewards such as money, trophies and prizes.

While some motives are clearly intrinsic (e.g. "I go cycling because it's fun") and some are clearly extrinsic (e.g. "I play professional sport because I get paid to do so"), others are less clear. For instance, how would you classify the motive "I exercise to control my body weight"? It seems more intrinsic than extrinsic but it's not totally intrinsic as the motive involves reasons for participation other than fun and enjoyment. For this reason Deci and Ryan proposed that viewing motives as either intrinsic or extrinsic is too simplistic and they developed a continuum of motivation called self-determination theory to explain this.

Self-determination theory

At one end of the continuum lies intrinsic motivation, where participation in the activity is for pure enjoyment and pleasure. On the other end of the continuum lies amotivation which is a complete lack of desire to participate in the activity. In-between these two extremes lie the different levels of extrinsic motivation, moving from the less intrinsic to the more self-determined levels (see Figure 11.1).

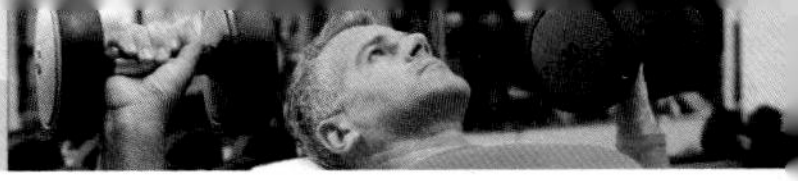

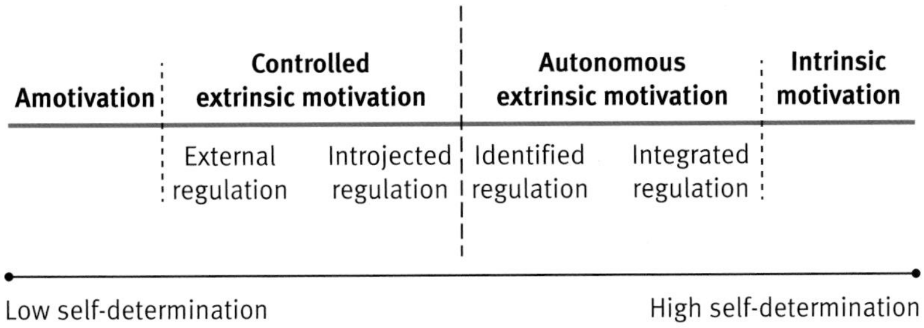

Amotivation	Controlled extrinsic motivation		Autonomous extrinsic motivation		Intrinsic motivation
	External regulation	Introjected regulation	Identified regulation	Integrated regulation	

Low self-determination   High self-determination

↑ Figure 11.1: The self-determination continuum

→ **External regulation** refers to behaviour that is driven by external forces rather than our own desire.
→ **Introjected regulation** is the first level of internalization and at this level we participate because we feel that we should in order to avoid disapproval or feelings of guilt.
→ At the **identified regulation** level we participate because we feel it's personally important to do so and we value the activity.
→ At the **integrated level** of self-regulation we participate because we feel the activity is a key part of ourselves.

Table 11.1 provides an example for each level of self-determination.

Amotivation	Paul has no desire to participate in sport or physical activity and avoids doing any exercise.
External regulation	Sara dislikes exercise but participates in walking and cycling because her doctor has advised her to do so in order to reduce her obesity level and improve her health.
Introjected regulation	Deborshi is in the school tennis team but doesn't really enjoy it and only participates because his parents and teachers want him to and he feels guilty if he doesn't.
Identified regulation	Kate attends aerobics classes because she wants to look good, as this is important to her.
Integrated regulation	Anna is a keen runner who gets personal satisfaction and achievement when she reaches her goals. She identifies herself as a runner when she introduces herself to others.
Intrinsic motivation	Davide participates in a variety of activities including golf, tennis, running and swimming. He takes part for the pure fun and enjoyment of it.

↑ Table 11.1: Examples of levels of self-determination in sport and exercise

TO THINK ABOUT

Rate your own levels of self-determination in the sports or physical activities that you currently participate in, or have previously participated in. Think about which ones you are most likely to continue, or why you dropped out.

Self-determination theory is based on the premise that there are three psychological needs that motivate all human behaviour (see Table 11.2).

AUTONOMY	COMPETENCE	RELATEDNESS
The need to feel autonomous, that is, to make our own decisions and to be in control of one's own behaviour, e.g. exercising because you want to, not because you are told to do so.	The need to feel competent and able to accomplish things, e.g. mastering a sports skill or improving your expertise in an activity.	The need to relate to others and feel a sense of belonging, e.g. being part of a team and feeling accepted and valued by your teammates.

↑ Table 11.2: The three psychological needs

As individuals, we strive to fulfill these needs in order to create a healthy psychological environment for ourselves. Sport and exercise activities provide many opportunities to fulfill these needs and quite often, this doesn't happen by chance. For instance the coach can give players the opportunity to lead parts of the session or to set their own goals for improvement in order to facilitate their self-determination.

McClelland–Atkinson Theory of Achievement Motivation

The link between the desire to achieve and sporting success is an obvious one. A strong need to achieve will be an important factor in determining how hard you train and how much effort you exert in competition. The need achievement theory of motivation was first put forward by McClelland and taken forward by Atkinson (Atkinson 1974; McClelland 1961) and argues that motivation is a balance between the motive to achieve success and the motive to avoid failure. When people enter into a sport or exercise situation, they do so with an approach–avoidance conflict. On the one hand, they are motivated because they want to succeed, but on the other hand they are also motivated because they want to avoid failure.

Achievement motivation = The desire to succeed − The fear of failure

According to McClelland and Atkinson, achievement motivation is a personality trait. For some, the desire to succeed outweighs the fear of failure and these individuals are said to be high in achievement motivation. For others, the fear of failure is the more important factor and these individuals are said to be low in achievement motivation. However, it is not only personality factors that predict behaviour but situational factors as well, such as the probability of success and the incentive for success. Thus, even if individuals are low in achievement motivation, if the probability of success is high and the rewards are great, they are likely to be motivated to participate.

KEY POINT

Need achievement theory argues that motivation is a balance between the motive to achieve success and the motive to avoid failure.

There are five components that contribute to need achievement theory, including personality factors, situational factors, resultant tendencies, emotional reactions and achievement-related behaviours (see Figure 11.2).

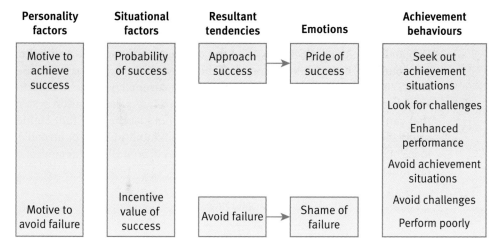

Personality factors	Situational factors	Resultant tendencies	Emotions	Achievement behaviours
Motive to achieve success	Probability of success	Approach success →	Pride of success	Seek out achievement situations
				Look for challenges
				Enhanced performance
				Avoid achievement situations
Motive to avoid failure	Incentive value of success	Avoid failure →	Shame of failure	Avoid challenges
				Perform poorly

↑ Figure 11.2: Need achievement theory

An individual's resultant behavioural tendency is derived by considering the personality factors in relation to the probability or incentive value of success. Weinberg and Gould (2003) suggested that the theory is best at predicting situations when there is a 50-50 chance of success.

The different behaviour patterns of high achievers and low achievers is outlined in Table 11.3. In such situations, high achievers seek out challenges because they enjoy competing against others of equal ability and performing challenging tasks. Low achievers, on the other hand, avoid challenges, opting for easier tasks where failure is less likely, or very difficult tasks where no one expects them to win. Low achievers avoid the negative evaluation associated with failure and a 50-50 chance of success causes maximum uncertainty and worry. Both high and low achievers want to experience pride and minimize shame, but high achievers focus more on pride, whereas low achievers focus more on shame and worry. High achievers select more challenging tasks, display high levels of effort, focus on the pride of success and continue to try hard in difficult situations. Low achievers avoid challenging situations, exert less effort and persistence and focus more on the shame of failure.

KEY POINT

For individuals who are high in achievement motivation, the desire to succeed outweighs the fear of failure. For others, the fear of failure is the more important factor and these individuals are said to be low in achievement motivation.

High achievers	Low achievers
→ Select challenging tasks	→ Avoid challenging activities
→ Display a high level of effort	→ Exert less effort when they take part
→ Continue to try hard in difficult situations	→ Exert less persistence when they take part
→ Focus on the pride of success	→ Focus on the shame of failure

↑ Table 11.3: Behaviour of high achievers versus behaviour of low achievers

Gill (2000) reviewed the research into need achievement theory on the choice of high and low difficulty tasks and found strong support for high achievers seeking out difficult tasks and low achievers' preference for easy tasks. However, according to Gill, the theory does not reliably predict sporting performance. That said, this approach has been very important in developing an understanding of motivation and serves as the framework in more contemporary motivational theories.

TO THINK ABOUT

Do you seek out or avoid tasks where there is a 50–50 chance of success? Why?

Attribution theory

Attribution theory focuses upon the reasons people use to explain their successes and failures. Information about the reasons for the outcome of an event affects

TO THINK ABOUT

Think about a recent successful and an unsuccessful sporting experience and consider whether your success was due mainly to ability, effort, difficulty of the task or luck.

the expectancy of future success and failure and also the feelings people experience, which in turn affects achievement behaviour.

Originally, Heider (1958) classified the attributions for success and failure into four categories: ability, effort, task difficulty and luck. However, Weiner (1985) identified that these attributions did not cover all possible reasons for success and failure. Consequently, Weiner provided a classification system that can be used for all possible attributions, not just the four that Heider originally proposed. These categories are: locus of stability (stable or unstable), locus of causality (internal or external) and locus of control (under control or not under our control) (see Figure 11.3).

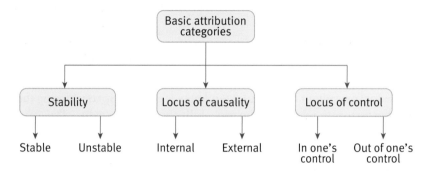

↑ Figure 11.3: Weiner's attribution categories

Consider the following example. A middle distance runner could attribute winning or losing a race to:

→ a stable factor such as ability, or an unstable factor such as luck
→ an internal cause such as effort, or an external cause such as the quality of the opposition
→ a factor they could control such as the race plan, or a factor out of their control such as the weather conditions.

Following a defeat there is a tendency for most people to adopt external attributions and blame other factors (e.g. luck), whereas after a success most of us tend to use internal reasons (e.g. effort or ability) to explain the outcome. This is known as the "self serving bias". If, however, an individual perceives that his or her failure is due to a lack of ability (which is both stable and internal) and their actions have no effect on the outcome of the task (are out of their control) then a state of "learned helplessness" can exist. In this situation, the individual feels doomed to failure and feels that nothing can be done about it.

Attributions have an important effect on expectations of future success or failure and affect emotional reactions. Attributing performance to stable, internal factors has been linked to pride and expectations of future success. For instance, taking the earlier example of the middle distance runner, if the athlete attributes his performance success to an internal cause (e.g. the training programme), he is more likely to feel pride and expect the outcome to occur again in the future. This in turn is likely to influence his future achievement motivation and to motivate him to continue to train hard.

Weiner (1985) established an interesting link between attribution theory and need achievement theory. It seems that individuals with a high need to achieve attribute their success to internal causes of ability and effort and their failure to lack of effort, while low need achievers attribute their failure to external factors and in some cases to a lack of ability.

Despite the logic and appeal of attribution theory, its popularity has decreased. It has been criticized on the basis that, although it may be useful in telling

KEY POINT

Attribution theory looks at whether an athlete puts their successes or failures down to luck, skill, the circumstances on the day or other factors.

us why things go wrong, it does not tell us how to put them right, as well as its lack of application to sport. It has also been criticized for focusing on why people expect to succeed, but not on why they want to succeed (Dweck, Elliott 1983).

Achievement goal theory

Achievement goal theory (Nicholls 1989) proposes that in achievement settings such as sport and exercise, an individual's main concern is to demonstrate high ability and to avoid demonstrating low ability. Ability, however, can be viewed in different ways based upon two states of goal involvement known as task involvement and ego involvement. When individuals are task involved, they focus on mastery of the task, the learning of skills, exerting effort, and self-improvement. In contrast, ego involved individuals focus on demonstrating superior ability compared to others and on winning in competitions with less effort than others.

According to achievement goal theory, three factors combine to determine motivation:

→ achievement goals
→ perceived ability
→ achievement behaviour.

Nicholls (1989) argued that perceived ability has a moderating effect on an individual's behaviours and that this effect is dependent on whether the individual adopts task or ego goals. When task goals are adopted and the individual is task involved, perceived ability is not relevant, since the criteria for success is self-referenced rather than comparative to others. In such circumstances, behaviours are most likely to be positive and the individual is predicted to persist in the face of difficulty, exert effort, choose challenging tasks and be interested in the activity.

On the other hand, when an individual adopts ego goals and is ego involved, perceived ability is of greater importance because the demonstration of ability compared to others is now highly significant to the individual. According to Nicholls (1989), in such circumstances, if perceived ability is high, positive motivational behaviours are predicted, as it is likely that high ability will be demonstrated. However, if perceived ability is low then more negative behaviours such as avoiding challenges, lack of effort, reduced persistence and the devaluing of tasks are predicted.

↑ Figure 11.4: Three key factors in the achievement goal approach

KEY POINT

Individuals who are task involved focus on mastery of the task, the learning of skills, exerting effort, and self-improvement. Whereas, ego involved individuals focus on demonstrating superior ability compared to others.

Achievement goal theory states that an individual's goal involvement in a particular situation is the combined result of his/her achievement goals (goal orientations) and the prevailing situational factors (motivational climate). Achievement goal orientations are an individual's proneness to be task or ego involved, which result from childhood socialization experiences at home, in the classroom or through previous experiences of sport and exercise activity. Although there is some evidence that these goal orientations can be influenced over time, they are relatively stable and unlikely to change in the short term. Nicholls argued that task and ego goal orientations are independent dispositional tendencies, which means that an individual can be high or low in either, or both, at the same time.

Task and Ego Orientation in Sport Questionnaire

In order to study differences in dispositional goal orientations in sport and exercise settings, Duda and Nicholls (1989) developed the "Task and Ego Orientation in Sport Questionnaire" (TEOSQ). Research has found a consistent pattern of motivational responses for task versus ego oriented individuals in sport and physical education settings. Task orientation has been positively related to effort, enjoyment, persistence, satisfaction and interest. In contrast, ego orientation has been negatively associated with enjoyment and interest and positively related to boredom. Furthermore, task oriented individuals have been found to be more intrinsically motivated than ego oriented individuals (Roberts 2001).

CASE STUDY

One of the first studies to examine the effects of combined levels of task and ego orientations was conducted by Fox et al. (1994). In this study, four groups were created for analysis based on mean splits of their levels of task and ego orientation, as measured by the TEOSQ. The groups were:
– high task/high ego
– low task/high ego
– high task/low ego
– low task/low ego.

The high task/high ego group emerged as having the highest perceived sport competence and enjoyment in sport, whereas, the low task/low ego group had the lowest. Fox et al. concluded that children dominated by a task orientation were more highly motivated than those dominated by an ego orientation, but the addition of ego orientation to a dominant task orientation may enhance sport enjoyment and does not appear to be motivationally detrimental. Further, the low task/low ego group was at highest risk of non-participation.

TO DO

Use the TEOSQ below to research the goal orientations of your classmates and work out the class average score for both task and ego orientation out of 5. Also consider how many of your classmates are high in both task and ego orientations.

Directions: Please read each of the statements listed below and indicate how much you personally agree with each statement by circling the appropriate response.

When do you feel most successful in sport? In other words, when do you feel an activity has gone really well for you?

I feel most successful in sport when ....

		1	2	3	4	5
1	I'm the only one who can do the skill.	Strongly disagree	Disagree	Neutral	Agree	Strongly agree
2	I learn a new skill and it makes me want to practice more.	Strongly disagree	Disagree	Neutral	Agree	Strongly agree
3	I can do better than my friends.	Strongly disagree	Disagree	Neutral	Agree	Strongly agree
4	The others can't do as well as me.	Strongly disagree	Disagree	Neutral	Agree	Strongly agree
5	I learn something that is fun to do.	Strongly disagree	Disagree	Neutral	Agree	Strongly agree
6	Others mess up and I don't.	Strongly disagree	Disagree	Neutral	Agree	Strongly agree
7	I learn a new skill by trying hard.	Strongly disagree	Disagree	Neutral	Agree	Strongly agree
8	I work really hard.	Strongly disagree	Disagree	Neutral	Agree	Strongly agree
9	I score the most points/goals.	Strongly disagree	Disagree	Neutral	Agree	Strongly agree
10	Something I learn makes me want to go and practice more.	Strongly disagree	Disagree	Neutral	Agree	Strongly agree
11	I'm the best.	Strongly disagree	Disagree	Neutral	Agree	Strongly agree
12	A skill I learn really feels right.	Strongly disagree	Disagree	Neutral	Agree	Strongly agree
13	I do my very best.	Strongly disagree	Disagree	Neutral	Agree	Strongly agree

Scoring

Add the task scores (questions 2, 5, 7, 8, 10, 12, 13), find the mean. A high score = high mastery orientation.

Add the ego scores (questions 1, 3, 4, 6, 9, 11), find the mean. A high score = high ego orientation.

The achievement goal theory approach has been criticized for having a Western and male bias and for only considering the two goals of task and ego. Fontayne et al. (2001) argued that people may hold multiple goals, each of which may influence their level of motivation for a particular social domain. Furthermore, limiting the study of motivation to the study of task/mastery and ego/social comparison goals could be considered reductionist, particularly when people from minority cultural groups are concerned.

Motivational climate

In addition to an individual's goal orientations, the particular environment or motivational climate created by the teacher, coach, peers or parents can induce a state of task or ego involvement in sport and exercise situations. Ames (1992) contended that the perceived motivational climate influences an individual's thoughts, feelings and achievement behaviours. Consistent with task and ego goal orientations, two climates have been found to be dominant in sport and educational environments: a performance (ego) climate and a mastery (task) climate.

→ In a **performance climate**, comparison with others is the most important source of information for self-evaluation; the focus is on winning and improvement is of little or no significance.

→ In a **mastery climate**, performance is evaluated in terms of personal mastery and improvement and not in comparison to others.

Research into perceptions of the motivational climate in sport and physical education (e.g. Carpenter, Morgan 1999) has demonstrated that perceptions of a mastery climate are related to a task goal orientation, intrinsic motivation, a preference for challenging tasks and beliefs that success is due to effort. Furthermore, a positive attitude, high satisfaction, low boredom and anxiety, high self-rated improvement, continued involvement and self-determined reasons for participation have also been associated with perceptions of a mastery climate.

In contrast, perceptions of a performance climate have been associated with high levels of worry, a focus on comparative ability and a preoccupation with enhancing one's social status.

Ames identified the dimensions of achievement situations that influence the motivational climate as the task, authority, recognition, grouping, evaluation and time structures (TARGET) (see Table 11.4). Manipulating these TARGET structures to be mastery focused has been found to improve pupils' motivation in physical education lessons, resulting in greater satisfaction with the activities, a more positive attitude towards the activity and a preference for more challenging tasks (Morgan, Carpenter 2002).

TARGET BEHAVIOUR	MASTERY/TASK	PERFORMANCE/EGO
Task	Self-referenced goals, differentiated	Comparative goals, undifferentiated
Authority	Students given leadership roles and involved in decision-making	Teacher makes all the decisions
Recognition	Private recognition of improvement and effort	Public recognition of ability and comparative performances
Grouping	Mixed ability and cooperative groups	Ability groups
Evaluation	Self-referenced; private consultations with teacher based on improvement and effort scores	Comparative and public
Time	Flexible time for task completion	Inflexible time for task completion

↑ Table 11.4: TARGET behaviours that influence motivational climate

Combining motivational climate theory with attribution theory may help us to understand why a perceived mastery motivational climate has consistently been associated with positive motivational outcomes. As Table 11.4 shows, a mastery motivational climate is associated with effort and self-referenced criteria for success. Attribution theory tells us that effort is seen as internal, controllable and unstable, thus allowing individuals to view success as achievable in the future with continued application of effort and, perhaps more importantly, to view failure as redeemable with greater effort.

THEORY OF KNOWLEDGE

Consider the following scenario in groups.

You are a physical education teacher and your learning outcome is to improve ball control/dribbling skills in a soccer lesson. The task you decide to use is a race between groups to be the first team to complete a dribbling relay running around fixed marker cones. In their desire to win, a number of participants cheat by cutting corners or running over the cones instead of around them.

Discuss the following in your groups:
→ Have you achieved your learning outcome?
→ Are you promoting a mastery- or ego-involving climate?
→ How could you change the session to promote a more mastery-involving climate?
→ How might a more mastery-involving climate impact on the learning outcome?

THEORY OF KNOWLEDGE

Theories play an important role in sport and exercise psychology. Why are theories useful for sport coaches and physical education teachers?

→ Motivation is defined as the "direction" and "intensity" of one's effort.

→ There are intrinsic and extrinsic motives for participation.

→ The self-determination continuum of motivation ranges from amotivation to intrinsic motivation.

→ McClelland and Atkinson's theory of achievement motivation is based upon the motive to achieve success and to avoid failure.

→ Attribution theory focuses on how people attribute success or failure to ability, effort, task difficulty or luck.

→ Achievement goal theory considers there to be three factors that determine motivation: achievement goals, perceived ability and achievement behaviour.

→ In task oriented goals an individual focuses on the mastery of the task, while in ego oriented goals the focus is on being better than others.

→ There are mastery and performance perceptions of the motivational climate.

→ The TARGET teaching/coaching behaviours influence perceptions of the motivational climate and the resultant motivational responses.

Self-study questions

1 Define motivation.

2 List three different theories of motivation.

3 State the *additive principle* of intrinsic and extrinsic motivation.

4 Describe attribution theory.

5 Distinguish between task and ego goal orientations.

6 Identify the six levels of the self-determination continuum.

7 Explain the difference between integrated and introjected regulation in self-determination theory.

8 Compare the typical behaviours of *high achievers* versus *low achievers* in achievement motivation theory.

9 Discuss the difference between goal orientations and motivational climate.

10 Suggest strategies that teachers or coaches can use to create a *mastery* motivational climate.

DATA BASED QUESTION

The goal orientations of a group of high school volleyball players were measured using the Task and Ego Orientation in Sport Questionnaire (TEOSQ) (Duda, Nicholls 1989). The results of three of the players are displayed in the table below, out of a maximum score of 5. Use this data to answer the following questions:

Student	Task orientation	Ego orientation
1	4.53	4.0
2	2.97	4.28
3	4.13	2.69

a Describe the goal orientation profile of each of the three students by describing the task or ego orientation as "high" or "low", e.g. high task, low ego. [1 mark]

  i Student 1 ....

  ii Student 2 ....

  iii Student 3...

b Calculate the mean task and ego orientation scores for all three players combined to two decimal places. [2 marks]

  i Mean ego =

  ii Mean task =

c Based on your knowledge of achievement goal theory and assuming the players all have similar levels of perceived ability:

  i Determine which of the players you think is most likely to "drop out" of the team if they lose the majority of their games, even though they are improving in their performances. [1 mark]

  ....

  ....

  ii Explain the reason for your decision. [2 marks]

Arousal, anxiety and performance

By the end of this chapter students should be able to

→ describe the terms "stress" and "arousal" and their application to human behaviour

→ identify the psycho-physiological responses that occur when humans are aroused

→ describe the transactional model of stress and anxiety

→ distinguish between two types of anxiety (somatic and cognitive)

→ evaluate descriptive theories of the anxiety–performance relationship

→ discuss the mechanism of attention in explaining how anxiety influences performance

→ describe the role of working memory

→ evaluate measurement approaches to investigate the anxiety–performance relationship.

Introduction

In this chapter we are going to look at the relationship between stress, arousal and anxiety and the effects these have on performance. Sport is a setting that individuals enter voluntarily and stress and anxiety are experienced regularly in both competitive and training situations. At the elite level it is considered by some that "the deciding factor is not the skill but the ability to perform it under stress" (Patmore 1986). This idea is often supported by elite athletes themselves and the occasions on which top level performers "choke" testifies to the fact that athletes must be able to control their internal states, in spite of the stressful situation, in order to produce peak performances.

The discipline of sport psychology has devoted much attention to understanding what happens under stress and, more importantly, how performers can be helped to perform under stress. In this chapter as well as developing an understanding of the key concepts and terms related to stress you will start to understand how our knowledge of it has progressed and developed.

Stress in humans

Although humans are highly developed in many ways, they are still animals and still respond to situations in a way that secures their evolutionary survival. As animals, we are programmed to respond to the stress of dangerous situations using rapid and pronounced arousal of the sympathetic division of the autonomic nervous system. This response is understood to be effective in preparing the individual to either run away from danger or to fight, either in self-defence or for food. This is sometimes referred to as the "fight–flight" response and is a highly functional response to prepare the body for high-intensity physical work. For example, increased heart rate assists in the transportation of oxygen while adrenaline promotes the release of stored energy such as liver glucose (glycogen). Together these increase the availability of energy to working muscles.

Stressful situations in modern life where the need for a highly physical response is less pronounced (think of an office worker being stressed) still prompt some of the same kinds of responses even though physical danger is not prevalent. Some of these responses may even have a negative impact on our performance. Imagine hurrying to school late on a day when you are reading in front of your class; rushing to take off your coat, open your bag and use fine motor control to get out the reading and hold it steady are tasks that would be impaired by the stress of being late.

Sport is interesting because it can benefit from some of the responses but be negatively affected by others. Even more interesting is that some performers have differential responses benefitting from some positive changes and with reduced levels of other more negative changes.

Early sport psychologists recognized the stressful nature of sport and sought to apply existing knowledge and research from other areas, such as clinical psychology and medicine to help them understand experiences and reactions. One particularly important source of understanding was the work of Hans Selye (1936, 1979), a medical doctor and endocrinologist who was an applied pioneer of stress research.

CASE STUDY

Hans Selye pioneer of stress research

Selye defined stress as "a non-specific response of the body to any demand made upon it" (Selye 1979). Using the term "non-specific" Selye was suggesting that the same sorts of responses would be elicited by any variety of stressful stimuli or stressors. Selye's initial work (published in the journal *Nature* in 1936) was based on exposing his research subjects to various stressors such as cold, surgical injury, production of spinal shock, excessive muscular exercise or intoxications with sub-lethal doses of diverse drugs.

These subjects were actually rats and this is the one key feature that limits the relevance of his work to understanding human responses because our brain contains a huge cortex which is not present in rats. The cortex is where humans engage in advanced thought processing including future-orientated thinking, worry and interpreting situations with meaning. The activity in the cortex means humans do not respond to all stressors uniformly like Selye's rats and as thinking styles also differ between individuals even the same stressor may produce quite different responses.

Selye's early work is still important and he contributed two other important points. Firstly he defined stress as a response. This is in line with the modern view of stress as a transaction between the individual and the environment. Secondly he introduced the idea that stress was not necessarily a negative response. For example, physiological adaptation through training is a response to stress, as is the sense of enjoyment or exhilaration that some individuals get from taking part in competitive sport or physical activity.

Selye used the terms "distress" and "eustress" to differentiate between negative and positive stress responses. Throughout this chapter keep in mind that while anxiety and worry may be negative consequences of stress, positive consequences also occur.

Psychological and physiological responses to stress

What happens to us when we are stressed? This question assumes that stress is one specific thing and in fact it may be easier to think of different categories of stress.

Time-limited "voluntary" stress	Amateur level competition—usually it is just for fun and does not determine other aspects of life.
Time-limited "compulsory" stress	A selection event to join an academy or gain a sports scholarship—the person feels compelled to take part in order to achieve another distant goal.
Stressful event sequences	A chain of related events—relocation means moving house, changing schools, losing friends, having to learn your way around etc.
Chronic stress	Long-term illness or overtraining—pervades life and has uncertain time course or outcome.
Distant stressors	An experience (usually traumatic) in the past that retains some impact on future responses.

↑ Table 12.1

The impact of stressors often depends on the specific type of stressor encountered. The danger of workplace stress to health is well documented in terms of coronary heart disease and is usually attributed to it being chronic (lasting for a long period of time). So it is important to remember that while stress is a very commonly used term it lacks precise meaning.

Furthermore the word "stress" can be used to mean an external force or influence, such as ambient temperature as a source of stress for desert marathon runners. Or stress can be used to describe an internal response that may be moderated by individual factors, so core body temperature may show that an acclimatized individual is under less stress than a non-acclimatized individual.

Stress can also be considered in terms of whether it involves a physical threat or danger to the individual (or someone close to them), or whether it relates to social evaluative concerns in which the persons feels that their status or position will be affected. A high school baseball fielder waiting for a high-ball is usually most concerned about messing it up because of social evaluative concerns—they don't want their skill to be shown as inadequate and they want their team to win. When going in to bat against a fast pitcher some of the concern now may be about getting hurt or injured (physical threat).

Interview a friend or family member who plays a sport and has recently been in a competition that was important to them. You are going to ask them about the time leading up to the competition, the day before and one hour before they competed. The interview will take between 20–25 minutes. Write down the questions you will ask and take notes on what they say. Timing is important and some approximate times are shown below to help you.

Give them a short explanation of what you would like to talk about, and why. Get their agreement they are happy to do this.

(2 mins)

Start by asking them to describe the competition to you and to explain why it was important to them

(4 mins)

Now ask them to think specifically about how they were 24 hours before the event.

(8 mins)

→ How did they feel physically?
→ What thoughts did they have in relation to the competition? How often during this time did they think about the event?
→ What feelings or emotions did they experience?
→ What actions and behaviours did they take that were directly a result of feeling or thinking about the competition?

Now ask them to think specifically about how they were one hour before the event.

Ask the same questions as before in relation to this time period.

(8 mins)

Thank your interviewee for their time and the information they have given you about their responses to this situation.

Arousal and performance

Under stress humans usually report symptoms of arousal. This concept of arousal exists along a continuum with states ranging from a very deep sleep-like state to excessive and uncontrolled activation of numerous systems that might be seen in the instance of a panic attack. Arousal is most commonly used to refer to arousal of the sympathetic division of the autonomic nervous system.

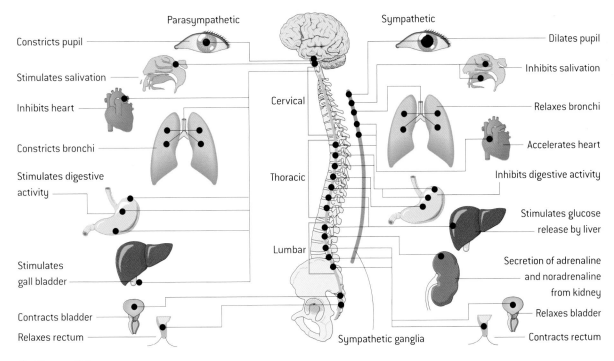

↑ Figure 12.1

Arousal, or autonomic arousal, is often considered to be the immediate response ("fight or flight") to a stressor and is governed by the sympathetic nervous system and corresponds to the alarm reaction of the general adaptive system. Autonomic arousal causes the sympathetic nervous system to close down any of the body's physiological systems that are non-essential to fight or flight and accelerates those that are essential. Generally as a consequence all parasympathetic activity is curtailed.

There are however some exceptions to this rule as the last item on the list of arousal symptoms for second world war combat pilots in Table 12.1 shows.

DURING COMBAT MISSIONS DID YOU FEEL	OFTEN %	SOMETIMES %	TOTAL %
pounding heart, rapid pulse	30	56	86
muscles tense	30	53	83
irritable	22	58	80
dry throat and mouth	30	50	80
"cold sweat"	26	53	79
"butterflies"	23	53	79
trembling	11	53	64
a sense of unreality	20	49	69
confused	3	50	53
weak or faint	4	37	41
unable to remember details or events of the mission immediately afterwards	5	34	39
sick to the stomach	5	33	38
unable to concentrate	3	32	35
that you had wet or soiled your pants	1	4	5

↑ Table 12.2: Symptoms of fear in combat flying based on reports of pilots during the second world war (from Shaffer, LF. 1947. "Fear and courage in aerial combat." *Journal of Consulting Psychology*. Vol 11(3). Pp137–143.)

One of the most obvious changes that occurs with arousal is an increase in heart rate and it remains one of the most frequently measured physical changes associated with an individual experiencing stress.

Heart rate under stress

Imagine standing at the top of a raging waterfall and preparing to abseil off the edge into the clouds of spray and the deafening roar as the water plunges over a rock shelf and falls down 50 meters. Imagine too that you have never abseiled before. What effect do you think this experience would have on your heart rate?

Look at the graph below of a 22-year-old facing this exact task.

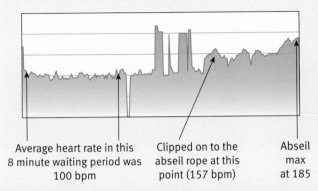

| Average heart rate in this 8 minute waiting period was 100 bpm | Clipped on to the abseil rope at this point (157 bpm) | Abseil max at 185 |

↑ Figure 12.2

Note that at points A and B the individual was getting into a harness (A) and then climbing over the protective railings to stand on the rocky edge near the abseil point (B). Then the performer was clipped onto the abseil rope and moved towards the edge. The small "notch" just before the profile finishes is a momentary "cardiac deceleration" just before going over the edge. This notch has been seen in contrasting situations (golf putting) and is associated with the moment when the performer commits to an action.

What might have been the key features of stress for this performer? Research suggests situations that are novel, unpredictable and where the person feels they do not have control and that they might be subject to social evaluation, are likely to cause psychological stress.

Now consider the heart rate of a 22-year-old rally driver completing a special stage of a major international event, say in ambient temperatures of 24°C (in car 34°C), with top speed over rough terrain reaching 130 kph. The driver has to drive a high-powered car, manoeuvring sharply with rapid braking and gear changes. To do so optimally the driver must combine three sources of information about the stage: a) the visible ground immediately in front of the car to avoid obstacles; b) the ground 100–200 meters further ahead to plan responses and c) listen to the pace notes read out by the co-driver that describe the stage and pre-planned driving strategy.

Now think about the stressors facing this performer and factors that might contribute to an elevated heart rate.

In the first case the elevation could be purely due to the anxiety associated with the situation. There is likely to be a high perceived risk (though as it is well managed by specialist staff it is actually quite small). However there is little physical demand, mental effort or significant environmental load. The heart rate elevation is "metabolically inappropriate" for the situation and would be almost entirely attributable to the perceived stress. Measuring heart rate when there is no other cause for a change can provide a good source of information about anxiety response.

In contrast the rally driver's heart rate can be considered a composite of the stressors encountered combined with mental and physical workload. It would be impossible to attribute values in any meaningful way to the array of factors, each of which would be expected to elevate heart rate. In this situation, with so many factors, heart rate cannot provide any clear index of anxiety.

Early attempts to understand changes to performance under stress attempted to describe these in terms of elevations in arousal. In fact as far back as 1908 Yerkes and Dodson suggested that for complex tasks there was an optimal level of arousal above and below which performance levels would decrease. Over time this idea has become known as the inverted-U approach because of the graphical shape of the proposed arousal-performance relationship (see Figure 12.3).

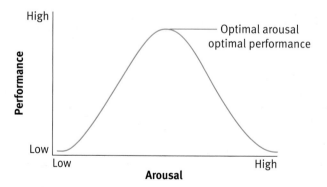

↑ Figure 12.3

The data on which the inverted-U approach was based was collected from a study examining the performance of mice learning to get through a maze under different conditions of electric shock. Surprisingly it is still often presented to explain performance of humans in sport settings even though there is little supporting evidence for this. Conceptually the inverted-U approach provides a simple description and this simplicity may partly explain why it is often used and remembered. However there is significant doubt over the value of this model, not least when we consider real-life examples of performers experiencing stress where the decline in performance level is not slow and progressive but rapid and dramatic.

The sudden and dramatic onset of "choking" in sport
Read the article below describing in detail the impact of stress on performance in this famous tennis example from a Wimbledon final.

Kafkaesque self-destruction as Graf seizes chance to take her fifth singles title

Too much choke ruins the Novotna engine

As a loser, Jana Novotna has achieved more lasting fame that many of the 35 winners of the 100 Wimbledon women's championships. She may struggle for a mention in the Guinness Book of Records, but shoots straight into a book of historic failures.

Her capitulation from 4-1, 40-30 in the final set to give Steffi Graf a fifth title, 7-6, 1-6, 6-4, began with a double fault. The second serve was heading in the general direction of St Mary's Church and was the start of one of the worst cases of "choking" ever witnessed on the world's most famous Centre Court.

"Choking" is the term for a player's loss of nerve at a crucial moment. Actors and singers occasionally forget their words, but can be prompted. A tennis player is isolated. The same applies in golf, where "yips" on the green have cost many a title, Bernhard Langer's putt in the Ryder Cup is readily called to mind. Snooker, lacking the physical endeavour to be classed as a sport by some writers, also induces moments of mental frailty. Steve Davis's miss on a pottable black which gave Dennis Taylor the opportunity to win the World Snooker Championship is a classic example. Similarly, a player in a team sport can feel all alone bearing the burden of responsibility. Consider the penalty misses by Stuart Pearce and Chris Waddle in the World Cup semi-final in Italy.

It is not always what can be seen that makes games fascinating, but the inner struggle, a perspiration of the mind.

Gabriela Sabatini, who was defeated by Novotna in straight sets in the quarter-finals, had the embarrassing experience at the recent French Open of losing a 6-1, 5-1 lead against Mary Joe Fernandez. Sabatini double faulted on match point, failed to convert four other opportunities, and lost 10-8 in the final set after saving four match points. Sabatini, it may be recalled, twice served for the Wimbledon title when defeated by Graf in 1991.

The 24-year-old Novotna's habit of seizing up after her abundant talent has taken her to the threshold of a major singles title has been well documented; hence the nickname, No-No Novotna.

Though few observers could have anticipated such a spectacular collapse on Saturday, the mortgages of regular tennis reporters were not being wagered on a Novotna triumph even as she arched her back and prepared to serve, one point away from 5-1 in the final set.

John Roberts
Tennis Correspondent

This was not the case at Sandown Park, I am informed. The "Sharks" in the betting ring decided that Novotna's price of 3-1 to win the match was too generous to be ignored. With Novotna leading 4-1, many of those punters returned their attention to the horses and ways of spending their Wimbledon gains.

After playing splendidly against an opponent who was straining for consistency with her famed forehand

WOMEN'S FINAL STATISTICS		
Graf won 7-6, 1-6, 6-4, in 2hr 14 min.		
Graf		**Novotna**
70%	First serve in	48 %
6	Aces	3
3	Double faults	7
55 %	Points won on serve	57 p%
102mph	1st serve speed (max)	112mph
92mph	1st serve speed (Ave)	97mph
21/35	Points won at net	38/65
43/101	Points won at baseline	34/71
49 %	Total points won	51 %
8/14	Game points won	10/17
5/11	Break points won	6/12

Novotna had reached the fraught stage when her actions would dictate whether she won or lost the most important match of her career.

Jo Durie, the stalwart of British women's tennis, once described critical errors in one of her matches as "a good double fault" to convey that she had been bold in going for her serves. By that reckoning, some of Novotna's double faults could be described as outstanding. She followed the one in the fifth game with three more to beckon Graf back in to the match at 4-4. By now, the Czech's racket hand had become as shaky as Martina Navratilova's towards the end of Thursday's semi-final.

The climax was Kafkaesque: dark foreboding, self-destruction, tears on the compassionate shoulder of a duchess. Perhaps there is something in the psyche of Czechoslovkian-born players that senses scudding clouds beyond the sunshine.

Jaroslav Drobny was no "choker". The only thing he ever ran away from was his nation's repressive regime. Even so, he was defeated in two finals before succeeding against Ken Rosewall, the perennial Wimbledon loser in 1954.

Ivan Lendl, whose forlorn quest for the Wimbledon title is a *cause célèbre* has won everything else. Yet he was considered a

"choker" by many of his peers until he retrieved a two-set deficit to triumph against John McEnroe at the 1984 French Open.

Novotna's coach, Hana Mandlikova, whose graceful talent ought to have bridged the generation gap between the Chris Evert/Navratilova era and the emergence of Graf, won the French, United States and Australian championships but lost two Wimbledon finals.

Navratilova, the most prolific of Wimbledon singles champions, with nine titles, has also experienced moments of uncertainty. Her errors in 1987 French Open final, for instance, eased Graf towards her first Grand Slam title. As Navratilova said at the time: "I don't know how many new ways I can find to lose matches."

What befell Novotna on Saturday may make people less surprised that players surround themselves with retinues of friends and gurus to help lift their spirits in times of need.

Novotna has been consulting Dr Jim Loehr, an American sports psychologist, and her damaged confidence was in a state of rehabilitation as soon as her tears had been dried away. The art of positive thinking dominated her interviews. "I don't think it's a horrible experience," she said. "I just feel it's very disappointing being really so close. I had the chance to lead for 5-1. Unfortunately, I double-faulted. But, you know, I decided to go for it the whole time, because it worked before in the matches against Sabatini and against Martina. I don't think it was nerves. I just went for it, and it didn't work at all."

"I would play exactly the same way, like I did today. I think I should be confident more than ever after this tournament. I just tried to stay focused on every point and just tried to work very hard. But it is known that once Steffi gets going she is very difficult to stop. And that is exactly what happened. I felt very good on the court. It's just a sad ending."

Graf, having made a characteristic clean execution, startled security officers by running up the steps to embrace her family in the guest box. Then, looking across at her distressed opponent, the 24-year-old German was as moved as everybody else in the arena.

When all was quiet, the line from Kipling over the door to the Centre Court came to mind:

"If you can meet with triumph and disaster
    And treat those two impostors just the same . . . "

Source : John Roberts, tennis correspondent, *Independent*, Monday 5 July 1993
http://www.independent.co.uk/sport/tennis--wimbledon-93-too-much-choke-ruins-the-novotna-engine-czech-challenger-descends-into-kafkaesque-selfdestruction-as-graf-seizes-chance-to-take-her-fifth-singles-title-1482979.html

CASE STUDY

The countdown to a major sports event is a stressful time for competitors and as the time gets shorter the symptoms of stress would be expected to increase. Using this logic, time-to-event designs have been used to investigate pre-competition anxiety.

In one such study 10 international standard marathon canoeists were measured for changes in hormonal concentrations at three different points: 24 hours before competition, 2 hours before and 1 hour before. In addition, in this study the canoeists were divided into groups based on whether they reported, via questionnaire, that they felt their anxiety symptoms were helpful and beneficial to performance (facilitators) or unhelpful and detrimental to performance (debilitators).

A great strength of this study was that it was conducted with national standard performers competing in a genuine competition of high importance to them as success would lead to selection for the world championships.

The results showed that individuals who felt their symptoms were positive (facilitators) for performance showed a different pattern of hormonal response to those who felt their symptoms were negative (debilitators).

↑ Figure 12.4a

Cortisol has often been referred to as a negative stress marker and in other (non-sport studies) it has been shown that the more extreme cortisol levels (either high or low) can impair aspects of cognitive function such as memory, vigilance and decision-making. In this particular study it would appear that high levels shown in debilitators means that they are more at risk of impaired thought processes.

In contrast the adrenaline reponses show the opposite effect with facilitators benefitting from a late surge in this hormone that is positively associated with physical performance, a vital ingredient to a good canoeing performance.

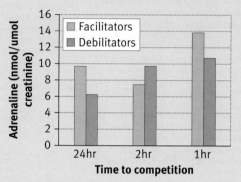

↑ Figure 12.4b

Reference

Eubank, M and Collins, D. 1997. "Individual temporal differences in pre-competition anxiety and hormonal concentration." *Personality and Individual Differences*. Vol 23, number 6. Pp 1031–9.

THEORY OF KNOWLEDGE

Examining the ways in which elite performers respond is fascinating because they appear to be capable of achieving incredible levels of performance. This is true not only of just physical feats of endurance, skill or strength but also of the mental ability to focus under the intense scrutiny of millions of spectators and demonstrate levels of commitment that normal members of the population cannot fully comprehend.

Working with this extraordinary group of people throws up a fundamental question for researchers who adopt a scientific model in attempting to establish theory in order to generalize findings to apply to the population and make

predictions. In psychological terms there is no reason to expect the individuals in this "group" to really be similar to one another as attempts to identify the personality of "champions" have consistently failed. The application of designs and statistical tests designed for making inferences to populations and generalized predictions could be challenged as illogical and inappropriate.

Is there any advantage to studying this group? How might research questions be framed and data analysed if there is no wider population to which the elite athletes belong?

To summarize there are several limitations to conceptualizing the arousal-performance relationship using the inverted-U relationship and in attempting to use an arousal-based approach to understanding the real-life experiences of sports performers.

The limitations of the inverted-U approach are:

→ a lack of credible weight of evidence on responses in sport
→ real-world performances are often comprised of several components and anxiety may affect different components in different ways
→ real-life declines are often sudden and rapid
→ descriptions of relationships do not provide explanatory mechanisms for the effects
→ arousal is not accurately defined (different elements may change independently of each other)
→ anxiety or other important cognitive processes associated with stressful performances are not included.

Sports performers certainly have elevated arousal levels when they experience stress; however, it is evident through systematic interview-based research that the most salient aspect of being stressed is anxiety. The construct of anxiety holds much more likelihood for explaining changes in performance and has been a serious focus for researchers of human performance for the past 60 to 70 years.

Anxiety

Anxiety has been defined as the "subjective evaluation of a situation, and concerns jeopardy to one's self-esteem during performance or social situations, physical danger, or insecurity and uncertainty" (Schwenkmezger, Steffgen 1989). Central to understanding anxiety is the view that it is based on the subjective experience, often called "relational meaning", of an event. In this way a situation is not stressful to an individual unless they perceive it to be so.

Anxiety has been found to be multidimensional comprising of both cognitive and somatic anxiety and possibly also a behavioural component.

→ Cognitive anxiety is the worry component and has been effectively defined by Borkovec as a chain of thoughts and images negatively affect-laden and relatively uncontrollable (Borkovec 1993).

→ Somatic anxiety is closely linked to physiological arousal and is best explained in terms of an awareness of physiological changes that provides a signal to the individual that they are anxious. So a performer who experiences some trembling and nausea may feel more anxious because these symptoms confirm to them that they are becoming anxious. This kind of physiological feedback and interpretation would support and enhance feelings of anxiety.

Determining levels of anxiety has one fundamental problem which is that it is primarily a cognitive function. Despite the very best technological advancements in brain imaging and scanning there is no immediate prospect of determining specific types of thought from such data sources. Consequently the only mechanism to assess what a person is thinking is to ask.

In anxiety research, questionnaires and interviews are the primary sources of data collection. Other techniques, such as diaries or real-time think aloud recordings, all fall same into the same general class of "self-report" data.

TO THINK ABOUT

Limitations of self-report data

Asking people to report anxiety states carries a number of limitations. Like many scientific measurements it is intrusive and hard to apply in real, time-pressured situations. However self-report data also has limitations if the respondent lacks sufficient awareness to accurately answer the questions.

There is also a danger that respondents may "manage" their responses to appear in a positive light. This is called *social desirability*. Questionnaires are also less robust to the effects of language comprehension, reading ability and educational background compared to a simple physiological measure.

There are steps that can be taken to reduce, although not remove, some of the limitations above. Can you think what could be done in relation to each of the issues listed?

In sport several questionnaires have been developed to assess anxiety, and one of the most used is the Competitive State Anxiety Inventory (Martens 1990). This questionnaire comprises 27 items and measures 3 related constructs: cognitive anxiety, somatic anxiety and self-confidence. Using this questionnaire during the time leading up to a competition, it has been reliably shown that somatic and cognitive anxiety are distinct from each other as they change at different rates over time.

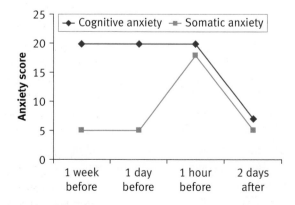

↑ Figure 12.5

CASE STUDY

Influence of anxiety on movement behaviour

Research showing that anxiety has a negative impact on performance outcome does not fully answer the question of why this would happen. One theory to explain this effect is that when individuals experience anxiety their movement becomes less fluid and efficient. Rob Pijpers and colleagues (2005) investigated this by monitoring movement of novice climbers to complete traverses (horizontal climbing) of an indoor climbing wall. To manipulate anxiety they used two identical 3.5 meter routes one high at 4.9 meters and one low at 0.3 meters. Total climb time was recorded and, using force induced electrical switches in each separate climbing hold, the total hold time and movement time were analysed.

On average total climbing time took much longer (22–50%) when the route was high compared to when it was low. Participants also reported significantly more anxiety and displayed significantly elevated heart rates (145.9 beats per minute at the greater height compared to 126.3 bpm).

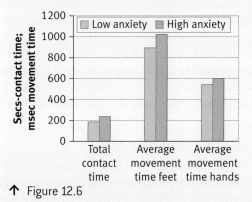

↑ Figure 12.6

As well as total time on the climb being longer, Pijpers and colleagues found that the total contact time (measured in seconds in Figure 12.6) was significantly longer for the climb at height. Using the pressure triggered timers on holds it was also possible to determine the time of movement—the time between the hand or foot leaving one hold and triggering the next. For both hands and feet the movement time was significantly longer climbing at height. An earlier study also found that climbing at height stimulated more "exploratory" movements indicative of the climbers being uncertain and hestitant in their movements.

The effects of anxiety on movement in this study would seem to have not just increased total time, but also had a negative impact on the nature of movements which were slowed and hesitant. The authors felt this data was consistent with one of the leading theories for explaining performance changes under pressure, the conscious processing hypothesis.

This hypothesis suggests that under pressure performers attempt to increase the degree of conscious control on movement. However many relatively well-learned movements become less effective, smooth and efficient when tighter step-by-step control is applied. In short increased efforts to improve performance actually result in worse performance ("choking").

Reference

Pijpers, J.R., Oudejans, R.R.D. and Bakker, F.C. 2005. "Anxiety induced changes in movement behaviour during the execution of a complex whole-body task." *The Quarterly Journal of Experimental Psychology*. Vol 58A. Pp 421–445.

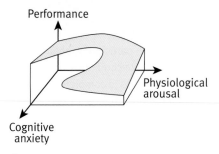

↑ Figure 12.7: Catastrophe Model (Hardy, Fazey 1987)

The concept of multidimensional anxiety formed the basis for a stronger understanding of the relationship between anxiety and performance among sport psychology researchers. In 1987 Hardy and Fazey presented the Catastrophe Model to explain the varied effects seen in real-life sports performances. The model presented was three-dimensional and centered on the concept of a "performance surface" to describe the combined effects of physiological arousal (closely allied to somatic anxiety although not the same) and cognitive anxiety on performance levels. The performance surface is best thought of as a soft sheet with a large fold at the front and a small ridge at the back.

Unlike inverted-U theory, the Catastrophe Model suggested that when cognitive anxiety was high (towards the front of the performance surface), continued increases in physiological arousal would result in a catastrophic decline in performance.

At the back of the model you will see the performance surface is shaped in a gentle inverted-U shape and suggest that at low cognitive anxiety physiological arousal will influence performance with a gradual increase to an optimal level followed by gradual decline.

One aspect of this model not evident from the diagram relates to what happens following a sudden catastrophic decline. Hardy and Fazey proposed that small reductions in physiological arousal were not sufficient to regain the level of performance. Instead they suggested that significant reduced arousal was required before the performers could begin to approach the same performance level again. The crucial aspect of this part of the model is that performance does not follow the same path when physiological arousal is increasing as when it is decreasing.

Limitations of catastrophe theory

Catastrophe theory was a significant development in understanding what happens to performance when anxiety increases because it considered the interaction between physiological arousal and cognitive anxiety. However the contribution of catastrophe theory failed to address two important issues.

→ A key requirement of any "theory" is that it identifies a mechanism to explain events. Catastrophe theory, whilst suggesting a relationship between anxiety, arousal and performance, did not offer any explanation as to why this relationship is thought to occur.

→ The model of catastrophe theory presented the idea of a "performance surface" (see Figure 12.7) but did not explain how it would be possible to accurately determine where a performer was on this surface. This significantly limited the potential for this theory to have real-world application.

The failure of catastrophe theory to offer a clear mechanism to explain the consequences of anxiety on performance, or to be practically useful, suggest that an alternative explanation was required. A viable explanation that has been linked to anxiety relates to the changes in attention. For many years it has been recognised that attention changes under conditions of anxiety, with increased anxiety being associated with decreased breadth and flexibility of attention. Under anxiety people seem to attend to less information, even ignoring information that is useful, and are not able to quickly move attention to different areas even when the situation demands this. However attention changes are not just symptoms of anxiety but have been suggested as a causal explanation of performance changes.

Attention, anxiety and performance

The work of Michael Eysenck and colleagues has been instrumental in developing a clear explanation of the way in which anxiety affects performance through attention processes. Attention is fundamental to performance, not only influencing the quality of information on which decisions are made by selecting all the correct cues to attend to, but of equal importance, by avoiding all of the distractions. Distractions can be deliberate (a dummy pass), due to conditions (a large noisy crowd), internal (fear of failing) and external (lots of moving opponents). Sometimes attending to factors normally of the highest relevance is a mistake and shows the performer has failed in attending to the most important cue at the time. Consider the example from the start of this chapter of Jean van de Velde in the final stages of the British Open golf championship in 1999. In golf the main objective is to get the ball in the hole in less shots than your opponent. However on this final hole, the situations demanded that he attend to a different and unusual goal. The well learned goal of "*fewest shots*" may have distracted him from the new goal that would have resulted in him winning the tournament.

Attentional processes are assumed to take place in and be organised by working memory (see case study "What is working memory?"). This limited capacity system is also easily affected by worry and the "uncontrollable thoughts and images of failure" that characterise worry use up valuable working memory capacity. Ultimately the combined demands of skilled execution and worry exceed capacity and, because worry dominates attention it can occupy attention space required for performance and produce a decline in performance level (see Figure 12.8).

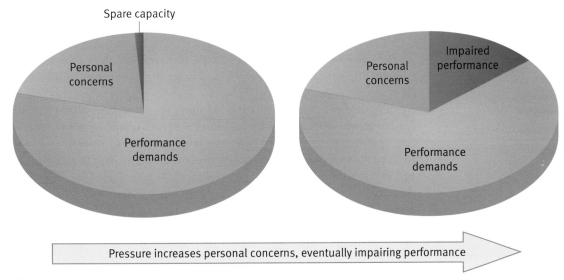

↑ Figure 12.8: Limited working memory capacity can be used up by anxiety

The concept of working memory capacity being exceeded suggests there is a period in which performance efficiency gradually declines although absolute performance level is maintained. You can think of this like energy consumption in two swimmers completing the same distance in the same time. One swimmer may be skilled and have a very efficient stroke requiring less energy to complete the swim. The novice can keep up to begin with by applying more effort but this reduced efficiency means they have less capacity in reserve. Performers also expend mental effort in performance and similar to physical energy may expend different amounts. As tasks increase in complexity more effort is required to complete them and as more distractions occur even more effort is required to maintain correct focus. **Processing Efficiency Theory** (proposed by Eysench and Calvo in 1992) emphasizes that the relationship between anxiety and performance is best explained by changes in efficiency rather than changes in absolute performance level.

$$\text{Processing efficiency} = \frac{\text{Performance}}{\text{Effort}}$$

This theory explains the sudden drop in observed performance level is actually the end phase of a more gradual reduction in processing efficiency which has then reached capacity limits. The role of attention in explaining anxiety effects has been further developed by identifying three key functions of attention which are illustrated below with reference to athletic sprinting.

ATTENTION FUNCTION	ROLE	CHANGE WITH ANXIETY
Inhibition	Prevent sprinter from focusing on apparent power and physical abilities of rivals	Focus on relevant "threat" of opponent's physique
Shifting	Enable focus on different factors in sequence: warm-up, coach instructions, holding room and keep arousal level in balance with breathing, recall positive memories, mentally rehearse race.	Cannot listen to coach properly whilst completing warm-up. Rehearsal of race fixates on perceived weakness in start.
Updating	Keep aware of time, where to be and when, monitor emotional state.	Constant checking required to avoid mistakes.

In summary, the work of Eysenck and colleagues on attention-based theories explaining anxiety and performance has resulted in proposing the following key relationships.

→ Anxiety increases are associated with performance efficiency decreases.
→ Cognitively complex tasks are affected more than simple tasks (because they require more capacity).
→ Anxiety results in attention being led more by immediate sensory input (e.g. what you see) and less by goal-directed plans (game strategy).
→ Susceptibility to distractions increases with increases in anxiety.
→ Performances requiring switching between two or more sub-tasks are more prone to error under anxiety.
→ Anxiety will reduce the frequency and accuracy of performers' ability to monitor and update information.

TO RESEARCH

Using the relationships between anxiety and attention described in this section, see if you can think of sport specific research designs that could test if these were correct.

CASE STUDY

What is working memory?

Imagine a basketball player beginning a match. In his head he is re-running the last instructions the coach said *"real fast in attack; don't let them boss you; keep the defensive shape"*. He also recalls long term memories about his opponents and their individual skills and preferences—a player who always spins to change direction, a player who always tries to go around the outside and another with a great three-point shot. For each opponent he decides how to play against them well. Simultaneously he becomes aware he feels a little sluggish, so claps his hands and does a couple of jumps telling himself to be sharp.

These activities all demonstrate working memory in action; replaying auditory material, extracting information from long term memory, making decisions, and comparing current with planned situations. Working memory has been likened to a "computer desktop", which processes (not just stores) internal and external generated information. However working memory is limited and too many processes at once will mean some are overlooked or not completed. It is also transitory which although means it does not become encumbered, does mean it may repeatedly go over processing which is especially relevant when we consider how it responds to anxiety and worrisome thoughts.

This effect is particularly evident when people are travelling and frequently check tickets and travel documents, but often cannot remember where they are when they are requested for inspection.

Influence of anxiety on simulated rally driving efficiency.

Individuals do not all respond in the same way to anxiety and those who have heightened response (high anxious) may find the impact on performance is greater than low anxious individuals. The effect of anxiety, according to Processing Efficiency Theory, may be more clearly shown in terms of effort used to achieve performance levels rather than just performance levels themselves. In this study Mark Wilson and colleagues asked participants to complete a self-report questionnaire to determine whether they were high or low anxious. Then they asked them to complete a simulated rally driving task based on a commercial computer game but with enhanced visual display, steering wheel, pedals and rally-car seat. The task was completed once in "low pressure" (told to drive as best as they can so research team could test the driving simulator equipment) and in "high pressure" (told their time would be compared to others and publicly posted in a league table of results, and the winner would receive a small monetary prize).

The researchers measured efficiency of car control (road position and speed control), gaze behaviour (using an eye-tracking device) and pupil dilation (changes are associated with effort). The performance of all drivers was worse with slower completion times in the high pressure condition, but high anxious individuals were affected much more than low anxious. It is also clear that all of the participants applied more effort in the high pressure condition.

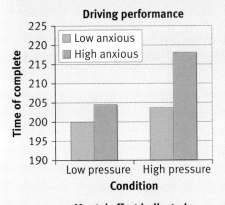

Driving performance

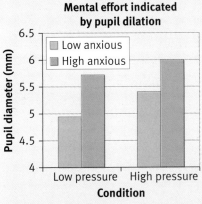

Mental effort indicated by pupil dilation

With increased effort and slower (worse) performance time the efficiency of performance under pressure decreased, consistent with processing efficiency theory.

Direct behavioural measures supported this with the high anxious participants despite applying more effort as pressure increased, showing less efficient search strategies with more frequent gaze fixations under high pressure. They also demonstrated much less efficient steering control with a high variation in movement of the steering wheel.

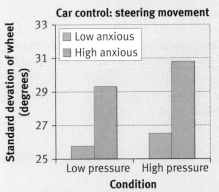

Gaze behaviour: search rate

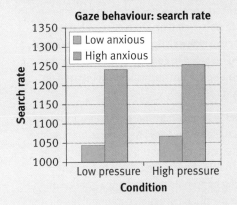

Car control: steering movement

Whilst this study showed reduced **performance level** in high pressure through slower race times, it also demonstrated that **performance efficiency** is also compromised under pressure. These affects were more evident in high anxious individuals than low anxious. The authors concluded that the results were consistent with the Processing Efficiency Theory but acknowledged that stronger evidence would be found in situations where performance level was maintained but effort increased. On reflection the driving task here was probably too hard in low pressure to allow room for compensatory increased effort to be used to maintain performance level as the pressure increased.

Wilson, M. et al. 2006. "The role of effort in moderating the anxiety-performance relationship: testing the prediction of processing efficiency theory in simulated rally driving." *Journal of Sports Sciences*. Vol 24. Pp 1223–1233.

The concept of working memory has important implications for all aspects of life that require cognitive activity. Tasks that are temporarily prioritised and occupy working memory space, such as conversations, inevitably result in less space for other tasks. Conversations demand perception and interpretation of the meaning of others as well as generation of one's own response. These may include recalling information from the past and considering what else you want to say in the conversation. Most of us can easily hold a conversation but struggle when we try to become involved in two conversations at once. Recent research has also shown that when people hold a conversation on a mobile phone their walking pace is slowed suggesting that elements of working memory involved in controlling where you are walking to and speed are not as available compared to without conversation.

When the second task becomes more complex and rapid such as driving, the effect is likely to be more pronounced and the consequences much more significant. In many places such as the UK there is legislation to prevent drivers from using hand-held mobile phones based on the assumption that the physical action compromises driving performance. In actual fact this legislation does not reflect the scientific research evidence which shows that driving performance is significantly impaired by both hand-held and hands-free mobile phone use. Jeff Caird and colleagues conducted a meta-analysis of the current research on driving and phone use. The meta-analysis approach enabled the results of 33 studies and over 2000 participants to be synthesized and analysed together providing much stronger evidence than a single study alone.

This meta-analysis found that drivers' reaction time was slowed on average by 0.25 seconds as a result of holding a conversation. There was no significant difference between hand-held or hands-free devices. Some have argued that whilst using a phone, drivers may slow down to compensate. There was some small indication that this does occur, but only with drivers using hand-held phones. This means that drivers using hands-free phones had equally impaired driving performance but took no compensatory action. The research is quite clear that having a conversation on a mobile phone significantly impairs driving performance.

The data even suggests that conversations with passengers are also distracting. However passenger conversation may be less influential if passengers cease or moderate conversation when they observe increased driving complexity. This modified style of conversation would provide strategic reduction in working memory load when more capacity is required for driving task, for example at a roundabout or junction which may lower the negative effects on reaction time.

→ What might be difficulties associated with making legislation based on this evidence?

→ What do you think might be the arguments made for and against using mobile phones whilst driving?

→ Who are the groups and organizations involved in this problem and what potential sources of influence do you think they may have on research, policy and legislation?

Caird, J.K., Willness, C.R., Piers, S., Scialfa, C. 2008. "A meta-analysis of the effects of cell phones on driver performance." *Accident Analysis and Prevention.* Vol 40. Pp 1282–1293.

Measurement of stress & anxiety

To research stress and anxiety effectively it is necessary to devise ways to measure these "constructs" in ways that are sufficiently valid and reliable to provide valuable information and understanding. The term "construct" is used to label an idea or concept that does not have a tangible form (e.g. you cannot touch or see it), but is created to explain a phenomenon. Some examples of other constructs might include fatigue, aggression or center of gravity. Each is determined through examining the outcome of usually two or more other primary measurements. The construct of anxiety has been measured in several different ways in the research outlined in case studies presented in this chapter.

One way of measuring the anxiety construct is to measure the changes we know that are associated with increased anxiety. So the symptoms and responses discussed earlier in this chapter, for example increases in heart rate, offer ways to measure anxiety. We can very broadly group these symptoms under five category headings (though note that strictly speaking biochemical would be a subset of physiological – but it warrants specific attention).

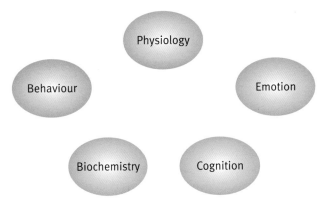

↑ Figure 12.9: Categories of stress responses and symptoms

Measuring changes under just one of these symptoms is a weak approach to determining if someone is anxious because changes may be due to other factors. For example if we measured the cortisol of football players turning up to training in the morning we might find it was higher than during the afternoon. However high cortisol does not mean the player is stressed or anxious as it is affected by other factors including a significant diurnal (daily) peak in the morning. To overcome this problem good research designs use a combination of measurements. When the results converge to provide a consistent picture then researchers can be more certain the measurement is valid. This process is often referred to as triangulation. Even though the word "**tri**angulation" suggests three measurements are used, the term is used for any combination of two or more measurements to increase validity.

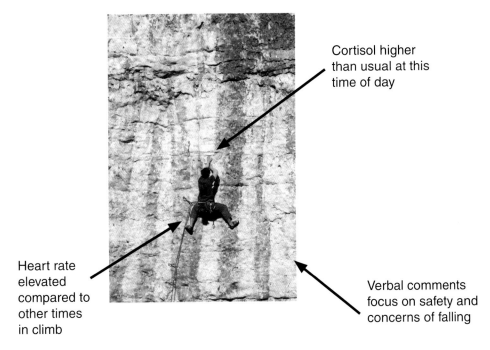

Cortisol higher than usual at this time of day

Heart rate elevated compared to other times in climb

Verbal comments focus on safety and concerns of falling

↑ Figure 12.10 Triangulating measurements improves validity of research

Measurement via self-report

Determining what a person feels or thinks (emotion and cognition) is largely dependent on asking them and usually this occurs via a questionnaire or interview. There are several potential problems associated with this approach that you were challenged to think about earlier in this chapter. There are strategies that can help to minimise, though never remove, the potential for this source of information to be inaccurate. Some of the more obvious problems and solutions are shown below.

PROBLEM	SOLUTION
Recall of thoughts and feelings after an event is dependent on memory	Ensure self-report is as close to event as possible (use field-based data collection or via phone?) Stimulated recall techniques (for example by film footage) may enhance recall.
Participants don't want to appear weak or anxious	Ensure participant information is treated confidentially, and individuals are not identifiable. Build trust with research team. Consider telephone interview with a researcher who does not know respondent's identity.
Outcome of event influences how they feel and what they remember. (success = positive recall; no success = negative)	Measurement "in-event" (especially in sports with breaks); use quick recorded "diary-entry" style or short single questions to be rated (e.g. on a scale of 1-10)
Participants do not understand what information is required from them.	Train participants including giving them feedback on type of quantity and depth of content (but avoid biasing content delivered). Check questions are easily understood.

There are several questionnaires that have been developed for use in sport settings that have established reliability and validity, this is important to enhance the quality of information. Non-sport specific questionnaires should not be used unless they are assessing the general tendency or predispositions of participants which are expected to affect general life as well as sport. Despite the limitations, self-report contains too much information of value to ignore so it has to be used, but with care, to provide the best possible information whilst accepting its limitations.

Conclusion

Performers in sport will always experience heightened arousal and very commonly stress and anxiety. Performing in such environments is directly associated with meeting challenges, excitement and later satisfaction and pride at one's achievement. So it seems that we should not strive to reduce or remove the stress or anxiety inherent in sporting situations. Performing in the presence of stress in sports settings may also teach people something that is of benefit them away from sports settings, in other parts of their life. Viewing sport in this way places it as a valuable learning opportunity to experience and practice a general life skill.

Understanding stress and anxiety in sport also emphasises the important distinction between performance situations that require physical and mental factors, such as most sports, in contrast with performance in an office or school setting where there is little physical component. Deep physical relaxation may help counter anxiety but is inappropriate for a sport performer who needs significant arousal levels to perform well. In contrast physical relaxation before a school exam may actually help performance in this mental task.

Finally, understanding how performers learn to effectively cope with anxiety provides useful information to develop better coping skills training. The research also shows clearly that how people respond to situations is partly dependent on the transaction between them and the stress source(s). This means that it is possible for a person to be taught how to modify their anxiety experiences through their own thinking processes, and by managing and using effective coping responses. In this way understanding developed through sport psychology research on performers who are good at coping can help provide the basis for helping all of us cope more effectively.

SUMMARY

→ Stress prompts the physiological system to become aroused through activation of the autonomic nervous system.

→ The "fight-flight" response is a global up-regulation of the body to prepare for fast high intensity action.

→ Sport performance where skilled execution, accurate timing and clear thinking are required may not be aided by strong arousal based responses.

→ Hans Selye emphasised that stress was response and proposed that stress could be considered as positive (eustress) or negative (distress).

→ Stress can be categorised by time limits of exposure and the extent to which it is voluntarily experienced or not.

→ Sources of stress can usually be defined with reference to two broad categories; 1) physical threat or danger, and 2) social-evaluative concerns.

→ Arousal based changes (e.g. elevated heart rate) can be used to indicate a response to stress but these measures can be compromised in sport research where physical workload masks stress response.

→ Many famous examples in sport show that under high stress performance levels can show sudden and dramatic declines.

→ Individuals respond differently to stress and may interpret their perceived anxiety as beneficial (facilitative) or detrimental (debilitative) to performance.

→ Interpretative differences highlight the transactional nature of stress which has an effect that is dependent on how the individual perceives a situation (and not just because of the nature of the situation itself).

→ Facilitative interpretations show a different biochemical response profile (cortisol) to debilitative interpretations. This suggests that physiological responses are influenced by psychological factors.

→ Cognitive anxiety (worry) is more important than arousal in understanding why and how performance is affected under stress.

→ Cognitive anxiety can prompt increased attempts to consciously control movements, paradoxically resulting in less efficient and effective performance.

→ Attention based models provide a strong theoretical explanation for how and why anxiety influences performance.

→ Cognitive anxiety occupies working memory space limiting availability for attentional resources from other tasks.

→ Performance efficiency is influenced by anxiety, but performance effectiveness can be maintained by increasing effort—up to a point.

→ Measurement of anxiety in sport requires combined approaches, triangulation and careful use of self-report data.

→ Research in stress and anxiety introduces a strong ethical dimension to designing and conducting studies.

→ Controlled scientific experiments rarely examine stress and anxiety at intensities equivalent to real world experiences.

→ Sport offers a perfect opportunity to study the impact of stress and anxiety on performance. Sport participants voluntarily and frequently experience stress and associated symptoms, have very high motivations to excel and engage in large volumes of practice to become skilled.

Self-study questions

1 Provide a definition for the following terms:

   a stress

   b arousal

   c anxiety.

2 Selye's idea of "a non-specific stress response" does not appear to hold true. What process do humans go through that may account for different responses?

3 Outline three major criticisms or weaknesses of the Inverted-U description of the arousal-performance relationship.

4 Sketch a graph showing the temporal patterning of physiological arousal and cognitive anxiety in the period prior to competition.

5 Identify two symptoms of stress that occur under each of the following five category headings:

   a physiology

   b biochemistry

   c emotions (feelings)

   d cognitions (thoughts)

   e behaviour.

6 Describe the concept of working memory and why it is relevant to sport performance.

7 Place the following key terms in the statements to match the ideas proposed by Processing Efficiency Theory.

   Key Terms: Effort, Performance levels, Cognitive anxiety, Efficiency

   _____ may not be affected by anxiety or stress.

   _____ of performance will be impaired by anxiety and stress.

   High _____ can be applied to offset potential threats to performance.

   _____ occupies working memory capacity reducing availability for other tasks.

8 Explain **two** key issues that are relevant to designing and conducting research in stress and anxiety.

Hardy and Parfitt (1991) examined changes in basketball free throw performance on the day before (high anxiety) and day after (low anxiety) an important competition. They manipulated physiological arousal by getting participants to complete shuttle runs and started either with the participant at near maximum heart rate, decreasing in bandwidths of 10 beats-per-minute (from maximum -10, -20, -30, -40), or starting from 40 beats below maximum and increasing. At each bandwidth participants completed a number of free throws to measure performance.

Below you can see the basketball shot scores from the day before competition, the high anxiety condition.

Heart rate bandwidths	Arousal increasing	Arousal decreasing
Max -40	19.88	21.25
Max -30	21.13	20.63
Max -20	21.25	12.75
Max -10	24.00	12.00
Max	11.37	12.63

Sketch out a graph with the five heart rate bandwidths along the x-axis (max -40 to max) and basketball performance on the y-axis. Now plot one line for increasing arousal (put an arrow on it pointing from left to right) and one line for decreasing arousal (arrow pointing in the other direction).

1 What performance scores were found when arousal was max -20?
2 What direction was arousal moving in to produce the highest performance score at max -20?
3 Describe what happens to performance when arousal increases from max -10 to max?

What does this data suggest would be the best physical arousal state (intensity and direction) for performing in high anxiety conditions?

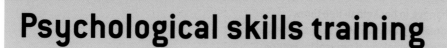

CHAPTER 13

Psychological skills training

OBJECTIVES

After reading this chapter, students should be able to:

→ discuss what is meant by psychological skills training and identify four key misconceptions about sport psychology

→ outline different types of goals and their uses

→ understand why goal setting works

→ evaluate the uses of mental imagery and provide examples of how it may be implemented in practice

→ outline relaxation techniques including progressive muscle relaxation (PMR), breathing techniques and biofeedback

→ outline self-talk techniques including thought stopping and self-talk.

> **❝** I don't care who you are, you're going to choke in certain matches. You get to a point where your legs don't move and you can't take a deep breath. You start to hit the ball about a yard wide, instead of inches. **❞**
>
> Arthur Ashe

> **❝** We all choke. Winners know how to handle choking better than losers. **❞**
>
> John McEnroe

THEORY OF KNOWLEDGE

Discuss the quote by Henry Ford that "Those who believe they can and those who believe they can't are both right."

Introduction

Even highly successful performers sometimes get affected by pressure during competitions. One big difference between those performers who succeed and those that don't is the way they manage their emotions and actions in difficult situations (e.g. Krane, Williams 2006).

One aim of a sport psychologist is to help athletes learn skills that they can use to take control, cope effectively and perform well under pressure. However, it is important to note that the application of sport psychology also has a major role to play in helping athletes manage their development, training and lifestyle over the course of their careers. This section examines several key interventions and evaluates their benefits and limitations.

Developing psychological skills

What are psychological skills?

Many people think that highly successful athletes are born winners or just happen to have the right type of personality to thrive. In fact, research into personality and sport performance has shown that personality factors account for only a very small percentage of eventual success. For example, a study by Rowley et al. (1995) concluded it was less than 1 per cent.

On the other hand, many researchers have shown that psychological skills can be learned in formal teaching settings through consistent training, as well as more informally through life or sport experiences. In other words, anyone can learn and improve their ability to use mental skills effectively, at any stage in their life.

Given the differences that have been identified between personality and psychological skills, it is important to clearly define what "psychological skills" are and present them in a form through which they can be learned and used easily. Vealey (1988) made an important distinction when she highlighted the difference between useful psychological states (e.g. confidence, motivation, concentration) and the skills that can be applied (e.g. goal setting, imagery, self-talk, relaxation) to help improve them. This is important because it is very difficult to just "be confident" without guidance, especially when someone feels low in confidence. For example, coaches often assume that athletes know how to "concentrate" or "relax" when they are told to do so from the touchline. However, they probably have never thought about how the athlete can do those things and are even more unlikely to have trained such skills. Because of this, it is important that athletes (and coaches) know what practical steps need to be taken to improve psychological states, and take time to practice them.

" Golf is 90 per cent mental, 10 per cent physical. "

Jack Nicklaus

What evidence is there that they work?

While the evidence shows that psychological skills can be taught, it is necessary to understand the importance of psychological training in improving performance. Anecdotally, it is clear to see that our mental state has a big role to play. For example, there are often stories in the media about sports people choking under pressure, and many top sports stars have been quoted highlighting psychology as one of the most, if not the most, important features of their sport.

However, while research supports the contention that psychology is very important, the evidence shows the need to take a more balanced, interdisciplinary view. For example, Kunst and Florescu (1971) highlighted the need to recognize that a range of different factors were important, with psychology accounting for approximately 35 per cent of performance variance.

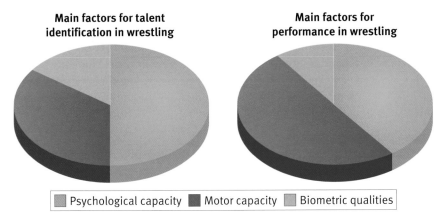

↑ Figure 13.1: Relative importance of psychological, motor and biometric factors in talent identification and performance in wrestling

Research into the impact of psychological interventions in sport generally shows they have a positive impact on performance and many Olympic athletes place a high importance on psychological preparation for success (Gould et al. 2002). While not all coaches and sports performers place a high value on sport psychology (Pain, Harwood 2004), there has been an overall increase in athletes seeking out sport psychology training over the last decade (Wrisberg et al. 2009).

The development process

For the most effective results, psychological skills must be trained systematically. In fact, they are acquired in much the same way as physical skills are and normally lots of commitment and perseverance is needed to make permanent changes.

Research by Pain and Harwood (2004) highlights there are a number of common misconceptions about sport psychology support.

Four common misconceptions

→ Psychology is a quick fix.
→ It is only required for problem athletes.
→ It is only pertinent for elite athletes.
→ Psychology isn't useful in a sport context.

There are three phases to the process of developing psychological skills.

Phase 1: General education phase

It is very important to incorporate a general education phase into psychological skills training (PST). This can be used to clarify what psychological skills are, how they can be trained, what role and level of commitment is required on the behalf of the psychologist, coach and athlete, and what improvements such training can bring. This helps to clarify expectations and understand the potential usefulness for any given individual.

Of course, every person has specific needs and circumstances and PST can be adapted to take on many different forms to best suit each individual. Equally, PST is not for everyone, which must also be respected.

Phase 2: Acquisition phase

The acquisition phase focuses on learning and understanding specific strategies and skills that will help to develop positive change where required. This phase will typically involve a thorough needs analysis of the athlete in their development and performance environment to ensure that PST is targeted at the athlete's needs. It will also focus on teaching the athlete how to implement strategies within the context of why they work. This is important because helping athletes to understand themselves, their emotions and behaviour in different situations will enable them to become independent problem-solvers when new or novel challenges arise. This forms part of the process of helping athletes self-regulate effectively (Richards 2011), which is an important overriding aim for many sport psychologists, and one that ultimately enables the athlete to function independently.

Phase 3: Practice phase

The final phase of the PST programme is the practice phase, which according to Weinberg and Gould (2011) has three primary objectives:

→ to automate skills through overlearning
→ to teach athletes to systematically integrate psychological skills into performance situations
→ to simulate skills athletes will want to apply in actual competition.

It is well documented that psychological skills cannot be taught effectively in isolation from the context in which they need to be applied (MacNamara et al. 2010). This is why in more formal PST settings, "homework" is set where the athlete practises different strategies under more realistic, sometimes increasingly pressured, situations. Regular evaluation is important as are meetings with the sport psychologist and/or personal reflections (e.g. logbook or journal) on the effectiveness of the strategies in different situations. These will enable the athlete to gain feedback, identify improvements and adjust and develop the strategies over time as required.

In addition to formal PST education, more informal experiences can occur through life and sport, leading to the development of increased mental toughness. For example, Bull et al. (2005) found that in young cricketers, a number of experiences facilitated psychological growth, including parental influence, exposure to foreign cricket, opportunities to survive setbacks, and needing to

TO THINK ABOUT

What experiences do you have from the non-sport areas of your life that help you in training or in a match or performance?

"earn" success. More recent research has highlighted the need for a more explicit use of real-life challenges to teach and embed coping skills (MacNamara et al. 2010), as well as the need for sport coaches (and significant others) to help develop mental resilience in athletes through the experiences they set up in their development environments (Martindale, Mortimer 2011).

Goal setting

As you can see from the quotes on this page, there are many anecdotes highlighting goal setting as an essential activity for success in life. As such, it will come as no surprise that goal setting is a well-established cornerstone technique in sport psychology.

Essentially a goal has broadly been defined as "what an individual is trying to accomplish; it is the object or aim of an action" (Locke et al. 1981). Locke and Latham (2002) highlighted that goals stimulate motivation and improved performance through one or more of the following mechanisms.

→ Goals focus attention.
→ Goals mobilize effort in proportion to the demands of the task.
→ Goals enhance persistence.
→ Indirectly, having goals encourages the individual to develop strategies for achieving them.

In other words, goals help direct and mobilize effort, while encouraging a problem-solving approach. Alternatively, goal setting has been shown to indirectly facilitate performance through knock-on effects on other psychological states. For example, Burton (1989) showed evidence of the positive effects of goals on performance through the manipulation of confidence and anxiety levels.

Types of goals

Different types of goals have been identified: outcome, performance and process goals.

→ Outcome goals relate to the outcome of an event, and usually involve a comparison with others (e.g. winning a race or being selected for a team).
→ Performance goals relate to a specific product of performance, which is normally relatively independent of others (e.g. swimming a certain race time or jumping a certain height).
→ Process goals relate to the processes that a performer will focus on during the performance (e.g. high knees or long stride pattern).

There are clear distinctions between the nature of these three types of goals (e.g. the extent of control the performer has over reaching their goal) and each of these goals has their own advantages and disadvantages within different contexts. For example, outcome goals can be useful for facilitating motivation in training, but have been shown to increase anxiety and irrelevant thoughts if used just prior to competition (Weinberg, Gould 2011). On the other hand, performance goals can help provide specific feedback about progress, and process goals can help provide a relevant focus in the middle of a race. Given these differences, it is perhaps unsurprising to see that using a combination of goal types has been shown to be more effective than using one alone (e.g. Filby et al. 1999).

Research into goal setting suggests that it is a technique that generally works very well. However, it has also been shown that if goals are not set properly they can impair the athlete's progress and be a major source of stress. Having said that, a broad review of the goal setting literature with collegiate, youth

KEY POINT

Psychological skills need to be learned in the same way that physical skills in sport are learned. The skills must be tailored to the needs of the individual athlete and it takes time and practice to develop them.

66 **Goals are not only absolutely necessary to motivate us. They are essential to really keep us alive.** 99

Bill Copeland

66 **Our goals can only be reached through a vehicle of a plan, in which we must fervently believe, and upon which we must vigorously act. There is no other route to success.** 99

Vincent van Gogh

TO DO

Write down five goals you have for different areas of your life, e.g. school, home life, hobbies.

TO DO

Break down your goals over time and identify what you need to do to make them happen.

What do I want to achieve?

Are there any milestones I need to reach along the way?

Long term:

Medium term:

Short term:

What do I need to do to give myself the best chance of achieving these goals?

1

2

3

and Olympic athletes revealed that almost all of the athletes used goal setting of some sort and found it to be effective.

Setting effective goals

The acronym SMARTER is often used for guidance when setting effective goals. While there are some merits in following the SMARTER guide (for example, it is easy to remember), rather confusingly many authors often use the acronym differently.

SMARTER goal setting
1) Specific
2) Measurable
3) Achievable
4) Realistic
5) Time-based
6) Exciting
7) Review

↑ Figure 13.2: SMARTER goal setting guidelines

Also, SMARTER guidelines do not present a full picture of the evidence, providing a rather simplistic overview. For a more full review of the goal setting literature see Hardy et al. (1996). Having said this, summary guidelines are still very useful, so a more substantial set of evidence-based goal setting principles are presented below.

1 Set specific goals

Research has shown that specific goals often lead to better performance than "do your best" goals or no goals (e.g. Tenenbaum et al. 1991). The more well defined you can make your goals the better. For example, "I want to be better at golf" can be made more specific, observable and measurable by changing it to "I want to lower my handicap from 5 to 3, by improving the accuracy of my iron play to the green from 100 yards". The more specific the goals, the more easily you can plan, practice and identify when you have been successful.

2 Set moderately difficult but realistic goals

Kyllo and Landers (1995) found that "moderately difficult" goals lead to the best performance, but they must be accepted by the athlete. However, Bueno et al. (2008) warned that if goals are perceived to be too difficult it can lead to learned helplessness. As such, it is important to try to find the right balance for the individual and adjust your goals when necessary—you will probably know if you are challenging yourself to the right level.

3 Set both short- and long-term goals—stepping stones to success

A combination of short- and long-term goals has been shown to be most effective (Kane et al. 2001). This is particularly true if long-term goals are broken down into relevant short-term goals which act as stepping stones, providing more regular feedback, ongoing focus and success experiences. Starting with a long-term goal in mind, then working backwards in time to form stepping stones to achieving your long-term goal is a common technique. Leading on from this, it is important to finish by identifying relevant practice goals and a good understanding of "what I want to achieve today".

4   Set a combination of outcome, performance and process goals

For every outcome goal that an athlete sets, there must be a range of different performance and process goals to support and underpin it (Filby et al. 1999). Remember the outcome goal (e.g. winning, getting selected, beating someone) often drives motivation while the process goals (e.g. technical, tactical, mental and/or physical tasks) and performance goals (e.g. specific times, splits, distances, shots) provide timely feedback and focus for day-to-day activities.

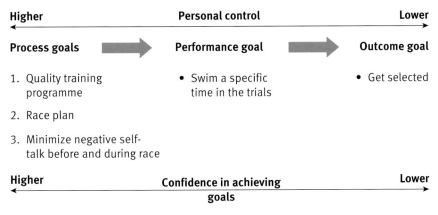

↑ Figure 13.3: Process goals can help improve a performance goal which, in turn, can lead to reaching an outcome goal

5   Always have training and competition goals

Athletes spend a lot of time practicing and relatively little time performing. Given the importance and specific nature of the deliberate practice required to improve (Ericsson et al. 1993), it is crucial that training goals are set, in addition to competition goals. Interestingly, Orlick and Partington (1988) found that one of the factors that differentiated between successful and less successful athletes was "setting practice goals". Doing this will ensure you remain focused, motivated through training and in competition.

6   Record your goals and make sure you get feedback on your progress

Research has shown the importance of recording goals and placing them where they can be seen as constant reminders. Furthermore, getting regular feedback on progress is an essential part of the process, enabling athletes to build confidence and motivation effectively over time. This will ensure you recognize and understand any progress and success on a regular basis.

7   Always identify strategies to help you be successful

Locke and Latham (2002) highlighted that goals work by encouraging someone to develop a plan of action. As such, this is a crucial part of the process of goal setting. It is common for sporting careers to have plenty of ups and downs, where challenges and barriers are encountered regularly. As such, identifying potential barriers, problem-solving and perseverance become crucial skills for negotiating the journey successfully.

8   Foster individual commitment to your goals and ensure you have adequate support

It is important that the aspirations of the individual are developed through goal setting in order to foster intrinsic motivation and commitment. As such, it is important to understand what an athlete really wants, encourage choice and perceptions of ability through the process. Furthermore, Dishman (1988) found that good support networks facilitated adherence to goal pursuit. As such, both of these aspects should be incorporated into the goal setting process.

KEY POINT

Setting goals is a useful tool for athletes. The best way to use them is to set a range of different types of goal.

Mental imagery

Imagery is "using all the senses to recreate or create an experience in the mind" (Vealey, Walter 1993) and is also sometimes known as mental practice or mental simulation. Imagery is a "central pillar" of applied psychology practice (Perry, Morris 1995) and has been shown to enhance motor task performance, increase muscular strength, and increase movement speed (e.g. Yue, Cole 1992; Pascual-Leone et al. 1995). The questions relating to "why" and "how" imagery works have intrigued researchers for decades and numerous theories have been proposed to explain the phenomenon (e.g. psychoneuromuscular theory, symbolic learning theory, attention-arousal theory and bio-informational theory). In addition, another possibility is "Possunt quia posse videntur" (they can because they see themselves as being able, Virgil, 20 BC), a concept that has been around for centuries. This suggests that imagery can have a positive effect on self-belief (e.g. sources of self-efficacy, Feltz 1984) and intrinsic motivation.

Currently, the most favoured theoretical stance for how imagery works is Lang's bio-informational theory (1977). This theory proposes that the same neural pathways in the brain used in performing skills are activated during the use of vivid imagery. This carries important implications for applied interventions as the same areas of the brain should be activated during imagery as during performance itself.

Indeed, Holmes and Collins (2001) suggest the extent to which this happens will determine the success of the imagery technique. They went on to devise seven elements to consider in the delivery of motor imagery-based interventions: Physical, Environment, Task, Timing, Learning, Emotion, Perspective (PETTLEP). The PETTLEP model of imagery is built on Lang's theory, but still requires testing and is far from complete. Nevertheless this model provides a way of incorporating all the relevant senses into an imagery intervention.

PETTLEP ELEMENT	JUDO EXAMPLE
Physical: Imagery should resemble as closely as possible the actual physical performance.	Stand on the mat with full judo kit on. Observe the session and attempt to take part in your mind or simulate competition fatigue by using imagery after a hard session
Environment: This should resemble as closely as possible the actual performance environment.	Complete imagery training session in the judo hall rather than at home. Use photos or video of new venues.
Task: Mirror the attention demands and changes of the actual practice.	Focus very specifically on performance and the internal feeling and emotions experienced.
Timing: Prepare for and execute movements in real time.	Experience the rhythm that you would normally use in performing throwing techniques.
Learning: If difficulties are envisaged, these should be included to keep it realistic.	You can still try new techniques in mental simulation. Also, it is important to change your imagery accordingly as real skills develop.
Emotion: Try to experience the feelings and emotions that you would if you were doing it for real.	Feeling of butterflies in your stomach as the fight begins. Use music to help facilitate these emotions.
Perspective: From the inside looking out as if you were actually performing (internal perspective) or viewing from the outside as if you were watching a recording of your performance (external perspective).	Use internal perspective for planning and executing techniques. Use external perspective to experience the aesthetic quality of the execution.

↑ Table 13.1: The PETTLEP model—a judo example

Of course, individuals will use imagery techniques differently depending on what type of activity is being performed (e.g. number of natural breaks in play and frequency of set plays/shots) and what level the athlete is performing at (e.g. novices may image a specific aspect of the skill, while experts may image the whole skill). Similarly, there may be a whole host of reasons why an athlete is using imagery as part of their preparation or performance (e.g. concentration enhancement, self-confidence, skill acquisition, emotional control, practice strategy, and coping with pain and injury—see Table 13.2). In addition, imagery may be integrated with other psychological skills as part of a wider performance intervention (e.g. imagery may feature as part of a pre-performance routine along with relaxation and self-talk techniques).

IMAGERY USE	EXAMPLE
Concentration enhancement	Rugby kicker using imagery as part of a pre-performance routine.
Self-confidence	Judo player seeing themselves throwing their competitor.
Skill acquisition	Novice tennis player images performing a serve before completing the task.
Emotional control	Golfer mentally practices making an important putt under pressure.
Practice strategy	Mountain biker mentally rehearses the route and how they will approach each part of the course.
Coping with pain and injury	An injured swimmer sees himself completing the next part of his rehabilitation successfully.

↑ Table 13.2: Various uses of imagery with examples

THEORY OF KNOWLEDGE

England is statistically the worst international football team when it comes to penalty shoot-outs. This article (See Figure 13.4) outlines some interesting reasons why some players struggle to score penalties under pressure.

Based on the information in this article and other relevant information you can find, design the content of a training schedule that would help players to learn to score penalties under pressure more regularly.

7th June 2010

Penalty takers must ignore keeper, study shows

Penalty takers hoping to snatch World Cup glory from their opponents in the final few shots of a match should completely ignore the goalkeeper and focus on where they want to kick the ball, scientists said on Monday.

Highlighting a new scientific study on how anxiety affects players in penalty shootouts, Greg Wood, a psychologist from Britain's Exeter University, said players under pressure needed to work to stay calm and not be distracted by the goalkeeper.

"We are naturally pre-conditioned to focus on things in our environment that we find threatening, and in a penalty competition the only thing that threatens the success of the kick is the goalkeeper, so we tend to focus on him and monitor his movements," he told a briefing in London.

"But instead, we should just look to where we're going to hit the ball... (and) ignore the goalkeeper.

"The control is with the kicker, and he must realize that, get confidence from it, and then align his eyes and let the eyes provide the brain with the necessary information for accurate shooting," he said.

Wood studied university-level soccer players who were fitted with eye-tracking technology and then subjected to various situations that would make them more or less anxious while they were trying to score penalties.

His study, which is due to be published in the Journal of Sports Sciences, found that the more anxious the players were, the more they focused on the main threat -- the goalkeeper -- and the more likely they were to shoot the ball at or near him -- making it easier for him to save the shot.

Goalkeepers, for their part, tended to focus on the ball or on the lower limbs of the kicker, not at the face or eyes, so there is little potential risk in a shooter focusing on his aim.

Penalty shootouts are likely to come into play in the final phase of the World Cup, which begins in South Africa on June 11.

In the knockout phase, which starts on June 26 and ends with the final on July 11, games which are drawn after extra time will be decided by penalties. Five players from each side take a kick, and then, if the scores are level, a "sudden-death" process starts. Since the format was introduced in 1982, there have been 20 shootouts in seven tournaments.

Wood said his research showed that the more a goalkeeper tried to distract a player -- for instance by jumping up and down or waving his arms about, the more likely the kicker was to focus on him and shoot the ball in his direction.

SPAGHETTI LEGS

His study quoted the former Liverpool goalkeeper Bruce Grobbelaar, who described in 2005 how he thought his distraction techniques had paid off in a big match.

"The biggest memory I have is the 1984 European Cup final against Roma and my 'spaghetti legs' routine during the penalty shootout that won us the trophy," Grobbelaar said.

"People said I was being disrespectful to their players, but I was just testing their concentration under pressure. I guess they failed that test."

Wood said his study backed Grobbelaar's suggestion.

"Whether it is a 'spaghetti legs' routine or simply the waving of arms, it seems that Bruce Grobbelaar was right," he said.

And if jumpy goalkeepers were not bad enough, the negative pressure of a history of poor performance in penalty shootouts is something a few teams will have to battle with, said Wood.

Teams such as England, the Netherlands, Yugoslavia, Mexico and Switzerland have all lost all of the World Cup penalty shootouts they have had to play in the past.

"When they're going up to take the kicks, this might play heavily on the minds of a penalty-taker," said Wood. "It almost becomes a self-fulfilling prophecy."

Source: Reuters

↑ Figure 13.4: Newspaper article related to penalty performance

Arousal a blend of physiological and psychological activity in a person, varying from deep sleep to intense excitement

Anxiety a negative emotional state in which feelings of nervousness, worry and apprehension are associated with arousal of the body

Choking the occurrence of inferior performance despite striving and incentives for superior performance

Relaxation techniques

Top level sports performers use a variety of skills and strategies to help them cope with pressured situations and among these relaxation is prominent. The ability to relax is considered important as a form of anxiety control and to ensure arousal levels are such that they will facilitate rather than debilitate performance. Additionally, literature in the area has identified that being relaxed during performance is one characteristic of peak performance although this is dependent on the sport (Krane, Williams 2006). For example, a golfer may benefit from feeling relaxed before performing, but a judo player almost certainly won't. This is because, in general, a higher level of arousal is required for certain sports such as combat sports than for others such as target sports.

Progressive muscle relaxation

Progressive muscle relaxation (PMR) is one of the most common forms of relaxation used in sport. Modern techniques are all variations of Jacobson's PMR (1938), so this is not a new phenomenon. The technique involves the systematic focus of attention on various gross muscle groups throughout the body and requires the individual to progress through the body, tensing and then releasing each of the muscle groups in turn.

PMR enhances greater self-awareness of degrees of body tension and the impact of this on performance. The goal of relaxation is to be able to achieve a relaxed state in seconds; however, as with developing any skill, it takes practice in order to be able to achieve this.

The PMR training schedule below illustrates how PMR can be practiced to reduce the amount of time it takes to achieve a relaxed state.

→ The first phase of training involves a 15-20 minute PMR session practiced twice a day (the use of PMR scripts or tapes can assist with this).
→ You can then move on to a release-only phase, which should take between 5-7 minutes to complete.
→ The time is reduced to a 2-3 minute version with the use of the self-instruction "relax".
→ The time is further reduced until only 20-30 seconds are required and then the technique is practiced in specific situations.

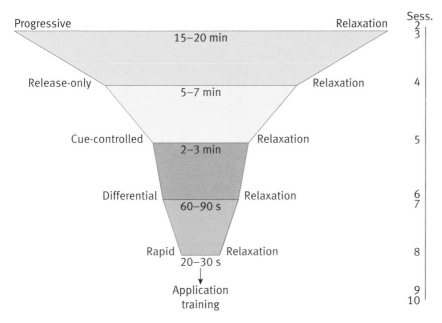

↑ Figure 13.5: Different components of applied relaxation (adapted from Hardy, Jones, Gould 1996, with permission)

It is extremely important to consider how the use of relaxation fits into athletes' pre-performance and performance routines. For example, the use of PMR just before a competition may not leave the performer in an optimum state. It is a technique that could be adapted for use both in the build up to and on the day of competition, however it would be most beneficial in its trained form as a rapid relaxation technique or if used as an aid to heighten awareness of unwanted tension. Only if sports performers are aware of any tension that may adversely affect their performance can they take measures to reduce or eliminate it.

Breathing techniques

Breathing techniques can be used to calm the body and distract the mind from the pressures of competition by giving the performer a specific task to focus on. The power of deep breathing as an aid to relaxation should not be underestimated. Not only does it increase the amount of oxygen in the blood, carry more energy to the muscles and facilitate the removal of waste products (Williams, Harris 2006) but a deep, regular and slow pattern of breathing is very relaxing to the body and mind (Cox 2007). Breathing techniques require regular practice in order for them to be used effectively in the build up to and during competition.

TO DO

Systematically tense and release each of the major muscle groups in your body. Start with your arms and hands, and then move on to your legs and finally to your face. Can you feel the difference between tension and relaxation?

TO RESEARCH

Look into how different sports use techniques such as PMR. How could it be useful in the sports you play?

TEST YOURSELF

Distinguish between cognitive anxiety and somatic anxiety.

TO RESEARCH

1 Outline the relationship between cognitive anxiety, physiological arousal and performance;

2 With reference to the following children's nursery rhyme explain why by thinking too much and drawing our attention inward about what we are doing we sometimes don't perform as well:

A centipede was happy quite,

Until a frog in fun

Said, 'Pray which leg comes after which?'

This raised her mind to such a pitch,

She lay distracted in the ditch

Considering how to run

Source: Katherine Craster, "The Centipede's Dilemma", 1871

THEORY OF KNOWLEDGE

Mindfulness is a whole-body-and-mind awareness of the present moment that is a cornerstone of Buddhist practice. Mindfulness is a means of paying attention in a particular way: on purpose and in the present moment. A controlled mental state has been shown to be a key element of maximizing performance.

Investigate the use of meditation and/or relaxation as one way of training your mind to be calm under the pressure of trying to produce your best performance in a major competition.

As with relaxation an awareness of effective and ineffective breathing is the first step towards breathing control. For example, under stressful conditions performers may hold their breath (e.g. just before a performance) or breathe rapidly and shallowly; both of which limit the amount of oxygen in the blood and increase muscle tension (Williams, Harris 2006; Weinberg, Gould 2011). One of the simplest forms of slow breathing is to breathe in to the count of four and breathe out to a count of eight. This technique encourages breathing control and provides a focus for the performer, so they are less likely to be distracted by irrelevant or unhelpful thoughts. When used in combination with relaxation and mental imagery, breathing techniques can assist athletes in reaching a hypnotic state. This may be particularly useful during a break or time out during a match or just before a performance (Weinberg, Gould 2011).

TO DO

Try deep and slow breathing by breathing in to the count of four and breathing out to a count of eight. What happens to your body when you do this?

Biofeedback

Biofeedback is the use of instruments to measure physiological systems (e.g. heart rate, muscle activation, brain waves, skin temperature) and feed that information back to the athlete (Wilson, Peper, Schmid 2006). Awareness of these systems and in particular whether they are operating to the optimal level can assist athletes in controlling them. For example, it has been shown that pistol shooters can not only lower their heart rates through the use of relaxation and breathing techniques, but can train themselves to shoot between heart beats, so as to reduce the amount of physiological variability involved at the point of release (Hatfield, Landers, Ray 1987).

Self-talk techniques

Self-talk is the internal dialogue that performers experience or in simpler terms, what athletes say to themselves. Although unseen and often unheard to the outside world, self-talk can have a powerful effect on a performer's self-image, perceptions, confidence, expectations and ultimately on their performance. The goal of self-talk interventions is to encourage the use of positive self-talk and limit the use of negative self-talk. The first step in ensuring effective self-talk is "awareness"—you can't change negative self-talk if you don't know it's there. Changing self-talk can be carried out through the use of thought logs (where athletes record thoughts and identify whether they are positive, negative or neutral), thought stopping (where negative thoughts are stopped by use of a verbal command such as "stop" or a visual image such as a "no entry" sign), and cognitive restructuring (where negative thoughts are restructured into positive ones).

TO DO

Can you identify whether these examples of self-talk are positive, negative or neutral?

SELF-TALK	REASON	POSITIVE, NEGATIVE OR NEUTRAL?
"I can't do this."	Missed long iron shot	
"Get stuck in."	Made a good early score	
"Keep playing positively."	Notice the opponent is giving up	
"You're so slow."	Unable to make a return shot	
"I must remember her birthday."	Saw her across the arena	
"Why is it not working?"	Hitting serves wide	
"That's it. Come on!"	Forced the opponent into making an error	

The use of self-talk can help performers to control their thoughts before, during and after performance. There are a number of benefits to this approach as the table below illustrates, along with example of each type of self-talk.

TYPE OF SELF-TALK	EXAMPLE
Attentional control (key words/cue words)	"Push."
Motivation	"This is my stage."
Negative thought stopping	"Stop."
Instruction	"Deep breath."
Skill acquisition (to focus attention on a particular skill element)	"Jump and flick."
Anxiety control (linked with attentional control and thought stopping)	"Just follow my routine."
Cultivate positivity (affecting self-efficacy)	"I can do this."

↑ Table 13.3: Types of self-talk with examples

TO THINK ABOUT

Can you think of more examples that could be used for each of the types of self-talk?

As with all applied interventions, consideration needs to be given to when and where self-talk would be most beneficial for the athlete. For example, positive self-talk can be built into an athlete's preparation plan or into their pre-shot routine as appropriate. It should be monitored regularly to ensure it is positive and that the correct type is being used to meet the required performance goals.

SUMMARY

→ Sport psychology is useful for performance enhancement as well as for managing training and a sporting lifestyle.

→ Two important concepts within PST are psychological states (e.g. confidence, motivation) and the psychological skills that can be applied to help improve them (e.g. goal setting, imagery, self-talk, relaxation).

→ While there are a range of factors associated with good performance, psychology has been shown to play a significant role.

→ Psychological skills are acquired in much the same way as physical skills, and as such, specific training is required.

→ Common misconceptions about sport psychology include: 1) psychology is a quick fix; 2) it is only required for problem athletes; 3) it is only pertinent for elite athletes; and 4) psychology isn't useful in a sport context.

→ Psychological skills can be developed both through formal teaching as well as more informal experiences. However, PST often has three phases: 1) general education phase; 2) acquisition phase; and 3) practice phase.

→ Goals work through one or more of the following mechanisms: 1) focus attention; 2) mobilize effort in proportion to the demands of the task; 3) enhance persistence; and 4) encourage the individual to develop strategies for achieving goals.

→ It is best to use a combination of different types of goals (e.g. outcome, performance and process goals).

→ The acronym SMARTER provides a simple way to remember some key aspects of effective goal setting, however, more in-depth guidelines are preferred.

→ Imagery is "using all the senses to recreate or create an experience in the mind" (Vealey, Walter 1993) and is also sometimes known as mental practice or mental simulation.

→ Holmes and Collins (2001) devised seven elements to consider in the delivery of motor imagery-based interventions: Physical, Environment, Task, Timing, Learning, Emotion, Perspective (PETTLEP).

→ Imagery can be used for concentration enhancement, self-confidence, skill acquisition, emotional control, practice strategy and coping with pain and injury.

→ Top level sports performers use a variety of skills and strategies to help them cope with pressured situations and among these relaxation is prominent.

→ Progressive muscle relaxation (PMR) is one of the most common forms of relaxation used in sport. This technique involves the systematic tensing and releasing of various gross muscle groups throughout the body.

→ Breathing techniques can be used to calm the body and distract the mind from the pressures of competition by giving the performer a specific task to focus on.

→ Biofeedback is the use of instruments to measure physiological systems (e.g. heart rate, muscle activation, brain waves, skin temperature) and feed that information back to the athlete (Wilson, Peper, Schmid 2006).

→ Self-talk is the internal dialogue that performers experience or what athletes say to themselves. Although unseen and often unheard to the outside world self-talk can have a powerful effect on a performer's self-image, perceptions, confidence, expectations, and ultimately on their performance.

→ The goal of self-talk interventions is to encourage the use of positive self-talk and limit the use of negative self-talk.

Self-study questions

1 List four common misconceptions about sport psychology.

2 Outline some evidence that suggests psychological skills can help improve performance.

3 Describe why goal setting works.

4 Outline three types of goals that Olympic athletes might use.

5 Describe guidelines for setting effective goals in a training programme.

6 Distinguish between internal and external imagery in sport.

7 Outline two examples of what imagery can be used for in an exercise setting.

8 Discuss why imagery works according to Lang's bio-informational theory (1977).

9 Explain what the acronym PETTLEP (Holmes, Collins 2001) stands for when using imagery.

10 Discuss how you would use PETTLEP imagery guidelines as part of imagery training.

11 Compare two different relaxation techniques.

12 Evaluate the use of relaxation techniques prior to sport performance.

13 Write a paragraph on the basic concepts of psychological skills training, and then list the key psychological skills with some examples of how these could be applied in practice.

DATA BASED QUESTION

A study was conducted examining elite (n = 65) and non-elite (n = 50) rugby players' use of psychological skills (imagery; self-talk), their experience of competition anxiety and their level of confidence during a match. The results are shown in the table below.

In relation to psychological skills, higher scores in the table are associated with greater use of the skills. With competition anxiety, higher scores for anxiety represent more anxiety, and a higher score for confidence is associated with more confidence.

	Elite (n=65) – mean (SD)	Non-elite (n=50) – mean (SD)
Imagery	15.29 (3.19)	13.10 (2.99)
Self-talk	16.32 (2.47)	14.71 (2.52)
Competition anxiety	14.06 (3.80)	15.26 (3.79)
Confidence	29.35 (4.55)	23.20 (5.18)

(Source: Neil et al. 2006. "Psychological skills usage and the competitive trait anxiety response as a function of skill level in rugby union." *Journal of Sports Science and Medicine*. Vol 5. Pp 415–23)

1 State which group used more self-talk. (1 mark)

2 Describe the differences between the elite and non-elite groups in relation to anxiety and confidence experiences. (2 marks)

3 Discuss the implications of these findings for psychological skills training. (3 marks)

CHAPTER 14

Overtraining, stress and burnout in adolescent athletes

OBJECTIVES

By the end of this chapter students should be able to:

→ define and differentiate between overtraining, staleness and burnout

→ identify the signs and symptoms of overtraining, staleness and burnout in young athletes

→ understand the reasons why burnout can occur

→ identify the remedial and preventative steps that can be taken to avoid overtraining and burnout in adolescent athletes.

Introduction

Participation in organized youth sports has increased in the last decade. Sports participation is now more accessible to all young people, from recreational play and school activities, to highly organized and competitive travelling teams, to pre-Olympic training opportunities. The variety of activities on offer has also grown from the traditional physical education activities such as football, hockey, netball and rugby, to include activities such as triathlon, rowing, boxercise, sports acrobatics, handball and various dance disciplines.

There are numerous physical, psychological and social benefits to engaging in sport from an early age. For example, youth sports programmes provide opportunities for individuals to build self-esteem, enhance social skills such as leadership and teamwork, acquire discipline, fight obesity, and improve general fitness and basic motor skills. However, because training has become more sport specific and continuous, overuse injuries are now common among young athletes (DiFiori 1999).

In 1992, up to 50 per cent of all injuries seen in pediatric sports medicine were related to overuse (Dalton 1992). If left unchecked, such overtraining can lead to burnout and, subsequently, complete withdrawal from sporting activity. Consequently, it is important that as youth sports participation continues to grow, the proper knowledge and support is available to athletes, parents and coaches in order to prevent the rise of overtraining injuries and burnout, while promoting the many benefits of continued participation. This chapter aims to highlight some of the issues associated with overtraining and burnout, and how they can be managed when working with adolescent athletes.

Overtraining

Overtraining the result of excessive physical training without adequate rest

Frequently, children are being directed into specializing in one or two sports from an early age (Matos, Winsley 2007; Brenner 2007; Gerrard 1993). This phenomenon is the product of coaches and parents who believe that in order to succeed and excel at senior level, it is necessary to start specific, intensive training well before puberty (Baxter-Jones, Mundt 2007). This "catch them young" philosophy has meant that many young athletes are training intensively and consistently by the time they become adolescents. As a result of this, they are often asked to engage in a level of training that would be considered exhaustive even for adults. This can often result in a syndrome known as overtraining.

Overtraining refers to a "syndrome that results when excessive, usually physical, overload on an athlete occurs without adequate rest" (US Olympic Committee 1998). Kreider et al. (1998) expanded on this by further examining the difference between overreaching and overtraining, already discussed in chapter 7. Overreaching refers to training beyond usual limits which leads to a short-term decrease in performance but can be effectively overcome with a short period of rest and recovery (Kreider et al. 1998). It is a normal part of the training process. However, overreaching can turn into overtraining if sufficient recovery time is not included in the young athlete's training programme. In this case overtraining will have a detrimental, long-term effect on performance. Matos and Winsley (2007) suggest that, in this respect, overreaching and overtraining are two ends of the same continuum.

A common question asked by all those involved or associated with youth sports is "how much training is too much?" Unfortunately, there are no scientifically determined guidelines to help coaches and parents define how much exercise is healthy and beneficial to the young athlete and what might be harmful and represent overtraining (Brenner 2007). In the past it was considered dangerous for young and adolescent athletes to engage in resilience training such as weightlifting. Now, however, research has shown us that when executed correctly, such resilience training can be safe and effective. In fact, it has the power to improve sport performance, enhance body composition, and reduce the rate of sport-related injuries (Matos, Winsley 2007).

Likewise training can also help children and adolescents improve their aerobic and anaerobic capacity. Therefore, rather than demonizing training, sports scientists, coaches, parents and athletes must be aware of what to look for and how to prevent the negative impacts of overtraining. In the following sections we will take a closer look at the physical and psychological impacts of overtraining, including staleness, overuse injuries and burnout. We will identify the signs and symptoms of overtraining and burnout, and consider what can be done to prevent such occurrences in young and adolescent athletes.

Physical impact of overtraining

Today, training for success is a fine balance between pushing oneself hard enough to develop the necessary fitness, strength and skills to achieve peak performance, and yet not too far so as to incur the negative consequences of overtraining. As mentioned above, overtraining can have a long-term negative impact on a young athlete's performance. Two avenues through which this may occur are overuse injuries and a syndrome known as "staleness". Each of these is considered in detail below along with an explanation of burnout.

Overuse injuries

Overuse is one of the most common factors that lead to injuries in the child or adolescent athlete. An overuse injury refers to micro-traumatic damage to a bone, muscle or tendon that has been subjected to repetitive stress without receiving sufficient time to heal (Brenner 2007). These types of injuries are categorized in four stages relating to the seriousness of the problem.

Overuse injury micro-traumatic damage to a bone, muscle or tendon that has been subjected to repetitive stress without receiving sufficient time to heal

TO THINK ABOUT

What injuries have you experienced as a result of playing sport? What about your classmates?

↑ Figure 14.1: Contusion injuries are likely to occur in contact sports such as rugby

These are presented below in Table 14.1.

Stage 1	Pain is experienced in the affected area after physical activity.
Stage 2	Pain is experienced in the affected area during physical activity, but does not restrict performance.
Stage 3	Pain is experienced during physical activity and does restrict the athlete's performance.
Stage 4	Chronic, unrelenting pain is experienced at all times, even at times of rest.

↑ Table 14.1: The four stages of overuse injuries

The most common places for overuse injuries to occur in children and adolescents are the ankle and knee, followed by the hand, wrist, elbow, shin and calf, head, neck and clavicle, shoulder, foot, back, hip and hamstring (Rice 1989). Younger children tend to sustain injuries to their head and other upper extremities (Adirim, Cheng 2003), such as their shoulder, clavicle and elbows, whereas older children are more likely to injure their lower extremities, such as the ankles and knees.

Adirim and Cheng highlight that the most likely injuries to be sustained by child and adolescent athletes are contusions and strains. Contusion injuries are bruises, caused by bleeding into the muscle or an area of soft tissue. Strains occur when a muscle or ligament is pushed or stretched beyond its limits. The severity of such injuries can range from a stage 1 on the overuse injury scale to a stage 4. Many younger athletes with these types of injuries may not even report them because they do not disrupt play or cause significant pain. Bruises are most common in sports such as football, hockey and rugby where contact or collision with another player is highly likely. Strains can occur in any sport, but are more common in sports where running is a key aspect of the game or event.

Muscle strains are common in older adolescents or adults, whereas younger athletes are more likely to experience strains at points in the body where tendon or cartilage meets the bone. Strains at these points are often caused by repetitive actions and overuse during periods of rapid growth. This explains why overuse injuries are commonly found at joints in the body, such as the ankle, knee and elbow. Treatment for child and adolescent injuries such as those described above includes rest, ice, compression and elevation (RICE). Athletes are often allowed to return to play when pain has subsided, and strength and range of motion in the affected body part has been restored (Adirim, Cheng 2003).

The risk that overtraining will lead to overuse injuries is more likely in child and adolescent athletes. There are physical, physiological and psychological differences between the young athlete and the mature, adult athlete that may cause them to be more vulnerable to such injury. Most of the physical and physiological reasons relate to the fact that the bodies of younger athletes have not finished developing yet. Below are some reasons that younger athletes are more susceptible to injury.

→ The growing bones of a young athlete cannot handle as much stress as the mature bones of adult athletes (Maffuli et al. 1992; Carter et al. 1988).
→ Compared to the rest of their bodies, children have larger heads, which can lead to a higher proportion of head injuries than in adult athletes (Adirim, Cheng 2003).
→ Because children are smaller and vary in size, generically produced protective equipment may not be appropriately sized and therefore not provide suitable protection.

- → Growing cartilage is more susceptible to stress which can be a factor in overuse injuries.
- → Repetitive activities can damage underdeveloped bones, muscles and tendons leading to adolescent-associated injuries such as spondylolysis, a stress fracture of the spine, commonly found in sports which promote repetitive hyperextension of the lower back, such as gymnastics.

↑ Figure 14.2: Repetitive hyperextension of the lower back makes young gymnasts susceptible to spondylolysis

Another reason that younger athletes are more susceptible to injury is that they are still developing the correct skills and techniques required to participate in specific sports. Their lack of developed motor skills can put them at risk of injury. A common example of this is an injury referred to as "Little League Elbow", named such because it is frequently found among young baseball players. Little League Elbow is caused by micro-tears where the cartilage meets the bone in the elbow joint. It commonly develops because the young player has not yet learned the proper throwing mechanics and is repeatedly throwing using just the arm rather than using the entire kinetic chain from foot to hand (Brenner 2007). Despite being named after baseball, Little League Elbow is an injury risk in any sport which requires athletes to execute a throwing action, including rounders, cricket, javelin, shot-put, dodgeball and handball.

TO THINK ABOUT

What specific techniques are required in the sports you play? How long did it take you to master them? Can very young athletes perform those skills correctly or do you need to have a certain level of strength or muscle control?

↑ Figure 14.3: If the correct techniques are not mastered, repetitive skills such as throwing may lead to injury

Psychologically, younger athletes are also more at risk of overuse injuries because they simply do not have the cognitive ability to associate vague symptoms of overtraining, such as fatigue and poor performance, with injury. Because of this, they are more likely to continue training when they are tired or even suffering from a stage 1 overuse injury, risking further, more serious injury.

Younger athletes are more likely to experience strains at points in the body where tendon or cartilage meets the bone. Strains at these points are often caused by repetitive actions and overuse during periods of rapid growth. Also younger athletes are still gaining the correct skills and techniques for their sport and may get injured as a result of poor technique.

Staleness the result of overtraining where there is no improvement in performance despite continued training

There are also added external psychological pressures on athletes at a younger age now in organized and competitive sports. Overenthusiastic parents or coaches may inadvertently place pressure on young athletes to compete, or overemphasize the importance of winning. Likewise, an increasing number of younger pupils are being given opportunities to compete for sports bursaries, which provide financial support throughout school, college or university.

Staleness

As we learned in chapter 7, training can be mapped onto a continuum, with the planned desirable training effects of overreaching at one end and the negative, detrimental training effects of unplanned overtraining at the other. In this respect overtraining is a process; it is something we do. Left unchecked, the process of overtraining can lead to a syndrome known as staleness.

Staleness refers to the initial failure of the body's adaptive mechanisms to cope with psychological and physical stress (Silva 1990). In practice, this manifests itself as a plateau, or drop, in performance. Despite continued or enhanced training, the individual's sporting performance remains at a consistent level, or even decreases, rather than improving as is expected with training. This concept is reflected in the American Medical Association's (1966) definition of staleness as the physiological state of overtraining which manifests itself as deteriorated athletic readiness.

Morgan et al. (1987) were very clear on the fundamental difference between overtraining as the process and staleness as the end result, or product, of that process. The concept that staleness is the result of overtraining is shared by many researchers within sports science (Morgan et al. 1987; Kenttä, Hassmen 1998; Polman, Houlahan 2004; Weinberg, Gould 2010). This inability to deal with training overload stress has resulted in performance decrements in athletes of all descriptions and disciplines (Polman, Houlahan 2004).

Burnout

In addition to the concepts of overtraining and staleness, there is also burnout to consider. Confusingly, the terms overtraining, staleness and burnout are often used interchangeably within medical and sports science literature to refer to the same construct. It is more accurate to consider these terms as separate entities, which are all linked together as part of the same continuum-based process (Kenttä, Hassmen 2004). As mentioned above, Morgan et al. (1987) were very clear that overtraining and staleness are fundamentally different as one refers to a process and the other a product, or outcome, of that process. However, staleness is not the final piece in the overtraining, staleness and burnout relationship.

Although some researchers and sports scientists have used staleness and burnout to refer to the same negative end state, Raglin (1993) has argued that burnout should be viewed as separate from staleness. Raglin suggests that there is a psychological difference between the two constructs, specifically stipulating that burnout is characterized by a loss of motivation that is not necessarily present in staleness. For example, a young swimmer suffering from staleness may be eager to continue training and competing but demonstrate a plateau or increase in his times in the pool. Comparatively, a young swimmer suffering from burnout would also demonstrate a drop in performance but this would also be coupled with a lack of motivation, or desire, to attend training or continue competing. The link between overtraining, staleness and burnout is shown in Figure 14.4.

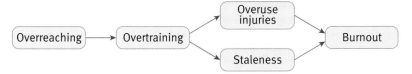

↑ Figure 14.4: The continuum-based process of how overtraining can lead to staleness, overuse injuries and, ultimately, to burnout

The concept of burnout did not actually develop within the sports science domain. It was first an area of interest and research within the occupational setting. Herbert Freudenberger (1974) was working with volunteers at a rehabilitation center in New York when he first defined burnout as a state of physical and emotional depletion resulting from work conditions. This was elaborated on by Christina Maslach, a social psychologist, who was investigating the gradual process of exhaustion, cynicism and reduced commitment in poverty lawyers. In 1984, Maslach and Jackson proposed that burnout comprised of three areas:

→ emotional exhaustion
→ depersonalization
→ a reduction in performance.

As with many constructs that develop in other domains yet are relevant to sports science, it is often necessary to assimilate the information and develop it in a way which is relevant and specific to the sporting environment and individuals. Questions regarding the appropriateness of the Maslach and Jackson (1984) conceptualization of burnout in a sporting domain prompted Raedeke et al. (2002) to develop an athlete-specific definition. They proposed that burnout refers to a withdrawal from sport because of a reduced sense of accomplishment, devaluation or resentment of the sport, and physical and psychological exhaustion.

Within the occupational domain it is widely accepted that burnout does not simply occur because of the presence of environmental or organizational stressors. Rather, it is considered to be the result of the interaction between these stressors and the intrapersonal characteristics which may help or hinder the development of burnout. This has been somewhat reflected in current sports science literature. In 2007, Gustafsson et al. found that there was no correlation between training load and burnout scores in 980 athletes from 29 different sports. These results suggest that not all athletes with high training loads will experience burnout. They also provide support for Raglin's (1993) proposal that staleness and burnout are different constructs, highlighting that while staleness results from overtraining, overtraining and staleness are not the only precursors to burnout in adolescent athletes.

Burnout in adolescent athletes has been an important issue for sports scientists over the past two decades, not least because of a large media interest in reporting and sensationalizing the dramatic demise of high profile sportspeople and the decline of young sports stars who fail to live up to their potential at senior level (Goodger et al. 2007). In 2002, the media reported that Martina Hingis, a tennis player who had won Wimbledon at the age of 16, was retiring from tennis at the age of 21 due to "burnout" and "repetitive ankle injuries".

Models of stress and burnout

A common understanding is that burnout involves a psychological and emotional element that is not present in overtraining or staleness. Often burnout is associated with a lack of motivation to continue participating within the sport (Morgan et al. 1987) and, in extreme cases, a complete withdrawal from a formerly enjoyed

Burnout a plateau in performance as a result of overtraining accompanied by a decrease in motivation to train

TO DO

Martina Hingis is one example of a sportswoman who excelled at a young age but was portrayed in the media as not living up to her potential. Can you think of other examples from other sports?

TEST YOURSELF

Explain what each of the following terms means:
→ overtraining
→ staleness
→ burnout.

KEY POINT

Burnout is not just a physical state, it is involves a psychological or emotional element as well. It can lead to a very talented and enthusiastic athlete giving up a sport altogether.

activity. However, the exact reasons why burnout occurs are still being debated. Two predominant models are Smith's (1986) Cognitive-Affective Stress Model and Coakley's (1992) psychosocial model (the Coakley Model). In order to understand Smith's model within the sporting context, we must first understand some generic principles of stress.

Transactional Model of Stress

It is now widely understood that stress is not a simple, linear process based on a stimulus-response basis. Instead, it is regarded as a complex, multidimensional relationship that results from an interaction between personal characteristics and environmental factors.

Lazarus and Folkman (1984) suggest that an individual will experience stress when they believe that an environmental stressor outweighs their ability to cope, or represents threat, loss or harm to their person. At the core of this Transactional Model of Stress lies the concept of appraisal: a particular environmental factor is only stressful if the individual appraises it to be so. This theory explains why people perceive different experiences or situations to be stressful and will react in different ways to the same situation.

Lazarus and Folkman highlight two stages of appraisal that are key in determining whether or not the stimulus will be determined as stressful: primary appraisal and secondary appraisal.

→ The **primary appraisal** process will determine whether the situation is: a) relevant or irrelevant to the individual, and b) benign-positive or representing potential harm, threat or loss to the individual. If the situation is relevant and presenting harm, threat or loss, it is likely to be viewed as stressful.

→ The **secondary appraisal** process assesses what might and can be done about the situation, including an assessment of relevant coping strategies and potential outcomes. If the potential harm, threat or loss outweighs the available coping resources, the person will experience stress. This process is depicted in the diagram below.

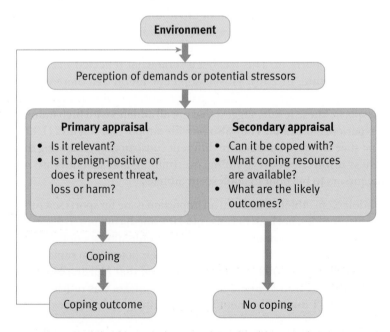

↑ Figure 14.5: The appraisal process (adapted from Richards 2004)

The outcome of the appraisal process directly influences whether or not an individual makes an attempt to cope with the situation. Coping is the constantly changing cognitive and behavioural effort exerted by an individual to manage a particular stressful situation (Lazarus, Folkman 1984). Both the appraisal process and the subsequent attempt to cope will have a direct influence on the individual's emotions.

The Cognitive-Affective Stress Model

The Cognitive-Affective Stress Model (Smith, 1986) defines burnout as "the psychological, emotional and physical withdrawal from a formerly pursued and enjoyable sport as a result of chronic stress." In this model Smith proposes that burnout in the young and adolescent athlete is due to an imbalance between perceived demands and coping strategies, which results in the negative experience of chronic stress.

Smith's model of burnout maps directly onto the Transactional Model of Stress proposed by Lazarus and Folkman. The burnout model consists of the following four stages:

1 situational demands

2 cognitive appraisal

3 physiological response

4 behavioural responses.

These progressive stages reflect environmental, psychological, physical and behavioural components that interrelate to create the burnout process. Furthermore, Smith stipulated that each stage of the process will be influenced by the young athlete's personality and level of motivation. This model is depicted in Figure 14.6 below.

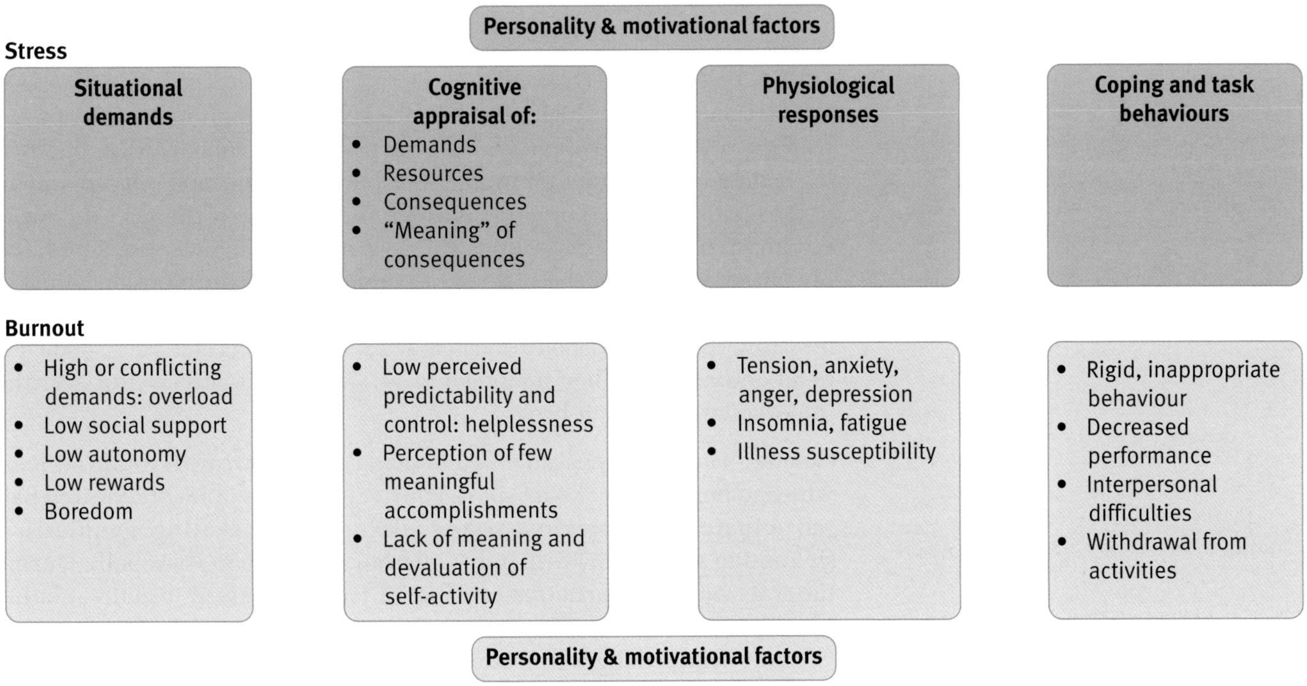

Personality & motivational factors

Stress

| Situational demands | Cognitive appraisal of:
 • Demands
 • Resources
 • Consequences
 • "Meaning" of consequences | Physiological responses | Coping and task behaviours |

Burnout

| • High or conflicting demands: overload
 • Low social support
 • Low autonomy
 • Low rewards
 • Boredom | • Low perceived predictability and control: helplessness
 • Perception of few meaningful accomplishments
 • Lack of meaning and devaluation of self-activity | • Tension, anxiety, anger, depression
 • Insomnia, fatigue
 • Illness susceptibility | • Rigid, inappropriate behaviour
 • Decreased performance
 • Interpersonal difficulties
 • Withdrawal from activities |

Personality & motivational factors

↑ Figure 14.6: Smith's (1986) Cognitive-Affective Stress Model of athlete burnout (adapted from Weinberg, Gould 2010)

As can be seen above, Smith's model of burnout suggests the following.

→ **Stage 1** High demands or pressures will be placed on the young athlete. Such demands may include an intense training schedule, pressure to win or external pressure such as schoolwork or exams.

→ **Stage 2** This stage is the athlete's appraisal process. As highlighted above, the outcome of this process will determine whether the environmental demands are perceived as stressful or not. Individuals will view the same situation in different ways. For example, one young dancer may thrive on the prospect of giving a public performance while another may find the idea highly stressful.

→ **Stage 3** The outcome of the young athlete's appraisal process may lead to physiological changes; an athlete under chronic stress may experience burnout symptoms such as anxiety, fatigue, insomnia and illness susceptibility.

→ **Stage 4** The physiological symptoms stimulate some sort of coping or behavioural action. For a burned-out athlete this may be a decrease in performance, a lack of desire to attend training sessions or, in extreme cases, complete withdrawal from the activity.

According to Smith's model the likelihood of whether an athlete will cope with stress or experience burnout will depend on individual personality characteristics and motivational factors. These moderating factors help explain why not all individuals with heavy training schedules burn out.

The Coakley Model of burnout

In 1992, Coakley introduced a model that would challenge stress-induced burnout theories such as Smith's Cognitive-Affective Stress Model. Coakley argued that burnout is a social phenomenon rooted in the social organization of sport itself.

According to the Coakley Model, burnout occurs for two main reasons.

→ The structure of high performance sport does not allow the young athlete to develop a normal, multi-faced identity.

→ The social environments of young athletes are organized in such a way that they have little or no control over events, and decisions about their own experiences.

Coakley suggests that high performance sports programmes are organized with the primary goal of producing peak performance outcomes as opposed to creating opportunities for overall social development, and self-assessment of the relationship of sport and non-sport life. Because of this goal, the social environment of an elite young athlete is usually highly constrained and organized, with either the coaches or parents making decisions on behalf of the individual. This leads to the athlete becoming disempowered to the point of realizing that participation in their particular sport has become a developmental dead end and that they no longer have any meaningful control over the important parts of their lives.

Coakley's model was based on 15 informal interviews with young athletes who had burned out of elite sport. Fourteen of the people interviewed had participated in individual sports (skiing, figure skating, gymnastics, swimming and tennis) with only one from a team sport (baseball). During the interviews all participants spoke of feeling stressed, usually relating it to a perceived lack of control over their lives in general. Consequently, Coakley acknowledges that stress is a factor in burnout but proposes it is a symptom rather than a cause, and emphasizes that the root of burnout in young athletes goes far beyond simply chronic stress, stress management abilities, emotional demands and consequences of sport participation, and individual resources.

Rather, Coakley concludes that adolescent burnout is best explained as a social problem rather than a personal failure, and is grounded in social organization as opposed to an individual character. According to this model, the young individuals more likely to experience burnout are highly accomplished athletes who have been heavily involved in a single sport for a relatively long period of time.

TO THINK ABOUT

Consider the top sports teams at your school. Are the athletes encouraged to play sport for their own enjoyment or to improve their performance so they can win trophies, titles and medals?

Empirical studies into athlete burnout

In 2007, Goodger et al. conducted a review of all athlete burnout studies within the then current peer-reviewed literature. They identified that there were only 27 empirical studies that related to athlete burnout. Perhaps the most influential of these is a series of three studies conducted by Gould et al. (1996a, 1996b, 1997) which together formed a large-scale investigation of burnout in junior tennis players from the United States.

The first study presented by Gould et al. (1996a) highlighted the need for research to test the burnout models that were predominant within the literature (such as: Smith 1986; Coakley 1992). In this primary study, Gould et al. used quantitative methods to compare the psychological differences between 30 burned out junior tennis players and 32 of their non-burned out counterparts. Gould et al. asked the young players to complete a number of psychometric tests designed to assess psychological characteristics such as motivation, perfectionism, trait anxiety, athletic self-perception and coping strategies.

Results indicated that the burned out players demonstrated significantly different psychological characteristics to their non-burned out colleagues, with burned out athletes demonstrating the following:

→ higher burnout scores
→ less input into training
→ more likely to have played in high school tennis
→ more likely to have played up an age division
→ higher withdrawal from training sessions
→ lower levels of external motivation
→ higher levels of a motivation
→ higher levels of withdrawal
→ higher levels of perfectionism
→ fewer uses of coping strategies
→ lower levels of positive interpretation and growth coping.

Following their initial study, Gould et al. concluded that in addition to a variety of personal and situational predictors, perfectionism plays a particularly important role in the development of burnout.

The second study in the Gould et al. series (1996b) adopted a more qualitative approach to investigating burnout. Extensive interviews were conducted with 10 of the junior tennis players identified as being the most burned out during the first study. These interviews identified that burnout symptoms fall under two major categories: physical and mental. They also highlighted that the reasons for burning out can be grouped into four main categories:

→ physical
→ logistical
→ social-interpersonal
→ psychological concerns.

Gould et al. point out that while their study suggested burnout was the result of an interaction between personal and situation factors, it was also heavily influenced by psychosocial factors. The data from the interviews was examined in relation to the major models of burnout.

Gould et al. (1996b) concluded that burnout is best viewed in terms of the general stages of Smith's Cognitive-Affective Stress Model of athlete burnout. They propose that this is because the model recognizes the importance of both personality and situational factors in the burnout process. However, Gould et al. also suggested that there may exist sub-strains of burnout within this process. Specifically, they identified a "social psychologically driven" form of burnout,

---

THEORY OF KNOWLEDGE

In their 2012 paper, Gustafsson and Skoog inform us that optimism is a personality disposition reflecting that good things will happen, whereas pessimism refers to the expectation of negative future outcomes. They highlight that it has been known for some time that optimists' perceptions of the world differ from those of pessimists and that this seems to have implications for the person's psychological well-being and general health. They go on to remind us that:

"Burnout is also found in athletes and is associated with negative outcomes such as performance impairment, reduced enjoyment, depressed mood and, potentially, sport termination."

(Source: Gustafsson, H.,Skoog, T. 2012. "The mediational role of perceived stress in the relation between optimism and burnout in competitive athletes." *Anxiety, Stress & Coping.* Vol 25, number 2. Pp :183–199.)

Discuss why promoting an optimistic attitude may be important in the setting of competitive and elite sports for avoiding burnout and increasing well-being in adolescent athletes.

which was further reduced into "athlete perfectionism" or "situational pressures" sub-strains. These conclusions are shown in Figure 14.7, which maps out Gould et al.'s (1996b) perception of how burnout may occur within a cognitive-affective stress-induced model.

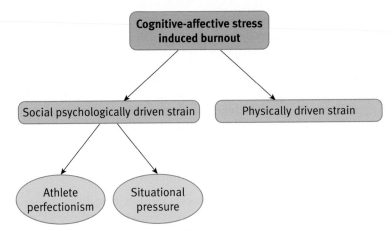

↑ Figure 14.7: The process of cognitive-affective stress-induced burnout in junior tennis players (adapted from Gould et al. 1996b).

The more qualitative approach to the second study allowed Gould et al. (1996b) to identify the importance of individual differences in the burnout experience. Because of this, the third study focused on identifying and recording the unique experiences of three individual players.

Gould et al. examined the profiles of three players who each represented different sub-strains of social psychologically driven and physically driven burnout (see Figure 14.7). The three case studies included:

→ a player characterized by high levels of perfectionism and overtraining
→ a player who experienced pressure from others and a need for a social life
→ a player who was physically overtrained and had inappropriate goals.

This study provided further support for the existence of various sub-strains within a stress-induced burnout model and highlighted the importance of recognizing the unique experience of each individual athlete when working with young, burned out athletes.

Identifying overtraining and burnout in child and adolescent athletes

When it comes to phenomena such as staleness and burnout, prevention is better than cure. Therefore it is important that sports scientists, coaches, parents, support staff and the young athletes themselves are made aware of the symptoms of overtraining and burnout. That way they can identify onset early on and take appropriate steps to curtail it. Symptoms of overtraining and burnout include:

→ decline in physical performance
→ decrease in appetite and weight loss
→ muscle tenderness
→ chronic muscle or joint pain
→ a higher incidence of head colds and allergic reactions
→ occasional nausea
→ disturbed sleep
→ elevated resting heart rate

→ elevated blood pressure
→ emotional instability
→ changes in personality/mood swings
→ *fatigue*
→ *lack of enthusiasm regarding training and competition*
→ *difficulty completing usual routines.*

(Note: the italic bullet points specifically characterize burnout, where as the other symptoms may reflect overtraining or burnout.)

Of course, the presence of just one of these symptoms may not represent overtraining or burnout. However, if several symptoms are persistently present in a young athlete it may imply something more serious. There are several physiological and psychological ways to identify if overtraining or burnout is the cause.

Sports scientists can run physical tests to check for increased oxygen consumption in the young athlete or check for increased heart rate following standard bouts of activity. All those involved can be mindful of any plateau or drop in performance of the young athlete. Furthermore, because burnout is not just a physical construct, it is also sensible to use psychometric measures to monitor changes in mood and general demeanour. A very simple way to monitor the athlete is to ask them to keep a training log detailing not only exercise but also diet, emotions, and general perceptions. There are also several psychometric tools that can be administered by a sports scientist. These include the perceived exertion scale, the Profile of Mood States (POMS) and the recovery-stress questionnaire for athletes. While these tools are not designed for the sole purpose of diagnosing burnout, they do measure characteristics or symptoms associated with burnout, such as changes in mood and stress levels.

Preventing burnout in child and adolescent athletes

Certain precautions can be taken by coaches, parents and sports scientists in order to help prevent overtraining, staleness and burnout at all stages of the process.

Brenner (2007) highlights that to prevent overuse injuries, a sound training regime is essential, and while repetition in training can be beneficial, it can also cause harm. As such, it is useful to remember that some sport-specific drills can use a variety of modalities. For example, aqua-jogging can prove a useful alternative to running on the track for athletics training. It provides the same benefits to the body without placing as much stress on developing muscles and joints.

Brenner also refers to the recommendation from the American Academy of Pediatrics Council on Sports Medicine and Fitness that training for a specific sporting activity should be limited to a maximum of five times per week, with at least one full day of rest. Furthermore, child and adolescent athletes should have two to three months off per year from their particular sport. During this they can take a physical and mental break from that sport, allow injuries to heal and work on strength conditioning and proprioception, an awareness of movement within joints and joint position, in an attempt to reduce the risk of future injury.

Based on the result of their second study, Gould et al. recommend that in order to prevent the onset of burnout, young athletes should take part in a sport for their own enjoyment rather than because of external pressures. They should also be encouraged to balance their primary sport with other activities in order to develop as an all-round athlete. Young and adolescent athletes should be allowed to take time off, do relaxing things and stop participation in that particular sport if it is no longer fun.

Furthermore Gould et al.'s studies amplify the importance of raising awareness among parents and coaches of the external pressures they can sometimes put on the young athlete and how this might affect them.

Some of the key preventative measures to prevent overtraining, staleness and burnout are:

→ alternate between easy, moderate and hard training sessions
→ eat sufficient carbohydrates to prevent glycogen depletion
→ keep workouts interesting, with age-appropriate games and fun practice sessions
→ take time off from organized or structured sports once a week to allow complete body rest
→ allow the young athlete to participate in other activities to keep them happy and allow them to develop a multi-faced identity
→ schedule in a two- to three-month break from a primary sport; this time can be used to focus on other activities or cross-training so skill and fitness levels are maintained
→ focus on wellness and teaching young athletes to be in tune with their bodies for cues to slow down or alter their training methods.

If a child is displaying symptoms of overtraining or burnout:

→ reduce their training intensity for several days
→ allow them to rest completely for a week
→ seek counselling or help from a sport psychologist.

TO RESEARCH

In this chapter we have discussed how too little recovery time can lead to overuse, injuries, staleness and ultimately burnout in child and adolescent athletes. Try visiting the website http://www.brianmac.co.uk/overtrn.htm and find the Total Quality Recovery (TQR) Process survey. This tool highlights whether your current level and quality of recovery from your primary sport is adequate to prevent overtraining. Have a go at completing the survey.

SUMMARY

→ As more young people are taking part in sport, the numbers of young athletes experiencing conditions such as overuse injuries and burnout are increasing.
→ Overtraining occurs when an athlete trains too hard without getting adequate rest.
→ Overtraining can lead to overuse injuries and staleness. Young athletes are particularly susceptible to injuries as their bodies are still developing.
→ Staleness is a product of overtraining where the young athlete's performance doesn't improve.
→ Burnout is different to staleness in that it is a psychological state as well as a physical one. The athlete may no longer want to take part in the sport and talented athletes may end up leaving the sport altogether.
→ There are steps coaches, parents and athletes can take to prevent burnout.

Self-study questions

1   Define overtraining, staleness and burnout.
2   Describe the four stages of overuse injuries.
3   List five of the psychological characteristics that burned out athletes displayed in Gould et al.'s (1996a) study of junior tennis players.
4   Compare Smith's Cognitive–Affective Stress Model of burnout and Coakley's Model of burnout in adolescent athletes.
5   Explain why child and adolescent athletes are more susceptible to overuse injuries than mature adult athletes.

Hope is a positive motivational state, and researchers have shown that high-hope individuals perform better than low-hope individuals in sport. Burnout among athletes is recognised as a serious problem and is associated with three burnout variables:

→ emotional and physical exhaustion

→ sport devaluation

→ a reduced sense of athletic accomplishment.

A study examined the relationship between hope and athlete burnout among 178 competitive athletes aged 15–20 years. The athletes completed the *State Hope Scale* questionnaire and the scores from this resulted in three groups:

→ low hope

→ medium hope

→ high hope.

The table below shows the mean scores (±SD) for the three burnout variables in the three groups, with a higher score indicating "more" or "greater".

	Low hope	Medium hope	High hope
Emotional/physical exhaustion	2.30 (0.62)	1.95 (0.64)	1.81 (0.65)
Sport devaluation	2.90 (0.60)	2.56 (0.61)	1.95 (0.64)
Reduced sense of accomplishment	2.31 (0.76)	1.90 (0.75)	1.61 (0.62)

(Source: Adapted from Gustafsson et al. 2010. "Exploring the relationship between hope and burnout in competitive sport." *Journal of Sports Sciences*. Vol 28, number 14. Pp. 1495–1504.)

1 Identify:
   a which group has the lowest standard deviation for a burnout variable (1 mark)
   b which burnout variable has the highest standard deviation. (1 mark)
2 Distinguish between the low hope and the high hope group. (3 marks)
3 Discuss causes of burnout in athletes. (4 marks)

CHAPTER 15

Physical activity and health

OBJECTIVES

By the end of this chapter students should be able to:

→ define the term hypokinetic disease

→ identify the major hypokinetic diseases

→ identify the main forms of cardiovascular disease

→ examine the role of exercise in lowering the risk of cardiovascular disease

→ explain the energy balance equation and discuss the causes of obesity

→ assess the role of exercise in preventing obesity

→ explain the causes and consequences of type 2 diabetes

→ examine the role of exercise in lowering the risk of type 2 diabetes

→ define the terms bone health and osteoporosis

→ assess the effects of exercise on bone health

→ describe how ageing affects various aspects of physical and mental function

→ assess the role of exercise in ageing

→ examine the relationship between exercise and psychological well-being

→ describe physical activity recommendations for health

→ evaluate the role of exercise for assisting in disease management.

> **All parts of the body which have a function, if used in moderation and exercised in labours in which each is accustomed, become thereby healthy, well-developed and age more slowly, but if unused and left idle they become liable to disease, defective in growth and age quickly.**
>
> Attributed to the Greek physician Hippocrates (c. 460–370 BC)

> **In their struggle for survival primordial humans had to maintain a high level of physical fitness. In their struggle for longevity, modern day humans are dying because of lack of physical exercise.**
>
> Dr Gunnar Erikssen, 2001

Introduction

In the 1850s average life expectancy was less than 50 years in most, if not all, countries worldwide. Over the last 150 years average life expectancy has increased in many countries and it is predicted that most babies born in developed countries since the year 2000 will celebrate their 100th birthdays.

This change in life expectancy is due to improvements in living standards resulting from the industrial and technological revolutions which have taken place in recent centuries, but one negative consequence of these revolutions is that modern-day life requires low levels of physical activity. The findings of many studies indicate that a physically active lifestyle is essential for optimal health.

According to the World Health Organisation (http://www.who.int/en/) "health is a state of complete physical, mental, and social well-being and not merely the absence of disease or infirmity". Thus, health is not defined solely by the absence of sickness and optimal health involves the ability to pursue life with physical and mental vigour.

This chapter will explore the ways in which physical activity can assist in lowering the risk of disease as well as aiding in the treatment of disease.

What is physical activity?

Physical activity may be defined as "any bodily movement produced by contraction of skeletal muscle that substantially increases energy expenditure" whereas exercise is "a subcategory of leisure-time physical activity in which planned, structured and repetitive bodily movements are performed to improve or maintain one or more components of physical fitness" (Howley 2001). Thus, the terms "physical activity" and "exercise" are distinct from each other but this distinction is not always helpful or necessary, and in this chapter the terms are used interchangeably.

Physical fitness can be divided into two main components: health-related fitness and skill-related fitness. These components can in turn be subdivided as indicated in Table 15.1 below.

HEALTH-RELATED FITNESS COMPONENTS	SKILL-RELATED FITNESS COMPONENTS
→ Cardiovascular fitness	→ Agility
→ Muscular strength	→ Balance
→ Muscular endurance	→ Coordination
→ Flexibility	→ Speed
→ Body composition	→ Power
	→ Reaction time

↑ Table 15.1: Health-related versus skill-related fitness

Hypokinetic disease

One of the earliest studies to suggest that exercise is important for health was conducted by Professor Jerry Morris who examined the prevalence of heart disease in bus drivers and bus conductors working on double-decker buses in London. Professor Morris discovered that the bus conductors experienced roughly half the number of heart attacks and sudden death due to heart attack than the drivers and he suggested that this was due to differences in the amount of occupational or working activity performed. It was estimated that the bus conductors climbed 600 stairs per day and they did this for 11 out of every 14 days, for 50 weeks per year, often for decades. In contrast the sedentary drivers sat for 90 per cent of their shift.

Many studies have since confirmed a link between high levels of physical activity and a lower risk of heart disease and these findings have been extended to other conditions and diseases also. This has led to the term "hypokinetic disease" meaning a disease associated with a sedentary (inactive) lifestyle. A variety of hypokinetic diseases have been identified including cardiovascular disease (CVD), some forms of cancer, obesity, type 2 diabetes, osteoporosis and mental ill-health.

Although the term hypokinetic disease is useful for emphasizing a central role for exercise in the maintenance of health, it is important to be aware that health is affected by a variety of factors beyond exercise including genetic predisposition, diet, smoking, alcohol consumption and other social and environmental factors, hence it would be an oversimplification to suggest that the sole cause of hypokinetic diseases is a lack of exercise.

The prevalence of a particular disease (or disease risk factor) may be calculated by dividing the total number of people with that disease (or disease risk factor)

Hypokinetic disease a disease associated with a sedentary or inactive lifestyle

TO THINK ABOUT

Over the last two to three centuries society has changed in many ways due to the effects of increased mechanization. Fewer and fewer occupations involve physical activity and humans now travel using cars, trains, buses and planes.

Think of the various ways in which mechanization and automation has removed physical activity from daily lives. How many examples can you think of?

by the total number of people in a sample group or population. It is used as an estimate of how common a particular disease (or disease risk factor) is in a population. It is contrasted with the term incidence which is an estimate of the number of new cases of a disease or disease risk factor. Many studies have observed a lower prevalence/incidence of disease in active/fit people than in inactive/unfit people.

Much of the evidence linking physical inactivity to an increased risk of disease comes from a branch of medical science known as epidemiology. Epidemiology studies the occurrence, transmission and control of epidemic (widespread) diseases and it usually involves studying large groups numbering tens of thousands, hundreds of thousands or even millions of individuals. Such studies are known as population-based studies.

Epidemiology a branch of medical science that studies the occurrence, transmission and control of epidemic diseases

Some epidemiological studies have examined physical fitness which may be considered an outcome of the volume and intensity of physical activity. In such studies the type of physical fitness most often examined is cardiovascular fitness. Many of these studies have found that people classified as physically fit are less likely to suffer from disease than people classified as physically unfit.

CASE STUDY

A study of men living in California, USA investigated the association between physical fitness and all-cause mortality risk (i.e. the risk of death from any cause). This study used a maximal treadmill test to quantify exercise capacity in metabolic equivalent of tasks or METs, which provides an indication of cardiovascular fitness.

Fitness was assessed in the men at baseline and they were then observed for an average of six years after this (known as the follow-up period). At baseline 3,679 of the men were diagnosed with cardiovascular disease (CVD) whereas 2,534 of the men did not have CVD. During the follow-up period 1,256 of the men died and within each group of men (i.e. those who had and those who did not have CVD) those with the lowest levels of fitness at baseline were approximately four times more likely to die during follow-up than those with the highest levels of fitness at baseline.

These findings suggest that high levels of fitness may lower the risk of death during a given period both in healthy men and in men who have pre-existing CVD.

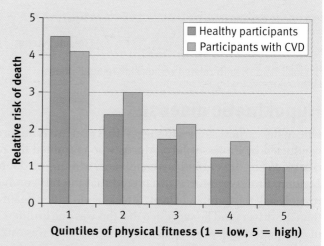

↑ Figure 15.1

Reference

Myers, J et al. 2002. "Exercise capacity and mortality among men referred for exercise testing." *New England Journal of Medicine.* Vol 346. Pp. 793–801.

Measuring physical activity

The abbreviation MET stands for metabolic equivalent of task and it is a measure of the energy expenditure of physical activity. For reference purposes 1 MET represents the oxygen consumption/energy expenditure at rest, equal to 3.5 millilitres of oxygen per kilogram of body mass per minute (ml $O_2 \cdot kg^{-1} \cdot min^{-1}$) or 4.184 kJ·kg^{-1}·hr^{-1} (1 kcal·kg^{-1}·hr^{-1}).

The MET unit can be used to describe the intensity of exercise by expressing oxygen consumption/energy expenditure during exercise as a ratio of that at rest. Hence a person running at 10 METs would be consuming 35 ml $O_2 \cdot kg^{-1} \cdot min^{-1}$ and expending 41.84 kJ·kg^{-1}·hr^{-1}.

METs are often used as a method of classifying physical activities in epidemiological studies. Moderate-intensity activities are defined as those requiring three to six METs whereas vigorous-intensity activities are defined as those requiring greater than six METs. Examples of moderate-intensity activities are brisk walking and slow cycling while examples of vigorous-intensity activities are jogging, playing soccer and skipping.

Cardiovascular disease

Cardiovascular disease (CVD) is the term given to a group of disorders of the heart and blood vessels. These disorders include hypertension (high blood pressure), coronary heart disease (CHD) also known as ischaemic heart disease, and stroke. According to the World Health Organisation CHD is the leading cause of death worldwide and was responsible for 7.25 million deaths in 2008 (13 per cent of all deaths worldwide). Stroke was the second leading cause of death globally in 2008, responsible for 6.15 million deaths (11 per cent of all deaths worldwide).

Coronary heart disease and stroke are particularly common in high income countries where they may account for more than 30 per cent of all deaths. A major cause of CHD and stroke is atherosclerosis which is a hardening of the arteries due to the accumulation of fat, cholesterol and other substances in the walls of the arteries forming hard structures called plaques. Atherosclerosis leads to a narrowing of arteries and eventually these can become blocked by a blood clot (thrombus). Pieces of plaque can also break off blocking arteries. If a blockage occurs in the coronary circulation (the blood vessels supplying the heart) then this will lead to a heart attack (also known as a myocardial infarction). If the blockage occurs in a blood vessel in the brain then the result is a stroke.

A blood-borne irritant injures or scratches the arterial wall exposing the underlying connective tissue.

Blood platelets and circulating immune cells known as monocytes are then attracted to the site of the injury and adhere to the exposed connective tissue. The platelets release a substance referred to as platelet-derived growth factor (PDGF) that promotes migration of smooth muscle cells from the media to the intima.

A plaque, which is basically composed of smooth muscle cells, connective tissue, and debris, forms at the site of injury.

As the plaque grows, it narrows the arterial opening and impedes blood flow. Lipids in the blood, specifically low-density- lipoprotein cholesterol (LDL-C), are deposited in the plaque. When pieces of the plaque break loose they can start clots that lodge in other parts of the vessel.

↑ Figure 15.2: Atherosclerosis

There are a variety of risk factors for CVD and these may be divided into modifiable and non-modifiable risk factors. Modifiable risk factors are those which may be influenced by lifestyle. Physical inactivity is a major modifiable risk factor for CVD. Many epidemiological studies have demonstrated an association between high levels of exercise and a lower risk of CHD.

Exercise may lower the risk of CHD by a variety of mechanisms.

→ Exercise may have direct effects on the heart, increasing the size of the coronary arteries and making them less likely to get blocked.

→ Exercise also improves endothelial function which means that arteries are able to vasodilate (open up) on demand to increase blood supply, reducing the chances of ischaemia.

TO RESEARCH

Physical activity is difficult to quantify accurately. A variety of methods are available to measure physical activity; some are very cheap and others are more expensive. These methods include physical activity questionnaires, pedometers, accelerometers, direct calorimetry, indirect calorimetry and doubly labelled water.

Find out about the methodology used for each of these techniques and create a table listing the advantages and disadvantages of each.

KEY POINT

Three major forms of cardiovascular disease are hypertension, coronary heart disease (CHD) and stroke. CHD and stroke account for a large percentage of deaths in high income countries.

TO DO

Find out the leading causes of death in your country. How many people in your country die each year from CHD and stroke and what percentage of total deaths is due to these two diseases?

→ Exercise may also reduce the risk of CHD by having a positive effect on other heart disease risk factors, for example, helping to prevent obesity, diabetes, hypertension and high blood cholesterol thus reducing the risk of blood clots forming.

→ One major positive effect of exercise is helping to maintain high levels of protective high density lipoprotein cholesterol (HDL-cholesterol). This lipoprotein is thought to play an important role in removing excess cholesterol from the body in a process termed "reverse cholesterol transport". Cholesterol is insoluble and is therefore carried within the bloodstream in lipoproteins. Two major lipoproteins are low density lipoprotein (LDL) and high density lipoprotein (HDL). These lipoproteins have different relationships with CVD. High levels of LDL-cholesterol increase the risk of CVD whereas high levels of HDL-cholesterol appear to protect from CVD. One important effect of exercise is that it raises HDL-cholesterol concentrations.

KEY POINT

High levels of LDL-cholesterol increase the risk of CVD while high levels of HDL cholesterol protect an individual from CVD.

MODIFIABLE RISK FACTORS	NON-MODIFIABLE RISK FACTORS
→ Cigarette smoking	→ Age
→ High blood pressure	→ Sex
→ High blood cholesterol	→ Ethnicity
→ Obesity	→ Family history
→ Diabetes	
→ Physical inactivity	

↑ Table 15.2: Risk factors for coronary heart disease

Risk factors can sometimes cluster together. A clustering of three or more risk factors together is sometimes referred to as the metabolic syndrome. Major components of the metabolic syndrome include dyslipidemia (high triglyceride (blood fat) concentrations and low levels of HDL-cholesterol), impaired glucose regulation or diabetes, obesity (particularly visceral/abdominal obesity, i.e. fat within and around the abdomen) and hypertension. This clustering of risk factors greatly increases the risk of CVD.

TO THINK ABOUT

Animal experiments are useful for exploring the mechanisms by which exercise can lower the risk of CHD. One example is a study conducted in monkeys. This study involved a sedentary group on an atherogenic (likely to cause atherosclerosis) diet and an exercising group also on an atherogenic diet. The exercising group ran on a treadmill for one hour three times each week over a two-year period.

At the end of the study both groups were found to have elevated total cholesterol concentrations but the exercising monkeys had higher levels of HDL-cholesterol. In addition, the degree of coronary artery narrowing caused by the atherogenic diet was much lower in the exercising monkeys than the sedentary monkeys. The authors concluded that "the benefits derived from such moderate exercise for one hour three times per week in the presence of hypercholesterolemia (high blood cholesterol) were less

atherosclerosis in wider coronary arteries supplying a larger heart that functioned at a slower rate" (Kramsch et al. 1981, p 1488).

Although animal experiments are useful for exploring mechanisms which may be difficult to assess in humans the findings may not be directly applicable, i.e. humans may not respond in the same way as animals. There are also ethical issues relating to animal experimentation. Think about the advantages and disadvantages of animal experimentation and draw up a list of reasons for and against animal testing.

Reference

Kramsch, DM et al. 1981. "Reduction of coronary atherosclerosis by moderate conditioning exercise in monkeys on an atherogenic diet." *New England Journal of Medicine*. Vol 305. Pp 1483–9.

Aside from playing a valuable role in lowering the risk of CVD (referred to as primary prevention), physical activity also has an important role to play in the treatment of CVD and in preventing a recurrence of cardiovascular disease events such as a heart attack (termed secondary prevention). In the past people who suffered a heart attack and survived were told to rest for many weeks afterwards but today people are encouraged to exercise soon after having a heart attack if possible. Studies suggest that heart attack patients who adopt a habit of regular exercise have a lower risk of death in the following years than those who remain sedentary. Exercise has also been shown to benefit people suffering other forms of CVD such as hypertension, peripheral vascular disease (narrowing of peripheral arteries, e.g. the femoral artery in the legs) and heart failure (inability of the heart of pump sufficient blood around the body for all of the body's requirements).

Obesity

Obesity is an excess of body fat to the point where health is endangered. Obesity is most commonly defined using the body mass index (BMI) which is calculated by dividing a person's weight in kilograms by their height in meters squared, i.e. $kg \cdot m^{-2}$.

A BMI ≥ 25 $kg \cdot m^{-2}$ indicates a person is overweight while a BMI ≥ 30 $kg \cdot m^{-2}$ represents obesity. The BMI provides an indirect assessment of body fat percentage.

In large groups of people BMI usually correlates highly with measurements of body fatness but BMI values can be misleading in some cases, e.g. weightlifters, bodybuilders, rugby players and American football players may have high BMI values due to a large muscle mass rather than high levels of body fat.

Very accurate assessments of body fat can be gained using sophisticated imaging techniques, including dual energy X-ray absorptiometry (DXA), magnetic resonance imaging (MRI) and computed tomography (CT), but these methods are costly and time consuming, and in the case of DXA and CT scanning the methods involve exposure to low doses of radiation.

Another method of classifying obesity is using a person's waist circumference (≥ 102 cm in men and ≥ 88 cm in women).

Obesity an excess of body fat that endangers health

Body mass index a measurement of body fat, calculated by dividing weight in kilograms by height in meters squared

	BMI $(kg \cdot m^{-2})$	RISK RELATIVE TO NORMAL WEIGHT AND WAIST CIRCUMFERENCE	
		MEN <102 cm WOMEN <88 cm	MEN ≥102 cm WOMEN ≥88 cm
Underweight	<18.5	Not increased	Not increased
Normal	18.5–24.9	Not increased	Increased
Overweight	25.0–29.9	Increased	High
Obesity (class I)	30.0–34.9	High	Very high
Obesity (class II)	35.0–39.9	Very high	Extremely high
Extreme obesity (class III)	≥40.0	Extremely high	Extremely high

Note: 102 cm = 40 inches, 88 cm = 35 inches

↑ Table 15.3: Classification of overweight and obesity by body mass index, waist circumference, and associated disease risk (i.e. type 2 diabetes, hypertension and cardiovascular disease)

There is concern about obesity worldwide because the prevalence of obesity has increased in most countries over the last few decades; in some countries one-quarter or more of the adult population are obese. Obesity increases the risks of many diseases and conditions, most notably type 2 diabetes but also cardiovascular disease, osteoarthritis and some forms of cancer.

Increases in the prevalence of obesity have been noted in children and adolescents as well as in adults in recent decades. This is a cause for concern because obese children have an increased risk of obesity in adulthood. Another concern is that obese children may experience stigmatization and bullying as a result of their condition.

TO RESEARCH

Obesity increases the risk of some forms of cancer and physical activity lowers the risk some forms of cancer.

Lack of exercise is not a risk factor for all forms of cancer. A convincing link between inactivity and cancer has only been established for two cancers so far: breast cancer and colon cancer.

For these two forms of cancer the relative risk in active versus inactive individuals is 20 to 30 per cent lower.

There is also some evidence that exercise can lower the risk of cancers of the endometrium, prostate, pancreas and lung but the evidence is not consistent and further research is required to clarify the relationship between these cancers and exercise.

Find out what advice is given relating to exercise and diet as a form of prevention of cancer by cancer charities such as Cancer Research UK.

TO RESEARCH

Investigate and make a list of the advantages and disadvantages of using BMI as a method of identifying obesity.

Find out the principles underlying dual energy X-ray absorptiometry, magnetic resonance imaging and computed tomography.

TO THINK ABOUT

Some obese people live long, healthy lives and are unaffected by type 2 diabetes, heart disease and cancer. Some obese people do not show any evidence of defective metabolism, e.g. they have normal levels of blood glucose and cholesterol. The term "benign obesity" has been used to describe such individuals. In view of this do you think that obesity should be classified as a disease?

Energy balance

According to the energy balance equation body mass is determined by energy intake and energy expenditure as follows:

→ Energy intake > energy expenditure = weight gain
→ Energy intake < energy expenditure = weight loss
→ Energy intake = energy expenditure = stable body weight

Underlying this apparently simple equation is a complex set of factors which affect energy intake and expenditure.

Energy intake and energy expenditure also influence each other. A reduction in energy intake will eventually lead to a reduction in metabolic rate and hence energy expenditure. An increase in energy intake will eventually lead to weight gain and an increase in metabolic rate to support a larger body mass. A variety of hormones influence appetite including the appetite stimulating hormone ghrelin and the appetite suppressing hormone leptin. Many environmental factors also influence food intake, including the availability and affordability of palatable (tasty) food.

Physical activity can assist in the prevention and management of obesity by increasing the energy expenditure side of the energy balance equation. Exercise helps by reducing both subcutaneous fat (fat underneath the skin) and abdominal visceral fat (fat within the abdomen). The American College of Sports Medicine recommends between 150 and 250 minutes of exercise each week (approximately 20 to 35 minutes of exercise each day) for preventing obesity. Some organizations recommend higher levels of exercise for preventing obesity, i.e. 45 to 60 minutes each day (approximately 5 to 7 hours each week). Even greater amounts of exercise may be required for weight loss. People who are successful at losing weight and maintaining weight loss frequently report high levels of exercise and moderate food intake.

Studies have also demonstrated that there are individual differences in the weight loss response to exercise, i.e. some people lose more weight than others, and it is difficult to predict which individuals will lose most weight. This may be partly due to individual differences in appetite and food intake responses to exercise. While most people do not appear to overeat after exercise this may happen in some cases.

Obesity is caused by a combination of genetic predisposition and environmental factors. In most cases genetic predisposition for obesity is polygenic (involving many different genes) but some rare monogenic (single gene) causes have been discovered.

An example is a defect in the ob gene which prevents fat cells from secreting the hormone leptin. Leptin suppresses appetite by acting on the hypothalamus (the appetite regulating center in the brain). As fat cells increase in size they secrete more leptin in an effort to suppress appetite (and increase energy expenditure) to prevent further weight gain. People who are leptin deficient report being constantly hungry and they develop obesity early in life. This can be treated with injections of leptin (see the before and after photographs below).

Most obese people are not deficient in leptin; most obese people have high leptin levels but appear to be insensitive to it.

Reference
Farooqi, I.S. and O'Rahilly, S. 2005. "New advances in the genetics of early onset obesity." *International Journal of Obesity*. Vol 29. Pp 1149–52.

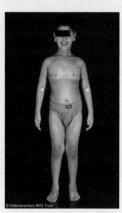

↑ Figure 15.3

A cross-sectional study conducted by Dr James Levine and his colleagues used devices known as inclinometers and accelerometers to assess posture allocation every half a second over a 10-day period in 10 lean and 10 obese people. Approximately 25 million data points on posture and movement were collected for each person.

No differences were observed between the groups in time spent lying down but obese participants spent 164 minutes longer sitting each day than lean participants. Conversely lean participants were upright for 152 minutes longer each day than obese participants. Interestingly both the lean and the obese participants classed themselves as "couch potatoes" and the difference in their activity levels was not due to structured exercise but rather to differences in daily activities such as sitting, standing, walking and talking. The researchers called this "non-exercise activity thermogenesis" (NEAT) and calculated that if the obese increased their NEAT to match that of the lean individuals they might expend an additional 350 kcal/day (1,464 kJ/day) and lose 15 kilograms in weight over a year (assuming that their energy intake did not change). Since both groups of individuals described themselves as couch potatoes one interpretation of these findings is that some people are "biologically programmed" to be sedentary and hence are likely to become obese.

Do you think this is true and what are the implications for obesity prevention and management if it is?

Reference
Levine, J. A. 2005. "Interindividual variation in posture allocation: possible role in human obesity." *Science*. Vol 307. Pp 584–6.

Read the passage below and then answer the questions which follow.

"It's a Monday morning. I'm in my clinic and the consultation with my first patient is just ending. We've discussed management of his obesity (BMI 34 kg·m⁻²) and prediabetes, and reviewed the healthy lifestyle changes that have been made. There's been an encouraging reduction in weight and waist circumference since I last saw him. I emphasize the importance of ongoing support from the dietitian and clinical psychologist, adjust metformin dosage, and discuss follow-up arrangements. The next patient is new to the clinic and is more severely obese (BMI 44 kg·m⁻²). She is referred from a sleep physician and has recently started continuous positive airway pressure therapy for her obstructive sleep apnoea. That treatment at least is going well—she recounts being more refreshed in the morning and less sleepy during the day. I review the blood test results and realize that she has prediabetes, dyslipidaemia, and probable fatty liver disease. Further history shows she has a number of psychological problems associated with her obesity and probable depression. Clinical examination reveals high blood pressure as well as thickened, pigmented skin at the base of her neck and in the flexures. I recognize

acanthosis nigricans, characteristic of insulin resistance. Management will be a challenge, what treatment options should I broach?

These are typical stories of the many patients with obesity-related chronic disease seen by medical practitioners. But what if I tell you that the clinic is in a children's hospital, with both patients aged only 11 years, and neither yet at high school?"

Questions

1 What factors might contribute to such high levels of obesity?

2 What can parents do to help children in this position?

3 What role should schools play in preventing and managing childhood obesity?

4 How do you think obese children might feel?

5 What social and psychological factors may affect obese children?

Reference

Baur, L. A. 2011. "Changing perceptions of obesity – recollections of a paediatrician." *Lancet*. Vol 378. Pp 762–3.

Type 2 diabetes

Diabetes is a disease characterized by elevated blood glucose concentrations, a condition known as hyperglycemia. In untreated diabetics blood glucose concentrations may be elevated to 10, 20 or even 50 mmol·L⁻¹ in comparison with values of around 5 mmol·L⁻¹ in healthy people.

There are two main forms of diabetes, namely type 1 and type 2 diabetes.

→ **Type 1 diabetics** do not produce insulin—type 1 diabetes is caused by an autoimmune destruction of the beta cells in the islets of Langerhans within the pancreas. These cells produce insulin which plays an important role in moving glucose from the blood into the liver, muscle and adipose tissue cells (where glucose provides a useful store of energy in the form of glycogen).

→ **Type 2 diabetics** are insensitive to insulin—type 2 diabetes is also characterized by hyperglycemia but this is due to insensitivity or resistance to the effects of insulin (known as insulin resistance) rather than a lack of insulin. People with type 2 diabetes often have high insulin values (hyperinsulinemia) and high glucose values.

If left untreated both forms of diabetes cause severe hyperglycemia, ill health and premature death.

The worldwide prevalence of diabetes has increased in recent years and is at approximately 10 per cent now. Most of these cases are type 2 diabetes. The major risk factors for type 2 diabetes are obesity (relating to overconsumption of food and physical inactivity) and family history. There is a particularly high prevalence of type 2 diabetes in certain ethnic groups. A well-documented example is that of the Pima Indians living in southern Arizona. A high prevalence is also observed in those of South Asian descent, e.g. those from India, Bangladesh and Pakistan.

Diabetes is a cause for concern because it is associated with a variety of health risks and premature mortality. The major health risks of diabetes are:

→ cerebrovascular disease (stroke)
→ retinopathy (a common cause of blindness)
→ coronary heart disease
→ nephropathy (damage to the kidneys)
→ peripheral vascular disease
→ neuropathy (damage to the nerves)
→ diabetic foot (resulting in ulceration and amputation).

CASE STUDY

Prior to the discovery of insulin in the early 1920s type 1 diabetes was a death sentence. Without insulin the body is unable to utilize glucose effectively for energy so muscle tissue is broken down instead in a process termed proteolysis.

The pictures here show one of the first patients to be treated with insulin. Muscle wasting is clearly evident in the panel on the left. The panel on the right shows the same young girl after treatment with insulin.

Reference
Bliss, M. 2007. *The discovery of insulin*. Chicago, IL. The University of Chicago Press.

↑ Figure 15.4

In recent decades cases of type 2 diabetes have emerged in children. Before this type 2 diabetes was considered to be an adult onset disease and this form of diabetes was often termed **adult onset diabetes**. The emergence of type 2 diabetes in children is thought to be related to environmental factors, i.e. poor diet and low levels of physical activity.

Many observational studies have demonstrated that active people are less likely to develop type 2 diabetes than inactive people. Intervention studies have also shown that a healthy diet and physical activity lower the risk of developing type 2 diabetes. Physical inactivity is an important risk factor for type 2 diabetes even in those with a family history of diabetes; those who are more active are less likely to develop type 2 diabetes than their inactive counterparts (although both groups are at greater risk than those without a family history of diabetes).

One of the main benefits of exercise is that it enhances insulin sensitivity and glucose tolerance. This effect can be seen after a single bout of exercise but frequent exercise is necessary for continued benefit. In contrast, periods of inactivity reduce insulin sensitivity and glucose tolerance as shown by bed rest studies. The enhanced insulin sensitivity achieved through exercise assists in maintaining healthy blood glucose concentrations by moving excess glucose out of the bloodstream. By preserving and/or increasing muscle mass, exercise also maintains a large storage area for glucose in the form of muscle glycogen. In addition to its role in lowering the risk of type 2 diabetes, exercising (and maintaining high levels of fitness) also benefits those afflicted with type 2 diabetes by reducing the risk of CVD and all-cause mortality.

Bone health

Bone is a dynamic tissue with high levels of metabolic activity. It acts as a support structure for the body as well as providing a reservoir for minerals, particularly calcium. The term **bone health** relates to the structure and density of bones.

Optimal bone health provides both strength and lightness so that moving the body around does not expend too much energy. The main determinant of bone strength is bone mineral density (BMD) which increases during growth, reaching a peak at between 35 and 45 years of age and decreasing gradually thereafter. Peak bone mass is higher in men than women and the decrease in bone mass with age accelerates sharply in women from the menopause to about 10 per cent per decade, levelling off to about 3 per cent per decade after the age of 75. Some women lose as much as 30 per cent of bone mass by the age of 70.

Decreases in BMD lead to lower bone strength making the bones more fragile and more likely to fracture. If BMD becomes too low this leads to the disorder osteoporosis (literally meaning "porous bones"). Osteoporotic fractures lead to disability, loss of independence and impairment of quality of life. They can also lead to the development of secondary complications as a result of long term hospitalization. Those most at risk of developing osteoporosis are females, people over 60 years old and people with a family history of osteoporosis. Other factors that increase the risk of osteoporosis include having a low BMI, a low calcium intake, cigarette smoking, experiencing early menopause and physical inactivity (although excessive exercise in young females who limit their food intake and maintain a low body mass can increase the risk of osteoporosis).

KEY POINT

Low bone mineral density can lead to osteoporosis which leaves a person more vulnerable to fracturing bones. Those most at risk are older women.

TO THINK ABOUT

Osteoporosis statistics

→ Osteoporosis is estimated to affect 200 million women worldwide, affecting approximately one-tenth of women aged 60, one-fifth of women aged 70, two-fifths of women aged 80 and two-thirds of women aged 90.

→ 1 in 3 women over 50 will experience osteoporotic fractures, as will 1 in 5 men.

→ By 2050, the worldwide incidence of hip fracture is projected to increase by 310 per cent in men and 240 per cent in women.

→ In women over 45 years of age, osteoporosis accounts for more days spent in hospital than many other diseases, including diabetes, myocardial infarction and breast cancer.

→ About 20–25 per cent of hip fractures occur in men. The overall mortality is about 20 per cent in the first 12 months after hip fracture and is higher in men than women.

→ It is estimated that the lifetime risk of experiencing an osteoporotic fracture in men over the age of 50 is 30 per cent.

Source: International Osteoporosis Foundation

http://www.iofbonehealth.org/facts-and-statistics.html

Osteoporosis is diagnosed by measuring BMD which can be assessed by dual energy X-ray absorptiometry (DXA) and computed tomography (CT). The World Health Organisation defines osteoporosis as a bone density 2.5 standard deviations below the mean for young, white, adult women, based on DXA scans.

Osteopenia (low BMD not reaching a threshold for diagnosis of osteoporosis) is identified when BMD is between 1 and 2.5 standard deviations below this mean. The photographs below show healthy lumbar vertebrae in early adult life (left panel) and lumbar vertebrae affected by osteoporosis (right panel).

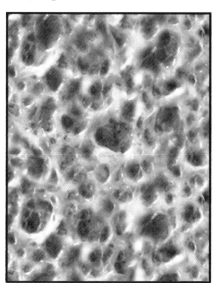 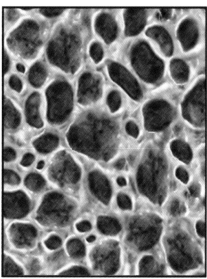

↑ Figure 15.5: Effects of osteoporosis

Weight-bearing physical activity is essential for bone health. Two main factors influence whether or not a person develops osteoporosis: their peak bone mass as a young adult and the rate of bone loss with ageing. Exercise can influence both of these factors. Childhood is a crucial time for optimizing bone health through exercise. Indeed some commentators have suggested that osteoporosis is a pediatric disease, implying that if bone mass is not optimized in childhood then osteoporosis is far more likely to occur in later life.

Aside from its role in increasing BMD early in life, weight-bearing exercise can also help to reduce the rate of bone loss from middle age onwards. Any weight-bearing exercise may be helpful but improvements in BMD are site specific (relating to the specific bones being stressed by exercise) and resistance training is more effective than endurance exercise.

Optimization of bone health in later life is particularly important for women. Women with a physically active lifestyle, including walking for exercise, have a lower risk of osteoporotic fracture of the hip than sedentary women. Moreover, many fractures are caused by falls and exercise can decrease the risk of falling by improving balance, strength and possibly coordination.

TO RESEARCH

Bone mineral density (BMD) is associated with many factors, including heredity, ethnic group, geographic region, environment, nutrition and lifestyle. For example, BMD values in black women exceed those in white women while values in Asian women are lower again, and BMD values of white women in the USA, Northern Europe and Kuwait are greater than those in Saudi Arabian and Lebanese women.

Find out what the typical values for men and women are in your country.

CASE STUDY

Childhood and adolescence are key periods for the development of BMD. This is clearly demonstrated by a study of the differences in bone mineral content (BMC) between the playing and non-playing arms of female tennis and squash players (mean age 28 years). The difference between each arm was two to four times greater in players who started playing before or at menarche (the start of menstruation) than in those who started playing more than 15 years after menarche. This suggests that physical activity before and around the time of puberty is particularly effective for increasing BMD.

Reference

Kannus, P. et al. 1995. "Effect of starting age of physical activity on bone mass in the dominant arm of tennis and squash players." *Annals of Internal Medicine*. Vol 123. Pp 27–31.

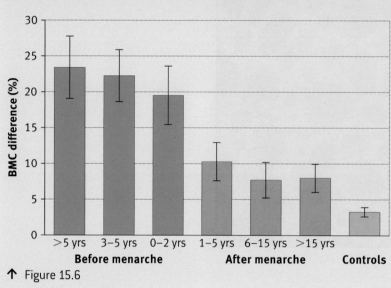

↑ Figure 15.6

Psychological well-being

So far this chapter has focused on the effects of exercise on physical health but there is also evidence to suggest that physical activity can benefit psychological well-being and mental health. Much of this evidence comes from cross-sectional and observational studies but some evidence is available from intervention studies. A variety of aspects are associated with psychological well-being but possibly the most frequently measured aspect is *mood*.

Mood refers to a set of feelings experienced on a day-to-day basis. Particular mood states may last for hours, days, weeks or even months. The term "mood" is distinct from the term "emotion" in that mood tends to be a longer lasting state whereas emotions are feelings generated in response to specific events and these feelings last for minutes or hours but not longer. Mood states are generally positive or negative in nature. Examples of positive mood states are happiness and vigour while examples of negative mood states are anger, anxiety, depression and fatigue.

Across a variety of study designs exercise and physical activity are consistently associated with positive mood, e.g. enhanced feelings of happiness and energy, decreased feelings of tension, fatigue and anger. There is also evidence supporting a role of exercise for enhancing self-esteem (due to changes in self-perceptions) and sleep quality (enabling people to fall asleep more quickly and to sleep more deeply and for longer). In addition there is some evidence that regular exercise has positive effects on women's experiences of menstruation, pregnancy and menopause. Such findings may apply both to healthy individuals and to those with disease and disability.

One key mood state linked to psychological well-being is depression. Here a distinction may be drawn between short-lived feelings of depression (a few hours to a few days) which may be considered non-clinical depression and longer term depression (lasting months or years) which interferes with personal and professional life and may be considered a mental illness. Clinical depression is a common disorder affecting about 121 million people globally and it is one of the leading causes of disability worldwide. High levels of physical activity are consistently related to lower levels of depression in population-based surveys, and meta-analyses of studies that have used exercise as a treatment for depression generally show a large effect size.

Less clear is the role of exercise in treating anxiety, defined as excessive worry over prolonged periods causing distress and interfering with everyday life. While exercise appears to have a small to moderate effect on reducing non-clinical (short-lived) levels of anxiety, there is insufficient evidence to make firm conclusions about the role of exercise in preventing and treating clinical anxiety disorders.

> **66** **Depression is a common mental disorder that presents with depressed mood, loss of interest or pleasure, feelings of guilt or low self-worth, disturbed sleep or appetite, low energy, and poor concentration. These problems can become chronic or recurrent and lead to substantial impairments in an individual's ability to take care of his or her everyday responsibilities. At its worst, depression can lead to suicide, a tragic fatality associated with the loss of about 850 000 lives every year. 99**
>
> World Health Organization

Effect size an objective and standardized measure of the magnitude of observed effect. We can compare effect sizes across different studies that have measured different variables, or have used different scales of measurement

How does exercise improve psychological well-being?

A variety of mechanisms have been proposed to explain how exercise enhances psychological well-being. These mechanisms may be broadly divided into physiological, biochemical/metabolic and psychological. No single theory explains the process fully and the effects of exercise are likely to operate through interacting mechanisms.

The following possible mechanisms link physical activity to psychological well-being (Biddle, Mutrie 2008).

→ Changes associated with an increase in core body temperature during and after exercise—the thermogenic hypothesis.

→ Increases in cerebral blood flow and oxygen supply to the brain as a consequence of frequent exercise.

→ Increases in endorphin production during and after exercise—the endorphin hypothesis. Endorphins may be considered an endogenous (produced within the body) form of morphine which function as neurotransmitters and are able to induce pain relief and feelings of well-being.

→ Changes in central serotonergic systems from exercise—the serotonin hypothesis. Serotonin is a neurotransmitter which contributes to feelings of well-being and happiness. A deficiency in serotonin may be a contributing factor to anxiety and depression.

→ Increases in the neurotransmitter noradrenaline, also known as norepinephrine. This may lead to a heightened sense of alertness and heightened vigour.

→ A "feel better" effect from exercise. This may enhance body image and feelings of self-worth and self-esteem from mastering new tasks. This in

TO RESEARCH

Strategies for enhancing adherence to exercise may be broadly divided into one of four categories:

→ Environmental approaches—for example, prompts, contracts, provision of footpaths

→ Reinforcement approaches—for example, rewards and feedback

→ Goal-setting approaches—for example, a target race time or distance to cover

→ Social support approaches—for example, involving family and friends.

Find out more about each of these approaches and the advantages and disadvantages of each for enhancing long-term exercise adherence.

KEY POINT

Exercise helps us to maintain functional and mental capacities as we age and reduces the risk of disease in later life, preserving our independence.

TO THINK ABOUT

Key facts about Alzheimer's disease

→ More than 35 million people worldwide have Alzheimer's disease.

→ Alzheimer's disease is a deterioration of memory and other cognitive domains that leads to death within three to nine years of diagnosis.

→ Alzheimer's disease is the most common form of dementia.

→ The principal risk factor for Alzheimer's disease is age. The incidence of the disease doubles every 5 years after 65 years of age.

→ Data on centenarians show that Alzheimer's disease is not necessarily the outcome of ageing.

→ Nevertheless, the odds of receiving a diagnosis of Alzheimer's disease after 85 years of age exceed one in three.

Reference

Querfurth, H. W. and LaFerla, F. M. 2010. "Mechanisms of Alzheimer's Disease." *New England Journal of Medicine*. Vol 362. Pp 329–44.

turn may provide a sense of personal control and serve as a distraction from negative or stressful aspects of life. Exercise may also make people feel better due to the positive social interactions it can facilitate.

Although it is clear that there are psychological benefits of exercise, it is important to realize that there are also barriers to exercise which may have psychological elements. These may be divided into:

→ **Physical barriers** for example, perceptions of being too old or too fat

→ **Emotional barriers** for example, shyness or embarrassment about exercising

→ **Motivational barriers** for example, lack of energy for, or enjoyment of, exercise

→ **Time barriers** for example, a perceived lack of time due to work and/or family life

→ **Availability barriers** for example, perceptions about a lack of equipment/ facilities and the feeling that there is no one to exercise with.

These factors need to be taken into consideration when planning and promoting physical activity programmes. Finally, it is important to recognize that too much exercise can have adverse psychological consequences, leading to negative addiction and adverse mood states with withdrawal.

Ageing

A major risk factor for many of the disorders discussed thus far is age and as people are living longer than ever before the prevalence of many of these disorders could increase in the coming years. Exercise has an important role to play in minimizing age-related deterioration in functional capacities and therefore the risk of disease in later life.

The role of exercise in preserving bone mass has already been addressed but exercise does far more than this. Regular exercise helps in preserving maximum oxygen uptake, muscular strength, muscular endurance, flexibility, balance and possibly coordination. Such benefits have been demonstrated even in adults in their 90s. The preservation of functional capacities is crucial for older adults so that they can maintain their independence. Tasks which young people take for granted can become a real challenge for older adults. These tasks include unscrewing the lids from jars, putting socks on, kneeling down to tie a shoelace, climbing in and out of a bath, climbing flights of stairs, getting out of an armchair, crossing the road in the time allotted at a pedestrian crossing and stepping onto and off buses and trains. Regular exercise helps to preserve mobility, reduces the risk of disability and maintains the capacity to perform a large variety of tasks essential for independent living.

Aside from its role in maintaining physical fitness recent research shows that exercise also plays an important role in helping to preserve mental function and reduce the risk of Alzheimer's disease as well as other forms of dementia. Several observational studies have shown that those who exercise more in middle and old age are less likely to experience cognitive impairment than their less active peers. Observational studies have also demonstrated a lower risk of dementia in active compared with inactive older adults. Support for a positive role of exercise for preserving brain health comes from very recent research demonstrating an association between physical activity levels and grey matter volume as well as a longitudinal training study showing that exercise can increase the size of the hippocampus and improve memory in older adults.

Prescription of exercise for health

Physical activity recommendations for health are provided by a variety of national organisations and also by the World Health Organization (WHO). The WHO provides guidelines for three specific age groups: 5 to 17 years, 18 to 64 years and 65 years and older. A summary of the guidelines for each of these groups is provided in Table 15.4 below. Further details can be found on the WHO website.

WHO EXERCISE RECOMMENDATIONS FOR THOSE AGED 5 TO 17 YEARS

→ Accumulate at least 60 minutes of moderate- to vigorous-intensity physical activity daily.

→ Physical activity of amounts greater than 60 minutes daily will provide additional health benefits.

→ Most of daily physical activity should be aerobic. Vigorous-intensity activities should be incorporated, including those that strengthen muscle and bone, at least three times per week.

WHO EXERCISE RECOMMENDATIONS FOR THOSE AGED 18 TO 64 YEARS

→ At least 150 minutes of moderate-intensity aerobic physical activity throughout the week, or do at least 75 minutes of vigorous-intensity aerobic physical activity throughout the week, or an equivalent combination of moderate- and vigorous-intensity activity.

→ Aerobic activity should be performed in bouts of at least 10 minutes duration.

→ For additional health benefits, adults should increase their moderate-intensity aerobic physical activity to 300 minutes per week, or engage in 150 minutes of vigorous-intensity aerobic physical activity per week, or an equivalent combination of moderate- and vigorous-intensity activity.

→ Muscle-strengthening activities should be done involving major muscle groups on two or more days a week.

WHO EXERCISE RECOMMENDATIONS FOR THOSE AGED 65 YEARS AND ABOVE

→ At least 150 minutes of moderate-intensity aerobic physical activity throughout the week, or at least 75 minutes of vigorous-intensity aerobic physical activity throughout the week, or an equivalent combination of moderate- and vigorous-intensity activity.

→ Aerobic activity should be performed in bouts of at least 10 minutes duration.

→ For additional health benefits: 300 minutes of moderate intensity aerobic physical activity per week, or 150 minutes of vigorous intensity aerobic physical activity per week, or an equivalent combination of moderate- and vigorous intensity activity.

→ Adults of this age group with poor mobility should perform physical activity to enhance balance and prevent falls on three or more days per week.

→ Muscle-strengthening activities should be done involving major muscle groups, on two or more days a week.

→ When adults of this age group cannot do the recommended amounts of physical activity due to health conditions, they should be as physically active as their abilities and conditions allow.

↑ Table 15.4: WHO physical activity guidelines

The WHO physical activity guidelines are designed to lower the risk of hypokinetic diseases but exercise is also important as a therapy for disease. The key aims of therapeutic exercise in people who have a hypokinetic disease are:

→ to allow them to make the most of their functional capacities
→ to alleviate or provide relief from symptoms
→ to reduce the need for medication
→ to reduce the risk of disease recurrence (secondary prevention)
→ to help overcome social problems and psychological distress.

When encouraging people to become more active it is important to bear in mind that there are a variety of barriers to physical activity including the risks of accident and injury during exercise. Exercise can also be difficult and/or dangerous for those with an uncontrolled disease such as unstable angina, poorly controlled diabetes or poorly controlled hypertension.

TO RESEARCH

Find out if there are any specific physical activity guidelines for your country.

TO RESEARCH

Although there are a variety of benefits to physical activity it is important to acknowledge and be aware of the potential hazards of exercise. These include the risk of accident and injury while exercising and playing sport, the risk of overtraining in those who perform excessive amounts of exercise and the risk that exercise may trigger a heart attack.

This latter risk is rare and is most likely to occur in sedentary older adults who have atherosclerosis and perform unaccustomed exercise. It also occasionally occurs in younger individuals who have a condition termed **hypertrophic cardiomyopathy**. Instances are very rare but there have been several high profile deaths due to heart attacks suffered during exercise including that of the 28-year-old Cameroon footballer Marc-Vivien Foé in 2003 and the 34-year-old Japanese footballer Naoki Matsuda in 2011.

Instances have also been noted in runners (see newspaper clip below).

Find out more about hypertrophic cardiomyopathy and what steps might reasonably be taken to reduce the risk of heart attack during exercise among those with this condition.

Daily Mail, Wednesday, August 7, 2002   Page 25

Top athlete killed by a heart attack at 33 may have trained too hard

Fatal dedication of man who ran himself to death

By Jaya Narain

A TOP athlete who died from a heart attack may have run himself to death because he trained too hard, it emerged yesterday.

John Taylor, 33, a fell and mountain runner who represented Britain, collapsed in his bedroom after he awoke with severe breathing difficulties.

His fiancee Kirstin Bailey, 29, tried to revive him, but he was found to be dead on arrival at hospital on Monday.

Now a post-mortem has found that the fell runner may have trained so hard he caused his heart to enlarge.

Doctors say this can happen to athletes who regularly undergo strenuous exercise.

On Saturday Mr Taylor, who ran for Bingley Harriers, helped his team win a gruelling fell race championship in Snowdonia despite a foot injury.

He completed the race comfortably and trained again on Sunday without any ill-effects.

Mr Taylor, who worked as a green-keeper at the Bradley Park Golf Club near his home in Skelmanthorpe, West Yorkshire, arrived early every day so he could run five miles around the course.

Last night, his parents said they were devastated that their son's commitment to the sport he loved had apparently led to his death.

Mr Taylor's mother June, 59, said: 'John was very fit and always took care of himself. He was never ill, and it is [...] probably caused by all that exercise. John was a sought-after runner and under pressure to take part in competitions all over the country.

'He loved running and found it difficult to say No. It seems his dedication to the sport has cost him his life.'

Miss Bailey, who was to have wed Mr Taylor next year, was being comforted by relatives.

Peter Moon, 54, a member of Bingley Harriers, said: 'John was a brilliant International athlete and a harrier for ten years.

Club coach Dennis Quinian added: 'John would compete on a weekly basis and trained every day.

'It is bizarre that he should collapse and die like this.

'If something like this could happen to John it could happen to anyone.'

Mr Taylor had been planning a trip to Switzerland next week where he was to have run in a mountain race and then had a holiday with his fiancee.

Medical experts say that if athletes develop an enlarged heart it can increase the volume of blood being pumped out.

j.narain@dailymail.co.uk

→ Modern day life is characterized by low levels of physical activity thus increasing the risk of hypokinetic disorders.

→ Major hypokinetic disorders include CVD, breast and colon cancer, obesity, type 2 diabetes and osteoporosis.

→ Regular exercise can lower the risk of hypokinetic disorders although other factors also play a role in these disorders.

→ Exercise lowers the risk of CVD through direct effects on the heart and circulation as well as through indirect effects on other CVD risk factors.

→ Exercise increases the energy expenditure side of the energy balance equation and assists in preventing obesity.

→ Exercise lowers the risk of type 2 diabetes by helping to maintain healthy body fat levels and by enhancing insulin sensitivity and glucose tolerance.

→ Exercise contributes to the preservation of bone mass reducing the risk of osteoporosis and bone fractures in later life, particularly in women.

→ Exercise preserves psychological well-being by enhancing mood and helping to combat anxiety and depression.

→ Exercise makes an important contribution to healthy ageing by preserving physical and mental function and, as a result, the ability to live independently and pursue life to the full.

→ Exercise is important as a therapy for a variety of diseases and conditions.

→ Physical activity guidelines for health recommend at least 60 minutes of exercise each day for children and 150 minutes of exercise each week (an average of 30 minutes each day) for adults.

Self-study questions

1 Define the term "health".

2 Define the terms "physical activity" and "physical fitness".

3 Briefly explain the findings of the bus driver/bus conductor study conducted by Professor Jerry Morris.

4 Discuss the meaning of the term "epidemiology".

5 Define and give a brief explanation of METs.

6 Identify and define three major forms of CVD.

7 Identify the major risk factors for CVD.

8 List the BMI cut-off points for underweight, normal weight, overweight and obesity classes I, II and III.

9 Explain the energy balance equation.

10 Explain what is meant by the term "benign obesity".

11 Discuss the exercise recommendations for weight control.

12 Explain the function of leptin.

13 Define and explain the term NEAT.

14 Distinguish between type 1 and type 2 diabetes.

15 List the health risks of diabetes.

16 Explain how exercise reduces the risk of type 2 diabetes.

17 Explain the term "osteoporosis".

18 Discuss the role of exercise for bone health.

19 Define the terms "mood" and "depression".

20 Explain the role of exercise in psychological well-being.

21 Explain the role of exercise in healthy ageing.

22 Give a brief summary of the WHO physical activity guidelines for health.

23 Briefly discuss the hazards of exercise.

DATA BASED QUESTION

1 Below is a list of various activities and their associated MET values. For each activity calculate the oxygen consumption in litres per minute $(L \cdot min^{-1})$ and energy expenditure in kilojoules per hour $(kJ \cdot hr^{-1})$ during 60 minutes of exercise for:

a an individual weighing 70 kg

b an individual weighing 90 kg.

Basketball, competitive	8	METs
Basketball, recreational	6	METs
Mountain bike racing	16	METs
Running at 19 km · hr^{-1}	19	METs
Soccer, competitive	10	METs
Swimming, front crawl, vigorous effort	10	METs
Walking at 6.4 km · hr^{-1} on a level firm surface	5	METs

2 What do you observe about the relationship between body mass, oxygen consumption and energy expenditure?

3 Can you think of any limitations of the MET system of classifying exercise intensity?

To find out more about METs and the MET values for a wide variety of physical activities go to the following website: http://sites.google.com/site/compendiumofphysicalactivities/home.

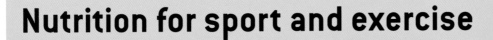

CHAPTER 16

Nutrition for sport and exercise

OBJECTIVES

By the end of this chapter students should be able to:

→ outline the components of the digestive system

→ describe the functions of enzymes

→ list the enzymes responsible for the digestion of carbohydrates, fats and proteins

→ describe the reasons water is essential to humans

→ explain how the body controls its water content

→ explain the causes of dehydration and why monitoring dehydration in athletes is important

→ explain the concepts of energy intake, energy expenditure and energy balance and why these are important to athletes

→ understand the importance of carbohydrates in sustaining energy levels during exercise

→ understand that proteins can't be stored in the body but must be eaten every day to maintain health

→ describe the use of supplements in the diet of athletes.

Introduction

Good nutrition is one of the foundations of good health. Nutritional intake below or in excess of our requirements can cause, or increase the risk of, numerous health problems, therefore making changes to a person's diet can help maintain and restore health.

In the general non-athletic population, good health cannot be improved further simply by adding nutrients to the diet. However, the diet of those involved in sport and exercise can be manipulated in a way that can have rapid, clear benefits for performance.

Historically the influence of diet on sports performance was not recognized. Indeed some thought that food and fluid ingestion during exercise would damage performance. This is the opposite to today's view of the link between nutrition and exercise with huge growth in an industry built around commercial sports drinks and foods. How things have changed in 100 years!

Digestion and absorption

The digestive system

The digestive system is a group of organs that are involved in the digestion of food (Figure 16.1). Digestion is the chemical and mechanical breakdown of food into nutrients. Table 16.1 summarizes the components of chemical and mechanical digestion. The function of the digestive system is controlled by the nervous system and a variety of hormones.

> ❝Don't get into the habit of eating or drinking in a marathon race: some prominent runners do, but it is not beneficial.❞
> JE Sullivan, 1909

> ❝To enjoy all the benefits of sport, athletes, whether they compete at the elite level or exercise on a recreational basis, should adopt specific nutrition strategies that can optimise mental and physical performance and support good health.❞
> International Olympic Committee, 2010

311

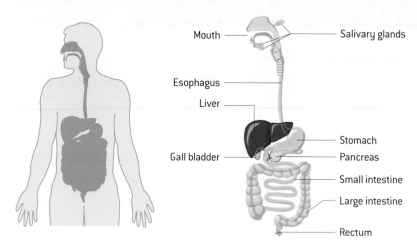

↑ Figure 16.1: Organs of the digestive system

DIGESTIVE COMPONENTS	CHEMICAL DIGESTION	MECHANICAL DIGESTION
Teeth		✓
Saliva	✓	
Stomach movements		✓
Gastric acid	✓	
Stomach enzymes	✓	
Small intestine enzymes	✓	
Bile	✓	
Pancreatic juice	✓	
Gut bacteria	✓	

↑ Table 16.1: Summary of how the different components of digestion can break down food mechanically and chemically

TO DO

Take a slice of white bread and chew it; chew, chew, chew continuously without swallowing. You may notice that it slowly begins to taste sweeter. What is happening?

Mouth and esophagus

Digestion begins in the mouth. We break down the food with our teeth mechanically by chewing. The saliva, secreted by salivary glands, contains enzymes which digest the food chemically. The ground food in the mouth is called a *bolus*. Saliva is also made of mucous which coats the bolus. This makes swallowing the bolus into the esophagus easier. With wave-like movements (peristalsis action) the esophagus transports the food into the stomach.

Stomach

The stomach is a hollow and muscular organ with an inner layer of expandable folds. These folds are called rugae and the hollow space is called the lumen. The stomach expands according to how much food and fluid we have in the lumen. This allows the stomach to store food for a short time.

The muscular contractions have further functions; they physically grind and mix the bolus into smaller particles (called chyme) and they regulate the emptying of the chyme into the small intestine. In the stomach the enzymatic digestion is initiated by the secretion of gastric juice by specific glands. The gastric juice contains hydrochloric acid, mucous, enzymes and hormones. The hydrochloric acid (gastric acid) activates digestive enzymes. Mucous is secreted to protect the stomach wall from damage by the acid.

Small intestine

The small intestine has an upper part (duodenum), a middle part (jejunum) and a lower part (ileum). In the upper part the mixing of chyme with digestive fluids from the liver and pancreas results in further chemical digestion taking place. The absorption of nutrients begins here and this is the main function of the middle and the lower part of the small intestine.

Absorption is the process where nutrients enter the bloodstream, either by diffusion or active transport. The wall of the small intestine is wrinkled and on each wrinkle there are small, finger-like structures called villi. Every single cell of the small intestine also has finger-like structures attached which are called microvilli (see Figure 16.2). The function of the wrinkles, villi and microvilli is to increase the surface area that can absorb nutrients.

The small intestine also transports undigested food and unabsorbed nutrients to the large intestine by characteristic contractions of intestinal muscles.

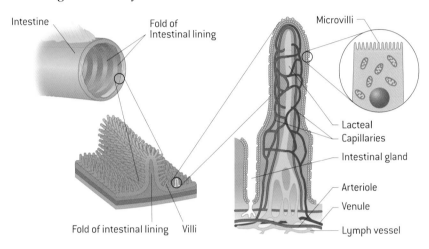

↑ Figure 16.2: Wall structure of the small intestine

Liver and gall bladder

The liver is an organ with multiple functions. In the process of digestion and absorption the liver has two functions:

→ the production and secretion of bile for digestion into the small intestine
→ the production of lymph for the transport of fat.

Bile is a complex fluid containing bile acid, cholesterol, bile salt, electrolytes, enzymes and fatty acids. The function of bile is to digest fat. When there is no need to digest fat, for example, when people are fasting, bile is stored in the gall bladder.

Pancreas

The pancreas produces a mixture of digestive enzymes and fluids that is secreted into the upper part of the small intestine. The fluids neutralize gastric acid which enters the small intestine with the chyme, therefore the fluids protect the wall of the small intestine from acid damage.

Large intestine

The large intestine is wider but shorter than the small intestine. The surface of the wall is characterized by intestinal glands instead of villi and microvilli. Digestion no longer takes place in the large intestine and most of the nutrients have been already absorbed. In the large intestine water and electrolytes from the chyme are absorbed. This contributes to the regulation of the water balance in the body. It also is the main organ in the formation of solid faeces. The large intestine can store faecal matter until it is discharged by intestinal muscle movements.

The large intestine is important in the absorption of vitamin K, produced by the gut bacteria. The gut bacteria play an important role in the breakdown of undigested carbohydrates.

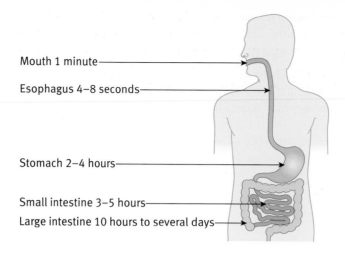

Mouth 1 minute

Esophagus 4–8 seconds

Stomach 2–4 hours

Small intestine 3–5 hours

Large intestine 10 hours to several days

↑ Figure 16.3: The time it takes for food to pass through the digestive system

Digestive enzymes

Enzymes are a class of proteins that support biochemical reactions, that is, they speed up or catalyse those reactions. Digestive enzymes are essential for the breakdown of carbohydrates, fats and proteins into small, absorbable molecules. For each macronutrient there are specific enzymes. Digestive enzymes are produced and secreted by salivary glands, stomach, pancreas, liver and small intestine. Table 16.2 shows the enzymes involved in macronutrient digestion and the organ of production and secretion.

MACRONUTRIENT	ENZYME	ORGAN
Carbohydrate	Amylase	Salivary glands
		Pancreas
	Sucrase	Small intestine
	Maltase	Small intestine
	Isomaltase	Small intestine
	Lactase	Small intestine
Protein	Pepsin	Stomach
	Trypsin	Pancreas
	Chymotrypsin	Pancreas
	Elastase	Pancreas
	Carboxypeptidase A	Pancreas
	Carboxypeptidase B	Pancreas
	Peptidase	Small intestine
Fat	Lipase	Salivary glands (only in infants)
		Stomach
		Pancreas
	Colipase	Pancreas
	Phospholipase	Pancreas
	Cholesterol esterase	Liver

↑ Table 16.2: Sources of enzymes for the digestion of carbohydrates, proteins and fats

Digestive enzymes are secreted in an inactive form and are only activated at the site of function to protect the secretion organs from any damaging, premature enzymatic action. Enzymes work most efficiently when the environment is optimal in temperature and pH value. The optimum temperature and pH is different for each enzyme. For example, different parts of the digestive system have a specific pH (Figure 16.4). This determines which enzymes we can find from mouth to large intestine and where the macronutrients are digested and absorbed.

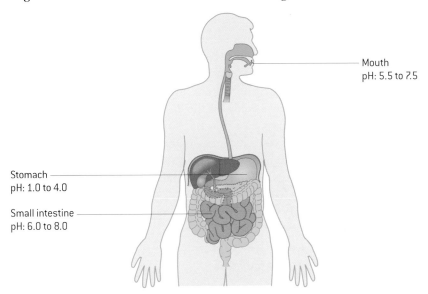

Mouth
pH: 5.5 to 7.5

Stomach
pH: 1.0 to 4.0

Small intestine
pH: 6.0 to 8.0

↑ Figure 16.4: Typical pH values found throughout the digestive system

Digestion and absorption of macronutrients

Carbohydrates

Carbohydrates are digested and hydrolysed to the sugars glucose, fructose and galactose.

The digestion of carbohydrates begins in the mouth. Complex carbohydrates such as starch and glycogen are broken down enzymatically by salivary amylase. However, once the food enters the stomach the low pH value of the stomach inhibits the enzyme. A more important role in the digestion of carbohydrates is played by the pancreatic amylase which is secreted into the upper part of the small intestine.

Amylase hydrolyses carbohydrates into the oligosaccharides maltose, maltotriose and α-limit dextrin. The enzymes needed to digest these molecules further are located in the microvilli-rich cell membrane, also called the brush-border membrane, of the small intestine. Maltase and isomaltase hydrolyse maltose, maltotriose and α-limit dextrin to glucose molecules. Other carbohydrates such as sucrose and lactose which enter the small intestine undigested are broken down by specific brush-border enzymes. Lactose is digested by lactase into glucose and galactose molecules, and sucrose is digested by sucrase into glucose and fructose molecules.

Monosaccharides are mostly absorbed in the upper and middle part of the small intestine. They travel through the brush-border membrane and the cytosol of the absorptive cells, pass the basolateral membrane and enter the capillary blood system. Figure 16.5 illustrates the transport of monosaccharides in the small intestine. Glucose and galactose are transported actively, which means that the molecules pass the cell wall with help of a transporter located in the brush-border membrane. The transport requires energy which is generated by the transporter called sodium glucose co-transporter (SGLT).

Fructose passes the intestinal wall by a process called facilitated diffusion. Another transporter (GLUT5) supports the transfer process of fructose into the cytosol. Glucose, galactose and fructose cross the basolateral membrane of the small intestine cells in a similar way to that used by fructose to enter the cell but facilitated by a GLUT2 transporter. All GLUT transporters transport the monosaccharides from the site with a high concentration (lumen of small intestine or cytosol) to the site with a low concentration (cytosol of intestinal cell or blood).

There are a few carbohydrates that escape digestion in the small intestine. A reason for this is that these carbohydrates have a particular chemical structure where the bonds can not be hydrolysed by the enzymes of our digestive system. Another reason is that these carbohydrates are enclosed in whole grains or are otherwise physically inaccessible for the digestive enzymes, for example, in fiber. These carbohydrates pass into the large intestine where they are digested by bacteria. In this so-called fermentation process carbohydrates are broken down to short-chain fatty acids. These two- to four-carbon fatty acids are easily absorbed by the cell of the large intestine.

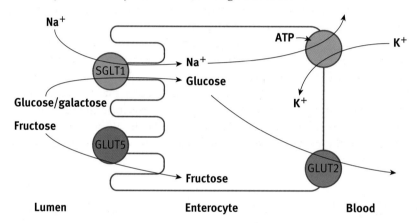

↑ Figure 16.5: Transport of monosaccharides through the brush border of a cell of the small intestine (enterocyte)

Proteins

Before proteins can be absorbed they need to be broken down into small peptides and amino acids. As shown in Table 16.2, there are numerous enzymes involved in the digestion of proteins. Most of the enzymes act on different parts of the molecular structures depending on the chemical characteristics of each protein.

The digestion of proteins starts in the stomach where the enzyme pepsin breaks proteins into larger peptides. About 15 percent of the dietary proteins are digested in the stomach. Most protein digestion takes place in the small intestine involving enzymes (proteases) secreted by the pancreas and brush-border enzymes. The pancreatic protease breaks proteins down into smaller peptides which are further digested into amino acids and peptides with chains of two to four amino acids by the brush-border proteases.

Amino acids are absorbed in the middle and lower part of the small intestine. They are carried across the intestinal cell into the blood by a range of mechanisms (passive diffusion, facilitated diffusion or active transport) depending on the type of amino acid, that is, whether they are hydrophobic, acidic, basic, neutral or aromatic. Most of the transporters are sodium dependent co-transporters.

Peptides, not longer than four amino acids, enter the cytosol with support of an H^+-dependent active transporter. In the intestinal cytosol these peptides are hydrolysed by cytoplasmatic peptidases into amino acids.

Fat

A challenging characteristic of fat for digestion and absorption is that it is not soluble in water, but has to be transferred through a watery environment in chyme (found in the stomach and small intestine), intestinal fluids, cytosol, lymph and blood.

Furthermore, the fat-specific digestive enzymes are all water-soluble and insoluble in fat so that they cannot access the molecules for their breakdown. The following processes overcome this problem.

→ **Emulsification** In the process of emulsification fat is dispersed into small globules. Stomach movements initiate emulsification which is completed in the small intestine. Bile, secreted from the liver and gall bladder into the small intestine, is required to emulsify dietary fat. Bile-coated fatty droplets can now circulate in fluids. Emulsification increases the surface area accessible to fat-hydrolysing enzymes (listed in Table 16.2). The products of fat digestion are free fatty acids, monoglyceride, cholesterol, cholesterol ester and lysophospholipids.

→ **Micelle formation** A micelle is a fat particle which consists of about 20 fat molecules. With bile acid all products of the fat digestion including fat-soluble vitamins form so-called mixed micelles. The "water-hating" (hydrophobic) part of fat digestion products is located in the center of the micelle while the "water-loving" (hydrophilic) parts form the surface. This enables the micelle to travel to the intestinal cell where the molecules diffuse into the cytosol (Figure 16.6). Fats eventually enter the blood via the lymph system.

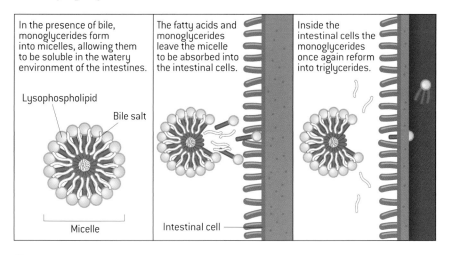

↑ Figure 16.6: Micelle formation and diffusion of fat molecules into the intestinal cells

→ **Repackaging into chylomicrons** The majority of fat is absorbed in the middle and lower part of the small intestine. Glycerol and fatty acid chains with less than 12 carbon atoms diffuse directly through the intestinal cell into the blood stream. Longer chain fatty acids, cholesterol, monoglycerides, and lysophospholipids are resynthesized into triglycerides, phospolipids and cholesterol esters in the cytosol. Together with specific transport proteins (apolipoproteins) resynthesized molecules are then incorporated into chylomicrons. Chylomicrons are another form of fat droplet; needed to transfer the water-insoluble molecules into the lymphatic vessel and later into the blood.

Water and electrolyte balance

Water is one of the defining features of all biological systems. It is essential for life in humans and in every other organism. There are multiple reasons why water is so essential.

→ Water is an effective solvent and this allows it to transport nutrients to cells, remove waste products from cells and transport other metabolites produced by cells such as hormones.

→ Water allows us to redistribute heat around the body and reduce body temperature through evaporation from the surface of our skin as we sweat.

→ Water makes an excellent lubricant as it is difficult to compress. For example, it is present around sliding surfaces in the body such as joint spaces and around tendons and muscles.

→ Finally water provides the aqueous medium essential for the biochemical reactions of metabolism inside and outside cells.

Body water

Around 50 to 70 per cent of total body mass is made up of water. The figure can vary greatly between people depending on how much body fat they have. The reason for this is that the fat present inside fat storage cells (called adiposites) does not contain any water. Therefore in overweight people a large proportion of body mass can be made up of tissue containing little water. Fat-free tissue on the other hand is comprised of 60 to 80 per cent water, so the leaner we are, the greater the percentage of our body mass that is water. The distribution of water in a typical healthy, non-overweight person is shown in Figure 16.7 below.

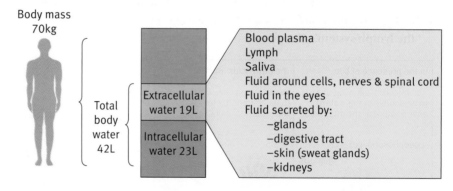

↑ Figure 16.7: The proportion of water in the body of a typical 70 kilogram person, and its distribution inside and outside cells

Intracellular (ICF) and extracellular (ECF) fluids are not just defined by their different locations; they are also very different in terms of the composition of solutes. One principle difference is that in ICF potassium (K^+) salts dominate while in ECF sodium (Na^+) salts dominate. The resulting concentration gradients across cell membranes are maintained by active transport (requiring ATP) which results in substantial, continuous energy expenditure. Although different in composition the overall concentration or osmolarity of ICF and ECF is the same.

Water balance

Day-to-day fluctuation in body mass is relatively small; even though there is a turnover of around 2.5 liters of body water per day in healthy people there is usually no substantial net gain or net loss of water (Figure 16.8). In non-exercising people the water losses of around 2.5 liters per day are replaced through ingestion of food, drinking fluids and oxidation of substrates (metabolic water).

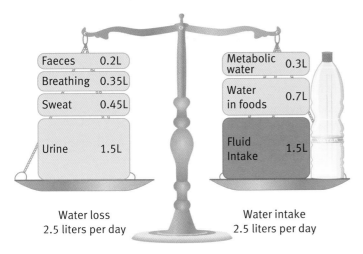

Faeces	0.2L
Breathing	0.35L
Sweat	0.45L
Urine	1.5L

Metabolic water	0.3L
Water in foods	0.7L
Fluid Intake	1.5L

Water loss
2.5 liters per day

Water intake
2.5 liters per day

↑ Figure 16.8: Water loss versus water intake

Negative feedback regulates water balance

When water balance is threatened and there is a net loss of body water, the concentration of body fluid increases. This change is detected in the hypothalamus and it responds by doing two things:

→ activates the sensation of thirst increasing the desire to drink fluids
→ secretes anti-diuretic hormone (ADH) which causes the kidneys to retain fluids and reduce urine production.

These two mechanisms "gain and retain" water; the consequence is increased water availability in ECF. The resulting dilution of solutes in ECF is detected in the hypothalamus and the response is the opposite of that described above. Thirst is "switched off" and ADH secretion is reduced (Figure 16.9).

Diuretic a substance that increases the rate at which urine is produced

KEY POINT

The amount of water in our bodies stays reasonably stable from day to day, with water lost through urine and sweat being replaced by water in our food and drink.

Hypertonicity

↑ Thirst
(water intake)

↑ **ADH**
(water retention)

Water loss

Set point

↓ Thirst
(no water intake)

↓ **ADH**
(water excrention)

Hypotonicity

↑ Figure 16.9: Control of water balance; negative feedback in action

The mechanisms above are a good example of how subtle changes in a biological variable are monitored by receptors which trigger a response that corrects the detected fluctuations within a remarkably narrow range of normal functioning (**set point**). This process is called negative feedback.

The kidney

The kidney controls retention and loss of water. Water and electrolytes are small molecules and are physically filtered from blood cells and large molecules in the glomerulus. This filtered fluid moves into the descending loop of Henlé into the medulla of the kidney (Figure 16.10).

→ The wall of the descending loop is permeable to water but not electrolytes. Since the surrounding medulla has a high osmolality water is absorbed passively into the medulla due to the concentration gradient; this increases the concentration and reduces the volume of fluid in the tubule.

→ The wall of the ascending limb of the tubule actively transports sodium chloride but is impermeable to water. Sodium chloride, but not water, is transported out of the fluid in the tubule therefore resulting in redilution of the now reduced volume of fluid.

→ In the collecting duct the reabsorption of water occurs and it is at this point that ADH is involved in regulation. The presence of ADH increases the permeability of the collecting duct wall increasing passive water reabsorption and reducing urine volume. Thus it is this phase which dictates the final urine volume and concentration.

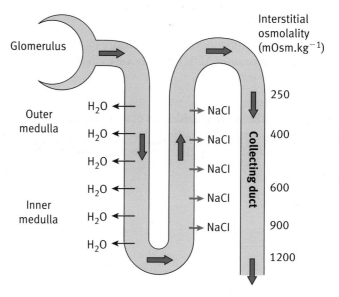

↑ Figure 16.10: Movement of fluid along a nephron (→) results in: a) exposure to osmotic gradients causing passive diffusion (→) and b) active transport mechanisms (→). This concentrates, dilutes and finally regulates urine volume and concentration.

Monitoring hydration status in athletes

The sensation of thirst is an indicator that our hydration status is not optimal and that we need to take in fluid to restore homeostasis. However, sometimes there is a need to have a more precise measure of hydration status, for example, in certain groups of patients or athletes. While becoming dehydrated is a potential health risk for all, a principle concern for athletes is that being dehydrated can impair performance in both competition and training. Current thinking is that athletes should aim to keep net fluid losses within an amount not exceeding two percent of their body mass. A number of methods exist to monitor hydration status; changes in body mass is one of the simplest.

Using body mass to monitor dehydration—a simple example

An athlete's fluid loss and fluid replacement strategy is being monitored during one of their training sessions. Their body mass is monitored before and after training and their drinking behaviour recorded. They attend training with a typical 750ml drink bottle and consume all of this during training.

Body mass prior to training	**75.8kg**
Body mass after two hours training	**74.1kg**
Fluids consumed during training	**750ml**
Urine produced during training	**0ml**

From this data we can estimate:

Total water loss from sweating (without fluid replacement)...
$$75.8 - 74.1 + 0.75 = \textbf{2.45L}$$

Total water deficit remaining after fluid replacement (750ml)...
$$75.8 - 74.1 = \textbf{1.70L}$$

This deficit is equivalent to...
$$1.70 / 75.8 = \textbf{2.2\%} \text{ of total body mass}$$

→ What are the assumptions in this simple approach?

→ What was this athlete's sweating *rate*?

→ What advice could this athlete be offered based on this data?

Analysing urine to monitor dehydration—simple approaches

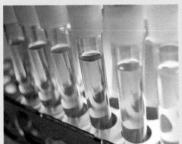

Urine colour chart

1
2
3
4
5
6
7
8

☞ The colour of urine can be used as a subjective indicator of dehydration, with a darker colour suggesting dehydration. Use of colour scales can assess this more objectively.

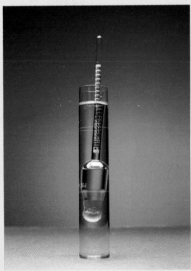

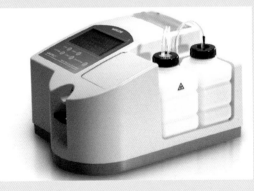

▲ A hydrometer measures the specific gravity of urine and offers a simple way of assessing the concentration of urine.

◀ Using an osmometer to measure freezing point in urine. Increased solute concentration reduces the freezing point and this can be used to quantify the osmolarity of urine.

↑ Figure 16.11: Simple ways to analyse urine

The analysis of urine offers another means of monitoring the hydration status of athletes. Loss of body water results in smaller amounts of more concentrated urine due to the effect of ADH. This means that concentrated urine is indicative of a dehydrated state and this is easily seen just by looking at the colour. Large amounts of pale urine are associated with a normal hydration while small amounts of darker-coloured urine indicate risk of dehydration.

Why do athletes need more fluid?

Water balance can be disrupted dramatically when we exercise or are exposed to hot environmental conditions. Much of the metabolic heat generated from muscle contraction during exercise is lost to the environment because of evaporation of sweat from the surface of the skin. Therefore sweat losses, which are small at rest, tend to be greater during exercise. Similarly, exposure to a warm climate will cause water loss due to an increased sweat rate. Both of these scenarios mean that fluid intake must be increased to compensate for losses and maintain fluid balance.

TO THINK ABOUT

When training and exercise occur in a hot climate maintaining fluid balance is even more challenging and can mean fluid intakes of up to 10 to 15 liters of water per day.

This Olympic athlete is using water during exercise in the heat.

→ Should he pour the contents of the bottle on himself or would drinking be more beneficial?

Exercising harder means increased rates of metabolic heat production which needs to be lost to the environment to control body temperature. Sweating faster helps achieve this but increases dehydration. This graph shows how faster running speeds up sweat loss; combining this with a hot environment makes the situation worse and fluid balance is harder to maintain.

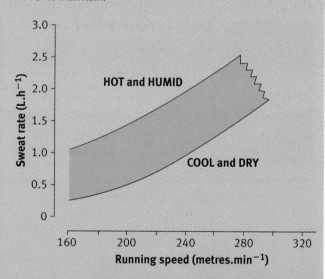

↑ Figure 16.12: Effect of exercise intensity on sweating rate in different environments

Dehydration during participation in sport and exercise is often unavoidable, however, the degree of fluid loss must be controlled. Exercise in a dehydrated state has health risks (e.g. heat stroke) and it can also impair sporting performance. Current evidence suggests that athletes should aim to not drop more than two percent of their body mass due to fluid losses.

Energy balance and body composition

Energy intake

Energy intake is confined to the chemical energy we ingest in foods. It is the macronutrient content (carbohydrate, protein and fat) of food which influences energy content.

→ Carbohydrate   1760 kJ.$100g^{-1}$
→ Protein   1720 kJ.$100g^{-1}$
→ Fats   4000 kJ.$100g^{-1}$

For example, foods which are high in fat are referred to as "energy dense" since fat has a higher energy content than both carbohydrate and protein. High energy content is directly linked to the ability to generate a large amount of ATP.

Energy expenditure

There are three routes by which the body expends energy:

→ basal metabolic rate (BMR)
→ thermic effect of feeding (TEF)
→ thermic effect of physical activity (PAL).

The basal metabolic rate (BMR) refers to the minimum energy requirement for maintenance of biological activity in the body, in other words to stay alive! These basic demands are the repair of body tissues, brain activity, membrane transport and the energy requirement for breathing and circulation. Since all metabolism in the body is ultimately aerobic BMR can be estimated by measuring the rate at which we consume oxygen from the air while at rest. Utilization of 1 liter of oxygen equates to expenditure of around 20 kJ of energy.

Thermic effect of food

This describes the energy needed to process food, that is, the energy needed to digest food and to absorb, transport and store the nutrients derived from it. This can be measured using the same approach as BMR whereby energy expenditure at rest is compared after fasting and after eating a meal.

Physical activity

Physical activity is defined as any muscle-driven movement which increases energy expenditure. This can include subconscious activities like fidgeting, or conscious efforts involving movement such as day-to-day activities, activity at work, walking and more vigorous efforts such as running, exercise training or participation in sports. Because there is so much variation in people's levels of physical activity this domain of energy expenditure is the most variable. The longer we exercise for, and the higher the exercise intensity, the greater the energy expenditure.

Relationship between intake and expenditure

Energy intake only occurs *intermittently* throughout the day when we eat food. However, we *constantly* expend energy and the rate at which this occurs is very variable. Therefore between meals the only way to ensure that we have sufficient energy to meet our requirements is to have stores of energy available in the body which can be used to synthesize ATP via the energy systems (Figure 16.13). Therefore our energy stores in the body even out the fluctuations in energy intake.

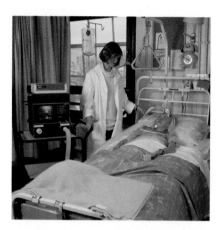

↑ Measurement of BMR. The Perspex hood over the head allows measurement of O_2 use and CO_2 production.

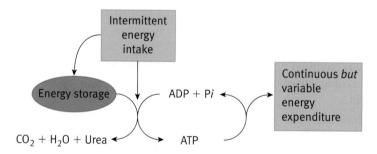

↑ Figure 16.13: Energy stores, including carbohydrate and fat, allow continuous energy expenditure even at times when energy from nutrients is not being ingested

The energy stores in the body comprise fats which we store in adipose tissue under the skin and carbohydrates in muscle and the liver. Although proteins in the body are plentiful and can be used as an energy source, they are not an energy store as such. This is because all proteins present in the body have a distinct biological role—breaking these down to meet an energy requirement will always be at the expense of other biological requirements and functions.

Energy balance

In the long term, energy intake and energy expenditure tend to be closely balanced in healthy adult humans, hence this relationship is referred to as the **energy balance** (Figure 16.14). In this state body mass does not change. If people habitually ingest food with an energy content which is greater than their total energy expenditure then chemical energy is stored in the body. Likewise if the diet has an energy content which is less than total energy expenditure then the energy stores must compensate for the deficit. Therefore disturbing the energy balance causes either a net gain in body mass or a net loss in body mass.

Body composition

When body mass gets heavier or lighter we can not be certain *what* has changed without exploring the composition of the body. Conversely the composition of the body can change without necessarily influencing body mass in a noticeable way.

Body composition is complex as there are many different tissues and materials which make up the body. A simple approach to describe body composition involves estimating the fraction of body mass which is made up of fat mass (FM) and the remainder which is termed fat-free mass (FFM).

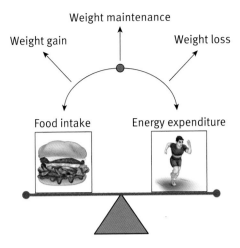

↑ Figure 16.14: The energy balance

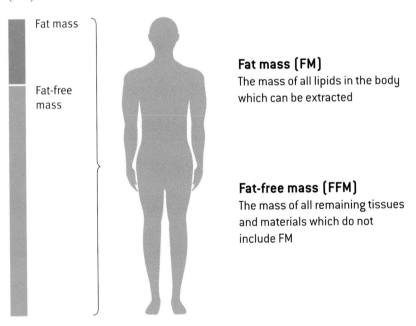

Fat mass

Fat-free mass

Fat mass (FM)
The mass of all lipids in the body which can be extracted

Fat-free mass (FFM)
The mass of all remaining tissues and materials which do not include FM

↑ Figure 16.15: A simple body composition model based on two compartments

You can visualize this in the legs shown in Figure 16.16, with the bone and muscle representing FFM and the adipose tissue contributing to FM. At the whole body level we can express the proportions of FM and FFM as a simple way of describing an individual's nutritional status.

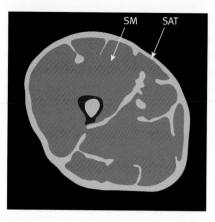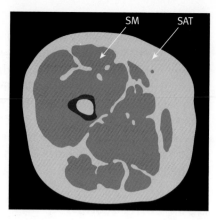

↑ Figure 16.16 MRI image representing a "slice" through the mid thigh of a trained, active person (left) and a sedentary, inactive person (right). There is a clear distinction between the fat-containing subcutaneous adipose tissue (SAT), skeletal muscle (SM) and the skeleton (femur).

How can FM and FFM be measured?

Expressing the amount of FM and FFM in kilograms or as a percentage of body mass is a simple idea but the actual measurement of this is problematic. The only truly reliable means of achieving this is by directly quantifying the amounts of tissues in the body. This can be done by the dissection of cadavers but of course this cannot be used on living people! Therefore more indirect approaches are needed but these give a less accurate measurement.

What are the typical levels of FM and FFM?

The amounts and relative proportion of FM and FFM vary with gender, age, genetics, diet and level of physical activity. Women tend to have a greater proportion of FM than men. If FM is either too low (<5 per cent for men and <12 per cent for women) or too high then health is threatened. For competitors in a range of sports the gender difference persists but there is also variation in FM and FFM across different sports (Table 16.3).

SPORT	GENDER	%FM	%FFM
Marathon	Male	3%	97%
	Female	15%	85%
Shot-put	Male	17%	83%
	Female	28%	72%
Long jump	Male	8%	92%
	Female	11%	89%
Gymnastics	Male	5%	95%
	Female	15%	85%

↑ Table 16.3: Relative amounts of fat mass (FM) and fat free mass (FFM) in male and female competitors in a range of sports

These data suggest that a low body fat may be important for weight-bearing endurance sports like running a marathon, "anti-gravity" sports like the long jump and aesthetic sports like gymnastics. However it seems even a relatively high body fat may be not a disadvantage for power sports like shot-put.

TO RESEARCH

The following methods can be used to assess body composition. Find how the following measures can used to make estimates of FM and FFM.
1 Skinfold calliper measures
2 Bioelectrical impedance
3 Underwater weighing
4 Dual x-ray absorptiometry (DXA or DEXA)

TO DO

Look at Table 16.3 and answer the following questions.
→ Can you think why a low percentage of FM may be advantageous for weight-bearing, anti-gravity and aesthetic sports?
→ Do these data suggest that shot-put athletes have the least amount of muscle?

All different shapes and sizes

All aspects of shape, size and composition of the body are linked to sporting success. Observation of athletes reveals obvious differences between sports, with endurance athletes tending to be small and slender while strength and power athletes tend to be muscular. In strength and power sports where body mass is not a limiting factor, the athletes may also have high levels of adipose tissue. This suggests there is optimal body morphology for success in different types of effort.

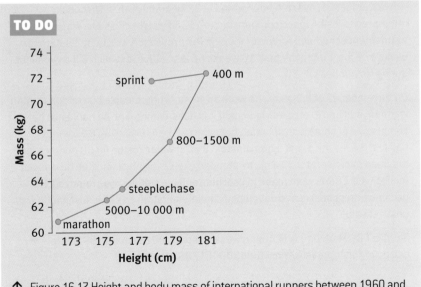

↑ Figure 16.17 Height and body mass of international runners between 1960 and 2005 (from O'Connor et al. 2007)

→ Why do sprinters (100 meters and 200 meters) appear shorter compared to the pattern of these data?

→ How many track athletes at the last Olympic Games got medals in *more* than one running distance?

What if body morphology differs from what is "ideal" for success in a sport? If we are too tall or too short there is of course nothing that can be done. However, body mass and body composition can be influenced, to some degree, by a combination of training and dietary behaviours.

→ **Gaining muscle mass (increasing FFM)** Appropriate strength training programmes can cause muscle hypertrophy. Bigger muscles mean more FFM. On the one hand this may increase muscle strength but there is a trade off since this must be offset against an increase in body mass. Not only must the correct training take place but the athlete must be in a positive energy balance and this must include an adequate protein intake. Any change occurs slowly over a long period of time.

→ **Reducing fat mass (decreasing FM)** Fat mass represents "dead weight" so a reduction may benefit performance in some circumstances. However the low energy intake associated with lean athletes, particularly women, has a number of potentially serious health problems.

→ **Dehydration** In sports such as rowing and judo athletes may compete in weight categories. Since an official weigh-in will often take place several hours before competition, there is a tendency for some competitors to deliberately restrict food and fluid intake in order to temporarily achieve a body mass which makes them eligible to compete in a weight class below their "normal" day-to-day body mass. The aim is to attempt to gain a weight advantage over an opponent, however, the trade off here is dehydration and low energy stores, both of which threaten rather than benefit performance. But the consequences can be much more serious than poor performance (see case study).

> **TO RESEARCH**
>
> In relation to health problems that can occur in women find out what is meant by the "Female Athlete Triad".

> **CASE STUDY**
>
> **In 1997 three collegiate wrestlers died after rapid weight loss before an official weigh-in.**
>
> "On November 21, over a 4-hour period, a 22-year-old man in Wisconsin attempted to lose 4 lbs to compete in the 153-lb weight class of a wrestling tournament scheduled for November 22. His preseason weight on September 6 was 178 lbs. During the next 10 weeks he lost 21 lbs, of which 8 lbs were lost during November 17–20.
>
> On November 21 at 5:30 a.m., he wore a vapour–impermeable suit under a cotton warm-up suit and exercised vigorously in a hot environment. An hour later, he complained of shortness of breath but continued exercising. By 8:50 a.m., he had lost 3.5 lbs. He drank approximately 8 oz of water, rested for 30 minutes, and resumed exercise. At 9:30 a.m., he stopped exercising and indicated he was not feeling well. Efforts were made to cool him, and his clothing was removed. He became unresponsive and developed cardiorespiratory arrest; resuscitation was unsuccessful."
>
> Source: CDC Morbidity & Mortality weekly report, 20 February 1998, http://www.cdc.gov/mmwr/preview/mmwrhtml/00051388.htm

Nutritional strategies

Nutritional intake can have a profound effect on exercise performance; the intake of carbohydrate can have a particularly noticeable effect.

Carbohydrate

Carbohydrate is used by both the aerobic and anaerobic systems to synthesize ATP. This means that carbohydrate plays a key role in driving muscle contraction across a very wide spectrum of exercise intensities. This can range from short-duration high-intensity exercise lasting less than one minute to longer duration endurance-type efforts lasting several hours, such as marathon running.

Despite the importance of glycogen for muscular work, the amount of carbohydrate in the body is relatively small. There is around 400 grams in muscle, 100 grams in the liver and a few grams circulating in the blood. Because the energy density is relatively low (1760 kJ.100g^{-1} compared to 4000 kJ.100g^{-1} in fat) it represents a limited source of energy. In healthy, active people there is sufficient glycogen to allow between one and a half and two hours of continuous activity. However, exercise intensity can affect the way glycogen is used up.

During moderate intensity exercise most muscular work is due to the activation of slow twitch fibers. As intensity increases fast twitch fibers are recruited too. Since glycogen is only used for energy metabolism within the cells in which it is stored exercise intensity changes the pattern of glycogen use within a muscle. Figure 16.18 shows how glycogen is depleted in type I fibers but more muscle glycogen remains in fast twitch muscle fibers after a long period of moderate cycling. This is because the slower twitch fibers would have been activated.

Since glycolysis is a very fast metabolic pathway it has the potential to use up glycogen very quickly! All-out cycling exercise of just 30 seconds can substantially reduce glycogen stores.

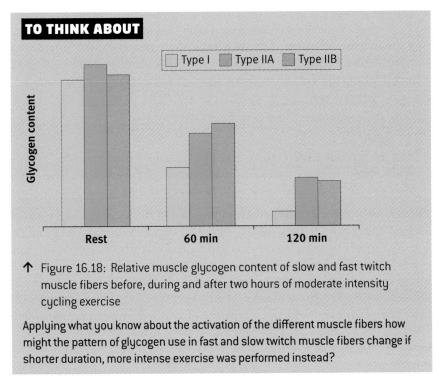

TO THINK ABOUT

☐ Type I ▨ Type IIA ▨ Type IIB

Glycogen content

Rest   60 min   120 min

↑ Figure 16.18: Relative muscle glycogen content of slow and fast twitch muscle fibers before, during and after two hours of moderate intensity cycling exercise

Applying what you know about the activation of the different muscle fibers how might the pattern of glycogen use in fast and slow twitch muscle fibers change if shorter duration, more intense exercise was performed instead?

Figure 16.19 shows the data from a classic exercise physiology study in 1966. Jonas Bergström (J.B.) and Eric Hultman (E.H.) sat on different sides of the same exercise bike, the first turning the left pedal with their right foot and resting the left, and their companion doing the opposite. Measures of muscle glycogen in each leg of both cyclists were made before and after one-legged cycling which they continued until they were exhausted. During recovery over the next three days the cyclists consumed a high carbohydrate diet.

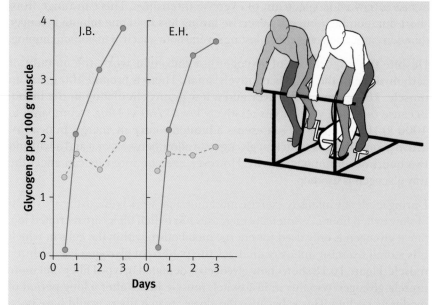

↑ Figure 16.19: Glycogen content of each leg of two cyclists (J.B. and E.H.) immediately after exhausting one-legged cycling and during three days of recovery (Bergström, Hultman 1966)

Endogenous originating internally
Exogenous originating externally

The study demonstrated several important concepts;

→ Muscle glycogen is utilized locally within the muscle in which it is stored.
→ Depletion of glycogen is connected with fatigue and exhaustion; when carbohydrate is limited, exercise is limited or prevented. The fatigue and drop in exercise capacity when carbohydrate runs out is sometimes referred to as "hitting the wall" by athletes who experience this.

In addition the study suggested that:

→ high carbohydrate intake during recovery can *restore* glycogen stores in 24 hours
→ rest and carbohydrate intake results in a "supercompensation" where additional glycogen is stored; in this example glycogen stores have more than doubled the initial levels seen in the rested legs.

The research of Bergström and Hultman started the idea that ingestion of carbohydrates can increase muscle glycogen stores. A similar effect can be achieved simply by reducing training and increasing carbohydrate intake; this avoids the need for hard exercise to empty the muscles of glycogen. This process is known by athletes as **carbohydrate loading** or **carbo loading**. Athletes do this because a larger glycogen store represents a greater energy store; this permits exercise to continue for longer before the glycogen store becomes depleted. This delaying of fatigue may be of particular value in long-duration endurance events or tournament-type situations where glycogen might run low.

If sports allow, it is possible to eat foods or drink fluids containing carbohydrate during exercise or between breaks in exercise. This is not replacing endogenous glycogen but it is providing an exogenous source of glucose in the blood which can be taken up by muscles and used as a substrate. Maintaining blood glucose helps reduce perceived level of effort and maintains concentration, both of which can benefit performance.

Types of carbohydrate

A plentiful supply of carbohydrate-containing foods is important in the lives of sportspeople. However not all carbohydrate-containing foods are equal! The physical structure of food and the chemical form of carbohydrate within it influence how efficiently carbohydrate is extracted and the rate and extent to which it increases the concentration of glucose in the blood after ingestion.

One approach to classifying foods is termed the *glycemic index* (GI). If a range of carbohydrate-containing foods are ingested, even if they contain the same amount of carbohydrate, the rate of its appearance in the blood can be very different (Figure 16.20).

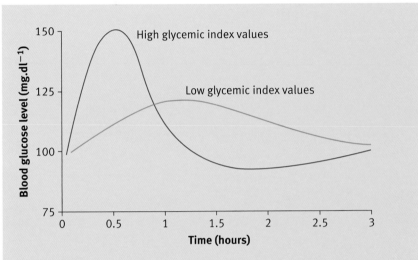

↑ Figure 16.20: The effect on blood glucose of foods with a high and low glycemic index

The glycemic index represents the ability of a food containing 50 grams of carbohydrate to raise blood glucose in comparison with a 50 grams reference dose of carbohydrate, usually given as glucose or white bread; these have a GI of 100. Sugary foods tend to have a high GI while high-fiber foods and those requiring greater physical and chemical digestion have lower values.

Foods	GI value
Jelly bean sweets	80
Kellogg's All Bran cereal	30
Kelloggs Corn flakes	72
White rice	50 to 70
Full fat cow's milk	30
Peanuts	14
Sports bar (Powerbar)	56
Carrots, raw	16
Carrots, boiled	30 to 50

Recovery from training

The same principles which allow carbohydrate loading can be applied to recovery after exercise. As athletes finish one training session they may already be thinking about the next one; this may be the following day or even later the same day. Therefore it is important to maintain high levels of muscle glycogen and replace quickly what has been used in training. It is the foods with a high GI value which provide the fastest, most efficient way of replacing glycogen.

TO DO

The web address given below links to a publication which contains an international table of GI values from foods from around the world: http://www.ajcn.org/content/76/1/5.full

→ Can you work out whether you had a low or high GI breakfast this morning?

→ Can you speculate whether a high or low GI breakfast is best for a morning of schoolwork?

KEY POINT

Carbohydrates are an important source of energy for athletes as they are used in different types of energy production. Athletes may choose to eat large amounts of carbohydrate-rich food before training or competition to increase glycogen stores. Likewise they may eat large amounts after training or competition to replace what has been used.

Protein

Unlike fat and carbohydrate there is no storage capacity for protein in the body. All protein is present with a specific biological function (e.g. as enzymes or structural proteins such as muscle). All protein in our bodies is in a state of flux, that is, molecules are constantly being broken down into their constituent amino acids and resynthesized (Figure 16.21).

The steady loss of amino acids from the body along with no storage means that a regular daily intake of protein is required to sustain biological function and health. The current level of intake recommended for healthy adults is 0.8 grams per kilogram of body mass per day ($0.8 \text{ g.kg}^{-1}.\text{d}^{-1}$).

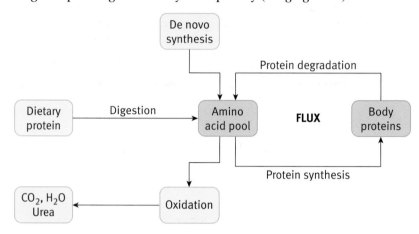

↑ Figure 16.21: Processes of protein and amino acid turnover

Influence of strength training and endurance training

The basic requirement for protein intake can increase in certain groups at certain times, such as in growing children, in people recovering from illness and in breastfeeding mothers. Also when people are engaged in exercise and training the requirements increase.

Table 16.4 shows how proteins are used in different groups of people.

POPULATION	AMINO ACID OXIDATION	MUSCLE REPAIR	MUSCLE HYPERTROPHY	DIETARY PROTEIN REQUIREMENT
Untrained people	✓	✓	✗	$0.8 \text{ g.kg}^{-1}.\text{d}^{-1}$
Endurance athletes	✓✓✓	✓✓	✓	$1.2 \text{ to } 1.4 \text{ g.kg}^{-1}.\text{d}^{-1}$
Strength athletes	✓	✓✓✓	✓✓✓	$1.2 \text{ to } 1.7 \text{ g.kg}^{-1}.\text{d}^{-1}$

↑ Table 16.4: Use of proteins in different groups of people

Meeting the requirements

Although protein degradation yields both essential and non-essential amino acids, net losses due to oxidation and metabolism means that dietary intake must include all amino acids.

Nutritional ergogenic aids

Sports drinks, bars and gels are products formulated around macronutrients and micronutrients. They are intended as a convenient means of ingesting fluid and/or macronutrients in an exercise setting when "normal" food may be impractical.

There are also numerous compounds and supplements that are not based on essential components of the diet which are marketed as commercial sports nutrition supplements. However there are few real "quick fixes" in sports nutrition and only a handful of these products are supported by good evidence (Table 16.5).

	MECHANISM OF ACTION	DOSAGE	BENEFITS	ADVERSE EFFECTS
Caffeine	CNS stimulant which can reduce the sensation of discomfort and effort during continuous exercise and increase force production during strength-type exercise.	2–6 mg per kg body mass before or during exercise. Sensitivity varies between individuals.	Increases exercise performance at a range of exercise intensities	Anxiety, insomnia, mild diuretic, weakly addictive
Creatine	Increases muscle creatine content, facilitates rapid PCr resynthesis in the rest periods during repeated high-intensity exercise. Creatine ingestion may also augment the effects of strength training by stimulating muscle anabolism.	15–20 g per day for 4–7 days followed by a maintenance dose of 2 g per day	Benefits exercise that relies on the PCr energy system such as strength, power and sprinting sports.	Increase in body mass may be detrimental for some.
Bicarbonate	Bicarbonate is a buffer which increases blood pH. This can increase tolerance to the H^+ generated by the lactic acid system during high intensity exercise.	0.3 g per kg taken before exercise	Increases performance during high-intensity exercise lasting 1–7 minutes	Bicarbonate can cause gastrointestinal upset.

↑ Table 16.5: Dietary supplements

Diet manipulation prior to competition

↑ These pictures show the different body shape of a long distance runner and a sprinter. Manipulation of the diet can be used to modify body weight and composition.

Nutritional manipulation of the diet can specifically be used to modify body weight and body composition. Some sports require smaller stature to compete in a lower weight class (e.g. boxing), to improve aesthetic appearance (e.g. gymnastics) or to increase physical performance (e.g. distance running). Athletes use various strategies to reach a low body weight. For rapid body weight loss, athletes cut down their fluid and total energy intake. Other athletes try to remove the perceived weight-gaining properties of body fat by following a diet high in carbohydrates (60–70 per cent of total energy intake) and low in fat (15–20 per cent of total energy intake). Both diets can have a harmful effect on health and can impair performance if done poorly and over a long period of time.

1 Why is it important for athletes to maintain a healthy diet and adjust their diet according to their energy expenditure and physiological requirements?

2 What are the reasons for diet manipulation prior to competition?

SUMMARY

→ Organs involved in digestion and absorption are the mouth, esophagus, stomach, liver, gall bladder, pancreas, small intestine and large intestine.

→ Specific enzymes in saliva, the small intestine and digestive juice produced in the stomach, liver, and pancreas are essential to break down carbohydrate, protein and fat molecules into smaller particles that can be absorbed.

→ Carbohydrates can only be absorbed into the bloodstream when broken down into simple sugars (glucose, fructose, galactose).

→ Protein molecules can only be absorbed into the bloodstream when they are broken down into peptides or amino acids.

→ Digestion and absorption of fat is a complex process because fat is not soluble in water, but has to be transferred through the watery environment of the digestive system, lymph and blood.

→ Fat is digested and absorbed through the processes of emulsification, micelle formation and repackaging into chylomicrons.

→ Fat molecules are digested into free fatty acids, monoglycerides, cholesterol, cholesterol esters and lysophospholipids which are transferred into the lymph stream before they enter the bloodstream.

→ Water is essential in humans; it is used for transport and thermoregulation, and acts as a lubricant.

→ The majority of human body mass consists of water (50–70%), the proportion is greater the less body fat we have.

→ In healthy humans water intake (from food and drink) is usually similar to water loss (from sweat and urine) this results in maintenance of a stable body mass

→ Turnover of around 2.5 liters of water per day typically occurs in healthy humans.

→ Water intake is controlled by thirst and water loss is controlled by the kidneys.

→ Severe dehydration can lead to death, dehydration of more than two percent body mass can reduce the exercise capacity of athletes.

→ Athletes may turn over substantially more than 2.5L per day due to increased sweat losses arising from exercise and training particularly if this occurs in a hot environment.

→ Energy intake describes the acquisition of chemical energy via ingestion of foods; carbohydrate 1760 kJ.100g^{-1}, protein 1720 kJ.100g^{-1} and fat 4000 kJ.100g^{-1}.

→ Energy expenditure describes use of chemical energy to perform metabolic work both at rest and during exercise.

→ Energy balance refers to the relationship between energy intake and expenditure; a positive energy balance leads to increased body mass and a negative energy balance leads to loss of body mass.

→ Body composition refers to the relative amounts of different tissues within the body.

→ A simple model of body composition divides the body into two compartments comprised of fat mass (all extractable lipids) and fat free mass (all remaining tissues).

→ The ideal proportion of FM to FFM among athletes varies from sport to sport.

→ Carbohydrate is used for energy across a wide range of exercise intensities.

→ A limited amount of carbohydrate is stored as glycogen in the liver and muscle.

→ Glycogen is used up during exercise; when it runs out exercise is limited or prevented – fatigue occurs.

→ Athletes may consume carbohydrates before exercise to increase glycogen stores (carbo loading), *during* exercise to provide additional carbohydrate, to spare their muscle glycogen, and *after* exercise to promote recovery of glycogen stores.

- → Glycemic index (GI) provides a measure of how accessible the carbohydrate content of different foods is; CHO foods with a higher GI are better for rapid post-exercise recovery.
- → Proteins in the body are only present with a specific biological function – there is no store of protein unlike fat and carbohydrate.
- → Constant turnover of body protein means that humans have a daily requirement of around 0.8 g. per kg body mass per day and this must include essential amino acids.
- → The daily requirement for protein is increased in athletes because they oxidize amino acids for energy, and muscle repair and hypertrophy.
- → Athletes may supplement their diet with nutritional ergogenic aids to increase exercise performance and tolerance.

Self-study questions

1 Define the main processes involved in digestion.

2 List the products of digestion of the macronutrients.

3 State the difference between fat mass and fat-free mass.

4 Describe the hormonal mechanism which helps maintain body water balance.

5 Distinguish between the effects of a positive and negative energy balance.

6 Outline the nutritional needs of a sprinter and a marathon runner.

7 Suggest why sports drinks are a popular nutritional intervention for athletes.

8 Explain why protein intake needs to be both regular and consist of high quality protein.

9 Discuss the ways in which poor nutrition might impair athletic performance.

DATA BASED QUESTION

A study (randomised, cross-over design; two separate days) compared the effectiveness of either a low-fat chocolate milk or a carbohydrate-electrolyte beverage (Gatorade sports drink) on recovery between morning and afternoon training sessions. The beverage (240 ml) was consumed immediately after the morning training session. The table below shows the composition of the two beverages.

Nutrient	Low fat chocolate milk	Gatorade
Energy (kJ)	669	209
Protein (g)	8	0
Fat (g)	3	0
Carbohydrate (g)	27	14
Calcium (mg)	300	0
Sodium (mg)	240	110

*The data are from www.tuscandairy.com and www.gatorade.com.

Immediately following the afternoon training session the subjects then completed a 20 m shuttle test to fatigue. The mean (±SD) time to fatigue for both trials is shown below.

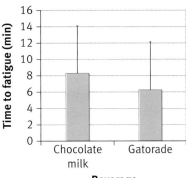

(Source: Spaccarotella, K.J., Andzel, W.D. 2011. "The effects of low fat chocolate milk on postexercise recovery in collegiate athletes." *J of Strength & Con Res,* Vol 25, number 4. Pp 3456–3460)

1 State which beverage contained the most protein.
(1 mark)

2 Identify from the graph which beverage consumption resulted in the best performance (1 mark)

3 Using the data in the table give a nutritional explanation for the difference in performance shown in the graph.
(1 marks)

4 What might athletes and coaches learn from these results? (4 marks)

CHAPTER 17

Internal assessment and practical work

Introduction

The internal assessment (IA) for the IB Diploma Programme course in sports, exercise and health science (SEHS) includes 40 hours of hands-on work in the laboratory and/or out in the field. The practical work is a chance for you to gain and develop new skills and techniques beyond your theory lessons. You should find this stimulating and challenging! This time includes 10 hours for the group 4 project, an interdisciplinary activity that all Diploma Programme science students must take part in.

Your performance is internally assessed by your teacher and externally moderated by the IB. Your work is marked against the five IA assessment criteria, with each criterion having a maximum mark of 6. The marks for each of the criteria are added together with the first three criteria each being assessed twice to determine the final mark out of 48 and this is then scaled to give a total out of 24 per cent. This is the contribution the practical work makes to your final mark for the course.

You will need to maintain a portfolio of your assessed written work for possible external moderation. External moderation aims to ensure that the practical component of the course has been carried out and that the standard of marking is standardized across all schools in the world doing the course.

When carrying out your IA work keep calm and remember that you are not penalized for seeking guidance; we encourage you to initiate discussions with your teacher to obtain advice and information. However, if you could not complete this work without substantial support, you will not be able to gain full marks. As part of the learning process, you will also be pleased to know that your teacher can provide you with feedback on your first draft of any internally assessed work.

Aims of SEHS practical work

The practical work has several aims.

→ It provides you with experience of methods and techniques used in sports, exercise and health investigations.
→ It develops your ability to analyse, evaluate and synthesize scientific information.
→ It strengthens your experimental and investigative scientific skills.
→ It engenders your awareness of the need for, and the value of, effective collaboration and communication during scientific activities, which is one of the main aims of the group 4 project.
→ It develops information and communication technology skills for the study of sports, exercise and health science.

How you will be assessed for each of these is described in Table 17.1 with the actual criteria appearing at the end of the chapter.

Design (D)

Aspect 1: defining the problem and selecting variables

Aspect 1: Formulate a focused problem/research question and identify the relevant variables.

Your teacher will give you an open-ended problem to investigate and you must generate your own focused problem or specific research question. Make sure you choose an area you are interested in. Consider exploring an issue that you genuinely wonder about.

Examples of teacher prompts and specific research questions relating to them appear in Table 17.1 below.

TOPIC	TEACHER PROMPT
Starting strategies	Investigate starting strategies to optimize acceleration in sprinting.
Sensory deprivation	Investigate the effects of sensory deprivation on performance.
Practice	Does practice make perfect?
Feedback	Investigate the effect of feedback on performance.
Physical performance	Investigate environmental factors on physical performance.
Fitness	Design an investigation on variations in the fitness levels of individuals.
Muscle fatigue	Investigate factor(s) that affect fatigue during isotonic and/or isometric contractions in specific muscle groups.
Ventilatory response	Design an investigation to characterize the cardiovascular response to various stimuli.
Joint movement	Investigate factors affecting the range of movement of joints.
Nutrient intake	Design an investigation that allows a comparison and evaluation of nutrient intake in different individuals.
Center of mass	Investigate how the position of the center of mass can affect athletic performance.
Trajectories	Investigate the trajectory characteristics of thrown objects.
Body responses	Investigate factors affecting heart rate, blood pressure, breathing rate, CO_2 production, skin temperature or rate of sweat production.
Assessment of physical activity	Using one or more methods, design an investigation to assess habitual physical activity in different groups.
Diet	Investigate the personal and/or social factors that influence dietary preferences.
Body composition	Using different methods, design an investigation to assess body composition.
Reaction time	Investigate reaction time as a component of the psychological refractory period.

↑ Table 17.1

First of all you need to decide which of the following types of investigation you are going to do.

→ Manipulate one independent variable to see the effect this has on another, the dependent variable, and examine the relationship between cause and effect.

→ Simply measure rather than manipulate variables, and look for relationships between them. Correlation research measures the degree of relationship between pairs of independent variables in a sample and because no independent variable is manipulated, no cause–effect relationship can be determined.

You can begin by modifying the general aim and indicating the variable(s) chosen for investigation. A clear, focused research question must state the dependent (measured) and the independent (changed) variables. The variables stated in the research question must be those that are directly measured. It is also good practice to include measurements in the research question, e.g. beats per minute (bpm), and this information must be included when you state your dependent variable.

Also, to ensure you gain a full range of data, you should use a minimum of *two to three* different values for the independent variable. Obviously, this will vary depending upon the time you have available for your investigation and the complexity of the task; for example, if your independent variable is temperature, you could collect data at 15°C, 20°C, 25°C and 30°C.

In addition, list all the *relevant controlled* variables (or monitored variables, if carrying out field work) along with the *confounding* variables. It is vital that your investigation is well controlled, and that the only thing that changes is the independent variable. Relevant variables are those that can reasonably be expected to affect the outcome and the number will vary from one investigation to another. Do not be afraid to say that there are variables that cannot be controlled but that you need to monitor (confounding variables) as they may influence your results.

Stating a hypothesis is no longer necessary; however, it is good practice and it will help you focus your investigation and provide a starting point for your conclusion. Your research hypothesis will predict the relationship between the independent variable and the dependent variable, in short, what you predict will happen.

Aspect 2: controlling variables

You must give clear descriptions of how you will control variables to ensure that only the independent variable changes. You could set this out as a table and also state why it is important to control the variable.

VARIABLE	HOW IS IT CONTROLLED?	WHY?
Skill level	All participants will have played competitive tennis for at least 5 years.	All players will be skilled experienced players and they should be in the associative phase of learning, as their performance will be more consistent and reliable.
Sample: Age, sex, number	20 females selected from a pool of 50 experienced players.	Results can be generalized and trends can be found for this sample if they are randomly selected.
Type of serve	Kick serve.	Results can be more reliable if all the participants are using the same type of serve.
Time of day	The experiment will take place between 3.00 – 4.00pm.	All participants will have relatively the same outside air temperatures and humidity levels.
Rest period between trials	A rest period of 10 minutes will be given after 10 serves, during which time participants will be allowed to drink water if desired.	All participants have a standard recovery time.
Feedback	No feedback from the test conductor or observers.	This ensures consistency and no external factors will affect the results.

↑ Table 17.2

Participants in your investigation must be described with justification for your sampling method (random, opportunity, self-selected). It may be enough to say that opportunity sampling was the easiest option and you chose whoever happened to be there at the time and was willing to participate.

Write a clear numbered method that will allow someone who does not know what you are doing to follow your experiment—imagine it is a recipe. A diagram along with a list of the apparatus is also helpful. You must quantify experimental details such as timings, concentrations, exercise intensity or duration and ensure that these variables are monitored and controlled. For example, ensure that all participants recover in the same supine position after exercise and in the same room with controlled environmental conditions. You must ensure that the time taken from completing the exercise to adopting the supine position and the first measurement being taken is constant, along with the frequency of measurements.

Remember to document how ethical guidelines were followed and explain how the briefing and debriefing were carried out. A copy of the consent form should be included in the appendices. Sometimes you may not want to let your participants know the exact aim of the study as it may affect your results. If this does not cause stress to the participant it is fine to inform participants at the end of the study.

If you use a test or standard measurement technique as part of your investigation, it should be referenced using a recognized citation style. For example, while planning an investigation to study the effect of habitual dietary intake on body composition you can select a method to measure body composition. This method may be found by referring to a primary source, a textbook, a website or teacher's notes.

Aspect 3: developing a method for collection of data

The investigation must allow you to generate sufficient numerical data for you to be able to demonstrate an analysis. A lack of data means that specific averages cannot always be processed (required for DCP aspect 2). It is ideal to have three to five repeats for each variable (e.g. temperature). In the heart rate experiment you would need to decide on the length of time the heart rate is recorded for and the frequency of taking measurements. A minimum of five subjects is also needed to undertake further statistical analysis such as standard deviation.

> Aspect 3: Develop a method that allows for the collection of sufficient relevant data.

Data collection and processing (DCP)

Aspect 1: recording raw data

The numerical raw data you collected (not averages) must enable you to answer the research question and enable you to carry out basic processing along with statistical analysis. This raw quantitative data should be recorded with a standardized predetermined degree of precision, e.g. to within one decimal place such as 5.5 cm, 8.5 cm etc. Appropriate raw quantitative data could consist of the heart rate readings and the time elapsed after finishing exercise. In addition the heart rate of the participant before taking exercise and the temperature of the room could be recorded.

> Aspect 1: Record appropriate quantitative and associated qualitative raw data, including units and uncertainties where relevant.

You are encouraged to make additional observations about your experiment as they may help you interpret or evaluate your results. Such data is often qualitative and it can be challenging to analyse, for example, the characteristics of the participant (age, gender, athletic history) or resting position/posture.

When a "design" has been set by the teacher, it may be that data gathered as a class has to be used in order for you to have sufficient data to carry out significant processing and the determination of uncertainties. If class data is to be used and DCP is to be assessed you must clearly present your own data. This can be achieved by either presenting your own data first or by clearly identifying your own data in a pooled data table. You must plan and produce your own data table; copying a table from other students will be counted as collusion.

Degrees of precision

All measured values have an associated uncertainty, therefore, all headings/ columns in data tables are required to have an accompanying uncertainty figure (+/− figure). The error is usually +/− one half of the smallest unit that can be measured. You may want to include human systematic error (e.g. when using a stopwatch) rather than mechanical error, for example, (+/− 0.5 seconds) would be appropriate for a stopwatch.

Examples of other appropriate degrees of precision appear in Table 17.3 below.

Weight (kg)	+/− 0.5kg
Height (cm)	+/− 0.5cm
Nomogram	+/− 2 kg.m.sec^{-1}
Heart rate monitor	+/− 6 beats min^{-1}
Stop watch (sec)	+/− 0.5 sec (e.g. 17.6 sec)

↑ Table 17.3

Tips for data collection and using tables
→ Table titles should be descriptive and include both the independent (changed) variable and the dependent variable (measured) and may start with the words: "Table showing the effect of…"
→ Try to fit all your data into a single table. Sketch the table beforehand, and try different ways of presenting the information if the first one does not work out.
→ Ensure the table headers are descriptive, for example, "Temperature of room 1" is much better than just "Temperature".
→ Every header requires appropriate units along with the error margin.
→ The number of decimal places must reflect the precision of the measuring instrument, for example, a thermometer can give one decimal place precision at best. You could read to the nearest 0.5°C only so don't plan to collect data to two decimal places..
→ All decimal places in a column must be consistent. For example, if you have a reading of 4 seconds and another one of 5.8, you must decide whether you will round up to whole numbers (in which case the values would be 4 and 6) or whether to have all values at one decimal place (4.0 and 5.8 respectively).
→ In your data table, repeats should be called "Trial 1", "Trial 2" etc.

Aspect 2: Process the quantitative raw data correctly.

Aspect 2: processing raw data

Data processing involves combining and manipulating raw data and transforming numbers into a form suitable for presentation, be it graphical, written or verbal. Within the heart rate investigation, data on the time taken to return to a normal heart rate could be recorded in a table or by graphical means such as a bar chart.

Your processed data can be presented separately or attached to the raw data table if it is clearly distinguishable. You must make sure your processed data is to the same level of precision as the raw data, i.e. to the same decimal places.

There are numerous ways of processing your data. Common ways include:
→ adding, subtracting
→ squaring, dividing
→ mean, mode, median range
→ percentage of the whole
→ percentage increase
→ rate
→ standard deviation
→ statistical tests.

Identify any anomalous results (if any) in your raw data by highlighting them in the tables or on the graph. If a reading is very different from your other data, you may leave it out of the processing and analysing stage. If you omit them, you must justify your decision.

Aspect 3: presenting processed data

Graph it! You are expected to decide upon a suitable presentation format for your *processed* data. Remember that when you present your data it is the processed data that should (usually) be graphed, not every individual trial.

Some tips for preparing your graph(s) include the following.

→ Title your graph in the same way as your data tables.

→ Graphs need to have appropriate scales, labelled axes with units and accurately plotted data points with a suitable best-fit line or curve.

→ The appropriate measurement must be on the relevant axis and it is good practice to include the error of measurement, e.g. time in seconds (+ 0.5 sec).

→ Where there is only one dependent variable it always goes on the y-axis, with the independent variable on the x-axis. If there are two independent variables they go along the x-axis, with the dependent variable on the y-axis. This is not always the case as there may not be an independent variable.

→ Use of data-logging software is appropriate if you decide on and input most of the relevant software settings (for labels, axes, units and graph title etc.) Reference any software used.

→ Error bars when used must be accompanied by an explanation of what these values mean. Remember that error bars show the spread of values around the mean and the more the data ranges from the mean, the less confident you can be that your data is statistically significant. For normally distributed data, about 68% of all values lie within ±1 standard deviation of (above or below) the mean and this rises to about 95% for ±2 standard deviations.

Aspect 3: Present processed data appropriately and, where relevant, include errors and uncertainties.

There are numerous ways of presenting your data. Common ways include:
→ scatter plots
→ bar charts
→ pie charts
→ histogram
→ kite diagrams
→ spreadsheet
→ tables
→ charts
→ flow diagrams.

Conclusion and evaluation

Aspect 1: concluding

A common mistake here is that students *describe* their results without *explaining* them. You must include data from your results to back up your findings and refer to the appropriate statistical test to discuss the significance of the data.

Here is an example of a good format to follow.

→ **Discuss** the trends in your data. You must refer to your graphs by name (which is easy to do if you numbered them "Graph 1", "Graph 2" etc.) and state what trends or patterns can be seen, *if any*. Do not imagine patterns if there are none!

→ **Compare** these to what you expected if measuring an already known or accepted value, *based on background research and the findings of others*. You are supposed to know something about the topic, so now is the time to bring in external information, usually from textbooks or peer-reviewed journals.

→ **Explain** your data by comparing with the literature value. Remember that literature must always be fully referenced. You should take care not to say that your results *prove* an explanation; the most you can say about empirical evidence is that it *supports* an explanation.

If your results are unexpected or show no pattern, discuss this. It is also fine to say your data is inconclusive, but attempt to suggest why this may be. Negative results that show no correlation when you had hoped to find one are very acceptable. Don't bend your data to fit what you think should happen; rather draw a conclusion as to your confidence in your results.

Another way to discuss findings is to consider whether the research was valid and the measurement was reliable.

Aspect 1: State a conclusion, with justification, based on a reasonable interpretation of the data.

Reliability is the extent to which the same reading is obtained each time a variable is measured.

Validity is the extent to which the measure actually measures what it claims to.

Aspect 2: Evaluate weaknesses and limitations.

Aspect 3: Suggest realistic improvements in respect of identified weaknesses and limitations.

When evaluating procedures you must comment on:
→ design
→ performance of procedure
→ method
→ equipment
→ precision and accuracy of measurement
→ quality and reliability of data
→ management of time.

Aspect 2: evaluating procedure(s) and aspect 3: improving the investigation

The evaluation is the final (and very important) part of the IA, so make sure you continue to follow the assessment criteria. Your evaluation could be presented as a table with three columns:

→ weaknesses
→ significance of weakness
→ suggested improvement.

The inclusion of a separate column for the significance of the weakness helps draw your attention to its significance in addition to solely identifying weaknesses. You should describe at least three major shortcomings, and more if you think there were more. For every weakness suggest a sensible improvement. Try not to include minor mistakes. The strongest evaluations will not rely on a simplistic evaluation, such as "the experimental study should have used a larger sample" or that more precise equipment should have been used.

WEAKNESSES	SIGNIFICANCE OF WEAKNESS	SUGGESTED IMPROVEMENT
The nomograms used to measure leg power may not have been an accurate representation as the scale was inconsistent in spacing values. Thus forcing the researchers to interpret the data, as investigators were required to estimate the distance, weight and leg power.	The significance of this error is very high, as the forced interpretation of data would lead to subjectivity, which makes the data, and conclusion, less reliable.	To improve the accuracy of the nomogram and reduce bias, an electron nomogram could be used or one with equal calibrations.
The use of thigh circumference as a measurement of leg muscle is subjective as a high value may be due to fat instead of muscle. Some participants also have longer bones, and thus a measurement of the circumference 10 cm above the knee may not be where the circumference is the largest.	This is quite a significant source of error as the investigation and leg power relies on leg muscle and not fat, and thus delimits our findings.	Instead of using thigh circumference in comparison to leg power, weight could be used. Measuring the thigh circumference halfway up the participant's thigh could eliminate the problem of varying bone lengths.

↑ Table 17.4

If you designed your own experiment, there are probably many areas that could be improved. In this section, you *may* be able to explain anomalous results, due to methodological difficulties.

Difficulties arising during the project

As you carry out your investigation, note down problems as you encounter them. Before you write your evaluation, list all the problems you came across and consider ways in which you could eliminate them if you were to carry out the investigation again. Now prioritize them. Make sure you can see the difference between a methodological shortcoming and a mistake.

Essentially, you are looking to ensure you have carried out a fair test, that is, the only variable you have changed is the independent variable. If any other variable inadvertently changed, it may affect your results, thereby making your conclusions less reliable.

For example, it is *not* a methodological error to "misread non-digital scales" but it *is* an error if you fail to use the same scales for all your measurements as other scales may be calibrated differently.

Ethics

The International Baccalaureate Organization has published a document called *Animal experimentation policy*, along with an *Ethical practice poster*; the advice given on these should be applied to all internal assessment work. When designing a study you must ensure that it is conducted in a way that represents the dignity of the participants, whether they are animals or human participants.

Ethical guidelines for IA include the following.

→ Laboratory or field experiments and investigations will be undertaken in an ethical way.
→ No experiments involving other people will be undertaken without their written consent and their understanding of the nature of the experiment.
→ Experiments involving body fluids must not be performed due to the risk of the transmission of blood-borne pathogens.
→ Experiments involving animals must be based on observing and measuring aspects of natural animal behaviour.
→ No experiment will be undertaken that inflicts pain on a human or live animal, or compromise its health in any way.
→ No experiment or fieldwork will be undertaken that damages the environment.
→ All presentations will respect the personal, political and spiritual values of others and there will be no intention to offend in remarks about race, gender or religious beliefs.

In addition to covering ethical issues in your method, another suggestion is to include in your conclusion how you addressed ethical issues within your IA. It is not a trivial matter. Sports and exercise scientists, indeed all scientists, must be able to demonstrate adherence to ethical principles and protocols.

Tips for submitting IA work

Here are some additional points to consider when submitting work for IA.

→ **Title page** The title page provides key information about you and your IA and should include your name, candidate number, the date and research question/problem.
→ **Introduction** The introduction can include literature sources and provide valuable background information to your IA along with your inspiration for this line of inquiry.
→ **References** In this section include a complete set of references to all the works cited in the study. An approved reference format should be used.
→ **Citation** The work of others, including information taken from different sources, should always be acknowledged and referenced using a recognized citation style.
→ **Appendices** In this section, include copies of any additional information, as well as materials used, such as standardized instructions, debriefing notes and informed consent letters. This section provides all the necessary materials so your research can be replicated. Each appendix should be numbered and have an appropriate title, for example, "Appendix 1: Nomogram to measure leg power."

The organization of the group 4 project will vary from school to school. You may be placed in a team consisting of students studying different group 4 subjects and asked to produce one project in response to an overarching theme, for example, "survival". In schools with larger numbers of students there may be several groups and each group may investigate a different theme.

Remember, you need to keep in mind aims 7, 8 and 10 as you develop your project.

Types of project

The project can be undertaken in a variety of ways as it may have a hands-on practical action phase or one involving purely theoretical aspects.

→ Designing and carrying out a laboratory investigation or fieldwork.

→ Carrying out a comparative study (experimental or otherwise) in collaboration with another school.

→ Collating, manipulating and analysing data from other sources, such as scientific journals, environmental organizations, science and technology industries and government reports.

→ Designing and using a model or simulation.

→ Contributing to a long-term project organized by the school.

Manipulative skills

Manipulative skills are assessed throughout the course and the assessment should be based on a wide range of manipulative skills. This is worth a total of 6 marks out of 48 for your internal assessment. It is your ability to follow instructions, carry out techniques and work safely which are assessed.

The group 4 project (10 hours)

The group 4 project is a collaborative activity where students from different group 4 subjects or schools work together to investigate a scientific or technological topic. The project you select should address aims 7, 8 and 10 of the group 4 subject guides.

→ Aim 7 requires you to develop and apply information and communication technology skills in the study of science.

→ Aim 8 relates to raising awareness of the moral, ethical, social, economic and environmental implications of using science and technology.

→ Aim 10 demands that you develop an understanding of the relationships between scientific disciplines and the overarching nature of the scientific method.

The emphasis is on interdisciplinary cooperation and the *processes* involved in scientific investigation, rather than the *products* of such investigation.

Personal skills

This assessment criterion only relates to the group 4 project. See details later in this chapter.

You will be assessed against the personal skills criterion in this project. This is worth a total of 6 marks out of 48 for your IB internal assessment. It is your involvement, your ability to work in a team and self-reflection that are assessed. After the project is completed you may be given a self-evaluation form to complete.

There are three parts to the group 4 project: planning, action and evaluation. Below is one approach to the group 4 project provided by Elaine Teale, Head of Science at UWCSEA (Dover), Singapore (2011).

Planning

The first planning meeting

Elect a chair and secretary in your project team. The chair should run the meeting and make sure that everyone gets a chance to express their views. The secretary should ensure that they have email addresses for every student in the team.

Throughout the planning and action phases, students will be documenting their project by collecting materials such as text, pictures, graphs and video relating to their work. You could store this information on a group blog. Make sure all members of the group know how to post information and then tag the information with labels that describe the aspects of the science project.

The blog could be used in two ways:

→ as a resource for the supervising teacher(s) to see how your group is working
→ as a collection of resources.

All members of the team should regularly contribute to the blog. Think of it as an online diary where you are recording what you have achieved and reflecting on your successes and failures. The emphasis should be on the cooperation between the team members and the processes involved in the investigation rather than the product. Your teacher may use it to help them make a final assessment of your personal skills and you will need it in order to put together your final presentation.

Discuss as a group a way to develop a project which can be completed in the time allowed. Topics are often broad, so there will be many interpretations. Remember you must follow the scientific method, as your project must be based on science or its applications.

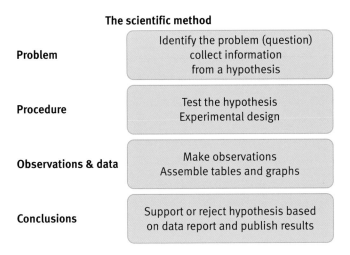

↑ Figure 17.1: The scientific method

The second planning meeting

At this meeting refine the question and design the investigation. If you have already done this in the first planning meeting, then you might want to start the action phase. Equipment orders must be submitted to your teacher and you must carry out a risk assessment to ensure that what you are planning is safe for participants and those observing them.

Action phase

During the action phase you are testing your hypothesis experimentally, collecting and analysing data and preparing your presentation. All members of the team should be engaged.

Keep the experiment simple. Keep aims 7, 8 and 10 in mind and think about the time you have available.

Remember to keep contributing to the blog.

Evaluation

In this phase of the project students share their findings with other students.

Presentation

If you are asked to put together a presentation you could use programs such as keynote, PowerPoint, or prezi, or you might want to make a video. In your presentation you could share your findings, along with both your successes and failures. Keep the aims in mind and also the collaborative effort of your team.

Assessment criteria

Below you will find the criteria that you will be assessed against.

Design

LEVELS/MARKS	ASPECT 1	ASPECT 2	ASPECT 3
	DEFINING THE PROBLEM AND SELECTING VARIABLES	CONTROLLING VARIABLES	DEVELOPING A METHOD FOR COLLECTION OF DATA
Complete/2	Formulates a focused problem/research question and identifies the relevant variables.	Designs a method for the effective control of the variables.	Develops a method that allows for the collection of sufficient relevant data.
Partial/1	Formulates a problem/research question that is incomplete or identifies only some relevant variables.	Designs a method that makes some attempt to control the variables.	Develops a method that allows for the collection of insufficient relevant data.
Not at all/0	Does not identify a problem/research question and does not identify any relevant variables.	Designs a method that does not control the variables.	Develops a method that does not allow for any relevant data to be collected.

Data collection and processing

LEVELS/MARKS	ASPECT 1	ASPECT 2	ASPECT 3
	RECORDING RAW DATA	PROCESSING RAW DATA	PRESENTING PROCESSED DATA
Complete/2	Records appropriate quantitative and associated qualitative raw data, including units and uncertainties where relevant.	Processes the quantitative raw data correctly.	Presents processed data appropriately and, where relevant, includes errors and uncertainties.
Partial/1	Records appropriate quantitative and associated qualitative raw data, but with some mistakes or omissions.	Processes quantitative raw data, but with some mistakes and/or omissions.	Presents processed data appropriately, but with some mistakes and/or omissions.
Not at all/0	Does not record any appropriate quantitative raw data or raw data is incomprehensible.	No processing of quantitative raw data is carried out or major mistakes are made in processing.	Presents processed data inappropriately or incomprehensibly.

Conclusion and evaluation

LEVELS/MARKS	ASPECT 1	ASPECT 2	ASPECT 3
	CONCLUDING	EVALUATING PROCEDURE(S)	IMPROVING THE INVESTIGATION
Complete/2	States a conclusion, with justification, based on a reasonable interpretation of the data.	Evaluates weaknesses and limitations.	Suggests realistic improvements in respect of identified weaknesses and limitations.

| Partial/1 | States a conclusion based on a reasonable interpretation of the data. | Identifies some weaknesses and limitations, but the evaluation is weak or missing. | Suggests only superficial improvements. |
| Not at all/0 | States no conclusion or the conclusion is based on an unreasonable interpretation of the data. | Identifies irrelevant weaknesses and limitations. | Suggests unrealistic improvements. |

Manipulative skills criteria

LEVELS/MARKS	ASPECT 1	ASPECT 2	ASPECT 3
	FOLLOWING INSTRUCTIONS	CARRYING OUT TECHNIQUES	WORKING SAFELY
Complete/2	Follows instructions accurately, adapting to new circumstances (seeking assistance when required).	Competent and methodical in the use of a range of techniques and equipment.	Pays attention to safety issues.
Partial/1	Follows instructions but requires assistance.	Usually competent and methodical in the use of a range of techniques and equipment.	Usually pays attention to safety issues.
Not at all/0	Rarely follows instructions or requires constant supervision.	Rarely competent and methodical in the use of a range of techniques and equipment.	Rarely pays attention to safety issues.

Personal skills criteria

	ASPECT 1	ASPECT 2	ASPECT 3
LEVELS/MARKS	SELF-MOTIVATION AND PERSEVERANCE	WORKING WITHIN A TEAM	SELF-REFLECTION
Complete/2	Approaches the project with self-motivation and follows it through to completion.	Collaborates and communicates in a group situation and integrates the views of others.	Shows a thorough awareness of their own strengths and weaknesses and gives thoughtful consideration to their learning experience.
Partial/1	Completes the project but sometimes lacks self-motivation.	Exchanges some views but requires guidance to collaborate with others.	Shows limited awareness of their own strengths and weaknesses and gives some consideration to their learning experience.
Not at all/0	Lacks perseverance and motivation.	Makes little or no attempt to collaborate in a group situation.	Shows no awareness of their own strengths and weaknesses and gives no consideration to their learning experience.

CHAPTER 18

Preparing for your exams

As you will be aware a significant amount of your overall grade for this course will come from your results in the external examination.

→ Marks from internal assessment   = 24%
→ Marks from external assessment (examination) = 76%

The examination is made up of 3 different papers:

Paper 1: (45 minutes) 30 multiple-choice questions on the core topics only.

Paper 2: (1 hour 15 minutes) Made up of short and long answer questions from the core topics only. It has two sections; In Section A all questions are compulsory, and in Section B you choose one question to answer from a selection of three.

Paper 3: (1 hour) Made up of short and long answer questions on the option topics only. You answer all questions on the options that you have studied in class.

These three separate papers are completed over two days. Papers 1 and 2 are completed on one day, and Paper 3 the day after.

An examiner is not able to cover all aspects of the course in only three hours of examination, so you need to be prepared to handle all aspects of the curriculum. This means that you need to put in significant time and effort in order to ensure that you know and understand the many different topics in the course. A simple plan such as the one on page 352 can be used to help in the organisation of your examination preparation.

Much of the information that we study is linked in some way, for example your knowledge of anatomy (Topic 1) will support your understanding in movement analysis (Topic 4); your knowledge of exercise physiology will support your understanding in aspects of Topic 6 as well as the option topics. With this in mind it could benefit you to approach your study by working through the core topics first, then revising the options you have learnt.

The resources you should be using to help you with your study are:

→ the curriculum guide: this has detailed information about each topic and teacher notes for each assessment statement, as well as the command terms that will be used to create the questions in papers 2 and 3
→ your textbook and any other study resource booklets
→ the Internet: it allows you to view aspects of the muscle very easily - for example, the "sliding filament theory" - search for it and look for the moving version.

A quick word about the curriculum guide

If we look at a part of the curriculum guide on the following page, it can tell you a lot of information that can help your study. You will know that each topic has subtopics, as indicated. Within this there are assessment statements which tell you what you will be expected to be able to do for the examination. As an example, in the examination you may be asked to:

Label a diagram of a motor unit.

In most cases the teacher's notes can help you by providing possible answers, or the scope of the expected answer. In this case the possible parts that you would be asked or expected to label are: limit to dendrite, cell body, axon, motor end plate, synapse and muscle.

What is also useful to realise is that the objective aspect is included. The objective refers to the type of command term (Table 2) that may be used to create the question you will be asked. The command terms are also available in the glossary of the curriculum handbook. The assessment statement above has an objective statement of 1. This means that it will only be asked at this level of difficulty. If the objective indicated is a level 2 or 3 then the question could come from that level or the one below; never from one above. For example, **Distinguish** anatomically between the axial and appendicular skeleton; **Distinguish** can be changed to any other suitable objective 2, or a suitable objective 1 command term such as **identify, annotate, state, list, label, define.**

Topic 4: Movement analysis (15 hours) ← Topic or option

4.1 Neuromuscular function ← Sub-topic

4 hours

	Assessment statement	Obj	Teacher's notes	
4.1.1	Label a diagram of a motor unit.	1	Limit to dendrite, cell body, nucleus, axon, motor end plate, synapse and muscle.	Assessment statement
4.1.2	Explain the role of neurotransmitters in stimulating skeletal muscle contraction.	3	Limit to acetylcholine and cholinesterase.	
4.1.3	Explain how skeletal muscle contracts by the sliding filament theory.	3	Include the terms myofibril, myofilament, sarcomere, actin and myosin, H zone, A band, Z line, tropomyosin, troponin, sarcoplasmic reticulum, calcium ions and ATP. **Aim 7:** Various online muscle contraction simulations are available.	Teacher's notes
4.1.4	Explain how slow and fast twitch fibre types differ in structure and function.	3	Limit fibre types to slow twitch (type I) and fast twitch (type IIa and IIb). Type IIa and IIb are high in glycogen content depending on training status. **Aim 8:** Implications of invasive techniques for taking samples, i.e. muscle biopsies. **Aim 9:** Implications of drawing conclusions from indirect measurements.	Objective

Your ability to understand what the command terms mean is very important, so that you are then able to answer the question in the way that has been asked. Spend time becoming familiar with these command terms as well as the assessed curriculum information.

Table 2: Command Terms

OBJECTIVE 1	
Define	Give the precise meaning of a word, phrase, concept or physical quantity
Draw	Represent by means of a labelled, accurate diagram or graph, using a pencil. A ruler (straight edge) should be used for straight lines
Label	Add labels to a diagram
List	Give a sequence of brief answers with no explanation

Measure	Obtain a value for a quantity
State	Give a specific name, value or other brief answer without explanation or calculation

OBJECTIVE 2	
Annotate	Add brief notes to a diagram or graph
Apply	Use an idea, equation, principle, theory or law in relation to a given problem or issue
Calculate	Obtain a numerical answer showing the relevant stages in the working
Describe	Give a detailed account
Distinguish	Make clear the differences between two or more concepts or items
Estimate	Find an approximate value
Identify	Provide an answer from a given number of possibilities
Outline	Give a brief account or summary

OBJECTIVE 3	
Analyse	Break down in order to bring out the essential elements or structure
Comment	Give a judgement based on a given statement or result of a calculation
Compare	Give an account of similarities between two (or more) items or situations, referring to both (all) of them throughout
Construct	Display information in a diagrammatic or logical form
Deduce	Reach a conclusion from the information given
Derive	Manipulate a mathematical relationship to give a new equation or relationship
Design	Produce a plan, simulation or model
Determine	Obtain the only possible answer
Discuss	Offer a considered and balanced review that includes a range of arguments, factors or hypotheses. Opinions or conclusions should be presented clearly and supported by appropriate evidence
Evaluate	Make an appraisal by weighing up the strengths and limitations
Explain	Give a detailed account including reasons or causes
Predict	Give an expected result
Show	Give the steps in a calculation or derivation
Sketch	Represent by means of a diagram or graph (labelled as appropriate). The sketch should give a general idea of the required shape or relationship, and should include relevant features
Solve	Obtain the answer(s) using algebraic and/or numerical and/or graphical methods
Suggest	Propose a solution, hypothesis or other possible answer

You will notice now that every assessment statement begins with a particular command term. In your curriculum guide you will find plenty of relevant questions that you can use to help you study. With some imagination you can easily change the assessment statements into new types of questions for yourself that will use a different command term and allow you to answer the question a different way. In the example above we looked at assessment statement 1.1.1 - **Distinguish** anatomically between the axial and appendicular skeleton.

This could become:

- → **Identify** the axial or appendicular skeleton.
- → **Annotate** on the diagram provided parts of the appendicular or axial skeleton.
- → **Define** the axial or appendicular skeleton.

You can use the assessment statements to help you condense and organise your notes. You should be able to condense and refine your notes by using techniques such as:

- → using bullet points
- → condensing paragraphs into shorter sentences or keywords
- → diagrams that summarise large amounts of information
- → cue cards.

Your new, condensed notes are what you then read over. Reading aloud is a good thing to do; then you see it, hear it, and you are moving too, so all of the learning modes are being used. It should get to a point where you use the assessment statement as a prompt that then triggers your notes, not reading any more, but simply saying the content to yourself with your notes beside you to remind you when needed. You need to really engage with the material so that the level of your understanding is as high as possible. As your understanding grows, you will discover connections between the different aspects of the curriculum and beyond - all of this will assist you in remembering the information.

We remember best when

- → we pay attention
- → are deeply engaged
- → the information has meaning for us and it makes sense
- → the information has connections.

There is no getting away from it; you have to put in a lot of time to ensure that you understand the material in this course. Those who develop good memory often do some of the following:

- → Organise their time well and set goals for themselves. This can be done with the aid of the Study Plan chart on the following page. You must look at studying as you would at any training programme.
- → Build up your brain endurance slowly (progressive overload) so you will be able to cope with the high demands. Start early.
- → Provide plenty of rewards, treats or breaks. Exercise is a great reward as it will give you balance and works your heart and lungs to help you cope with stress. When it is really bad weather or time for just a short break, try juggling! Put the breaks on your chart.
- → Insert your exam times so you can see when they are. This can also let you see where to put your subjects to ensure you have given balance to your plan.
- → Study for periods of about 40-50 minutes with at least 10 minutes break between. Remember to hydrate yourself.
- → Minimise distractions.
- → Create a glossary of terms and ideas you have difficulty remembering or understanding. This can be done each week as you move through the topics. Sometimes you may feel like you are learning another language. It is important that you give yourself some time to understand these new terms.
- → Each day on the chart has 8 time slots to use. Adjust it to suit your needs. Put all of your commitments on the chart so you can plan around everything you do.

Study Plan								
Date	Time slot	Monday	Tuesday	Wednesday	Thursday	Friday	Saturday	Sunday
Insert date here								
Insert date here								

Examination strategies

It is important that you have checked and double checked your examination time and place. You should also ask someone else check this with you as well. It would be a tragedy to have put in the many hours of study to then have this wasted because you had the wrong day or time written down.

Paper 1

→ Remember this is a multiple-choice paper with 30 questions on the core topics only.
→ You have 45 minutes for this paper.
→ Your answers will be put onto a separate answer sheet.
→ When you are working through the questions it is critical that you take your time with each one by reading the question carefully and then looking at each of the possible answers. This will allow you to identify the best possible answer. If you rush yourself you may misinterpret the question.
→ Use a highlighter to identify key phrases and terms.

For example:

What is the term given to the volume of air comprising of vital capacity and residual volume?

→ Try to answer the question before you look at the alternatives.
→ Eliminate incorrect answers.
→ Do not second guess yourself. Examiners do not write questions to trick you. Trust your instincts. Often the first response is the correct one.
→ If you come across a difficult question which you are unsure of, skip it and move to the next one. This will give your brain time to process it and you may be assisted by any one of the questions that follow it.

→ At the end check your answer sheet for gaps and work on these first, then go back over each question again and check what you have put down. If there is still time, check again.

Paper 2
→ As mentioned earlier, this paper is 1 hour 15 minutes long.
→ It is made up of short and long answer questions from the core topics only.
→ It has 2 sections: Section A in which all questions are compulsory, and Section B where you answer one question from a selection of three.

You will be allowed 5 minutes reading time with this paper (but note that no writing can be done during this time). Use this time to look at Section B and identify which question would suit you best. When selecting in Section B, be sure to be aware of the big mark questions - it can be easy to pick one where you know the answers to the initial questions which will be worth fewer marks, but you may not be so strong in the last few questions where the marks are often worth the most. Also use this time to look through Section A and get your brain ready for what is to come.

Once you can write in this paper it could be useful to go back to specific sections and jot down quick notes to yourself which will guide your answers later on in the paper. Then go to the start and work through Section A.

The first question in Section A will begin with some form of stimulus, such as a table of data or a graph. The initial questions will possibly get you to draw information from this.

Remember the following:
→ You will need your ruler and calculator.
→ Be sure you include units on any figures asked for. This includes %.
→ As with Paper 1, read the questions carefully so you are sure that you know what is being asked for.
→ Check the number of marks that the question is offering - this will indicate the number of points you need to make.
→ If you need extra space to write then use refill pages.
→ Check diagrams and tables carefully. Highlight units and look for a key to assist in interpreting the graph or table.
→ Separate your ideas. Do not bundle all your answers into one long sentence.
→ Check your spelling and use of terms. For example, Glycogenolysis, Glucose, Glucagon and Glycogen can all be easily confused.

In this paper and **Paper 3** your understanding of the command terms is vital.
→ **Compare** questions can be assisted with the use of a Venn diagram.
→ **Outline** and **Explain** are two terms that can be mixed up.
→ **Outline** requires you to give a brief account or summary. For example: *The heart rate of X-C Skiers in the graph rises at a steady rate as intensity increases.*
→ **Explain** questions require you to give a detailed account of causes, reasons or mechanisms. The explanation would include information like: *As the body works harder the breakdown of ATP produces a greater volume of carbon dioxide which is detected in the various sensory areas of the body, such as in the aorta, which in turn triggers a response from the medulla oblongata. So in this situation the heart beats faster.*

Paper 3
→ This will be completed the next day and you will have 1 hour to complete this.
→ The paper will include four sections - one section for each of the four option topics.
→ You must ensure that you only select the two questions (20 marks each) that you would have done with your teacher. Sometimes the questions in

the other options which you have not studied look enticing, but it is very dangerous to assume that you will be able to answer it with the type of terminology and depth required.

→ You have half an hour for each section.

→ The format of the questions follows a similar line to that experienced in Paper 2.

→ Your knowledge of the command terms is important.

→ As well as reading the question carefully, make sure that you are aware of the number of marks that the question is worth as this will guide you as to how many points you need to make if this is not already stated in the question.

→ A stimulus such as a table, diagram or graph will start the question and draw you into the topic.

→ The questions will come from across the sub-topics of the option, so you will need to be confident with the broad scope of the option.

→ Use the marks awarded as a guide to the depth of the response required.

→ There are often multiple answers to a question, however try to resist the urge to write down everything you know about a particular topic. Be precise and to the point.

Example 1

A1. d) Discuss **one** physiological response to exercising in the heat for a prolonged period of time. [3]

Possible answer:

Dehydration;

Thickening of the blood making it harder for the heart to maintain the same cardiac output;

Reduction of the oxygen available to working muscles;

Cardiovascular drift / increase in working heart rate.

The student would be awarded 3 marks even though they have listed four points. They haven't overstated the answer but have given enough information to receive the full marks.

Example 2

D1. e) Discuss the possible advantage to a canoeist of consuming sports drinks, bars and gels as a nutritional ergogenic aid during an event. [2]

Possible answer:

This is a portable nutrition option whilst canoeing. It is a practical option that will help the athlete.

The student would only be awarded 1 mark from the possible 2 marks available. The two ideas listed here are similar. They haven't developed or listed another advantage.

To get full marks they need to indicate something additional. For example, one of the following would have been sufficient:

These drinks and foods deliver fluid and carbohydrate during exercise.

They are legal and ethical options.

They improve performance by increasing glycogen stores.

To help you get used to the format of the different papers it is a good idea to use and practice on as many old examination papers as you can. Ask your teacher for the mark schemes to assist you with understanding how marks are awarded.

Useful websites

→ BBC website for exam preparation, revision planning, planning motivation and control
www.bbc.co.uk/scotland/brainsmart/success

→ Agonistic and antagonistic muscles
www.teachpe.com/multi/types_muscle_prime_movers_agonists_synergists_new.htm

→ Revision on the heart
www.teachpe.com/cross/the_heart.htm

→ Movements at the joint
www.teachpe.com/multi/types_movement_at_joint_flexion_extension_rotation_etc.htm

→ Types of fitness
www.teachpe.com/cloze/health_related_fitness.htm

Sample exam questions

These questions are taken from specimen papers, © IB Organization 2012.

Paper 1

1   Which best describes flat bones?

    A   Complex and varied in shape, such as the vertebrae

    B   The type of bones found in the skull and the shoulder blade

    C   Bones that are longer than they are wide

    D   Bones found in the wrist and ankle

2   The table below shows the respiratory rates and lung volumes for an endurance-trained athlete.

Respiratory rates and volumes	Recorded results
Pulmonary ventilation	61.0 litres min^{-1}
Tidal volume at rest	0.5 litres
Maximal tidal volume	3.9 litres
Vital capacity	6.2 litres
Residual volume	1.2 litres

[Data from W L Kenny, J H Wilmore and D L Costill, (2012), *Physiology of Sport and Exercise*, 5th Edition, Champaign, IL: Human Kinetics, 267]

What is the total lung capacity?

    A   7.4 litres

    B   6.7 litres

    C   4.7 litres

    D   10.9 litres

3   What needs to be considered when recommending a balanced diet?

   I   Habitual physical activity level of the person

   II Age of the person

   III Climate where the person lives

   A I only

   B I and II only

   C II and III only

   D I, II and III

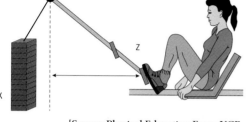

[Source: Physical Education Exam VCE Units 1 and 2, Malpeli/Telford ©2008, Cengage Learning Australia. Reprinted with the permission of Cengage Learning Australia.]

4   The diagram on the left demonstrates an athlete performing a leg press. Which correctly identifies the fulcrum, effort and load for this first class lever?

   A X = Fulcrum, Y = Effort and Z = Load

   B X = Fulcrum, Y = Load and Z = Effort

   C X = Load, Y = Effort and Z = Fulcrum

   D X = Load, Y = Fulcrum and Z = Effort

5   What are the information processing mechanisms that match the numerals in the diagram below?

Information from display → Sense Organs → I → II → III → Muscular System

	I	**II**	**III**
A	Effector mechanism	Perceptual mechanism	Decision Mechanism
B	Decision Mechanism	Perceptual mechanism	Effector mechanism
C	Perceptual mechanism	Effector mechanism	Decision Mechanism
D	Perceptual mechanism	Decision Mechanism	Effector mechanism

6   The mean (± SD) exercise heart rate of a group in a physical education class is 155 beats per minute (bpm) (± 14). What percentage of the group has an exercise heart rate between 141 bpm and 169 bpm?

   A 5%   **C** 85%

   B 68%   **D** 95%

Paper 2

1   A study was undertaken of Asafa Powell during his 100m sprint for a world record of 9.74s in Italy in 2007. The graphs below represent the impulse recorded from a single footfall (from first contact to the foot leaving the ground). Each graph represents a different stage of the sprint.

[Source: adapted from J Rhodes, (2008), Biomechanics, *PE Review*, 3 (2), pages 21-25. Reproduced in adapted form by permission of Philip Alan Updates.]

Early stage (0–20 m)

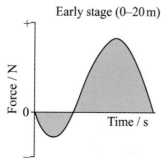

Middle stage (50–70 m)

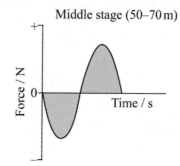

Final stage (80–100 m)

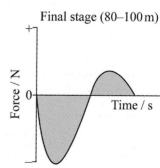

a) Define the term *impulse*. [1]

b) Net impulses are a combination of positive and negative impulses. Describe the net impulse during the 100m sprint for each of the following stages:

   i) Early stage [1]

   ii) Middle stage [1]

   iii) Final stage [1]

c) Compare the acceleration of Asafa Powell in the early stage to the final stage of the 100m sprint. [2]

Usain Bolt, the winner of the 100m sprint at the 2008 Olympics, reaches his peak velocity later in the sprint than Asafa Powell.

d) Using the information above, predict how Usain Bolt's middle stage force-time graph would be different from Asafa Powell's for the 100m sprint. [2]

The frames below were captured from a cyclist.

[Source: images captured by *Siliconcoach Video Analysis Software*. Used by permission.]

e) i) State the type of movement occurring at the cyclist's right hip from Frames 1 to 3. [1]

   ii) State the type of muscle contraction that is occurring from Frames 1 to 3 in the vastus medialis of the right leg. [1]

f) Explain the concept of reciprocal inhibition in relation to the action occurring at the right knee of the cyclist from Frames 1 to 3. [3]

2 Compare the heart rate, stroke volume and cardiac output of trained rowers versus untrained rowers during rest and exercise. [5]

3 Outline the two continua of motor skills classification below. Illustrate your answers using sporting examples.

a) Fine and gross [3]

b) Externally and internally paced skills [3]

4 Discuss **two** advantages and **two** disadvantages of sub-maximal tests of fitness. [4]

Paper 3
This question is a sample question from Section A

1 A study was undertaken to compare the effects of training programmes on 3km running performance time. The subjects were divided into 3 groups and trained twice a week for 10 weeks. Each training session lasted for 60 minutes.

Group	Method of training
1	High-intensity running bouts with a work-to-rest ratio of 1:1
2	High-intensity running bouts with a work-to-rest ratio of 1:3
Control	Steady state running

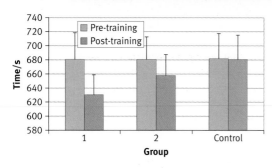

[Source: Reprinted from Journal of Science and Medicine in Sport, 10/1, F Esfarjani and P Laursen, Manipulating high-intensity interval training: Effects on VO_2 max, the lactate threshold and 3000 m running performance in moderately trained males, pages 27–35, Copyright (2012), with permission from Elsevier.]

The graph on the left shows the pre-training and post-training 3 km running performance times.

a) **i)** State the two different methods of training used in this study. *[2]*

     ii) Compare the pre-training 3 km running performance times of the three groups. *[1]*

     iii) Identify which group had the most improved post-training 3 km running performance time. *[1]*

     iv) Suggest **one** reason why the work-to-rest ratio has resulted in a difference in the post-training running performance times between groups 1 and 2. *[1]*

     v) Identify a different training method that could be used to improve a 3 km running performance time. *[1]*

This question is a sample question from Section B

2 **a)** Using an example from a sport event of your choice, distinguish between internal and external imagery. *[4]*

     b) Explain when to use imagery to improve your sports performance. *[3]*

This question is a sample question from Section C

Regular brisk walking reduces the risk of chronic health problems. A study investigated the perceived barriers elderly people had against walking in their neighbourhood. The table below shows details of the types of perceived barriers pre (before) and post (after) attending a 12 month neighbourhood "walking the way to health" scheme led by trained walk leaders.

Perceived barriers *I would walk around my neighbourhood, but ...*	% response pre-walking scheme	% response post-walking scheme
I have no one to walk with.	25.4	20.5
there is nowhere pleasant to walk near my home.	8.0	11.7
I worry about my personal safety.	30.5	19.1
I worry about being knocked down by a cyclist riding on the pavement.	10.8	17.0
I worry about tripping over broken paving stones.	17.9	23.5
there is too much traffic on the roads where I live.	17.6	22.1

[Source: adapted from British Journal of Sports Medicine, 2007, 41, pages 562–568; reproduced with permission from the BMJ Publishing Group]

3 **a)** Identify which was the greatest perceived barrier before attending the walking scheme. *[1]*

     b) Calculate the percentage for worrying about tripping over broken paving stones after attending the walking scheme. *[1]*

     c) Comment on **one** positive outcome of this study in relation to the perceived barriers to walking. *[2]*

     d) Describe three strategies for enhancing adherence to exercise. *[3]*

This question is a sample question from Section D

4 Explain why endurance athletes require a greater water intake. *[4]*

For the mark schemes for the questions included in this chapter, go to:

www.oxfordsecondary.co.uk/ ibsport

GLOSSARY

Actin and myosin contractile proteins responsible for movement

Adenosine triphosphate (ATP) a molecule created from biochemical energy in organic molecules by catabolic reactions

Afferent neurons neurons that carry sensory information

Anabolism the metabolic process of creating more of a certain substance or tissue

Antecedent previous or pre-existing factor known to increase self-efficacy

Anterior in front of or nearer to the front

Anteriorly concave curves inwards at the front

Anteriorly convex curves outwards at the front

Anxiety a negative emotional state in which feelings of nervousness, worry and apprehension are associated with arousal of the body

Arousal a blend of physiological and psychological activity in a person, varying from deep sleep to intense excitement

Balanced diet a diet that provides all nutrients in the right amount in order to maintain health and prevent nutrient excess or deficiency diseases

Beta blockers drugs that reduce the influence of adrenaline on the body

Body mass index a measurement of body fat, calculated by dividing weight in kilograms by height in metres squared

Burnout a plateau in performance as a result of overtraining accompanied by a decrease in motivation to train

Catabolism the breaking down of molecules

Cell respiration the controlled release of energy in the form of ATP

Choking the occurrence of inferior performance despite striving and incentives for superior performance

Cytokines proteins that regulate the process of inflammation which is common in all forms of tissue damage and is an important part of the healing process for damaged tissue

Dietary guidelines recommended amounts of foods, food groups or meals

Dietary recommendations recommended amounts of essential nutrients in the diet

Distal further away from where a limb attaches to the body

Diuretic a substance that increases the rate at which urine is produced

Diuretics substances that increase removal of water from the body

Double blind experiment an experiment in which neither the participants nor the experimenters know who has been given the placebo

Effect size an objective and standardized measure of the magnitude of observed effect. We can compare effect sizes across different studies that have measured different variables, or have used different scales of measurement

Efferent system the motoneurons that carry information to the muscles

Endogenous originating internally

Endurance capacity how long a person can continue to exercise before they become exhausted

Endurance performance how much distance/work can be completed in a given time, or how quickly a given distance/amount of work can be completed

Epidemiology a branch of medical science that studies the occurrence, transmission and control of epidemic diseases

Exogenous originating externally

External located on or near the surface

Frostbite the continued cooling and freezing of cells

Frostnip the initial freezing of the superficial skin tissue

Gas exchange the transfer of oxygen and carbon dioxide between the systems

Homeostasis the condition in which the body's internal environment remains relatively constant, within physiological limits

Hyperthermia an elevated body temperature, usually above 39°C (102°F)

Hypokinetic disease a disease associated with a sedentary or inactive lifestyle

Hypothermia low body temperature that has different clinical categories depending on the severity

Inferior below or further away from the head

Internal located inside or further away from the surface

Joule a unit of energy. In nutrition, joule (J) is the energy obtained from food that is available through cell respiration

Lateral further away from the midline of the body

Learning a relatively permanent change in performance resulting from practice or past experience

Macrocycle the name of the athlete's training programme for an entire year or season

Masking agents a substance or agent that hides the presence of another substance or agent

Medial closer to the midline of the body

Mesocycle a block of training composed of several week-long microcycles

Microcycle a weekly training programme

Motor unit a single motoneuron and the muscle fibres which it innervates

Obesity an excess of body fat that endangers health

Overreaching pushing the body beyond its limits for a short period of time to stimulate a training response

Overtraining the result of excessive physical training without adequate rest

Overtraining training too often or at too high an intensity over a prolonged period of time

Overuse injury micro-traumatic damage to a bone, muscle or tendon that has been subjected to repetitive stress without receiving sufficient time to heal

Performance a temporary occurrence, fluctuating over time

Placebo effect a positive effect that cannot be attributed to the properties of the placebo itself but must be due simply to the person's belief that the placebo works

Posterior behind or nearer to

Proximal nearer to where a limb attaches to the body

Reliability is the extent to which the same reading is obtained each time a variable is measured

Scalar a measurement that only has size

Sleep disturbances not only fewer hours spent sleeping but also increased movement during sleep that reduces the quality of sleep

Staleness the result of overtraining where there is no improvement in performance despite continued training

Steroids a class of chemical substances that can be found in the body and can also be synthesized

Striated appearance of light and dark stripes

Superior above or nearer to the head

To articulate to form a joint

To innervate to supply an organ or other body part with nerves

Training the systematic repeated performance of structured exercise sessions over a period of time

Undertraining not providing the body enough stimulation for performance to improve by training too infrequently or at too low an intensity

Validity is the extent to which the measure actually measures what it claims to

Vector a measurement that has both size and direction

VO₂max the maximal rate of oxygen uptake and represents someone's maximal aerobic capacity

INDEX